IS IT A
COINCIDENCE

that Lee Harvey Oswald's address book contained the name and home address of a CIA counter-intelligence officer?

that a series of CIA pictures of "Oswald" in Mexico show a man 6 feet tall, 200 pounds, in his 30s?

that two living witnesses can tie Oswald and Ruby together?

that Dallas police questioned Oswald for eleven hours and say they made no transcript, notes, or tape recordings?

that David Ferrie, Oswald's friend, was an employee of Mafia chieftain Carlos Marcello?

that Jack Ruby made several trips to Cuba after Fidel Castro took power?

—OR A
CONSPIRACY?

COINCIDENCE OR CONSPIRACY?

PRODUCED BY THE
COMMITTEE TO INVESTIGATE ASSASSINATIONS
UNDER THE DIRECTION OF
BERNARD FENSTERWALD, JR.,
AND COMPILED BY MICHAEL EWING

ZEBRA BOOKS

KENSINGTON PUBLISHING CORP.

ZEBRA BOOKS

are published by

KENSINGTON PUBLISHING CORP.

521 Fifth Avenue

New York, N.Y. 10017

Copyright © 1977 by the Committee to Investigate Assassinations, Inc.

All rights reserved. No part of this book may be reproduced in any form or by any means without the prior written consent of the Publisher, excepting brief quotes used in reviews.

For further information, address inquiries to the Committee to Investigate Assassinations, Inc., 2101 L. Street N.W., Washington, D.C. 20037.

First Printing: April, 1977

Printed in the United States of America

CONTENTS

PREFACE	9
ONE/PRINCIPALS	17
TWO/THE WARREN COMMISSION	71
THREE/POLITICOS	121
FOUR/PLOTS TO KILL CASTRO	155
FIVE/THE INTELLIGENCE COMMUNITY	174
SIX/HOOVER'S FBI	247
SEVEN/THE MAFIA CONNECTION	268
EIGHT/THE SECOND OSWALD	383
NINE/THE DALLAS POLICE	407
TEN/THE NEW ORLEANS PROBE	450
ELEVEN/THE CUBANS	481
TWELVE/LINKS TO WATERGATE	500
THIRTEEN/NEGLECTED OR SPURNED WITNESSES	556
FOURTEEN/BIT PLAYERS AND VICTIMS	565

DEDICATION

This book is dedicated to those politicians who have taken the lead in persuading Congress to re-open the Kennedy killing.

The first is Senator Richard S. Schweiker of Pennsylvania, a courageous member of Senator Church's Senate Committee to Study Intelligence Activities. Despite massive skepticism and great odds, Senator Schweiker insisted that the Committee take at least a preliminary look at possible Cuban involvement in the Dallas murder as well as the role of the CIA and the FBI in a cover-up.

The second is Representative Thomas Downing, a veteran Democrat from Newport News, Virginia. Once he became interested in the case, Tom Downing used all of his great energy and his spotless record of intergrity to see that the House of Representatives began a serious re-study of the JFK murder. He rounded up more than a hundred co-sponsors of the resolution and shepherded it through the powerful Rules Committee and the whole House. He worked a minor miracle when he achieved a vote of 280 to 65 in favor of the resolution.

Our amateur Committee to Investigate Assassinations pledges all possible assistance to the official Select Committee. Through their efforts, the American people, albeit belatedly, may learn the details of the fate of their martyred leader.

                BERNARD FENSTERWALD, JR.
                Executive Director
                Committee to Investigate Assassinations

Washington, D.C.
December, 1976

PREFACE

For most Americans, and for many people around the globe, the events of November 22, 1963, remain vivid and horrifying. Yet, there are some young people today who are vitally interested in those events but who were either unborn then or too young to have personal recall. And, after all, more than thirteen years have passed, dimming all of our memories somewhat.

On that traumatic fall day, President John F. Kennedy was ending an arduous political tour of Texas. While he was riding through Dealey Plaza in downtown Dallas, several shots rang out. The President was struck first by a non-fatal shot which transited his neck and then by another shot which exploded his head. Texas Governor John Connally, who was sitting on a jump-seat immediately in front of the President, was hit by a single bullet which went through his rib cage and wrist and lodged in his thigh.

Both Kennedy and Connally were rushed to nearby Parkland Hospital. For all intents and purposes, the President was dead on arrival; but Governor Connally was saved and is alive and well in Texas today. Vice President Lyndon Johnson, who was in another car in the parade, was sworn in as President about two hours after the shooting.

Less than an hour after the assassination, a Dallas police officer, J.D. Tippit, was shot and killed on a back street several miles from Dealey Plaza. The facts surrounding his death were disputed at the time and remain confused to this day. There were conflicting reports as to whether he was killed by one person or two and the description of that person or persons. In any event, a few minutes after this second shooting, a young man was arrested in a nearby theater and charged with Tippit's murder. This man was subsequently charged with the assassination of the President. He was, of course, Lee Harvey Oswald, a twenty-four-year-old ex-Marine.

Oswald had grown up in New Orleans and had joined the Marines at age seventeen. He was a radar operator in the very highly classified U-2 program in the Far East and California. After an early discharge in 1959, he "defected" to the USSR for two and one-half years, marrying a young Russian woman named Marina before his return to the United States in June of 1962. Upon his return he lived in Dallas and New Orleans, working at odd jobs. He is alleged to have taken a trip to Mexico shortly before the assassination.

After his arrest, Oswald was held for almost 48 hours in the Dallas Police Station. He was questioned intensively for eleven of these hours by Dallas Police and the FBI, but it is claimed that no tape, transcript, or comprehensive notes of the interrogation were made. He was represented by no lawyer. While he was being transferred to the County jail, he was fatally shot by Jack Ruby while an enormous television audience watched in horror. The shooting took place in the basement of the Dallas jail, within feet of scores of Dallas police, FBI agents, etc.

The *real* Jack Ruby and his motive remain clouded in mystery to this day. After one abortive trial and on the eve of the second, Jack Ruby died in jail without "talking." Even the cause of his death is the subject of considerable doubt. Recently, it has been disclosed that Ruby was an FBI informant and had ties to the Mafia and probably to the CIA; many of the facts surrounding these "connections" were hidden from the President's Commission which investigated the murders.

Chief Justice Earl Warren was reluctantly persuaded by President Lyndon Johnson to head this seven-man investigating group. Other members were Gerald Ford, then Minority Leader of the House of Representatives; Rep. Hale Boggs, who later disappeared in an airplane somewhere off Alaska; Senators Richard Russell and John Cooper; Allen Dulles, former Director of Central Intelligence; and John McCloy, a banker and ex-intelligence officer. The Commission studied the assassination from December, 1963, until September, 1964, when they issued a lengthy report, followed shortly thereafter by 26 volumes of Hearings and Evidence.

The Warren Commission concluded that Oswald was a "lone-nut killer," who acted on his own and without the assistance of anyone. They concluded that there was no conspiracy, domestic or international. They could assign no clear motive to Oswald's action. As to Ruby, they accepted his statement that he killed Oswald to prevent the necessity of having Mrs. Kennedy return to Texas for a trial of Oswald. To fit the facts to their conclusions, the Commission adopted the much disputed "single bullet" or "magic bullet" thesis. In briefest outline this central thesis is as follows:

It was known that all the shooting took place in approximately six seconds. The alleged murder weapon, an ancient Italian Carcano, was a single shot and could be loaded, aimed and fired a maximum of three times in six seconds. One shot hit the curb, so all of the damage to the President's neck and head and to the Governor's ribs, wrist and leg would have, of necessity, have meant a second gunman, i.e., a conspiracy. Thus, goes the theory, one of the three bullets missed the target, one exploded the President's head, and a single bullet did all of the damage to both men. Even more remarkable, although breaking several bones, the bullet came out pristine, as though it had hit nothing.

Almost immediately after the issuance of the Report, a spate of books and articles appeared which disputed the Commission's basic conclusions. Many of the more responsible ones, including Sylvia Meagher's *Accessories After the Fact* and Josiah Thompson's *Six Seconds in Dallas*, clearly demonstrated the physical impossibility of the "single bullet" theory and the improbability of many of the other basic conclusions and remarked upon the almost endless number of strange "connections" and leads which were ignored by the Commission .... in a seeming desire to make the facts fit their conclusions.

In the 1967-69 period, New Orlean's District Attorney Jim Garrison attempted to "solve" the case through the prosecution of David Ferrie and Clay Shaw. His efforts ended in a debacle, but recent revelations of several House and Senate investigating Committees have shown that many of his basic beliefs were nowhere near as "crazy" as most people had once believed. In fact, he appears to have been on the right track (Cubans, CIA & Mafia) before he derailed.

More recently, there have been a number of further reviews of the Warren Commission's conclusion. There was a complete whitewash of them in 1974, conducted by the so-called Rockefeller Commission, under the tutelage of David Belin, formerly counsel to the Warren Commission. Representative Don Edwards of California held hearings on the FBI's destruction of crucial evidence in the case. The Senate Intelligence Committee, chaired by Senator Frank Church, conducted an investigation of the CIA-Mafia plots against the Castro brothers and concluded that all of the facts surrounding the plots were wrongfully withheld from the Warren Commission. A subcommittee of the Church Committee, consisting of Senators Richard Schweiker and Gary Hart, conducted a preliminary survey into the questioning of CIA-FBI cooperation (or lack thereof) with the Warren Commission, and they concluded that many leads were not followed and much information was withheld.

One of the major problems confronting investigators of the JFK murder is the unavailability of crucial documentary evidence. President Johnson began the process of hiding the evidence when he signed an executive order in 1965 which provided that all of the Warren Commission's materials would be kept in the National Archives but which also permitted the various government agencies, such as the CIA and FBI, to require the continual classification until the year 2039 of their records which had gone to the Commission. This is bad enough in itself, but the situation is much worse than the public (and most government officials) realize. In the case of the CIA, only a fraction of their total records found their way to the Commission in the first place. Taking the CIA assassination files as a whole, there is no doubt that after thirteen years the vast majority remain classified in whole or in part. In a Freedom of Information lawsuit brought by the Committee to Investigate Assassinations for production of those records, it was revealed that the "Oswald 201 File" alone contained 1194 documents. These documents ranged in length from one page to hundreds of pages. Of the 1194 documents, only 66 were made public in their entirety. And after two years, only this one file has ever been reviewed and indexed despite pressure from Judge John Sirica's court. Harold Weisberg, the dean of the critics, has made a concerted effort to get at the FBI's records and with similar results. The stonewalling continues in 1977 unabated. Only a Congressional Committee with subpoena power — and guts and persistence — will ever see all of the files, and then, in all likelihood, only after a lengthy court battle over "executive privilege."

What follows in this book is not a rehash of the shortcomings of the Warren Commission with respect to the physical evidence in the case. We do not discuss the ballistics and medical evidence. We do not demolish the "single bullet theory" for the one hundred and first time. We believe that responsible critics have done this in spades over the past several years.

After an in-depth study of these matters of physical evidence for a decade, we have concluded that the Warren Commission was simply wrong in its basic conclusion that Oswald was a "lone-nut killer." It is our firm conviction that there had to be at least two riflemen, hence some sort of conspiracy. And the latest Gallup poll shows that more than 80% of the American people agree with us. *What we are interested in is who shot John F. Kennedy and why.*

We do not pass judgment on why the Commission reached the wrong result. We do know, of course, that much information was withheld from them by the government agencies which did their investigating, especially the FBI and CIA.

In an effort to get a step nearer to the *who* and *why*, what we do concentrate on is the almost endless series of "coincidences" which have cropped up in the past thirteen years and which seem to defy credulity if one insists upon clinging to the "no conspiracy" theory of the Warren Commission. Strung end to end, we believe that they spell conspiracy with a capital C.

Although the members of the Committee to Investigate Assassinations, mostly professional people joined in a non-profit corporation, have done considerable original investigation and research, we do not wish to leave the impression that most of the material in this book is original. Some was found buried in the Warren Commission's 26 volumes of evidence. However, a large part of it is attributable to the sizeable corps of dedicated critics who have worked on this case since 1963. In each case we hope that we have given credit where credit is due. If we have failed here or there, we apologize to our friends.

CHAPTER ONE

Principals

While the resignation of Richard M. Nixon from the Presidency in August, 1974, brought a swift conclusion to the seemingly endless hemorrhage of revelations about the broad range of Watergate crimes and related corruption, the years 1975 and 1976 saw the continued disclosure of other areas of governmental wrongdoing and conspiracy; disclosures only partially muted by the public numbness in the aftermath of Watergate.

With the Senate and House Intelligence Committee probes during the past two years, the FBI, CIA, and other intelligence agencies have replaced Richard Nixon and his men as the prime targets of continuing investigation by several diverse bodies, including the Congress, press, and courts.

With the steady stream of disclosures relating to circumstances surrounding the Kennedy assassination, new areas of information have come to light on each of the key principals in the case.

The Senate Intelligence Committee's extensive accounting of the CIA-Mafia assassination conspiracies against Fidel Castro in the early 1960s, uncovered a broad range of new information pertaining to President Kennedy: his strong efforts to undermine the Castro regime in 1961 and 1962; his subsequent secret communications with the Castro government, aimed at detente, in 1963; Attorney General Robert Kennedy's discovery of the CIA-Mafia assassination conspiracies against Castro in May, 1962. These areas will be covered in depth in later chapters.

During this same period, 1975 and 1976, new information — indeed ominous information — also surfaced regarding the young Texan accused of assassinating President Kennedy, as well as the man who in turn murdered him two days later.

As will be seen later, one of the most startling disclosures of 1975 revealed that Lee Oswald had delivered a secret note to the Dallas FBI Office during the days immediately preceding the assassination — a secret note that was flushed down the toilet by FBI agent James Hosty several hours after Oswald was shot to death in the basement of the Dallas City Jail by Jack Ruby. The incident had been covered up for over eleven years by senior officials of the FBI. While there have been reports that the secret Oswald note contained a threat against the FBI (for allegedly harassing him), its actual subject or contents have never been determined despite lengthy investigations aimed at doing just that.

The Senate Intelligence Committee's Final Report on the Kennedy Assassination noted that after Oswald's secret FBI note was first disclosed in 1975, the Bureau at first claimed to have had no knowledge of it:

> The Bureau's initial file review failed to develop any information indicating that Oswald had ever visited the FBI field office in Dallas or that he had left a note.[1]

The Senate committee went on to report that as controversy over the episode grew, the FBI finally was able to come up with an accounting of this document — an accounting which unfortunately contained some important gaps:

> FBI interviews with Personnel assigned to the Dallas field office in 1963 established that:
>
> (1) Lee Harvey Oswald did visit the office some two or three weeks prior to the assassination;
>
> (2) Oswald asked to see [Special Agent] James Hosty, and upon being informed that he was not in, left a note for Hosty; and
>
> (3) the note was destroyed after the assassination.
>
> The evidence developed by the Bureau contained sharp conflicts. The investigators failed to establish:
>
> (1) whether the note was threatening in nature; and
>
> (2) at whose instructions the note was destroyed.[2]

It was also in 1975 that new information came to national attention concerning the relationship between Jack Ruby and the FBI. The new information came to light in a Warren Commission document which had been withheld from the public since 1964. The new document, consisting of a letter from FBI Director J. Edgar Hoover to J. Lee Rankin, Commission General Counsel, disclosed that the Dallas FBI Office had "contacted [Jack Ruby] on eight occasions" for possible service as an FBI informant.[3]

The previously secret document (which some members of the Commission staff claim they had been unaware of), indicated that several of those occasions on which the Dallas FBI "contacted" Ruby had been around the same period in 1959 when Ruby was visiting a close friend in Havana, Cuba — a friend whom the Warren Commission noted was associated with the Mafia's casinos there.[4] J. Edgar Hoover's February 27, 1964 letter to the Commission also stated that "Ruby was never paid any money" by the Dallas FBI, and also was never officially a Bureau informant.[5] However, as defenders of the Warren Commission conclusions have even pointed out, this repeated Ruby-FBI contact clearly indicates something other than just a random relationship. Interestingly, the actual FBI "302" interview reports on the Ruby-FBI meetings have not been released and there is no clear indication that they were ever furnished to the Warren Commission.[6]

In late 1976, even more surprising information about Oswald came to light through previously classified documents secured under the provisions of the Freedom of Information Act.

On October 1, 1976, after years of recurring speculation and allegations concerning such a possibility, the Associated Press disclosed:

> Contrary to sworn testimony, the CIA once considered using accused Presidential assassin Lee Harvey Oswald as a source of intelligence information about the Soviet Union, according to a newly released CIA document.
>
> In sworn testimony before the Warren Commission, former CIA Director Richard Helms said the Agency never had "or even contemplated" any contacts with Oswald.
>
> The newly released document, written by an unidentified CIA officer three days after President John F. Kennedy was killed in Dallas, on November 22, 1963, says that "we showed intelligence interest" in Oswald and "discussed . . . the laying on of interviews."
>
> The unidentified officer added that, "I

do not know what action developed thereafter."[7]

The article further states:

When he appeared before the Warren Commission in May of 1964, Helms, then head of the agency's clandestine services, testified under oath that "there's no material in the Central Intelligence Agency, either in the record or in the mind of any of the individuals that there was any contact had or even contemplated with Oswald."[8]

The November 25, 1963 CIA memorandum (Document No. 435-173A) contained other details about the possible use of Lee Oswald for intelligence purposes, and states that this possible CIA contact with Oswald had originally been discussed "sometime in Summer, 1960."[9] The memo further states that the CIA officer who originally proposed using Oswald couldn't remember whether the idea "was discussed while Oswald and his family were en route to our country [from the Soviet Union] or if it was after their arrival."[10]

This previously secret report notes that one of the reasons the Agency considered using Lee Oswald was that they "were particularly interested in the information Oswald might provide" on industrial activities in Russia as well as "[biographic information] that might help develop foreign personality dossiers."[11] The CIA official who first discussed the Agency's potential use of Oswald, ended his memorandum by stating:

> I was phasing into my next cover assignment [deletion] at the time. Thus, I would have left our country shortly after Oswald's arrival. I do not know what action developed thereafter.[12]

Several months before this previously-classified CIA information had been made public, the Senate Intelligence Committee disclosed other CIA interest that may have also led the agency to Lee Oswald in 1963. In their Final Report of June 23, 1976, the Committee states:

> The CIA also took an interest in the Fair Play for Cuba Committee with which Oswald was associated. According to [an] FBI document, on September 16, 1963, the CIA advised the FBI that the "agency is giving some consideration to countering the activities of [the FPCC] in foreign countries."[13]

The September, 1963, FBI document cited by the Senate Committee went on to state that the "CIA is also giving some thought to planting deceptive information which might embarrass the [Fair Play for Cuba] Committee in areas where it does have some support."[14] Interestingly, as Senate investigators have pointed out, Fair Play for Cuba Committee member Lee Oswald made what the Warren Commission itself regarded as a highly mysterious visit to Mexico City during the last week of that very month, September, 1963.[15]

In November, 1975, then CIA Director William Colby stated "We had no contact with Mr. Oswald . . . No contact with him before he went to the Soviet Union. No contact with him after he returned from the Soviet Union. No contact with him while he was in the Soviet Union."[16] While no solid proof that the CIA was actually somehow involved with Lee Harvey Oswald has yet emerged, few observers would now regard such a prospect as remotely as they would have in 1963.

In November, 1975, CBS News correspondent Dan Rather questioned former CIA executive Victor Marchetti about the CIA's possible contact with Lee Oswald. Marchetti, a former Executive Assistant to the Deputy Director of the CIA, is the author of what has come to be regarded as the most authoritative book on the intelligence establishment. Their dialogue provided an illustration of just how far the realm of educated speculation has advanced in the Kennedy case; few in Washington have ever sought to denigrate the credentials or integrity of Marchetti.

Rather: John McCone, then the CIA Director, swore to the Warren Commission that the Agency had never communicated with Oswald in any way, directly or indirectly. Do you think this eliminates the possibility that the Agency debriefed Oswald on his return from the Soviet Union, or that he was in some other way connected or contacted with the CIA?

Marchetti: I think John McCone should know better than to ever make such a blanket statement with regard to the CIA, after having been director of that Agency. I would think he would want to add to that, "to my knowledge." They could very well have dealt with him [Oswald] without McCone ever being informed. I think the CIA knows more about the circumstances surrounding the Kennedy assassination that has not yet been made public about their relationships with Oswald, and that the agency has covered up. I am going on the assumption that the CIA had nothing to do with the Kennedy assassination. I cannot believe, to this day, that the CIA, as an institution, the people running the CIA that I knew, would have been party to any sort of a crime of this sort: murdering a President of the United States. This doesn't mean that there may not have been individuals, either acting on their own, or — or who were only remotely connected with the Agency in some capability as a contract agent, or formerly a contract agent, who may have been involved.[17]

President John F. Kennedy

"I wish I weren't going to Texas," remarked President Kennedy to Press Secretary Pierre Salinger a few hours before he left on his fatal visit to Dallas in late November of 1963.[18] President Kennedy dreaded making the lengthy political trip to Texas. His mission, in part, was to stem a raging feud between Governor John B. Connally, Senator Ralph Yarborough, and Vice President Lyndon B. Johnson.

Kennedy in fact was warned to cancel his trip to Dallas — the bastion of heated right-wing politics — by several close associates, including Senators J. W. Fulbright, Hubert Humphrey, Wayne Morse, and U.N. Ambassador Adlai Stevenson, as well as Evelyn Lincoln, his personal secretary. All feared the possibility of some violent act against the President, presumably by extremist right-wing elements that had grown increasingly virulent in that city.

While various people expressed fear for the safety of the young President, the prospect of assassination was one with which Kennedy had long been acquainted. Kenneth O'Donnell, President Kennedy's White House Chief of Staff and Appointments Secretary, remembers that Kennedy "often talked about how easy it would be for somebody to shoot at him with a rifle from a high building."[19]

With thirteen years of steadily growing public doubt about who murdered President Kennedy now at its high point — with the investigative functions of the House and Senate now committed to re-opening the case — a review of the issues, conflicts, and forces at work during the brief Kennedy Presidency of two years and ten months becomes a necessary step in determining the motive and means of its brutal and mysterious end.

"The only thing that surprised us when we got into office, was that things were just as bad as we had been saying they were," is how President Kennedy described the national state of affairs to a friend in the press after taking office.

While the tumultuous thirteen years following his death have produced a massive amount of writings on the history of the Kennedy Administration, there are many aspects of President Kennedy's brief tenure in office that have attracted little attention until recently, as revelations of internecine battles within the Federal Government — including crimes, conspiracies, and cover-ups, and mysterious relationships such as the CIA-Mafia "partnership" — have finally come to the surface.

With the painful exposure of some of these darker sides of the post-war American government, new light is being shed on the image of President Kennedy and his administration. Coming to the surface is a portrait of a President increasingly fearful of the ways and means of the American intelligence establishment, in particular the CIA; a President striving, often in vain, to reassert Constitutional authority over the already self-propelling clandestine operations of the military and CIA; a President and his brother, the Attorney General, seeking to harness the full investigatory resources of the Federal bureaucracy against the alarming penetration of organized crime into virtually every segment of American society; and finally, the discovery by the same President and

Attorney General of a highly secret (and highly active) assassination apparatus within the government, being run by a mysterious amalgamation of organized crime leaders, CIA officials, and equally anti-Kennedy Cuban-exile operatives. And, perhaps also, the same President beginning increasingly to voice some degree of speculation (always in private, of course) as to the possibility of some of these same forces conspiring to take illegal action against himself, possibly through some kind of overthrow or assassination.

While Kennedy's fondness for spy novels is well known, his appreciation of the delicacy and occasional brutality of the political process in this country was even more prescient. As might be expected, the devastating Bay of Pigs fiasco (coordinated by the CIA, the Agency's Cuban-exile operatives, and, unbeknownst to Kennedy, the Mafia) clearly seems to have played a large part in Kennedy's eventual strong mistrust of the military and intelligence establishments. The President would later use the Bay of Pigs crisis as an analogy in discussing the idea of a President being removed from office through an overthrow or other illegal means. The President's remarks were made in a private conversation with his long-time close friend (and Undersecretary of the Navy) Paul B. Fay. Fay reports that Kennedy discussed "the possibility" of such a takeover "very calmly" and in some detail, stating:

> It's possible. It could happen in this country, but the conditions would have to be just right. If, for example, the country had a young President, and he had a Bay of Pigs, there would be a certain uneasiness. Maybe the military would do a little criticizing behind his back, but this would be written off as the usual military dissatisfaction with civilian control. Then if there were another Bay of Pigs . . . the military would almost feel that it was their patriotic obligation to stand ready to preserve the integrity of the

nation, and only God knows just what segment of democracy they would be defending if they overthrew the elected establishment.[20]

Paul Fay reports that Kennedy deeply resented the CIA's assumption that the President would finally agree to launch an attack of American armed forces against Cuba, during the Bay of Pigs invasion, to salvage the remnants of the CIA's disastrous Cuban exile invasion force. Fay reports that Kennedy said, "We're not going to plunge into an irresponsible action just because a fanatical fringe in this country puts so-called national pride above national reason."[21]

With the Bay of Pigs having long figured as a possible motive behind the JFK killing by various Warren Commission critics, a review of that event is relevant. Ever since the assassination, various investigators have theorized that either pro-Castro Cubans or anti-Castro Cuban exiles were involved in the assassination, a theory that was only narrowly investigated by the Warren Commission, the CIA, and the FBI, according to the Senate Intelligence Committee Report of June 1976.

Beyond the disastrously coordinated CIA logistics during the Bay of Pigs invasion, President Kennedy privately placed the next largest amount of blame on some of the Cuban exiles themselves, and particularly on some of their leaders. Former Kennedy aide Pierre Salinger has written of the inability of the CIA and the Agency's Cuban-exile operatives to maintain the necessary security for the operation:

> The volatile leaders of the Cuban Revolutionary Council in exile — the political arm of the brigade — were just as heedless of security. Only nine days before the landing, the Council's President, Dr. José Miro Cardona, told the press in Miami that an uprising against Castro was "imminent."

JFK was livid. He said to me in his office a week before the invasion: "I can't believe what I'm reading! Castro doesn't need agents over here. All he has to do is read our papers. It's all laid out for him."[22]

Kenneth O'Donnell, Kennedy's White House chief of staff, recalls Kennedy stating, "Everybody in Miami knew exactly when those poor fellows were going to hit the beaches, but the only people in Cuba who knew about it were the ones who were working in Castro's office."[23] O'Donnell has further recalled Kennedy grimly remarking shortly before the invasion, "If we decided now to call the whole thing off, I don't know if we could go down there and take the guns away from them."[24]

At the time, Kennedy had no way of knowing how close he was to the truth. A year after the assassination, reporter Haynes Johnson disclosed that some of the CIA officials and Cuban exiles involved in the invasion had indeed made secret plans to "countermand" any decision to call it off. In his lengthy book, *The Bay of Pigs*, reporter Johnson, now of the *Washington Post*, disclosed that some of the CIA field coordinators had instructed their Cuban exile men to stage a "spontaneous" mutiny at their training grounds and go ahead and launch the invasion on their own, if Kennedy cancelled their orders.[25] According to Johnson, these same CIA officials had further instructed their Cuban exile teams to seize and jail them (the CIA field coordinators) at the training camps in order to make the proposed "spontaneous" mutiny look believable.[26]

While various CIA, Cuban exile community, and Pentagon sources would later try to place most of the blame for the disastrous invasion on President Kennedy (with the CIA's Bay of Pigs coordinator E. Howard Hunt being the most vociferous in trying to establish Kennedy's "guilt"), the official investigation into the failure of the invasion placed the blame squarely on the doorstep of the CIA and the military. Theodore Sorensen, former Special Counsel to President Kennedy, noted:

> The proximate cause of their [the Cuban exile forces] defeat, according to the full-scale investigation later conducted under the chairmanship of Gen. Maxwell Taylor was a shortage of ammunition, and the reasons for the shortage illustrate all the shortcomings of the operation.[27]

Sorensen, Kennedy's closest policy aide, went on to detail the CIA's disastrous role in canceling a convoy containing desperately needed ammunition enroute to the embattled exiles, then being pounded on the shores of Cuba by Castro's forces. As Sorensen noted, the CIA's invasion coordinators "called off the convoy without consulting the President."[28] While some CIA and Cuban exile defenders have maintained that the fiasco could be traced to an alleged decision by President Kennedy to withdraw "air cover" from the exiles' bombing raids against Castro's air bases, no evidence has ever come to light through the years to support this allegation. Indeed, as Sorensen noted, the CIA's stated "plan was to destroy Castro's air force on the ground before the battle began ... That plan failed."[29]

Sorensen and other observers have further noted that President Kennedy approved, although reluctantly, a limited air cover operation during the final hours of the invasion. The CIA requested this last-ditch air cover (of unmarked American Navy jets) as a means of trying to escort the Cuban exiles, own planes (outmoded and poorly equipped B-26s provided by the CIA) to Cuba.[30] However, as Sorensen has noted, the Navy jets requested by the CIA also fell victim to the Agency's bungled planning operations:

> . . . receiving their directions from the CIA, they [the Cuban exile B-26s] arrived on the scene an hour before the [American] jets, who received their directions from the Navy; and whether this tragic error was due to a difference in time zones or instructions, the B-26s were soon downed or gone, the jet mission was invalidated before it started, and without ammunition the exiles were quickly rounded up.[31]

Sorensen, who was asked by President Kennedy to assemble official material relating to the Bay of Pigs for use in the memoirs he planned to write after leaving the Presidency, has also noted other key mistakes in the CIA's invasion planning:

> . . . the immediate [invasion] area was not suitable for guerrilla warfare, as the President had been assured, the vast majority of brigade members had not been given guerrilla training, as had been assured; and the eighty mile route to the Escambray Mountains to which he had been assured they could escape, was so long, so swampy, and so covered by Castro's troops that this was never a realistic alternative.[32]

Finally, Sorensen concludes, the CIA's own general refusal to heed the advice of other parties involved in the invasion planning, and of course its uneven mask of secrecy, also had its toll on the final outcome:

> The CIA's close control of the operation, however, kept the President and the Cuban exile force largely uninformed of each other's thinking; and its enthusiasm caused

it to reject the clear evidence of Castro's political and military strength which was available from British and State Department Intelligence and even from newspaper stories.[33]

Interestingly, the subsequent negotiations of 1961 and 1962 (between the United States and Castro) for the release of the several hundred Cuban exiles captured and imprisoned by Castro provides one of the more telling examples of the CIA's continuing efforts to assassinate Fidel Castro — plots which were taking place without the knowledge of President Kennedy (or even CIA Director John McCone).[34] Attorney General Robert F. Kennedy had personally taken on the responsibility of coordinating a nationwide fund-raising campaign to collect fifty-three million dollars' worth of drugs, medical equipment, tractors, and baby food to be paid to the Castro government as ransom for the imprisoned Cuban exiles. This figure had been agreed upon by Castro and a bipartisan committee of prominent Americans (including Dr. Milton Eisenhower and Eleanor Roosevelt) after a long series of delicate negotiations. The man who had been selected by the Kennedy Administration to complete these negotiations was attorney James Donovan. In November, 1975, the Church Senate Intelligence Committee revealed that the CIA (acting under the authorization of Deputy Director Richard Helms) had sought to involve attorney Donovan — unknowingly — in another plot to assassinate Castro.[35] According to the Senate Committee, this assassination plot was conceived in "early 1963" by CIA officials Desmond Fitzgerald and William Harvey, with Harvey's previous experience in the CIA-Mafia assassination conspiracies apparently being brought to bear.[36] The Senate Intelligence Committee Report stated that the secret plan "involved having James Donovan [who was negotiating with Castro for the release of prisoners taken during the Bay of Pigs operation] present Castro with a contaminated diving suit . . . Donovan was not aware of the plan."[37]

This plot had been proposed after CIA official Desmond Fitzgerald had unsuccessfully sought to have "an exotic seashell rigged to explode deposited in an area where Castro commonly went skin-diving."[38]

According to the Church Report:

> The [CIA] Technical Services Division bought a diving suit, dusted the inside with a fungus that would produce a chronic skin disease (Madura Foot), and contaminated the breathing apparatus with a tubercule bacillus. The Inspector-General's Report states that the plan was abandoned because Donovan gave Castro a different diving suit on his own initiative. Helms testified that the diving suit never left the laboratory.[39]

It was not until April and May, 1962, that the President and the Attorney General learned of the CIA-Mafia assassination conspiracies against Castro, according to the Report of the Senate Intelligence Committee in late 1975.[40] As Kennedy finally began to understand the scope and deadly nature of some of the CIA's activities conducted behind his back, his anger toward the Agency apparently continued to increase. According to then-Senator George Smathers of Florida, a long-time friend of the President, Kennedy increasingly spoke privately of the need for reforming the CIA. Smathers has recalled:

> I remember him saying that the CIA frequently did things he didn't know about . . . He complained that the CIA was almost autonomous. He told me he believed the CIA had arranged to have Diem and Trujillo bumped off.[41]

In an effort to exert greater Presidential control over the activities of the CIA, John Kennedy had successfully sought the "voluntary" resignation or retirement of both CIA Director Allen Dulles and CIA Deputy Director Charles Cabell after the Bay of Pigs disaster. While waiting a "decent interval" as a matter of courtesy before making the two CIA leaders leave office, Kennedy was determined to put the Agency under new restrictions of accountability. Kenneth O'Donnell has written:

> The Bay of Pigs experience brought several significant changes in the Kennedy administration. The operations and authority of the CIA, which had had a free hand under Eisenhower, were limited and tightened . . . And Bobby Kennedy took on a larger general role as his brother's personal troubleshooter. [42]

Interestingly, it was the second crisis involving Cuba, the Cuban Missile Crisis of October, 1962, that has provided one of the more fascinating pieces of information regarding President Kennedy's reported fears of disloyalty inside the military establishment and CIA. This information concerns the Soviet Union's perception of alleged forces within the American government which may have threatened President Kennedy.

This startling account, which was first disclosed in the secret memoirs of Nikita Khrushchev smuggled out of Russia in 1969 and published in 1970, has received little public attention. In his tape-recorded memoirs, the former Russian leader told of a previously secret meeting between Attorney General Robert Kennedy and Soviet Ambassador Anatoly Dobrynin at the height of the Cuban Missile Crisis in late October, 1962.

In his memoirs (published under the title *Khrushchev Remembers*) the deposed Soviet leader set forth an account of this RFK-Dobrynin meeting, reported to him by Ambassador Dobrynin shortly after it occurred:

> Robert Kennedy looked exhausted. One could see from his eyes that he had not slept for days. He himself said that he had not been home for six days and nights. "The President is in a grave situation," Robert Kennedy said, "and he does not know how to get out of it. We are under very severe stress. In fact, we are under pressure from our military to use force against Cuba. Probably at this very moment the President is sitting down to write a message to Chairman Khrushchev. We want to ask you, Mr. Dobrynin, to pass President Kennedy's message to Chairman Khrushchev through unofficial channels. President Kennedy implores Chairman Khrushchev to accept his offer and to take into consideration the peculiarities of the American system. Even though the President is very much against starting a war over Cuba, an irreversible chain of events could occur, against his will. That is why the President is appealing directly to Chairman Khrushchev for his help in liquidating this conflict. If the situation continues much longer, the President is not sure that the military will not overthrow him and seize power. The American Army could get out of control."[43]

While Nikita Khrushchev may, of course, be regarded by many as a questionable source, the fact that he included this alleged information in his memoirs (compiled in lonely exile) nevertheless is interesting. Why Khrushchev would invent such a strange episode cannot readily be seen. Whether Dobrynin will confirm the Khrushchev account waits to be seen, as he presently refuses comment on the matter. At least one informed intelligence source has speculated that the Russians may possibly in fact possess a tape recording of this actual RFK-Dobrynin meeting, which Khrushchev indicates was held at the Russian Embassy in Washington. It would indeed appear quite possible (or even likely) that any such meetings at the Russian Embassy would have been recorded by the Soviets during the Missile Crisis. However, there has been no confirmation of this conjecture.

While the whole subject of the reported fears of President Kennedy as to some kind of uncontrollable "rogue elephant" within the CIA or possible plotting by officers in the military or intelligence communities is something which must be approached with great caution and perhaps even greater skepticism, interesting fragments of information continue to surface. Theodore Sorensen wrote about JFK's reaction, several months before the assassination, to the best-selling book *Seven Days in May*:

> Communications between the Chiefs of Staff and their Commander-in-Chief remained unsatisfactory for a large portion of his term. Enjoying a popular novel, *Seven Days in May*, about a fictional attempt by a few military brass to take over the country, the President joked, "I know a couple who wish they could."[44]

Arthur Schlesinger subsequently elaborated that President Kennedy had told him that *Seven Days in May* was a book that had met with his firm approval, as "a warning to the nation."[45] Years after the best-selling novel had been made into a popular motion picture, the director of the film, John Frankenheimer, revealed that John Kennedy not only liked the book but had been involved in the decision to make it into a movie. The noted director disclosed:

Those were the days of General Walker and so on . . . President Kennedy wanted *Seven Days in May* made. Pierre Salinger conveyed this to us. The Pentagon didn't want it done. Kennedy said that when we wanted to shoot at the White House he could conveniently go to Hyannis Port that weekend.[46]

Lee Harvey Oswald

Over thirteen years after the assassination of President John F. Kennedy, a seemingly impenetrable mystery still surrounds the actions and alleged role of the twenty-four-year-old youth who was murdered less than forty-eight hours after being charged with planning and carrying out the killing. Every investigator and investigation is led to the same strange question: Who was Lee Harvey Oswald and what really was his state of mind?

Was he really the lonely, embittered, and somewhat shallow leftist with a long-time streak of repressed violence that the Warren Commission portrayed? Was he actually a sophisticated agent or informant of some Federal agency or right-wing group operating under complex cover during his adult years, as alleged by many Warren Commission critics? Or was he "just a patsy" (in his own words of November 22, 1963) embroiled and framed in a conspiracy not of his own making?

"The fact that a decade has gone by and we are still unable to understand, fathom, or even really document all of his [Oswald's] connections — which seem to stretch practically to hell and back — shows things to be a little less tidy than the Warren Commission claimed,". a leading Congressman associated with the renewed interest in the Kennedy case has remarked. As will be seen through the maze of information on Oswald in forthcoming chapters, much of it supplied through recent declassifications of previously secret assassination documents, the Oswald connections do indeed stretch ominously far. And, throughout the mysteries relating to Lee Harvey Oswald runs the recurrent puzzle around which so much evidence makes so little sense: *motive*.

The Warren Commission itself was never able to set forth an actual motive behind Lee Oswald's alleged decision to assassinate President Kennedy — which the Commission concluded he formulated and then carried out, acting alone. It was the lack of any readily apparent motive for Oswald's alleged actions which fueled speculation of a conspiracy almost from the beginning. The search for a clear motive was one search which even the Warren Commission itself admitted had been unsuccessful. In its final Report, the Commission admitted the paucity of any real evidence of any real motive, and stated that, "The Commission does not believe that it can ascribe to him any one motive or group of motives."[47] While briefly noting such things as the accused assassin's alleged "hostility to his environment," and his alleged inability "to establish meaningful relationships with other people," the Warren Commission chose not to make any judgment of why the man they said killed the President actually did so. Former Warren Commission Counsel Joseph Ball later confided to author Edward Jay Epstein that the Commission's brief suggestion that

Oswald may conceivably have acted out of such things as "hostility to his environment" were actually "cliches that belonged in a television script."[48]

Sylvia Meagher, widely acknowledged as one of the most respected Warren Commission critics, has devoted years of meticulous research to probing the possible motivations of the alleged assassin, and has noted:

> If there is one area in which all the testimony is consistent and unambiguous it is Oswald's friendly and even admiring attitude toward President Kennedy. Witnesses of varying background and beliefs testified to Oswald's favorable feelings about the President...[49]

In her book, *Accessories After the Fact*, Meagher has catalogued the citations of various Warren Commission witnesses who had pointed out Oswald's attitude or feelings toward President Kennedy:

> Michael Paine (2H 399), Paul Gregory (9H 148) and George De Mohrenschildt (9H 255) testified that Oswald was an admirer of President Kennedy and had praised him. Lillian Murret, Oswald's aunt, said that he had liked the President and admired his wife. (8H 153) Marilyn Murret, her daughter, confirmed that Oswald had spoken favorably of the President.[50]

During his lengthy interrogation on the afternoon and evening of November 22, 1963, accused assassin Oswald had in fact stated, "I haven't any views on the President. I like his family very much."[51] As Sylvia Meagher further notes:

> No one who knew Oswald reported that he had ever said or done anything which sug-

gested animus toward President Kennedy or his family. Consequently, Oswald's alleged reply that he had no views on the President was actually an understatement; he might have, but did not, protest that he had always entertained friendly feelings for the President: there were withnesses to corroborate this.[52]

Based on information that became available in the summer of 1976, it would appear that the Warren Commission was not the only group interested in trying to reach some understanding of Oswald's possible motives. While it was previously known that the CIA was in the business of preparing highly secret psychological profiles of world leaders (with President Kennedy receiving one such CIA profile of Nikita Khrushchev prior to his Summit meeting with the Soviet leader in Vienna in 1961) new information about the CIA's psychological evaluation specialists was disclosed in June, 1976. James Keehner, a former CIA psychologist who had been instrumental in developing the Psychological Assessment System (PAS) for the CIA Technical Services Division, disclosed that the CIA psychological assessment specialists had at one time conducted studies of Lee Harvey Oswald and the assassin of Robert F. Kennedy, Sirhan Sirhan.[53] In an article on James Keehner's work for the CIA, writer Maureen Orth disclosed the following:

> The CIA assessed Sirhan Sirhan when Robert Kennedy was assassinated, and concluded he was insane. Keehner says he knows of no official assessment of Lee Harvey Oswald but he says that CIA psychological experts studied Oswald on their own and concluded he was incapable of killing the President by himself. (One of the CIA employees who worked on the Oswald material confirmed both the study and the conclusion.)[54]

While the CIA has never publicly released any of the psychological studies prepared by its specialists, a secret psychological profile of Dr. Daniel Ellsberg was released by the Ervin Senate Watergate Committee in 1974. In that instance, it was disclosed that Watergate conspirator E. Howard Hunt, the head of the White House Plumbers, had ordered the preparation of the secret CIA psychological profile of Ellsberg, in an effort to establish what Hunt claimed was Ellsberg's "mental instability."[55]

It was not until the final drafting of the Warren Commission Report in the summer of 1964 that the Commission members were finally faced with having to spell out the alleged motivation of the accused assassin. By then, the Commission staff had gone to some length to establish "what made Oswald tick." This effort had perhaps reached a veritable peak during the questioning of a former high school classmate of Oswald, Edward Voebel. During the Commission's questioning, a Warren Commission staff counsel asked Voebel:

> Did you have any impression as to whether he [Oswald] had a feeling that there were things that should have been accorded him by way of possession or attainment of worldly goods, of which he had been deprived because his father had predeceased him?[56]

Voebel's response, that he and Oswald "were just boys" who had "a fairly good time, as all boys our age seemed to do," was no doubt a disappointment to the Commission staff.[57]

Interestingly, it was Lee Oswald's older brother, Robert Oswald, viewed by the Warren Commission as one of its most helpful witnesses, who provided one of the more damning accounts of the Commission's efforts to establish Lee Oswald's motive.

Robert Oswald has disclosed that in July, 1964, as the Warren Commission was wrapping up its investigation, he received a telephone call from Commission Counsel Wesley Liebeler.[58] Liebeler told Robert Oswald that he was calling from an "isolated cabin or ski lodge" in Vermont where he was trying to write the Warren Report's section on the motives of Lee Harvey Oswald.[59] According to Robert Oswald, Liebeler very candidly asked him if he could come up with any explanation of his brother's motivation, stating "When you want to know something, you go directly to the man who should know the answer."[60] Robert Oswald has written:

> I was astonished by the question . . . here, suddenly, after taking the testimony of hundreds of witnesses, a member of the Commission staff was asking me to answer during a brief telephone conversation one of the most important questions about the entire case.[61]

With the sudden murder of Lee Oswald by Jack Ruby less than forty-eight hours after Kennedy's death — a murder which also seemingly lacked a clear motive — the lips of the accused Presidential assassin were forever sealed. While the accused man lay moaning on the floor of the police basement, dying of a gaping point-blank stomach wound inflicted by Ruby, it became apparent that whatever he knew, if anything, was going to remain a mystery. While the Warren Report omitted his account of Oswald's dying moments, Dallas Police Detective B.H. Combest had provided Commission Counsel Leon Hubert with the following information:

> *Combest:* He was moaning . . . and I laid him down on the floor and removed the handcuffs that he had on him . . . At the time I asked him and talked to him trying

to get him to make a statement to me at the time. Especially, after I realized how serious the wound was. When we first asked him he appeared to comprehend what I was saying . . . I told him was there anything that he wanted me to tell anybody or was there anything he wanted to say right now before it was too late . . . trying to let him know if he was ever going to say anything he was going to have to say it then.

Hubert: And do you think you used language to him to convey to him your idea that he was dying?

Combest: Yes, sir.

Hubert: Did you get any indication that he actually understood what you were trying to convey to him?

Combest: When I first started asking him he did. He looked up at me, seemed to recognize that I — who was talking to him . . .

Hubert: But, didn't say anything?

Combest: No sir, just shook his head and I said, "Do you have anything you want to tell us now," and he shook his head . . .[62]

While the young accused assassin still remains an enigma thirteen years after the President's murder, the varying perceptions of Lee Oswald by the immediate members of his family provide some insight into the complexity of his background and activities.

Marina Oswald

"Marina Oswald has lied to the Secret Service, the FBI and this Commission repeatedly on matters which are of vital concern to the people of this country and the world," wrote Warren Commission Counsel Norman Redlich in an internal Commission memorandum in 1964.[63] Commission Counsel Redlich — who was expressing his discontent over the inclination of Commission members Warren, Ford, and Dulles to give strong credence to most of Marina Oswald's testimony — was accurate in describing as a liar the young attractive widow of the accused assassin. As will be seen, the Russian-born wife of Lee Harvey Oswald later became the Warren Commission's "star witness" against her husband, providing testimony which would of course have been inadmissible in any court of law, under the long-established American system of legal jurisprudence which forbids such testimony by a wife against her husband. With the death of Lee Oswald two days after the President's assassination, however, the privileged legal relationship of Marina Oswald to her husband Lee came to an end.

Within a few short weeks of the assassination, Marina Oswald would be called as the Warren Commission's first official witness and would provide the most damaging testimony against her husband of any of the hundreds of people contacted during the Commission's nine-month investigation. However, as Redlich noted, Marina's testimony would also be filled with unresolvable contradictions, "misstatements," and, even worse, clear fabrications.

Marina Oswald appeared before the Warren Commission as a witness on four separate occasions, beginning on February 3, 1964 and concluding in September of that same year, shortly before the Warren Report was prepared for release.

Marina Oswald's initial reaction to hearing news of her husband's arrest on the afternoon of November 22, 1963, had been most supportive, as might be expected even of a wife whose marriage was not going all that well. In the immediate days after the assassination, Marina Oswald became famous, partly as a result of her defense of her husband in heavily accented broken English: "Lee good man. Lee not shoot anybody." However, as detailed examination of her various sets of testimony has over the years shown, Marina's views were quite susceptible to change, particularly after she became a ward of the Federal authorities in the days following Oswald's murder by Jack Ruby.

At one time (early in her Commission testimony) Marina Oswald testified that Lee had not only been "a good man," but also a good husband.[64] In later testimony Marina stated that he had been a bad husband.[65] While at one point she identified the Mannlicher-Carcano rifle found on the sixth floor of the Texas School Book Depository as what she called "the fateful rifle of Lee Oswald," she later testified (after again viewing the same rifle) that she was not sure it was Lee's gun.[66] At another point in her testimony, Marina spoke of a pistol that she said her husband owned.[67] However, later on she testified that she didn't know her husband even had a pistol.[68]

While Marina Oswald had initially defended her husband by saying, "Lee good man. Lee not shoot anybody," she subsequently told the Warren Commission of what she alleged were two other assassination attempts or plans by her husband: trying to kill General Edwin Walker, the extremist general mustered out of the armed forces, and former Vice President Richard M. Nixon.[69] Still later, after becoming the Commission's key witness implicating her husband as the assassin of John F. Kennedy, she surprised the members of the Warren Commission with yet another twist in her checkered testimony. Marina told the Commission that she believed that "Lee did not have President Kennedy as a prime target when he assassinated him."[70] When a startled Congressman, Hale Boggs, then asked who was the target, Marina answered, "I think it was Connally. That's my personal opinion that he perhaps was shooting at Governor Connally, the Governor of Texas."[71]

One of the clearer illustrations of the weakness and unreliability of the testimony of Marina Oswald came with her allegation that her husband Lee had also once planned to assassinate former Vice President Richard M. Nixon. According to Marina, she vaguely remembered Lee saying that he was going to kill Nixon when the former Presidential candidate made a visit to Dallas.[72] While the Warren Commission had the FBI interview Nixon and his secretary, Rose Mary Woods, in an unsuccessful effort to learn of any such Nixon trip to Dallas, Marina Oswald stuck to her story. She further testified that she had finally locked Lee inside their bathroom in order to prevent him from going out and shooting Nixon at some undefined point in time.[73] Unfortunately for that part of her story, the Warren Commission established that there was no such lock on the outside of the Oswald bathroom, nor any such lock (capable of locking Lee inside) on any of the Oswald residences.

Though many Warren Commission critics have long questioned whether Marina Oswald's testimony about her husband killing President Kennedy could readily be believed — while her strange testimony about the Nixon attempt remained without any foundation — the Warren Commission obviously believed it could.

However, the Warren Report did take brief (but sympathetic) notice of Marina's flawed story of Lee's plan to shoot Richard Nixon:

> Marina Oswald might have misunderstood her husband . . . In the absence of other evidence that Oswald actually intended to shoot someone at this time, the Commission concluded that the incident, as described by Marina Oswald, was of no probative value in the Commission's decision concerning the identity of the assassin . . . [74]

Author Sylvia Meagher points out the inherent problems of this episode and other related matters:

> In other words, the Commission concluded, mainly or exclusively on the basis of Marina Oswald's testimony, that Oswald had (a) made a prior attempt to kill, in an attack on General Walker, (b) purchased and possessed a rifle, (c) stored that rifle in the Paine garage, and (d) removed it in order to assassinate the President; yet the Commission also concluded that the incredible story of the thwarted attempt on Nixon, which fell apart at every point, in no way raised the issue of Marina Oswald's credibility.[75]

Indeed, as the various assassination researchers continue to point out, Marina Oswald's testimony is replete with such inconsistencies and contradictions relating to such crucial matters as Oswald's contacts with the FBI in New Orleans and in Dallas; his alleged use of various aliases; his possible practice with some kind of rifle, and other questions relating to his rifle and alleged ammunition. One classic example was provided early in Marina's testimony when she stated that she had not been telling the truth about her husband's alleged possession of a rifle. During the exchange, her Secret Service interpreter interrupted and noted in English that Marina recognized that she must now "tell the truth" since she was now under oath:

> *J. Lee Rankin:* Did you ever see him clean the rifle?
>
> *Marina Oswald:* Yes. I said before I never had seen it before.
>
> *Secret Service Interpreter:* She says she was not sworn in before. But now inasmuch as she is sworn in, she is going to tell the truth.[76]

Needless to say, a great deal of speculation continues to relate to the enigmatic Marina Oswald and her knowledge of her equally enigmatic husband. Marina Oswald clearly seems to have deliberately (and, quite possibly, criminally) concealed evidence of various actions relating to her late husband. While it is known that Marina Oswald viewed the FBI with considerable fear (sometimes refusing to be questioned by them without the presence of other investigators in the same room) and while it has long been suggested by various sources (including the Warren Commission staff) that she may have felt pressured by FBI agents to "amend" some parts of her testimony, her role in the investigation remains highly illusory.

In recent years the Russian background of Marina Oswald (formerly Marina Prusakova) has come under renewed attention. The Warren Commission itself had noted that Marina's uncle Ilya had attained the rank of colonel in the Russian MVD, the governmental ministry that includes the KGB.[77] Although theories have been advanced of such disparate concepts as the KGB using Marina as an agent to manipulate Oswald into killing the American President, or Oswald being recruited by the CIA to romance Marina, the niece of a Russian KGB official, while doing undercover work in that country, most assassination investigators believe the truth about Lee Oswald and his wife still remains out of reach.

Robert Oswald

Robert Oswald, the older brother of Lee Harvey Oswald, has long been the subject of sympathy among those who have studied the Kennedy case. Soft-spoken, intelligent, Oswald's brother was viewed by the Warren Commission staff as one of the more helpful witnesses to appear before the Commission. Chairman Earl Warren reportedly viewed it as "a tragedy" that "such a fine man" could be embroiled in a national nightmare by the actions of his "twisted" brother. Some observers have noted the parallel of Edwin Booth, the noted nineteenth century actor whose career was shaken when his brother John Wilkes Booth assassinated President Lincoln. Robert Oswald, who still shies away from interviews or other publicity, has always believed that his brother Lee did in fact murder President Kennedy:

. . . based on the findings of the Warren

Commission, in my opinion there is only one conclusion, and that is that Lee did assassinate the President of the United States and also killed Officer Tippit.[78]

While staunchly defending the Federal government's identification of his brother Lee as the Dallas assassin, stating, "I do not believe any of the investigating groups deliberately concealed facts or manufactured evidence to fit some preconceived theory," Robert Oswald has voiced some degree of criticism over some aspects of the Warren Commission's investigation. In a book published in 1967, Robert Oswald voiced his displeasure over the performance of one Warren Commission member in particular:

> Gerry Ford struck me as a very ambitious young man who saw his assignment on the Commission as an opportunity to get some public attention. The way he walked, the way he talked, his entire manner, seemed to bear out this interpretation.[79]

Robert Oswald has also cautiously expressed some question as to whether or not another assassin may have been involved with his brother Lee. In particular, he questions the controversial "single-bullet theory," set forth by the Warren Commission in concluding that Lee Oswald acted alone. Robert has stated:

> The Commission may have convinced some people that the one bullet caused the extensive injuries to two men and then emerged in that [barely damaged] condition. It has not convinced me, partly because of the vagueness of its report on its own efforts to demonstrate the reasonableness of its theory. I feel that these tests, like many of the others carried out with the Mannlicher-

Carcano, were ill-conceived, unrealistic, and finally meaningless.[80]

Robert Oswald also has faulted officers of the Dallas Police Department for refusing to allow him to see his brother Lee for anything longer than a brief meeting, during Oswald's two-day imprisonment. Robert Oswald has described the short meeting he had with Lee on the day following the assassination:

> As we talked that Saturday afternoon before his death, I felt that the police interrupted our conversation just when we were approaching the point where he might have said something that would have made his motives clear to me even if he did not say in so many words that he had killed President Kennedy. This, of course, is pure speculation.[81]

Interestingly, Robert Oswald has written that his brother had voiced a short warning of sorts at the beginning of their meeting on the day before Lee was murdered by Ruby. Robert has written that upon entering the visitors' cubicle in the Dallas jail, Lee told him, "This is taped."[82] After telling Lee that he didn't care whether they were being taped or not, Robert states that he had the following brief exchange with his brother, Lee Harvey Oswald:

> . . . I finally asked him bluntly, "Lee, what in the Sam Hill is goin' on?"
> "I don't know," he said.
> "You don't know? Look, they got your pistol, they got your rifle, they've got you charged with shooting the President and a police officer. And you tell me you don't know. Now, I want to know just what's going on."
> He stiffened and straightened up, and his

facial expression was suddenly very tight.

"I just don't know what they're talking about," he said, firmly and deliberately. "Don't believe all this so-called evidence."

I was studying his face closely, trying to find the answer to my questions in his eyes or expression. He realized that, and as I stared into his eyes, he said to me quietly, "Brother, you won't find anything there."[83]

Marguerite Oswald

Marguerite Oswald, the mother of the accused assassin of President Kennedy, now aging and in ill health, has of course long been one of the more vocal defenders of her son. Commonly characterized by the Warren Commission, the press, and other observers as a hurt, embittered, and accusatory woman, Marguerite Oswald has said that her son Lee Harvey Oswald was probably a secret agent of the U.S. government, most likely the CIA, and that one of his missions had been "defecting" to the Soviet Union, and later doing various undercover work in New Orleans and Dallas. Unlike the other critics of the Warren Commission, however, Mrs. Oswald strangely enough has said that from the very beginning. While for years her charges often precipitated questions about her sanity more than anything else, intervening events and disclosures now tend to cast somewhat different light on "the assassin's mother." Lee Oswald's brother, Robert, has described his mother's longtime belief:

> My mother has managed to convince herself that Lee was recruited by a secret agency of the United States government after he enlisted in the Marines. He was sent to Russia on some unexplained confidential mission, she believed, then brought back to the United States to carry out some other secret assignment — perhaps the assassination of President Kennedy. She is certain that all of his actions in the final months of his life were carried out at the direction of the CIA or some similar organization.[84]

"He never did tell me why he went to Russia," Mrs. Oswald has stated, "[but] I have my own opinions. He spoke Russian, he wrote Russian, and he read Russian. Why? Because my boy was being trained as an agent, that's why."[85] According to Mrs. Oswald, Lee's alleged service as some kind of secret agent was only natural as "we are a military family."[86] While never producing any real evidence to substantiate her charges, the highly emotional Mrs. Oswald has long accused the Warren Commission of deliberately conspiring to "frame" her son:

> If my son was an agent of the United States, this should be known . . . Did Chief Justice Warren have to whitewash something the public don't (sic) know about? Did he know my son was innocent? Who used my son?

52

My son was killed on cue . . .[87]

While Mrs. Oswald has not been able to supply any documentary evidence to support her allegations, she has inadvertently provided a small piece of information that has recently been of interest to Senate and House probers and other investigators. It is believed, in fact, that this information may be of considerable use in tracing the CIA's awareness and coverage (through file reports and other data) of Lee Oswald's activities in the Marine Corps and his subsequent defection to the Soviet Union.

Jean Stafford, who wrote a book about Mrs. Oswald in 1966, *A Mother in History*, has written of a letter that Mrs. Oswald sent to Soviet Premier Nikita Khrushchev in the summer of 1960, inquiring as to the whereabouts and well-being of her son, the defector. Mrs. Oswald was at that point fearful over the fact that her letters to her son in Russia had been returned to her unopened. As will be seen, the interesting thing about the letter from Mrs. Oswald to Khrushchev is that recent disclosures clearly indicate that the CIA must have intercepted and photographed it at some point before it left the United States.

Mrs. Oswald (who possesses a copy of her original letter) has described her letter of July 19, 1960 to the Soviet Premier, as follows:

> I stated that Lee had gone to Russia in September of 1959 and that I had one letter from him in January, but my letter to him was returned and I never heard from him again. I asked Mr. Khrushchev to supply me with any information about his whereabouts, if he was working and so on and so forth . . . [88]

Even though Mrs. Oswald states that she "did not receive an answer from Mr. Khrushchev," this letter must have been processed through the CIA's Office of Security, according to previously secret information about CIA activities disclosed by the Senate Intelligence Committee in 1975 and 1976. The Senate Committee disclosed two CIA "mail intercept projects" which had secretly opened and examined mail sent overseas from the U.S. to Communist countries, during a twenty-year period.

According to the Senate Committee, all mail sent from the U.S. to the Soviet Union was opened during that period, presumably including Mrs. Oswald's letter to Khrushchev. According to the Senate Intelligence Report, "more than two hundred and fifteen thousand letters to and from the Soviet Union were opened and photographed by CIA agents in New York. Copies of more than fifty-seven thousand of these letters were also disseminated to the FBI."[89] Thus, it seems probable that the CIA (and perhaps the FBI) has yet another piece of information about Lee Oswald — his mother's letter of inquiry to Khrushchev — in their files which has heretofore never been disclosed. For over ten years, Warren Commission critics have meticulously documented discrepancies that are apparent in the listings and inventories of classified documents compiled by the CIA and FBI relating to Lee Oswald and the assassination. Many critics have long maintained that both agencies appear to be holding back other "classified" assassination documents which the Warren Commission and public have never known about.

In any event, the CIA's secret mail intercept project (code-named HTLINGUAL by the Agency's Counterintelligence Staff and SRPOINTER by the Office of Security) must indeed have netted Mrs. Oswald's letter to Russia, and thus there must be another previously undisclosed CIA file entry on

Oswald's activities in Russia. While disclosing that "a team of about four (CIA) Office of Security personnel screened and photographed this mail" to Russia, the Senate Intelligence Committee more importantly noted that copies of all these intercepted letters "were indexed, filed, and are retained even today."[90]

Jack Ruby

"I am not a gangster."[91]

"There was no conspiracy."[92]

Thus spoke Jack L. Ruby on June 7, 1964, during his appearance before the Warren Commission, in which he provided his characteristically graphic version of why he had snuffed out the life of the man charged with planning and carrying out the assassination of John F. Kennedy.[93] Ruby testified:

> No one . . . requested me to do anything. I never spoke to anyone about attempting to do anything . . . No underworld person made any effort to contact me. It all happened that Sunday morning.

> The last thing I read was that Mrs. Kennedy may have to come back to Dallas for a trial for Lee Harvey Oswald and I don't know what bug got ahold of me ... suddenly the feeling, the emotional feeling came within me that someone owed this debt to our beloved President to save her the ordeal of coming back.[94]
>
> I had the gun in my right hip pocket, and impulsively, if that is the correct word here, I saw him [Oswald] and that is all I can say . . . I think I used the words, "You killed my President, you rat." The next thing I was down on the floor.[95]

Jack Ruby would stick to that same story — of murdering Lee Oswald only out of a compassionate desire to spare Jackie Kennedy the agony of returning to Dallas for Oswald's trial — to the very end. Shortly before his death on January 3, 1967, just a month before controversial New Orleans District Attorney Jim Garrison would bring the Kennedy assassination back to national attention, Ruby had reaffirmed his Warren Commission testimony and again claimed that he had acted without guidance from any source and only to spare Mrs. Kennedy further sorrow.

However, less than three months after he died from a reported blood clot stemming from a case of terminal cancer, the veracity of Jack Ruby's testimony about why he had murdered the alleged Presidential assassin was irrevocably shattered.

On March 27, 1967, *Newsweek* magazine disclosed the contents of a handwritten note that Ruby had given to one of his attorneys, Joseph Tonahill, several months after the assassination, during a discussion in his Dallas jail cell.[96] The contents of the Ruby note read as follows:

> Joe you should know this. Tom Howard

> [Ruby's earlier lawyer] told me to say that I shot Oswald so that Caroline and Mrs. Kennedy wouldn't have to come to Dallas to testify. OK?[97]

With the disclosure of the previously secret Ruby note and other information which has come to light in recent years, the entire basis of Jack Ruby's Warren Commission testimony has been brought into serious question. A review of that testimony, from June 7 and July 18, 1964, dramatically illustrates the length to which Jack Ruby sought to establish that he had acted without guidance from any source, and only to spare the President's widow the grief of having to return to Dallas for Oswald's trial:

> I felt very emotional and very carried away for Mrs. Kennedy, that with all the strife she had gone through . . . that someone owed it to our beloved President that she shouldn't be expected to come back to face [the] trial of this heinous crime. (Warren Commission Volume 5, p. 197)

> [I saw] a small comment in the newspaper that, I don't know how it was stated, that Mrs. Kennedy may have to come back for the trial of Lee Harvey Oswald.
> That caused me to go like I did; that caused me to go like I did. (Warren Commission Volume 5, p. 198)

> I walked down those few steps [to kill Oswald] and . . . I wouldn't say I saw red — it was a feeling I had for our beloved President and Mrs. Kennedy. (Warren Commission Volume 5, p. 199)

> All that blended into the things that, like

> a screwball, the way it turned out, that I thought that I would sacrifice myself for the few moments of saving Mrs. Kennedy the discomfiture of coming back to trial. (Warren Commission Volume 5, p. 200)

> I was very much broken up emotionally, and I constantly repeated that I didn't want Mrs. Kennedy to come back to trial... (Warren Commission Volume 5, p. 206)

> I never called the man [Oswald] by any obscene name because as I stated earlier, there was no malice in me. He was insignificant, to my feelings for my love for Mrs. Kennedy and our beloved President... Anything I said was with emotional feeling of I didn't want Mrs. Kennedy to come back to trial. (Warren Commission Volume 5, p. 206)

> ... I was so carried away emotionally that I said ... "If something happened to this person [Oswald] that then Mrs. Kennedy won't have to come back for trial there." (Warren Commission Volume 14, p. 549)

In the years since the death of President Kennedy, significant new areas of evidence have arisen pertaining to Ruby's associations with powerful organized crime leaders as well as anti-Castro exile operatives associated with some of those same Mafia figures. This new evidence directly contradicts the Warren Commission conclusion that while Ruby may have been an acquaintance of some minor "underworld" gambling figures, he was not actually involved with organized crime. As will be seen (see the chapter on "The Mafia Connection") Jack Ruby now clearly appears to have had various dealings with several syndicate figures who were closely associated with Santos Trafficante, the Florida Mafia leader, who served as a key coordinator of the CIA-Mafia assassination conspiracies against Castro. As will be seen, the implications of some of this new information — which was of course unknown to the Warren Commission — are quite serious.

Interestingly, the Warren Commission's central effort to probe Jack Ruby's alleged ties to the Mafia and/or various Cuban activities — an investigative effort aimed at utilizing the considerable resources of the CIA — was eventually stymied. Several Senate investigators who worked on the Senate Intelligence Committee's review of the Kennedy assassination investigation have voiced their belief that this Warren Commission effort to probe Jack Ruby's ties provides the clearest example of the CIA's lack of cooperation with — or obstruction of — the Warren Commission probe.

The episode began on March 12, 1964, when key members of the Warren Commission staff met with the CIA's Deputy Director for Plans, Richard Helms, and some Helms' aides. The Warren Commission investigators gave Helms a lengthy official Commission memorandum requesting CIA investigative assistance pertaining to the Commission's probe of Jack Ruby.[98] The Commission memorandum, titled "Jack Ruby — Background, Friends, and Other Pertinent Information," contained an extensive accounting of information indicating possible Ruby ties to organized crime figures, as well as various Cuban activities.[99] The Warren Commission quite naturally viewed the CIA as a prime source of potential information for several key areas outlined in the memo.

As can be seen, this memo set forth an extensive array of information for the CIA to investigate, both on Ruby's personal background and possible associations:

. . . Ruby is considered to be a highly emotional person. He speaks with a lisp, has been described as soft-spoken, is generally well mannered and well dressed, but is given to sudden and extreme displays of temper and violence. He is known to have brutally beaten at least 25 different persons either as a result of a personal encounter or because they were causing disturbances in his club.

He is said to have effeminate mannerisms and is alleged by some to be homosexual. However, there is no direct evidence of any homosexual behavior. Although he has never been married, he is known to have dated and at one time was known as a "ladies' man." In recent years, some of the women toward whom he has shown interest have indicated that he had perverted attitudes toward sex. One male witness describes an occasion when he [engaged in a perverse sexual act] with one of his dogs and apparently derived great pleasure from it . . .

To generalize, it can be said that, while living in Dallas, Ruby has very carefully cultivated friendships with police officers and other public officials. At the same time, he was peripherally, if not directly connected with members of the underworld.

Ruby is also rumored to have been the tip-off man between the Dallas police and the Dallas underworld, especially in regard to enforcement of the local liquor laws.

. . . His associations with strip teasers and cheap entertainers brought him into constant contact with people of questionable reputations. Ruby operated his businesses on a cash basis, keeping no record, whatsoever — a strong indication that Ruby himself was involved in illicit operations of some sort.

> When it suited his own purposes, he did not hesitate to call on underworld characters for assistance.[100]

Referring to areas of possible conspiratorial involvement, the Warren Commission memorandum outlined the following further information for the CIA to investigate:

> In about 1959, Ruby became interested in the possibility of opening a gambling casino in Havana. He was in contact at that time with a friend, Lewis J. McWillie. Insufficient evidence is available on that episode to evaluate Ruby's connection with any Cuban (anti-Castro or pro-Castro) groups. Ruby is also rumored to have met in Dallas with an American Army colonel (LNU) and some Cubans concerning the sale of arms. A Government informant in Chicago connected with the sale of arms to anti-Castro Cubans has reported that such Cubans were behind the Kennedy assassination . . .
>
> On balance, it may be said that Ruby's primary interest in life was making money. He does not seem to have had any great scruples concerning the manner in which he might do so. However, he has usually been careful to avoid prosecution by law enforcement authorities . . . His primary technique in avoiding prosecution, was the maintenance of friendship with police officers, public officials, and other influential persons in the Dallas community.
>
> It is possible that Ruby could have been utilized by a politically motivated group either upon the promise of money or because of the influential character of the individual approaching Ruby. If he is a sex deviate, blackmail is also possible.[101]

Finally, after setting forth several sets of information concerning Jack Ruby's relationships with a number of rather mysterious people (including several alleged "underworld" and Teamster Union figures), the Warren Commission memorandum came to a final area of information. Stating that "the following groups and places seem significant in looking for ties between Ruby and others who might have been interested in the assassination of President Kennedy," the Commission listed a handful of groups, including, "The Las Vegas Gambling Community," the "Teamsters Union," and "The Dallas Police Department."[102]

With the Warren Commission investigation then operating at its peak, the Commission staff waited eagerly for the CIA response from Deputy Director for Plans Richard Helms, who would become Director of the Agency two years later. The Commission waited nine weeks — and still there was no response from Helms.

Finally, on May 19, 1964, Warren Commission General Counsel J. Lee Rankin sent a letter to Helms asking for an immediate response to the Commission's request of two months earlier. The Rankin letter stated:

Dear Mr. Helms:

At a meeting on March 12, 1964, between representatives of your Agency and this Commission a memorandum prepared by members of the Commission staff was handed to you which related to the background of Jack L. Ruby and alleged associates and/or activities with Cuba.

At that time we requested that you review this information and submit to the Commission any information contained in your files regarding the matters covered in the memorandum, as well as any other analyses by your representatives which you believed might be useful to the Commission.

As you know, this Commission is nearing the end of its investigation. We would appreciate hearing from you as soon as possible whether you are in a position to comply with this request in the near future.[103]

The Warren Commission staff then waited for what it finally thought would be an early response to its second request pertaining to Ruby. Well over three months later, the Commission was still waiting.

Finally, on September 19, 1964 (as the actual Warren Commission Report was already being set in type at the Government Printing Office), an astonished Commission staff received the official CIA response in the form of a brief memo from Thomas Karamessines, an assistant to Richard Helms. The CIA memo stated:

Reference is made to your memorandum of 19 May 1964, requesting that this Agency furnish any information in its files relative to Jack Ruby, his activities and his associates ... An examination of Central Intelligence Agency files has produced no information on Jack Ruby or his activities. The Central Intelligence Agency has no indication that Ruby or Lee Harvey Oswald ever knew each other, were associated, or might have been connected in any manner.[104]

A former senior counsel to the Warren Commission recently remarked, "If we had known then that after six months of delaying, all they would come up with was that little memo, things would have been a lot different." When asked why the Commission hadn't pushed Helms harder, or whether the Commission shouldn't have suspected such a response after the long delay, the same former Commission counsel replied, "Those are questions that just get back to the climate thing. The times and feelings were a lot different then."

Thus, little or no information on the mysterious Ruby and such things as his known travels to Cuba and ties to pre-Castro Cuban gambling operatives of the Mafia was to be received from the CIA. Oswald's killer remains an equally enigmatic figure even after his lengthy appearances before the Warren Commission. As from the beginning, the same ominous questions remained. Was Ruby's story about murdering Oswald only out of explosive sympathy for Jacqueline Kennedy really credible? If it wasn't, had he either known Oswald or been a part of an assassination conspiracy? And, were Ruby's numerous ties to seeming underworld figures significant?

The importance of Jack Ruby to the Kennedy assassination case is crucial. For it is the Ruby connection which could provide the greatest likelihood of unraveling the cover-up of the assassination conspiracy, if in fact one does exist. For assuming that Jack Ruby silenced Lee Oswald as part of the alleged conspiracy, then one can also reasonably assume that the conspiracy at that point was falling apart, had gone haywire, and was otherwise about to come undone. Something must have gone wrong.

The base assumption of the alleged Ruby involvement would be that Oswald had to be silenced — that he could have supplied either direct or indirect information leading to other people involved in the Kennedy murder. The fact that the young accused assassin was murdered so soon after the President's death — just forty-eight hours later — would seem to emphasize the urgency with which this alleged silencing was needed.

From that assumption, one reaches perhaps the

central point involved in the alleged Ruby connection. If Oswald somehow came to be captured alive, and placed in the position of possibly naming others involved, how had this happened? Surely something quite serious must have gone wrong with the plan in the immediate minutes and hours after the President was struck by the fatal shots. What thus seems probable is one of two simple things: either Oswald was supposed to have gotten away, through a carefully planned escape, or he was supposed to have been killed even earlier — before he was apprehended by the Dallas Police.

Some Warren Commission critics, suspicious about various aspects of the case involving Dallas Police officers, have speculated that Officer J. D. Tippit, who was allegedly killed by Oswald during his escape, may have been assigned to the early silencing of the assassin — a silencing that went awry when Oswald "outdrew" the Dallas patrolman. (See reference to Officer J.D. Tippit and other Dallas officers in the chapter on "The Dallas Police.")

The concept that the alleged powerful conspirators involved would have actually planned for Oswald's getaway (perhaps by leaving the country) has long seemed questionable to various investigators and researchers of the Kennedy case. Assuming that there was such a conspiracy, the best evidence would seem to indicate that the conspiracy had been designed to result in the identification of a single man — a 24-year-old politically "leftist" Texas man — as the lone and perhaps deranged assassin. The strong consensus of the various Warren Commission critics has long been that this "lone assassin" concept — or framing — would have been integral to any conspiracy. The prospect of the alleged assassin actually escaping, and the national and international manhunt that would have resulted (complete with closing the borders and a wave of public terror) seems to be exactly the opposite of what such conspirators would have sought. The ability of young Oswald to vanish and escape would in all likelihood have been regarded as confirmation that he had received some help, and that there were indeed some sophisticated co-conspirators involved.

Finally, assuming that such an assassination conspiracy did exist, it has been suggested that the best argument that it was premised upon was the partial or total framing of a "lone assassin," who would be killed early on, is that this is what actually happened — and that is what worked. Even assuming that some serious hitch in the plan occurred between November 22nd and November 24th, causing Ruby to have to carry out the urgent silencing of Oswald at that time, it can be said that if this was in fact what happened, whoever planned it that way got away with it for at least thirteen years.

Interestingly, as will be seen later, there is an intriguing piece of information surrounding Jack Ruby's immediate movements after the assassination that has received scant attention by both the public and the critics of the Warren Commission. Namely, that according to his own testimony, Jack Ruby stood "about three feet away from Oswald" in the Dallas Police headquarters, just twelve hours after the assassination.[105] And further, that Ruby would at first admit that he had had his gun with him during this first encounter with Oswald, but would later tell the Warren Commission, "I lied about it. It isn't so. I didn't have a gun."[106]

Thus, as can be seen from the mysterious Ruby note that surfaced after his death in early 1967, Ruby's extensive testimony about killing Oswald "out of love for our beloved President" and to "spare Mrs. Kennedy" the necessity of attending Oswald's trial, was actually a legal ploy apparently created by his first lawyer, Tom Howard. The only clear conclusion from the note seems to be that Ruby felt that he had to conceal the real reasons why he shot Oswald to death.

Further, the largely overlooked fact that Ruby first actually stood within feet of Oswald just twelve hours after the assassination, possibly with a gun in his coat, seems to indicate a strong possibility that the stalking of the young accused assassin had already begun.

1. *Senate Intelligence Committee Report on the Kennedy Assassination*, p. 95.
2. Ibid.
3. Letter of February 27, 1964, from FBI Director J. Edgar Hoover to Warren Commission General Counsel J. Lee Rankin; Warren Commission Document 1052.
4. FBI Report of March 26, 1964, "Jack L. Ruby, Lee Harvey Oswald - Victim;" Warren Commission Docoment 686d.
5. Warren Commission Document 1052.
6. Ibid.
7. Associated Press, *Washington Post*, October 1, 1976.
8. Ibid.
9. CIA memorandum, "25 November 1963 - Subject: Mr. Lee Harvey Oswald," Document No. 435-173A.
10. Ibid.
11. Ibid.
12. Ibid.
13. *Senate Intelligence Committee Report on the Kennedy Assassination*, p. 65.
14. Ibid.
15. January 27, 1964 Warren Commission Session Transcript, pp. 186-187.
16. *CBS Reports Inquiry*, "The American Assassins," Part Two, November 26, 1975.
17. Ibid.
18. Pierre Salinger, *With Kennedy* (Garden City, N.Y., Doubleday and Company, Inc., 1966), p. 3.
19. Kenneth P. O'Donnell and David F. Powers, *Johnny, We Hardly Knew Ye* (New York: Simon and Schuster, Pocket Books Edition, 1973), p. 19.
20. Paul B. Fay, Jr., *The Pleasure of His Company* (New York: Harper and Row, 1966), pp. 174-175.

21. Ibid., pp. 172-173.
22. Salinger, *With Kennedy*, p. 146.
23. O'Donnell and Powers, *Johnny, We Hardly Knew Ye*, p. 316.
24. Ibid., p. 312.
25. Haynes Johnson, *The Bay of Pigs* (New York: W.W. Norton and Company, 1964), p. 76.
26. Ibid.
27. Theodore C. Sorensen, *Kennedy* (New York: Bantam Books Edition, 1966), p. 334.
28. Ibid., p. 335.
29. Ibid., p. 336.
30. Ibid., p. 335.
31. Ibid.
32. Ibid., p. 338.
33. Ibid., p. 342.
34. *Senate Intelligence Committee Report on Foreign Assassinations*, pp. 102, 148, 154-155.
35. Ibid., p. 85.
36. Ibid., p. 86.
37. Ibid., p. 85.
38. Ibid.
39. Ibid., p. 86.
40. Ibid., p. 131-133.
41. Jack Anderson column, January 19, 1971; Tad Szulc, "Cuba On Our Mind," *Esquire*, February 1974.
42. O'Donnell and Powers, *Johnny, We Hardly Knew Ye*, pp. 320-321.
43. Nikita S. Khrushchev, Edward Crankshaw, ed., *Khrushchev Remembers* (Boston and Toronto: Little, Brown and Company, 1970), pp. 497-498.
44. Sorensen, *Kennedy*, p. 684.
45. Arthur M. Schlesinger, Jr., *The Imperial Presidency* (New York: Popular Library Edition, 1974), pp. 198, 417.
46. Charles Higham and Joel Greenberg, *The Celluloid Muse: Hollywood Directors Speak* (New York: Signet Books, 1972) p. 92.
47. *Report of the Warren Commission on the Assassination of President John F. Kennedy* (New York: Bantam Books, Inc., 1964), p. 399. (Hereafter referred to as Warren Commission Report.)
48. Edward Jay Epstein, *Inquest* (New York: Viking Press, 1966), p. 152.
49. Sylvia Meagher, *Accessories After the Fact* (New York, Indianapolis, Kansas City: The Bobbs-Merrill Company, Inc., 1967), p. 234.

50. Ibid., p. 245.
51. Ibid., p. 233.
52. Ibid., p. 234.
53. Maureen Orth, *New Times*, June 25, 1976.
54. Ibid.
55. Senate Watergate Committee Final Report, 1974, pp. 1135-1144.
56. *Hearings Before the President's Commission on the Assassination of President Kennedy* (Washington, D.C.: Government Printing Office, 1964, 26 volumes.) Warren Commission Volume 8, pp. 11-12.
57. Ibid.
58. Robert Oswald, *Lee* (New York: Coward-McCann, Inc., 1967), p. 228.
59. Ibid.
60. Ibid.
61. Ibid.
62. Warren Commission Volume 12, p. 185.
63. Epstein, *Inquest*, pp. 96-97.
64. Warren Commission Volume 1, p. 32.
65. Warren Commission Volume 5, pp. 594-595.
66. Warren Commission Volume 1, p. 119; Warren Commission Volume 5, p. 611.
67. Warren Commission Report, p. 174.
68. Warren Commission Document 344.
69. Warren Commission Volume 1, p. 16; Warren Commission Volume 5, pp. 387-388.
70. Warren Commission Volume 5, p. 607.
71. Ibid.
72. Warren Commission Report, p. 189; Warren Commission Volume 1, p. 16: Warren Commission Volume 5, pp. 387-388.
73. Ibid.
74. Warren Commission Report, p. 189.
75. Meagher, *Accessories After the Fact*, p. 241.
76. Warren Commission Volume 1, p. 14.
77. Warren Commission Report, p. 370.
78. Oswald, *Lee*, p. 198.
79. Ibid., p. 190.
80. Ibid., p. 212.
81. Ibid., p. 218.
82. Ibid., p. 143.
83. Ibid., p. 144.
84. Ibid., p. 216.
85. Jean Stafford, *A Mother in History* (New York: Bantam Books Edition, 1966), p. 32.
86. Ibid., p. 28.
87. Ibid., pp. 17-18.

88. Ibid., pp. 64-65.
89. *Senate Intelligence Committee Final Report*, Book Three, 1976, p. 567.
90. Ibid., pp. 561, 571.
91. Warren Commission Volume 5, p. 204.
92. Ibid., p. 212.
93. Ibid., p. 204.
94. Ibid., pp. 198-199.
95. Ibid., pp. 199-200.
96. *Newsweek*, March 27, 1967.
97. Ibid.
98. Warren Commission Exhibit 2980, Warren Commission Volume 26, pp. 467-473.
99. Ibid.
100. Ibid.
101. Ibid.
102. Ibid.
103. Ibid.
104. September 19, 1964 memorandum from Acting CIA Deputy Director for Plans Thomas Karamessines to Warren Commission General Counsel J. Lee Rankin, "Information Concerning Jack Ruby (aka Jack Rubenstein) and His Associates."
105. Warren Commission Volume 5, p. 189.
106. Warren Commission Volume 14, p. 552; Warren Commission Volume 5, p. 205.

CHAPTER TWO

The Warren Commission

Of the controversial Warren Commission investigation, former Commission member Gerald R. Ford would subsequently write: ". . . the monumental record of the President's Commission will stand like a Gibraltar of factual literature through the ages to come."[1]

While Ford's tendency toward overstatement ("President Nixon is the greatest President in our lifetime") may have been another result of his service on the Warren Commission, his sentiments at that time were widely shared. While the Warren Commission was originally intended to be the ultimate in "blue ribbon" commissions, sweeping away the early speculation and suspicions of an assassination conspiracy, the Commission's performance would, in later years, become the subject of unrelenting doubt and comprehensive criticism — doubt which would finally lead to a Congressional reopening of the entire Kennedy case.

John J. McCloy, another member of the Warren Commission, and also a strong defender of its conclusions, ironically provided the single earliest — and now, the most damagingly prophetic — analysis of the task that confronted the Commission. At the first Commission session, December 5, 1963, Commission member McCloy stated:

> The Commission is going to be criticized
> . . . no matter what we do, but I think we
> would be more criticized if we were simply
> posed before the world as something that
> is evaluating government agencies' reports,
> who themselves may be culpable.[2]

Earl Warren

Earl Warren, the Chief Justice of the Supreme Court, was the man selected by President Johnson to head the "blue ribbon commission" charged with investigating the murder of President John F. Kennedy. Chief Justice Warren later disclosed that Johnson had had to arm-twist him into taking the position. Warren later said it was "the worst nine months" of his life. It wasn't until long after the Commission had ended its work that the nature of the pressure President Johnson had put on Justice Warren became known.

In an internal Commission memo released years later, Staff Counsel Melvin Eisenberg wrote about

Warren's first meeting with the Commission staff on January 20, 1964, during which Warren explained how President Johnson had "pressured" him into heading the investigation. In the memo, Eisenberg wrote:

> The President stated that rumors of the most exaggerated kind were circulating in this country and overseas . . . Some rumors went as far as attributing the assassination to a faction within the government wishing the presidency assumed by President Johnson. Others, if not quenched, could conceivably lead the country into a war which could cost forty million lives. No one could refuse to do something which might help prevent such a possibility . . . . He placed emphasis on the quenching of rumors, and precluding further speculation.[3]

Just three days after that meeting, Warren told the other members of the Commission that the Attorney General of Texas had informed him of persistent rumors in Texas indicating Lee Harvey Oswald had been an operative of the FBI. Thus, less than three days after informing the Commission staff that President Johnson had spoken of rumors "attributing the assassination to a faction within the Government," Earl Warren was confronted with other rumors of an equally disturbing nature. A previously secret transcript of the Warren Commission's session of January 27, 1964, sets forth this information. The transcript (declassified and released to long-time assassination researcher Harold Weisberg in late 1974) reveals that Commission General Counsel J. Lee Rankin told how the Texas authorities had informed him of the rumors about Oswald and how he had informed Warren:

> I called the Chief Justice immediately and went over and told him the story . . . and it

was the consensus of the meeting that we should try to get those people up here, including the District Attorney, Wade, the Attorney General, Special Counsel with the Attorney General Leon Jaworski, and Bob Storey, and Mr. Alexander, the Assistant District Attorney in Dallas.

We asked them to all come up, and they did on Friday. At that time they were — they said the rumors were constant there that Oswald was an undercover agent, but they extended it also to the CIA, saying that they had a number assigned to him connecting with the CIA, and gave that to him, and none of them had any original information of their own.[4]

While it has now been established that both the CIA and FBI withheld significant information from the Warren Commission, most observers believe the single most important area of information withheld relates to the CIA's use of the Mafia between 1960 and 1963 to try to assassinate Fidel Castro. The Senate Intelligence Committee concluded that the CIA made at least eight attempts on Castro's life during that period. Recent information has established that it was not until early 1967 — over three years after the Kennedy assassination — that Earl Warren first learned of those CIA-Mafia assassination plots. According to the June 1976 Senate Committee Report, "The Investigation of the Assassination of President John F. Kennedy: Performance of the Intelligence Agencies," Warren learned of the secret plots from columnist Drew Pearson:

In late January of 1967, *Washington Post* columnist Drew Pearson met with Chief Justice Earl Warren. Pearson told the Chief Justice that a Washington lawyer had told him that one of his clients said the United

States had attempted to assassinate Fidel Castro in the early 1960s, and that Castro had decided to retaliate.[5]

As will be seen later, the "Washington lawyer" and "his client" (whose names were withheld by the Senate Intelligence Committee when their report was issued) were men who had, in fact, had direct knowledge of the CIA-Mafia plots against Castro. And, as will further be seen, when their actual names became publicly identified (in late August 1976) the entire Kennedy case became shrouded in even more compelling mystery and urgency.

In any event, the Washington lawyer claimed to represent some clients who had once been involved in U.S. Government-sponsored assassination plots against Fidel Castro. According to this lawyer, his clients became aware — through their involvement in this plot — of certain information pertaining to the subsequent assassination of President Kennedy. The Senate Committee Report goes on to state that Chief Justice Warren decided to refer the information to James J. Rowley, the Director of the U.S. Secret Service. According to the Senate Report, Rowley testified that Warren thought the information should be investigated:

> The way he (Chief Justice Warren) approached it, was that he said he thought this was serious enough and so forth, but he wanted to get it off his hands. He felt that he had to — that it — had to be told to somebody, and that the Warren Commission was finished, and he wanted the thing pursued, I suppose, by ourselves or the FBI.[6]

The Senate Committee Report goes on to state that Secret Service Director Rowley then referred the information to FBI Director Hoover. On February 15,

1967, Hoover and the FBI decided that "no investigation will be conducted regarding the allegation made . . . to Chief Justice Warren."[7] The Senate Intelligence Committee found fault with the FBI for refusing to pursue the information, especially since the FBI had already been aware to some extent that the CIA had once used Mafia leaders to try to murder Castro. The Sentate Report disclosed that the FBI supervisor in charge of dealing with the matter had not been able to explain the FBI's actions:

> When asked why the FBI did not investigate such a serious allegation, particularly in light of Director Hoover's testimony before the Warren Commission that the assassination case would always remain open, the [FBI] supervisor responded, "I understand your thinking and I can't truthfully and logically answer your question because I don't know."[8]

According to the Senate Report, President Lyndon B. Johnson had, in the meantime, become aware of the information supplied by Drew Pearson to Earl Warren, and had decided to push the FBI into investigating it at once. President Johnson suggested that the FBI interview the Washington lawyer who had been the source of Pearson's information. Hoover's closest aide, Clyde Tolson, received a memo from FBI aide Cartha DeLoach on March 17, 1967, in which DeLoach stated that Johnson aide Marvin Watson had ordered that the interview take place.

> Watson stated that the President still desired that the FBI conduct the interview in question. I told Watson that, under the circumstances, we had no alternative but to make this attempt; however, I hoped he

and the President realized that this might be putting the FBI into a situation with District Attorney Garrison, who was nothing more than a publicity seeker.[9]

Finally, on March 31, 1976, the FBI interviewed the lawyer who had been the source of the Pearson information. According to an official FBI memo written about the interview, the lawyer had stated that he had clients who had further relevant information:

> His clients, who were on the fringe of the underworld, were neither directly nor indirectly involved in the death of President Kennedy, but they faced possible prosecution in a crime not related to the assassination and through participation in such a crime they learned of information pertaining to the President's assassination.[10]

The FBI memo goes on to state that the lawyer's clients claim to have been involved in a CIA plot to assassinate Fidel Castro and that the "project almost reached fruition when Castro became aware of it."[11] According to the same FBI memo, Fidel Castro at that point decided to retaliate:

> Castro therafter employed teams of individuals who were dispatched to the United States for the purpose of assassinating President Kennedy. The lawyer stated that his clients obtained this information "from 'feed back' furnished by sources close to Castro."[12]

The Senate Intelligence Committee Report states that neither the FBI nor CIA came up with evidence to support these allegations, and further notes that the lawyer's clients were unwilling to volunteer to be interviewed for any further information. While the

Senate Report notes that this episode involving Drew Pearson and Earl Warren finally triggered an internal investigation by the CIA's Inspector General into the history of the CIA-Mafia assassination conspiracies against Castro, that same CIA investigation proved to be highly limited. According to the Senate Report, the key CIA analyst involved in the matter "was not asked to determine whether there were any connections between CIA assassination operations and the assassination of President Kennedy."[13]

At the time the Senate Intelligence Committee Report was released in late June of 1976, there was considerable speculation as to who the unidentified "Washington lawyer" and "his client" actually were. Beyond wanting to comply with the two men's requests for anonymity, the Senate Committee was known to have felt that the disclosure of their names might in some way endanger them. Unfortunately, subsequent events indicated that perhaps just the opposite had been true.

Six weeks after the Senate Report was issued, the "client" — CIA-Mafia assassination coordinator John Roselli — was found murdered. Two weeks after Roselli's mutilated body was retrieved from a barrel floating off Miami (on August 7, 1976), his identity as the unnamed "client" of the "Washington lawyer" was finally revealed. On August 22, 1976, *Washington Post* reporters Ron Kessler and Laurence Stern disclosed that John Roselli was the unnamed source of the mysterious information sent through Drew Pearson in 1967 to the Secret Service, FBI, CIA, and President Johnson.[14] Kessler and Stern also disclosed that the unnamed "Washington lawyer" was Edward P. Morgan, the prominent D.C. attorney who at one time represented CIA-Mafia assassination coordinator Robert Maheu, as well as Maheu's employer, billionaire Howard Hughes.[15]

Days after the *Washington Post* disclosure, columnist Jack Anderson further reported that John Roselli had indicated that some of his syndicate colleagues from the CIA-Mafia plots had in fact been the men who had subsequently assassinated President Kennedy.[16] According to Anderson, who had interviewed Roselli repeatedly over the years, the murdered Mafia leader also claimed that Fidel Castro may have also been involved in the plots — along with the Mafia.

Senate Intelligence investigators have confirmed the basic outlines of Roselli's allegations, as set forth in the *Washington Post* and Anderson accounts. All agree that Roselli privately charged that the Mafia had recruited pro-Castro activist Lee Harvey Oswald for the assassination of the President. Jack Anderson reported:

> According to Roselli's version, Oswald may have shot Kennedy or may have acted as a decoy while others ambushed him from closer range. When Oswald was picked up, Roselli suggested, the underworld conspirators feared he would crack and disclose information that might lead to them. This almost certainly would have brought a massive U.S. crackdown on the Mafia.
>
> So Jack Ruby was ordered to eliminate Oswald, making it appear as an act of reprisal against the President's killer. At least this is how Roselli explained the tragedy in Dallas.[17]

In any event, within days the Roselli murder and its various chilling implications had resulted in a new wave of serious and — more importantly — sustained suspicion in Washington — suspicion which soon led to a vote in the House of Representatives to re-open the Kennedy assassination investigation.

Were he alive today, Earl Warren would certainly be a key witness in the review of this strange episode pertaining to John Roselli's 1967 allegations. As the Senate Intelligence Committee's account shows, he witnessed firsthand the almost total "reluctance" of the FBI, Secret Service, and CIA to investigate the explosive Roselli allegations.

A former member of the Senate Committee has recently stated, "You can bet one thing: if it hadn't been for Drew Pearson, Warren, and L.B.J. pushing the thing [Roselli's allegations] we would never have even been told about it."

Allen Dulles

Another of the seven members of the Warren Commission was Allen Dulles, former Director of the CIA. While Dulles has previously been criticized for some of his activities as a member of the Commission — including his strong advocacy of the controversial "single-bullet theory" — more recent disclosures reveal that he was directly involved in keeping information from others on the Commission. Specifically, as the Church Senate Intelligence Committee investigations have shown, one crucial area of information was concealed by Dulles: the existence of the secret assassination apparatus set up by CIA officials, jointly coordinated by powerful Mafia leaders and Robert Maheu, and authorized by Dulles and others to assassinate Fidel Castro.

It has been suggested by various Warren Commission critics (most recently, Senator Richard Schweiker) that Castro may have learned of the secret CIA-Mafia assassination plots against him, and he may have retaliated by having President Kennedy assassinated. Other observers have speculated that some of the same elements involved in the CIA-Mafia assassination apparatus — particularly the top Mafia leaders and the various Cuban exiles on their payroll — may have been behind the Kennedy assassination. There has been speculation that the organized crime leaders involved with the CIA in plotting the Castro assassination may have subsequently been in a position to "blackmail" or pressure the CIA into covering up possible Mafia involvement in the assassination of President Kennedy.

Thus, as the Church Committee has pointed out, the existence of the secret CIA-Mafia assassination conspiracies against Castro (which lasted from late 1960 to at least mid-1963) would have been a crucially significant area for the Warren Commission to analyze. Yet Allen Dulles never revealed these plots to his Commission colleagues. According to the detailed Senate Intelligence Committee report on the CIA-Mafia plots:

> In August, 1960, the CIA took steps to enlist members of the criminal underworld with gambling syndicate contacts to aid in assassinating Castro.[18]

The Senate Intelligence report went on to disclose that the two top CIA officials involved in setting up this secret assassination group, Deputy Director for Plans Richard Bissell and Director of the Office of Security Sheffield Edwards, both stated that CIA Director Allen Dulles had personally approved the secret assassination planning. The Senate report says:

Bissell recalled that "in the latter part of September" there was "a meeting in which Colonel Edwards and I briefed Mr. Dulles and General Cabell" about the plan to assassinate Castro. Bissell testified that "Colonel Edwards outlined in somewhat circumlocutious terms the plan that they had discussed with syndicate representatives." He stated that Edwards had said: "That contact had been made with [the underworld], that a plan had been prepared for their use . . . that the plan would be put into effect unless at that time or subsequently he was told by Mr. Dulles that it should not be."[19]

According to the Church Committee Report, the conspiracies against Castro continued for another three years, involving a handful of top CIA officials as well as Chicago Mafia leader Sam Giancana, Florida Mafia leader Santos Trafficante, and Howard Hughes' top deputy, Robert Maheu.[20]

In confirming the serious implications of withholding this information from the Warren Commission, several former Warren Commission staff counsels have stated that knowledge of these conspiracies against Castro would have comprehensively altered the basic direction and complexion of the Commission's investigation.

David W. Belin, a former Warren Commision counsel who remins a strong defender of its conclusions, has himself called for a re-opening of the Kennedy case on the basis of this information that Dulles and the CIA withheld.[21]

However, the fact that Allen Dulles was well-equipped for keeping a secret was no surprise to the other Commission members. The transcript of the Commission's January 27, 1964 session (declassified and released to Harold Weisberg in 1974) contains an illuminating discussion between former spy chief Dulles and his colleagues regarding the accountability of the CIA. It shows the other Commission members were somewhat surprised by Dulles' explanation of the Agency's accountability. The discussion began when Congressman Hale Boggs pointed out the apparent difficulty of determining whether a person, in this case Lee Harvey Oswald, had ever been connected with the CIA in any way. Boggs asked Dulles whether or not CIA records and registries would have shown that U-2 pilot Gary Powers, was employed by the CIA at the time his plane was shot down during the course of a surveillance overflight for the CIA:

> *Rep. Boggs:* Let's say Powers did not have a signed contract but he was recruited by someone in CIA. The man who recruited him would know, wouldn't he?
>
> *Mr. Dulles:* Yes, but he wouldn't tell.
>
> *The Chairman:* Wouldn't he tell it under oath?
>
> *Mr. Dulles:* I wouldn't think he would tell it under oath, no.
>
> *The Chairman:* Why?
>
> *Mr. Dulles:* He ought not to tell it under oath. Maybe not tell it to his own government but wouldn't tell it any other way.
>
> *Mr. McCloy:* Wouldn't he tell it to his own chief?
>
> *Mr. Dulles:* He might or might not. If he was a bad one, then he wouldn't.[27]

While Commission Chairman Earl Warren was recoiling from the Dulles admission that CIA men would feel free to commit perjury on behalf of the

Agency in such a matter, John McCloy further queried Dulles about the question of to whom the CIA answers. McCloy asked, "Suppose the President of the United States comes to you and says 'Will you tell me, Mr. Dulles?'"

> *Mr. Dulles:* I would tell the President of the United States anything, yes, I am under his control. He is my boss, wouldn't necessarily tell anybody else, unless the President authorized me to do it. We had that come up at times.
>
> *Mr. McCloy:* You wouldn't tell the Secretary of Defense?
>
> *Mr. Dulles:* Well, it depends a little bit on the circumstances.[23]

Later during the same discussion, McCloy once again returned to the question of ascertaining whether Lee Oswald had in any manner ever been recruited by the CIA. McCloy asked Dulles if "you would know in this case who, if there was anybody, who would have hired Oswald, who it would be?" To which Dulles answered, "Certainly within an area, certainly no one had authority to do it. Now someone might have done it without authority. The CIA has no charter to hire anybody for this kind of work in the United States. It has abroad, that is the distinction."[24]

What many Dulles critics have described as his penchant for secrecy and his tendency to shade the meaning of covert operations apparently came under question from President Kennedy as well. JFK had allowed Dulles to remain as CIA Director when he first took office, but three months later, following the disastrous Bay of Pigs Invasion, had given him his walking papers. It was no secret that Kennedy placed a great deal of the blame for the failure on Dulles, who had been on an out-of-town speaking engagement at the time of the invasion. He later remarked to an aide who had been involved in the operation, "Dulles was shrewd enough to beat his ass out of town before those men hit the beach." Kennedy confided the scope of his misgivings about Dulles to Arthur Schlesinger:

> "I probably made a mistake in keeping Dulles on . . . I have never worked with him, and therefore I can't estimate his meaning when he tells me things . . . I must have someone there [at CIA] with whom I can be in complete and intimate contact — someone from whom I know I will be getting the exact pitch. I made a mistake in putting Bobby in the Justice Department. He is wasted there . . . Bobby should be in CIA."[25]

John J. McCloy

John McCloy, former diplomat and architect of the post-war American intelligence establishment, also served as one of the seven members of the Warren Commission. McCloy, who is still a strong defender of the Commission's work, was a prime mover of its efforts to portray Oswald as a lone deranged assassin, who acted out of what was, according to McCloy, "killer instinct."[26] It was John McCloy who successfully mediated the hot dispute within the Commission over the proposed adoption of the crucial "single-bullet theory." In his authoritative account of the Commission's investigation, *Inquest*, Edward Jay Epstein gives the following account of McCloy's role:

> . . . Ford said he was closest to the position that both men were hit by the same bullet, and Senator Russell was furthest away. In fact, Russell reportedly said he would not sign a Report which concluded that both men were hit by the same bullet.
>
> Both Dulles and McCloy said that they believed the most reasonable explanation of the assassination was that both men were hit by the same bullet. The Commission was thus more or less evenly split on the question, with Ford, Dulles, and McCloy tending toward the conclusion that both men were both hit by the same bullet, and Russell, Cooper, and Boggs tending toward the conclusion that both men were hit by separate bullets . . .
>
> McCloy said it was of vital importance to have a unanimous Report. He proposed, as a compromise, stating that there was evidence that both men were hit by the same bullet but that "in view of other evidence, the Commission could not decide on the probability of this."
>
> There then followed what was described as "the battle of the adjectives." Ford wanted to state that there was "compelling" evidence. McCloy finally suggested that the adjective "persuasive" be used, and this word was agreed upon.[27]

While John McCloy and Allen Dulles were old friends, having previously worked together on a number of occasions, they had at least one known disagreement during their tenure on the Warren Commission. The transcript of the January 27, 1964 Commission session disclosed that McCloy and Dulles differed over the question of whether someone as young and inexperienced as Lee Harvey Oswald could have been serving as a secret operative of the FBI. Allen Dulles offered the view that "this fellow was so incompetent that he was not the kind of fellow that Hoover would hire . . . Hoover didn't hire this kind of a stupid fellow . . . "

McCloy, Dulles, and Warren then had the following exchange:

> *Mr. McCloy:* I wouldn't put much confidence in the intelligence of all the agents I have run into. I have run into some awfully stupid agents.
>
> *Mr. Dulles:* Not this irresponsible.
>
> *Mr. McCloy:* Well, I can't say that I have run into a fellow comparable to Oswald but I have run into some very limited mentalities both in the CIA and FBI.
>
> *The Chairman:* Under agents, the regular agents, I think that would be right, but they and all other agencies do employ undercover men who are of terrible character.
>
> *Mr. Dulles:* Terribly bad characters.[28]

With the disclosure by Seymour Hersh of the *New York Times* in 1975 of the active relationship between the CIA and Mafia, questions have been raised about John McCloy's possible knowledge of that link. The investigations of the last two years have revealed that the CIA-Mafia connection developed over a period of twenty to thirty years, with roots as far back as World War II. In that early instance, top Mafia leaders, including Lucky Luciano, Meyer Lansky, and Frank Costello, had actively aided the OSS (the forerunner of the CIA) in various wartime activities.[29] This early OSS-Mafia collaboration had come to be known as "Operation Underworld" in U.S. intelligence circles. Due to John McCloy's close involvement in OSS affairs during that period, it has been suggested that he may have been aware of the Mafia's involvement with the American intelligence establishment.[30] However, this has never been confirmed.

J. Lee Rankin

J. Lee Rankin served as General Counsel to the Warren Commission and thus held the single highest-ranking staff position on the Commission. Rankin was the man in overall charge of the Commission investigation and served as the Commission's chief liaison to both the CIA and FBI.

Lee Rankin also was the official go-between through whom all communications between Commission members and Commission staff were passed. Thus, as one former Commission Counsel has stated: "It was, very simply, a Rankin operation."

J. Lee Rankin has long been a prime target of various critics of the Warren Commission who trace a great many of its investigative deficiencies directly to him. While many of these criticisms are legitimate and can be documented, perhaps the most damaging criticisms of the Warren Commission, and J. Lee Rankin specifically, have come from other lawyers who served on the Commission staff with him.

Former Warren Commission Counsel Wesley Liebeler related an incident to Edward Jay Epstein which illustrates the serious problem that staff members had with General Counsel Rankin. Liebeler recounted how he had prepared a comprehensive twenty-six-page memorandum for submission to Rankin, a memorandum which methodically outlined serious deficiencies in the evidence in the final draft of a key chapter of the Warren Commission Report, pertaining to identification of Lee Harvey Oswald as the single assassin. Liebeler reported that Rankin curtly dismissed his objections, stating, "No more memorandums. The Report has to be published."[31]

In another instance, Warren Commission Counsels William Coleman and Wesley Liebeler compiled a substantial amount of Commission information supporting the testimony of Mrs. Sylvia Odio, a wealthy Cuban exile activist who swore that she had been approached by Lee Oswald and two right-wing Cuban exiles in Dallas during the same time the FBI and CIA said Oswald was in Mexico. Mrs. Odio's testimony raised a number of crucial questions that struck at the heart of several of the Commission's most basic conclusions about the alleged Presidential assassin. (See detailed reference to Sylvia Odio and her testimony in the chapter on "The Second Oswald.") When Warren Commission Counsel Liebeler attempted to bring his assessment of the mysterious Odio matter to General Counsel Rankin's attention, Rankin angrily responded, "At this stage, we are supposed to be closing doors, not opening them."[32]

As noted earlier, it was J. Lee Rankin who first informed the actual Warren Commission members (on January 22, 1964) that the Attorney General of Texas had some unconfirmed information regarding Lee Harvey Oswald's possible position as a secret operative of the FBI. During the session of January 22, 1964, Rankin explained that such allegations of an Oswald-FBI connection would be difficult to check out. In the years since the Commission ended its work, critics have placed heavy blame on Rankin (whose position made him Commission liaison to J. Edgar Hoover) for its unwillingness to pursue these allegations by independently investigating such possible FBI links — without relying on the FBI to do the investigation. In any event, it was during this meeting that Lee Rankin outlined the problem:

> . . . It was being rumored that he [Oswald] was an undercover agent. Now it is something that is very difficult to prove out. There are events in connection with this that are curious, in that they might make it possible to check some of it out in time. I assume that the FBI records would never show it, and if it is true, and of course we don't know, but we thought you should have the information.[33]

During that same Warren Commission meeting, Rankin also stated:

> It is going to be very difficult for us to be able to establish the facts in it. I am confident that the FBI would never admit it, and I presume the records will never show it, or if the records do show anything, I would think their records would show some kind of a number that could be assigned to a dozen different people according to how they want to describe them. So that it seemed to me if it's really happened, he [Oswald] did use postal boxes practically every place that he went, and that would be an ideal way to get money to anyone that you wanted as an undercover agent, or

anybody else that you wanted to do business that way without having any particular transaction.[34]

After serving as Corporation Counsel of New York City, J. Lee Rankin is now in private law practice in New York, and he has generally declined to discuss his role in the Warren Commission's investigation. In late 1973, as the Watergate crisis heightened, President Nixon and Charles Colson sought to involve Rankin in the White House "tapes dispute" being arbitrated between Nixon and the Special Prosecutor. In this little-known episode, Nixon and Colson had recommended to the prosecutors that J. Lee Rankin be used to edit out "national security" portions of the secret Watergate tapes. (See further references to this matter in the chapter on "The Link to Watergate.")

Senator Richard B. Russell

Senator Richard Russell, the highly respected Chairman of the Senate Armed Services Committee, also chaired the important Subcommittee on CIA Oversight as well. A southern conservative who held the distinction of having warned against American involvement in Vietnam as far back as the early 1950s, Russell was widely regarded as one of the Senate's most

91

intelligent members, in the words of Majority Leader Mike Mansfield. Before his death on January 4, 1971, Senator Russell (then President Pro Tempore of the Senate) had been a close friend and political confidante of his fellow Georgian, Jimmy Carter.

In recent years, there has been a growing series of indications that Senator Russell was deeply disturbed by the performance of the Warren Commission, and even more deeply disturbed by the denial of certain information to it by both the CIA and FBI. As will be seen, Russell's doubts about the integrity of the Commission's conclusions finally became public in January, 1970.

During the course of a secret Executive Session meeting on January 27, 1964 (first disclosed in a transcript provided to Harold Weisberg ten years later), Senator Russell drew an admission from Allen Dulles that the CIA and/or the FBI would never publicly admit that Lee Oswald had worked for them, if that had in fact been true. This transcript sets forth the following account of the agency's "deniability" prerogative:

> *Sen. Russell:* If Oswald never had assassinated the President or at least been charged with assassinating the President and had been in the employ of the FBI and somebody had gone to the FBI they would have denied he was an agent.
>
> *Mr. Dulles:* Oh, yes.
>
> *Sen. Russell:* They would be the first to deny it. Your [CIA] agents would have done exactly the same thing.
>
> *Mr. Dulles:* Exactly.
>
> *Sen. Russell:* Say I never heard about the

man who may have been on the payroll for five years.[35]

The same transcript, which had remained "classified" until 1974, despite long legal battles for its release by several Commission critics, revealed the depth of feeling by Senator Russell, Congressman Hale Boggs, and General Counsel Lee Rankin, that the FBI had "a closed mind" about the possibility of an assassination conspiracy from the outset:

> *Mr. Rankin:* Part of our difficulty in regard to [the investigation] is that they [the FBI] have no problem. They have decided that it is Oswald who committed the assassination, they have decided that no one else was involved, they have decided that —
>
> *Sen. Russell:* They have tried the case and reached a verdict on every aspect.
>
> *Rep. Boggs:* You have put your finger on it.[36]

Years later, as will be seen, Richard Russell expressed strong suspicion over the still-mysterious trip by Lee Harvey Oswald to Mexico City in late September, 1963, less than eight weeks before the assassination. The strange lack of information about this trip — and the fact that the limited data about it was coming from CIA sources — was also set forth in the previously classified January 27, 1964 Warren Commission transcript:

> *Mr. Rankin:* We do not have enough information about that to know what happened there [Mexico City] except we do have information that he tried to get a visa at the Cuban Embassy, and he tried to get a visa at the Soviet Embassy, and we know

the hotel he stayed at, and we have a very
limited report from the hotel keeper about
most of it to the effect that they knew
nothing about him, didn't even know that
he came or went, although there were seven
days between the time he went down on
the 26th, and the 3rd when he came back.[37]

At that point in the meeting, Senator Russell asked, "Who has been doing the investigating in Mexico?" In response, General Counsel Lee Rankin answered, "The CIA has been working with us in regard to that area, and the FBI has an attaché there who has done some work but most of it has been by the CIA."[38]

It was not until more than six years later that Senator Richard Russell publicly voiced his doubts about the Warren Commission conclusions — the first former Warren Commission member to do so. On January 19, 1970, the *Washington Post* disclosed that Senator Russell was ending his past silence about the Commission's findings, and in fact now believed that there had been a criminal conspiracy behind the Presidential murder.[39]

Of Lee Harvey Oswald, Senator Russell stated, "I think someone else worked with him."[40] Russell went on to disclose that the accused assassin's mysterious trip to Mexico City in September 1963 had become a key area of his suspicion:

There were too many things — the fact that
he [Oswald] was at Minsk [in the Soviet
Union] and that was the principal center for
educating Cuban students . . . some of the
trips he made to Mexico City and a number
of discrepancies in the evidence, or as to
means of transportation, the luggage he had
and whether or not anyone was with him —
caused me to doubt that he planned it all
by himself.[41]

In 1974, Harold Weisberg, the longtime Kennedy assassination researcher and former Senate investigator, disclosed that he had assisted Senator Russell in an effort to locate a missing Warren Commission transcript from the September 18, 1964 session.[42] The Senator stated that he and some other Warren Commission members had discussed a number of deficiencies in the Commission's findings during that meeting. However, as Weisberg later informed Russell, the official transcript (prepared under the personal direction of General Counsel Rankin) had contained no mention of the doubts expressed by Russell and others during that late session. According to Weisberg, Senator Russell "was shaken" by his discovery of the missing transcript sections.[43] Weisberg has written that Russell "asked me to conduct a further investigation to prove whether or not there still existed a transcript of the executive session Russell had forced on September 18, just before publication of the Report, which went to press less than a week later . . ."[44] Efforts to locate the missing sections proved unsuccessful, and while Weisberg has pursued the issue of transcript deletions in the courts, no final determination of the matter has yet been achieved.[45] Weisberg has written that General Counsel J. Lee Rankin appears to have been instrumental in the handling of the September 18th transcript, and he may have been responsible for the strange deletions.[46]

In a supplemental affidavit filed in U.S. District Court in late April of 1974, Harold Weisberg stated:

> Privately Senator Russell told me that he was convinced that there were two areas in which Warren Commission members had been deceived by Federal agencies responsible for investigating the assassination of President Kennedy. These two areas were: (1) Oswald's background; and, (2) the ballistics evidence.[47]

Congressman Hale Boggs

"You have got to do everything on earth to establish the facts one way or the other. And without doing that, why everything concerned, including every one of us is doing a very grave disservice."[48] Thus House Majority Leader Hale Boggs delivered an admonishment of sorts to his Warren Commission colleagues on January 27, 1964. Along with Senator Richard Russell, and to a lesser degree, Senator John Sherman Cooper, Congressman Boggs served as a beacon of skepticism and probity in trying to fend off the FBI and CIA's efforts to "shade" and indeed manipulate the findings of the Warren Commission.

Like Russell, Boggs was, very simply, a strong doubter. Several years after his death in 1972, a colleague of his wife Lindy (who was elected to fill her late husband's seat in the Congress) recalled Mrs. Boggs remarking, "Hale felt very, very torn during his work [on the Commission] . . . he wished he had never been on it and wished he'd never signed it [the Warren Report]." A former aide to the late House Majority Leader has recently recalled, "Hale always returned to one thing: Hoover lied his eyes out to the Commission — on Oswald, on Ruby, on their friends, the bullets, the gun, you name it . . . "

Almost from the beginning, Congressman Boggs had been suspicious over the FBI and CIA's reluctance to provide hard information when the Commission's probe turned to certain areas, such as allegations that Oswald may have been an undercover operative of some sort. When the Commission sought to disprove the growing suspicion that Oswald had once worked for the FBI, Boggs was outraged that the only proof of denial that the FBI offered was a brief statement of disclaimer by J. Edgar Hoover. It was Hale Boggs who drew an admission from Allen Dulles that the CIA's record of employing someone like Oswald might be so heavily coded that the verification of his service would be almost impossible for outside investigators to establish. Boggs and Dulles had the following exchange:

> *Rep. Boggs:* So I will ask you. Did you have agents about whom you had no record whatsoever?
>
> *Mr. Dulles:* The record might not be on paper. But on paper [we] would have hieroglyphics that only two people knew what they meant, and nobody outside of the Agency would know and you could say this meant the agent and someone else could say it meant another agent.[49]

Congressman Boggs had been the Commission's leading proponent for devoting more investigative resources to probing the connections of Jack Ruby. With an early recognition that "the most difficult aspect of this is the Ruby aspect," Boggs had wanted an increased effort made to investigate the accused assassin's murderer.[50]

Boggs was perhaps the first person to recognize something which numerous Warren Commission critics would write about in future years: the strange variations and dissimilarities to be found in Lee Harvey Oswald's correspondence during 1960 to 1963. Some critics have advanced the theory that some of Oswald's letters — particularly correspondence to the American Embassy in Moscow, and later, to the Fair Play for Cuba Committee — may have been "planted" documents written by someone else. In 1975 and 1976, the investigations of the Senate Intelligence Committee and other Congressional groups disclosed that such uses of fabricated correspondence had been a recurring tool of the FBI's secret domestic COINTELPRO [Counter Intelligence] program as well as other intelligence operations. In any event, Warren Commission member Boggs and Commission General Counsel Lee Rankin had early on discussed such an idea:

> *Mr. Rankin:* They [the Fair Play For Cuba Committee] denied he was a member and also he wrote to them and tried to establish as one of the letters indicate, a new branch there in New Orleans, the Fair Play For Cuba.
>
> *Rep. Boggs:* That letter has caused me a lot of trouble. It is a much more literate and polished communication than any of his other writing.[51]

It is also known Boggs felt that because of the lack of adequate material from the FBI and CIA the Commission members were poorly prepared for the examination of witnesses. According to a former Boggs staffer, the Congressman felt that lack of adequate file preparation and the sometimes erratic scheduling of Commission sessions served to prevent those same sessions from being adequately substantive. Consequently, Boggs cut down his participation in these sessions as the investigation stretched on through 1964.

Author Sylvia Meagher has cited one of the more telling examples of the frequent inability of the Warren Commission to coordinate its members' involvement in these sessions, as illustrated by the following exchange in Warren Commission Volume 3:

> *Chairman Warren:* Senator Cooper, at this time I am obliged to leave for our all-day

conference on Friday at the Supreme Court, and I may be back later in the day, but if I don't, you continue, of course.

Sen. Cooper: I will this morning. If I can't be here this afternoon whom do you want to preside?

Chairman Warren: Congressman Ford, would you be here this afternoon at all?

Rep. Ford: Unfortunately, Mr. McCloy and I have to go to a conference out of town.

Chairman Warren: You are both going out of town, aren't you?

Sen. Cooper: I can go and come back if it is necessary.

Chairman Warren: I will try to be here myself. Will Mr. Dulles be here?

Mr. McCloy: He is out of town.[52]

On April 5, 1971, House Majority Leader Hale Boggs took the floor of the House to deliver a speech that created a major stir in Washington for several weeks. Declaring that FBI Director J. Edgar Hoover was incompetent and senile, and charging that the FBI had, under Hoover's most recent years adopted "the tactics of the Soviet Union and Hitler's Gestapo," Boggs demanded Hoover's immediate resignation.[53] Boggs also charged that he had discovered that certain FBI agents had tapped his own telephone as well as the phones of certain other members of the House and Senate.[54]

In his emotional House speech, Boggs went on to say Attorney General "Mitchell says he is a law and order man. If law and order means the suppression of the Bill of Rights ... then I say 'God help us.'"[55] As the *Washington Post* noted, "The Louisiana Democrat's speech was the harshest criticism of Hoover ever heard in the House ... It was the first attack on Hoover by any member of the House leadership..."[56]

At the time, Boggs' startling speech created a sensation in Washington. Observers were uncertain as to his exact motivations in demanding Hoover's resignation, and there was an immediate critical reaction from Hoover's various defenders. It has been reported that sources within the FBI and the Attorney General's office began spreading stories that Boggs was a hopeless alcoholic. However, it was not until almost four years later that the motivation behind Boggs' outburst came into clearer focus.

On January 20, 1975, the *Washington Post* and other news organizations reported that solid evidence had been uncovered about the existence of what Hoover and the FBI had long denied they possessed: secret damaging dossiers on various members of the House and Senate, compiled through various forms of surveillance.[57]

On the following day, January 21, 1975, *Washington Post* reporter Ron Kessler made a further disclosure:

> ... the son of the late House Majority Leader Boggs has told The *Post* that the FBI leaked to his father damaging material on the personal lives of critics of its investigation into John F. Kennedy's assassination.
>
> Thomas Hale Boggs, Jr. said his father, who was a member of the Warren Commission, which investigated the assassination and its handling by the FBI, was given the material in an apparent attempt to discredit the critics [of the Warren Commission].
>
> The material, which Thomas Boggs made available, includes photographs of sexual activity and reports on alleged communist affiliations of some authors of articles and books on the assassination.[58]

The *Washington Post* went on to report:

> Boggs, a Washington lawyer, said the experience played a large role in his father's decision to publicly charge the FBI with Gestapo tactics in a 1971 speech alleging the Bureau had wiretapped his telephone and that of other Congressmen.[59]

As will be seen, the details about the FBI's secret surveillance of the leading critics of the Warren Commission were later reviewed by the Senate Intelligence Committee in 1975. The Senate investigators finally established that FBI Director Hoover not only had prepared secret "derogatory dossiers" on the critics of the Warren Commission over the years, but had even ordered the preparation of similar "damaging" reports about staff members of the Warren Commission.[60] (See reference to J. Edgar Hoover in chapter on "Hoover's FBI.") Whether FBI Director Hoover intended to use these dossiers for purposes of blackmail has never been determined.

Although it was not until eleven years after the murder of John F. Kennedy that the FBI's crude harassment and surveillance of various assassination researchers and investigators became officially documented, other information about it had previously surfaced.

Mark Lane, the long time critic of the Warren Report has often spoken of FBI harassment and surveillance directed against him. While many observers were at first skeptical about Lane's characteristically vocal allegations against the FBI, the list of classified Warren Commission documents that was later released substantiated Lane's charges, as it contained several FBI files about him. Lane had earlier uncovered a February 24, 1964 Warren Commission memorandum from staff counsel Harold Willens to General Counsel J. Lee Rankin. The memorandum revealed that FBI agents had Lane's movements and lectures under surveillance, and were forwarding their reports to the Warren Commission.[61]

In March, 1967, the official list of secret Commission documents then being held in a National Archives vault included at least seven FBI files on Lane, which were classified on supposed grounds of "national security." Among these secret Bureau reports were the following: Warren Commission Document 489, "Mark Lane, Buffalo appearances;" Warren Commission Document 694, "Various Mark Lane appearances;" Warren Commission Document 763, "Mark Lane appearances;" and Warren Commission Document 1457, "Mark Lane and his trip to Europe."[62]

In at least one documented instance, the CIA had been equally avid in "compiling" information on another critic, the noted European writer Joachim Joesten, who had written an early "conspiracy theory" book, titled *Oswald: Assassin or Fall Guy* (Marzani and Munsell Publishers, Inc., 1964, West Germany). A Warren Commission file (Document 1532), declassified years later, revealed that the CIA had turned to an unusual source in their effort to investigate Joesten. According to the document, which consists of a CIA memorandum of October 1, 1964, written by Richard Helms' staff, the CIA conducted a search of some of Adolph Hitler's Gestapo files for information on Joesten.[63]

Joachim Joesten, an opponent of the Hitler regime in Germany, was a survivor of one of the more infamous concentration camps. The Helms memorandum reveals that Helms' CIA aides had compiled information on Joesten's alleged political instability — information taken from Gestapo security files of the Third Reich, dated 1936 and 1937.[64] In one instance, Helms' aides had used data on Joesten which had been gathered by Hitler's Chief of S.S. on November 8, 1937.[37] While the CIA memorandum did not memtion it, there was good reason for the Third

Reich's efforts to compile a dossier on Joesten. Three days earlier, on November 5, 1937, at the infamous "Hossbach Conference," Adolph Hilter had informed Hermann Goering and his other top lieutenants of his plan to launch a world war by invading Europe.[66]

In late 1975, during a Senate Intelligence Committee hearing that featured the questioning of top FBI officials, Senator Richard Schweiker disclosed other secret FBI surveillance of Warren Commission critics. Senator Schweiker disclosed new information from a November 8, 1966 memorandum by J. Edgar Hoover, relating to other dossiers on the critics. According to Schweiker, "Seven individuals [were] listed, some of their files . . . not only included derogatory information, but sex pictures to boot."[67] During the Senate Committee session, Schweiker also disclosed that "we came across another FBI letter several months later on another of the critic's personal files. I think it is January 30, 1967. Here, almost three months apart, is an ongoing campaign to personally derogate people who differed politically. In this case it was the Warren Commission [critics]."[68]

As will be seen in the chapter on "Links to Watergate," copies of the FBI's "derogatory dossier" on another leading Warren Commission critic, associated with Mark Lane, were later distributed through the Nixon White House by secret Nixon investigator John Caulfield, John Dean, and H. R. Haldeman's top aides.

Still further information relating to FBI-CIA surveillance of the Warren Commission critics was disclosed in January, 1975 by Senator Howard Baker and the *New York Times*. On January 17, 1975, the *Times* disclosed that Senator Baker had come across an extensive CIA dossier on Bernard Fensterwald, Jr., the Director of the Committee to Investigate Assassinations, during the course of Baker's service on the Senate Watergate Committee.[69] Senator Baker was then probing various areas of CIA involvement in the Watergate conspiracy. The *New York Times* reported that Baker believed the dossier on Fensterwald indicated that the Agency was conducting domestic activities or surveillances — prohibited by the Agency charter's ban on domestic involvement.[70]

Among the items contained in the CIA dossier on Fensterwald was an Agency report of May 12, 1972 titled "#553 989." The CIA report indicated that this detailed surveillance was conducted under the joint auspices of the CIA and the Washington, D. C. Metropolitan Police Intelligence Unit. D. C. Police involvement with the CIA, which in some cases was illegal, subsequently erupted into a scandal which resulted in an internal police investigation in 1975 and 1976, as well as a Congressional investigation.

The May 12, 1972 CIA report on Fensterwald states:

> On 10 May 1972, a check was made at the Metropolitan Police Department Intelligence Unit concerning an organization called The Committee To Investigate Assassinations located at 927 15th Street, N.W., Washington, D. C. . . .
>
> On 10 May 1972, a check was made (DELETION)
>
> On 11 May 1972, a physical check was made of 927 15th Street . . . to verify the location of the above-mentioned organization. This check disclosed that the Committee To Investigate Assassinations is located in room 409 and 414 of the Carry Building.[71]

After setting forth a room by room analysis of the offices and businesses located on the same floor as the Committee, the report went on:

A discreet inquiry was made with (DELETION) of this building showing no government interest concerning the Committee To Investigate Assassinations. This source stated that on a daily basis that traffic coming and going from this office is very busy. This source stated that on a daily basis the office is operated by two individuals one of whose name is Jim.[72]

Former Warren Commission member Hale Boggs would no doubt have been pleased that these activities of the FBI and CIA were finally brought to light. As his son has pointed out, Boggs' denunciation of J. Edgar Hoover in April of 1971 was based in part on his knowledge of the FBI's murky surveillance of Warren Commission critics.[73] Whether Boggs believed the FBI's surveillance of him was based on the fact that he himself had privately become a fierce critic of Commission's conclusions is not known.

On October 16, 1972, Hale Boggs vanished during a flight in Alaska from Anchorage to Juneau. Despite a thirty-nine-day search by the Air Force, Navy, and Coast Guard, no trace of the twin-engine plane on which Boggs was traveling has ever been found.

Had he been alive today, Boggs would probably have become Speaker of the House, having held the number two leadership post in the Congress at the time of his disappearance. There is no doubt Boggs would have been a singularly important figure in any re-opening of the Kennedy case.

David W. Belin

David Belin served as an Assistant Counsel to the Warren Commission and has emerged through the years as one of its most outspoken defenders. Several years ago, Belin authored *November 22, 1963: You are the Jury*, in which he strongly defended the conclusions, thoroughness, and integrity of the Commission's nine-month investigation. Belin places the blame for the fact that most Americans disbelieve the Warren Report's conclusion — that Oswald acted alone — on "critics, irresponsible critics who have deliberately and grossly misrepresented the [Warren Commission] record to the American public."[74] Despite David Belin's strong belief that there was no conspiracy involved in the Kennedy assassination, he has called for a Congressional reopening of the case, to "contribute toward restoration of credibility in Government," and to show that the various critics are wrong. He states:

> I think it would be very helpful for the American public to learn how easily they can be misled and exploited by people that sensationalize the facts, and that have not told them the truth, and how the media perhaps has been taken advantage of.[75]

He also stated:

> ... I think that fact that the CIA concealed from the Warren Commission any evidence of the fact that there were plots being directed against Castro was absolutely reprehensible...
>
> No member of the legal staff of the Warren Commission knew about CIA plots directed against foreign leaders, including Castro. I don't know of any member of the Commission, other than Dulles, that knew that the CIA had been involved, and I have specifically discussed this with some of the living members.[76]

In a Face the Nation interview on CBS in November, 1975, Belin fervently defended the Warren Commission, even going so far as to claim that since a conspiracy has never been uncovered, one probably in fact does not exist. In that interview Belin and CBS newsman Daniel Schorr had the following exchange:

> *Belin:* I don't happen to believe that Oswald was a part of any conspiracy, and as a matter of fact, the very fact that twelve years have passed and there really is no concrete evidence of any conspiracy, is in itself evidence of the fact there was no conspiracy.
>
> *Schorr:* Or that it was a very good one.[77]

Burt W. Griffin

Burt Griffin served as a counsel to the Warren Commission, and like some of his colleagues, has been accused of at least one specific attempt to affect the testimony of a key assassination witness whose testimony ran counter to the Warren staff's conclusions. However, unlike most of his fellow Warren Commission alumni, Burt Griffin has advocated a re-opening of the entire Kennedy case, stating in late 1975 that "extremely serious questions" have yet to be fully resolved about aspects of the Presidential murder.

Mark Lane was the first to point out that a key witness had stated that Griffin had attempted to affect that witness' testimony and had apparently sought to place key parts of the testimony "off the record," where it would, of course, never be recorded. Over the years, serious questions have been raised regarding the frequent use of "off the record" discussions between the Staff and various witnesses, which sometimes occurred during key phases of testimony that may have differed from the Commission's own suppositions and conclusions.

The episode involving Burt Griffin and a key witness relating to Jack Ruby's plans to murder Oswald provides a significant example of the "off the record" technique used by some Warren Commission staffers. The episode revolves around Griffin's questioning of Dallas Police Sergeant Patrick Dean, who had conducted the first interrogation of Jack Ruby. According to Sergeant Dean, Jack Ruby told him that he had been planning to kill Oswald for over two days.[78] This was a statement that would have raised what one Commission staffer called "horrendous problems." The Warren Commission had already concluded that Jack Ruby acted on a wild impulse and had planned the murder only minutes before he actually shot Oswald. Any other interpretation of Ruby's actions and motivation, particularly a confession of premeditated murder, would necessarily lead to a complete re-examination of Ruby's movements and associations during that period — something which the Commission wished to avoid.

Dean testified that Commission Counsel Griffin tried to badger and pressure him into changing his testimony about Ruby's plans during an "off the record" discussion. Sergeant Dean provided the following account of how he said Griffin dealt with him:

> Well, after the court reporter left, Mr. Griffin started talking to me in a manner of gaining my confidence in that he would help me and that he felt that I would probably need some help in the future.
>
> Mr. Griffin took my reports, one dated February 18, subject of it was an interview with Jack Ruby, and one dated November 26, which was my assignment in the basement.
>
> He said there were things in these statements which were not true and, in fact, that both these statements, he said there were particular things in there that were not true, and I asked him which portions did he consider not true, and then very dogmatically he said that "Jack Ruby didn't tell you that he entered the basement via the Main Street ramp."

And of course I was shocked at this. This is what I testified to, in fact, I was cross-examined on this, and he, Mr. Griffin, further said, "Jack Ruby did not tell you that he had thought or planned to kill Lee Oswald two nights prior."

And he said, "Your testimony was false, and these reports to your Chief of Police are false. . . ."

I quoted Ruby just about verbatim, and since he didn't believe me, and I was saying that they were true, we might as well terminate the interview.

Mr. Griffin then got back on the record, or before he did get back on the record, he said, "Well now, Sgt. Dean, I respect you as a witness, I respect you in your profession, but I have offered my help and assistance and I again will offer you my help and assistance in that I don't feel you will be subjecting yourself to loss of your job," or words to that effect, "if you will go ahead and tell me the truth about it."[79]

Griffin denied Dean's charges, maintaining that he had never intimidated any Commission witness. In later years, Burt Griffin became director of the legal services program of the Office of Economic Opportunity during the Nixon Administration.

William Coleman

William Coleman served as another counsel to the Warren Commission and was in charge of "Area IV" of the investigation: "Possible conspiratorial relationships." In early 1975, President Gerald Ford appointed Coleman to his Cabinet, as Secretary of Transportation.

William Coleman played a key role in probing Mrs. Sylvia Odio's testimony that Lee Harvey Oswald had been involved with a right-wing anti-Castro group in Dallas. The testimony by Mrs. Odio, who, Coleman concluded, "checked out thoroughly," provided one of the most significant areas of evidence regarding Lee Oswald's possible use of a "left-wing" pro-Castro "cover" in the assassination. (See reference to Sylvia Odio in the chapter on "The Second Oswald.")

William Coleman also was the principal author (along with Warren Commission Counsel David Slawson) of a key Commission memo which is still the subject of intense interest by various Kennedy assassination investigators. The Coleman-Slawson memorandum is a quite lengthy analysis of various "conspiracy scenarios" based on legitimate Warren Commission documentation. However, the entire memo has never been publicly released. Instead, various Freedom of Information requests filed with the National Archives have resulted in the de-classification of segments and partial paragraphs of the memo.

Daniel Schorr of CBS News was instrumental in securing the release of further portions of the classified memo in 1975. Commission critics had long sought access to the segment dealing with the possibility that Lee Harvey Oswald might have been a "double agent" posing as a "pro-Castro" activist while actually being involved with "anti-Castro" Cuban exiles. This concept has gradually become a leading theory of many Warren Commission critics and is one of the central areas being probed by the House and Senate investigations.

When substantial portions of the "double agent" section of the Coleman-Slawson memorandum were released in 1975, many observers were surprised to see that the concept had been articulated so well by the two Warren Commission staffers. Though it was noted that Coleman and Slawson had not been allowed to pursue the "double agent" theory to the extent they wished, many Commission critics noted that the memo is evidence that at least two Warren Commission staffers understood the dynamics of such a theory. In the memo, William Coleman and David Slawson wrote:

> The evidence here could lead to an anti-Castro involvement in the assassination on some sort of basis as this: Oswald could have beome known to the Cubans as being strongly pro-Castro. He made no secret of his sympathies, and so the anti-Castro Cubans must have realized that law enforcement authorities were also aware of Oswald's feelings and that, therefore, if he got into trouble, the public would also learn of them. The anti-Castro group may have even believed the fiction Oswald tried to create that he had organized some sort of large, active Fair Play for Cuba group in New Orleans. Second, someone in the anti-Castro organization might have been keen enough to sense that Oswald had a penchant for violence that might easily be aroused ... On

these facts, it is possible that some sort of deception was used to encourage Oswald to kill the President when he came to Dallas. Perhaps "double agents" were even used to persuade Oswald that pro-Castro Cubans would help in the assassination or in the get-away afterwards. The motive of this would of course be the expectation that after the President was killed Oswald would be caught or at least his identity ascertained, the law enforcement authorities and the public would then blame the assassination on the Castro government, and the call for its forceful overthrow would be irresistible. A "second Bay of Pigs invasion" would begin, this time, hopefully, to end successfully.[80]

Ramsey Clark

Ramsey Clark, who later served as Attorney General under President Johnson, was one of the Justice Department officials who worked in a liaison capacity with the investigation being conducted in 1964 by the Warren Commission. In 1967, Attorney General Clark became the subject of criticism by various Warren Commission critics, including New Orleans

District Attorney Jim Garrison. On March 2, 1967, the day after District Attorney Garrison announced the arrest of businessman Clay Shaw on charges of conspiring to assassinate President Kennedy, Attorney General Ramsey Clark stated that the FBI had already investigated Shaw "in November and December of 1963," and had "cleared" him of any involvement.[81] The Associated Press account of Ramsey Clark's remarks stated:

> . . . Clark said today the Federal Bureau of Investigation already has investigated and cleared Clay L. Shaw — a businessman arrested in New Orleans — of any part in the assassination of President John F. Kennedy.
>
> . . . Clark said the Justice Department knows what Garrison's case involves, and does not consider it valid.
>
> Clark said Shaw "was included in an investigation in November and December of 1963."
>
> "On the evidence that the FBI has, there was no connection found between Shaw and the assassination of the President in Dallas on November 22, 1963," Clark said.[82]

Ramsey Clark's statement proved to be completely inaccurate. No such investigation of Clay Shaw by the FBI or Justice Department ever took place. Within a matter of days, Attorney General Clark retracted his statement, without explaining his apparent misinformation. In a March 12, 1967, Face the Nation interview on CBS, Clark declined to comment on his previous inaccurate remarks about Clay Shaw, stating "it would be inappropriate for me to comment on the case. . . "[83] In the same interview, CBS correspondent George Herman questioned the Attorney General about the FBI's secret classified files on David Ferrie, the other key assassination suspect in Garrison's investigation. Herman asked: "Now Mr. Ferrie has been dead several weeks, and the Ferrie material is still classified and I wonder if that is at the order of the FBI and the Justice Department?" Clark replied, "No, those documents are under the general jurisdiction of the General Services Administration at this time."[84]

This statement was also inaccurate, as the Ferrie documents had specifically been classified under orders from FBI Director J. Edgar Hoover and his aides. The Ferrie documents were also subsequently withheld from Jim Garrison by the Justice Department when Garrison subpoenaed them for his investigation.

Later, Garrison officially requested Ramsey Clark to appear for questioning relating to the role of the FBI in investigating the Kennedy murder. However, Attorney General Clark refused to testify and once again stated that there was "nothing new" to Garrison's investigation.[85]

Ramsey Clark was also the subject of criticism a year later when he announced that there was "no sign of conspiracy" in the assassination of Martin Luther King, just days after King was shot to death, and several weeks before James Earl Ray, the alleged assassin, had even been apprehended.

Interestingly, former Attorney General Clark disclosed some information in 1975 that raises questions about J. Edgar Hoover's handling of the King assassination case: specifically, the FBI's arrest of James Earl Ray. The episode, as related by Ramsey Clark, may shed some light on Hoover's method of dealing with important investigations, including assassination probes. Clark's largely overlooked information raises the possibility that Hoover and his top aides withheld certain information from the Attorney General pertaining to the imminent arrest of James Earl Ray.[86] Clark's information further suggests that Hoover and the FBI also deliberately coordinated the timing of the actual arrest of Ray to coincide with the funeral of Robert F. Kennedy — thus scoring a public relations "coup" for the FBI. In his interview with Ovid Demaris (published in 1975, in the book *The Director*), Ramsey Clark disclosed the following sequence of events:

> We'd been searching for James Earl Ray, the assassin of Dr. King, and I had been in daily contact with them about it. I'd go over and see the evidence and hear what they had and they'd send me reports . . . They were showing me everything. . .
>
> The day of Bob Kennedy's funeral I went up to St. Patrick's . . . When I came out of the church, an agent said, "Mr. Attorney General, Mr. DeLoach says that it's urgent that you call him immediately." When I called them, they said that they had captured James Earl Ray in London and that he had tried to hold it up until after the funeral but he couldn't hold it up because Scotland Yard or somebody was saying, "We can't do that," and so they released the story apparently during the church service. I was a little puzzled by that. . . I got back to Washington and some of my people were really upset because they said there had been this long typed announcement of the arrest, that it had been laid on their desk either the night before or that morning.[87]

When Demaris noted that, "It sounds like they wanted to release it at that precise time," former Attorney General Clark concluded:

> I never have understood why. I mean, it's too bizarre for me to understand, but for some reason they decided they'd remind everybody the FBI was still on the job about that time of day and they did. I think I could have taken that. I mean, it's an idiosyncrasy and kind of a petty one, but the thing I couldn't take was that I believed that I'd been lied to, and you can't function that way. I'd been told with some elaboration that they'd tried to hold up and couldn't do it when in fact it had been just the opposite, that they had held up just to release it at that time.[88]

The former Attorney General also went on to disclose that he had suspended J. Edgar Hoover's close aide, Cartha DeLoach, from his position as FBI liaison, as a result of this incident. [89]

On the last day that Clark served as Attorney General, he ordered the Justice Department to withhold from New Orleans District Attorney Jim Garrison the X-Rays and photographs from the autopsy of President Kennedy. Garrison had subpoenaed these items in connection with his unsuccessful prosecution of Clay Shaw, and his subpoena had been upheld by a judge in Washington, D.C. Clark, however, appealed the judge's ruling, and the materials were never in fact produced.[90]

1. Gerald R. Ford, *Portrait of the Assassin* (New York: Simon and Schuster, Inc., 1965), pp. 451-452.
2. Warren Commission Session Transcript, December 5, 1963.
3. Warren Commission internal memorandum, by Melvin Eisenberg, February 17, 1964.
4. Warren Commission Session Transcript, January 27, 1964; Weisberg, *Whitewash IV*, pp. 36-121.
5. *Senate Intelligence Committee Report on the Kennedy Assassination*, p. 80.
6. Ibid.
7. Ibid., p. 81.
8. Ibid., p. 82.
9. Ibid., p. 83.
10. Ibid., p. 84.
11. Ibid.
12. Ibid.
13. Ibid., p. 86.
14. *Washington Post*, August 22, 1976.
15. Ibid.
16. Jack Anderson column, September 7, 1976.
17. Ibid.
18. *Senate Intelligence Committee Report on Foreign Assassinations*, p. 74.
19. Ibid., pp. 94-95.
20. Ibid., pp. 74-77, 80-85.
21. *Washington Star*, November 23, 1975.
22. Warren Commission Session Transcript, January 27, 1964; Weisberg, *Whitewash IV*, pp. 60-63.
23. Ibid.
24. Ibid.
25. Arthur M. Schlesinger, Jr., *A Thousand Days* (Boston: Houghton Mifflin, 1965), p. 276.
26. Epstein, *Inquest*, p. 152.
27. Ibid., pp. 149-150.
28. Warren Commission Session Transcript, January 27, 1964; Weisberg, *Whitewash IV*, p. 72.
29. *New York Times*, March 10, 1975; R. Harris Smith, *OSS: The Secret History of America's First Central Intelligence Agency* (New York: Dell Publishing Co., Inc., 1973), pp. 85-86.
30. "The Mafia, the CIA, and the Kennedy Assassination," Milton Viorst, *The Washingtonian*, November 1975.
31. Epstein, *Inquest*, pp. 146-147.
32. Ibid., p. 103.
33. Warren Commission Session Transcript, January 22, 1964.
34. Ibid.

35. Warren Commission Session Transcript, January 27, 1964, pp. 143-144; Weisberg, *Whitewash IV*, pp. 52-53.
36. Ibid., pp. 171-172; p. 80.
37. Ibid., p. 186; p. 95.
38. Ibid, p. 187; p. 96.
39. *Washington Post*, January 19, 1970.
40. Ibid.
41. Ibid.
42. Weisberg, *Whitewash IV*, pp. 20-23.
43. Ibid., p. 21.
44. Ibid.
45. Ibid., pp. 198-209.
46. Ibid.
47. Ibid., p. 209.
48. Warren Commission Session Transcript, January 27, 1964, p. 144; Weisberg, *Whitewash IV*, p. 53.
49. Ibid., p. 152; p. 61.
50. Ibid., p. 172; p. 81.
51. Ibid., p. 199; p. 108.
52. Warren Commission Report, Volume 3, p. 55.
53. *Washington Post*, April 6, 1971, April 7, 1971.
54. Ibid.
55. Ibid.
56. Ibid.
57. *Washington Post*, January 20, 1975.
58. Ibid., January 21, 1975.
59. Ibid.
60. *Senate Intelligence Committee Report on the Kennedy Assassination*, pp. 47, 53.
61. February 24, 1964 Warren Commission memorandum from Harold Willens to General Counsel J. Lee Rankin; Mark Lane, *A Citizen's Dissent* (New York: Fawcett Crest Edition, 1969), pp. 33-38.
62. Warren Commission Documents 489, 694, 763, 1457.
63. October 1, 1964 CIA memorandum, Richard Helms staff, sent to Warren Commission General Counsel J. Lee Rankin; Warren Commission Document 1532.
64. Ibid.
65. Ibid.
66. Louis L. Snyder, *Encyclopedia of the Third Reich* (New York: McGraw-Hill, Inc., 1976), p. 171.
67. *Senate Intelligence Committee Final Report*, Volume 6, p. 181.
68. Ibid.
69. *New York Times*, January 17, 1975.
70. Ibid.
71. CIA memorandum, "12 May 1972 — #533 989."
72. Ibid.

73. *Washington Post*, January 21, 1975.
74. Face the Nation, CBS, Interview with David W. Belin, November 23, 1975.
75. Ibid.
76. Ibid.
77. Ibid.
78. Warren Commission Report, Volume 5, pp. 255-256; Mark Lane, *Rush to Judgment* (New York: Fawcett Crest Edition, 1967), pp. 334-336.
79. Ibid.
80. Memorandum to the Warren Commission, from William Coleman and W. David Slawson. Undated.
81. *Washington Star*, March 2, 1967; *Washington Post*, March 3, 1967.
82. *Washington Star*, March 2, 1967.
83. Face the Nation, CBS, Interview with Attorney General Ramsey Clark, March 12, 1967.
84. Ibid.
85. Garrison, *A Heritage of Stone*, pp. 17-18.
86. Demaris, *The Director*, pp. 229-230.
87. Ibid.
88. Ibid.
89. Ibid.
90. *New York Times*, January 20, 1969, January 21, 1969.

CHAPTER THREE

Politicos

When the U.S. House of Representatives voted overwhelmingly in mid-September 1976 to reopen the investigation of the assassination of President Kennedy almost exactly twelve years after the Warren Commission Report was issued, the nation was in the midst of another Presidential campaign. While public (and official) interest focused on the Dallas murder once more, the real cost of the assassination to American democracy became evident. As some critics and students of the Warren Commission have noted, there has not been a single Presidential election in the past sixteen years whose outcome wasn't directly affected, indeed altered, by assassination:
— The electoral mandate of John F. Kennedy in 1960 was exploded on the streets of Dallas, Texas after less than three years of incumbency;
— The election of Lyndon B. Johnson to a full term in 1964 was the election of a man whose

name would never have been placed at the top of the Presidential ballot had he not succeeded to the Presidency through accident;
— The election of Richard M. Nixon in 1968, after a campaign which saw the death by assassination of his strongest (and most likely) opponent Robert Kennedy;
— The re-election of Richard M. Nixon in 1972 by a landslide margin that had been only a few points wide prior to the elimination, through a crippling assassination attempt, of a candidate whose potential third-party bid would have provided a siphoning off of much of that same landslide margin.

Author Robert Sam Anson, in recording some of the effects of the Kennedy assassination on the American political process, points out what many have observed is the continuing malignancy of that process — a malignancy that many believe has grown steadily since the President's murder in a crowded Texas Plaza:

John Kennedy's death defies simple rationality. Its impact is as much emotional as political, discerned better by psychologists than historians. The assassination, more than any other event, gave the succeeding decade its shape and form. For the generation that came to political consciousness in the 1960s, the assassination is the seminal happening . . . Even today his death is the emotional demarcation between hope and promise and bitterness and despair. The polls confirm what the gut feels: never since Dallas have Americans invested so much trust in their government. Each year, since 1964 onwards, the figures have become worse; declining confidence in government, in the church, in the family, in the inevitability of change for the better. The first spadeful of earth in what has come to be the "credibility gap" — but is really the chasm we feel in ourselves — was turned over in Dealey Plaza.[1]

One way or another, the JFK murder, its investigation by the Warren Commission, and now its reinvestigation have intimately involved and affected most of the top political leadership in the country since 1963. They have very directly affected the lives and/or political career of four Presidents (Kennedy, Johnson, Nixon, and Ford): two Vice Presidents (Rockefeller and Mondale); two Supreme Court Justices (Warren and Powell); five Presidential hopefuls (Robert Kennedy, John Connally, and Frank Church); and two Vice Presidential hopefuls (Schweiker and Baker). Let us examine briefly how these top political figures are tied into the matter.

Lyndon B. Johnson

Riding just a few cars behind President Kennedy, Vice President Lyndon B. Johnson was immediately shoved to the floor of his automobile by a Secret Service agent as shots echoed through Dealey Plaza. Shortly after arriving at Parkland Hospital, Johnson was told that President Kennedy's head wound had proved fatal. Kennedy aide Kenneth O'Donnell informed him, "The President is dead, Mr. President."

In the immediate aftermath of the killing, President Johnson appointed the Warren Commission to conduct the official investigation. Johnson publicly supported the Warren Commission's finding that Oswald had acted alone, and often publicly stated that he had no doubts about it. However, in recent years it has become evident that Johnson privately believed that there had in fact been a secret conspiracy behind the murder, a conspiracy that he was afraid to mention publicly.

While several of Johnson's close associates have now confirmed his reported belief in a conspiracy, the first documented evidence on paper of LBJ's suspicions came only this past year, as the Church Senate Intelligence Committee conducted its investigation into the activities of the FBI and CIA.

In a previously secret FBI memo first disclosed by Senator Richard Schweiker on December 3, 1975, President Johnson's suspicions were clearly recorded. In the memo (dated April 4, 1967), J. Edgar Hoover's third closest aide, Cartha DeLoach, informed Hoover's single closest aide, Clyde Tolson, that Marvin Watson (a top Johnson aide) had informed DeLoach that President Johnson "was now convinced" that the CIA had somehow been involved in the Kennedy assassination.[2]

While only fragments of this DeLoach/Tolson memo have been publicly released, other information received from reliable Senate sources has emerged. During Senator Schweiker's questioning of DeLoach about the memo, DeLoach disclosed that several weeks before it was written, Johnson had requested all FBI files on Robert Maheu and Sam Giancana.[3] Maheu and Giancana, together with Meyer Lansky's deputy, Santos Trafficante, had (according to the Church Committee) been the men used by the CIA to set up a secret assassination apparatus in the early 1960s for intended use against Fidel Castro.[4] Sources close to the Church Committee report that the Senators on the Committee (and their staff) were generally stunned to discover the Johnson view set forth in the secret DeLoach/Tolson FBI memo.

Previously, President Johnson had spoken privately of his belief that there was a conspiracy behind the Kennedy murder, but never before had his strong suspicions of CIA involvement surfaced.

In the spring of 1975, Walter Cronkite of CBS News released a portion of an interview with former President Johnson that had been filmed in 1969. This portion of the interview, which dealt with the Kennedy assassination, had originally been withheld from broadcast at Johnson's request, on grounds of "national security."

In the Cronkite interview, finally released six years later, Johnson stated that, "I don't think that they [the Warren Commission] or me or anyone else is always absolutely sure of everything that might have motivated Oswald or others that could have been involved. But he was quite a mysterious fellow, and he did have connections that bore examination."[5]

In November, 1975, in an interview with Dan Rather of CBS, Joseph Califano, a former top aide to LBJ, and now President Carter's Secretary of Health, Education and Welfare, disclosed that, "He [Johnson] used to say that — that he thought in time, when all the activities of the CIA were flushed out and when — then — then maybe the whole story of the Kennedy assassination would be known."[6]

In December, 1975, in testimony before the Church Committee, former FBI official Cartha DeLoach also testified that President Johnson had grown fearful that he himself would be assassinated, and had taken the unprecedented step of ordering the use of FBI agents to supplement his Secret Service protection. In his testimony, DeLoach stated, "The President of the United States, following the assassination of President John F. Kennedy, became somewhat obsessed with the fact that he himself might be assassinated . . . it was very apparent to personnel of the FBI that the President was obsessed with fear concerning possible assassination."[7]

John Connally

Texas Governor John Connally was the other victim of November 22, 1963, barely living through the gaping chest and back wounds suffered at the hands of the same person or persons who shot President Kennedy. "Oh, my God, they are going to kill us all," Connally screamed as a bullet tore into his back, plowed through his chest, glanced off two ribs, exited his chest, slammed into his wristbone and finally came to rest in his thigh.

The most important piece of eyewitness testimony provided by Connally (and his wife Nellie) centers on the entire basis of the controversial "single-bullet theory." Very simply, the Connallys, the closest witnesses to the actual shooting, both flatly state that the President and Connally were hit by separate bullets. Both state flatly that the "theory" of a single bullet is absolutely inaccurate. Connally and his wife have testified that they remember "to a moral certainty" that a *second separate bullet* hit Connally just a second or so after the first bullet hit Kennedy.[8] Though Connally still states that he believes the Warren Commission findings of a "lone assassin" are correct, he has never explained the contradictions inherent in this firm recollection that he and Kennedy were hit by separate bullets — bullets which both the Warren Commission and its league of critics have shown would have been fired too quickly to have both come from Oswald's antiquated gun.

Thus, inexplicably, Connally's public position remains as one of the more puzzling accounts of the shooting: he believes there was only one assassin, yet he also insists the "single-bullet theory" is absolutely untrue. Interestingly, Connally's doctors also firmly backed up his account of the shooting when they re-examined the medical and photographic evidence of the assassination, during a probe by *Life* in November, 1966.[9] (*Life* finally called for a total re-opening of the Kennedy case on the basis of the many contradictions and weaknesses inherent in the "single-bullet theory.")

While some defenders of the Warren Commission have tried to "shake" John and Nellie Connally's recollections, most observers credit both of them with having particularly detailed and accurate memories of the shooting. In one gruesome instance, Connally states that he clearly remembers seeing a light gray piece of President Kennedy's brain, "the size of a man's thumbnail," that had been blown forward in the car following the final fatal head shot.

Richard M. Nixon

The politician who went on to finally become President five years after John Kennedy was murdered is emerging as the subject of increasing interest by various critics of the Warren Commission findings.

Some of the growing speculation about Nixon stems from various pieces of information which connect certain areas of the Watergate mystery (particularly some of the Watergate participants) to various events surrounding the Kennedy assassination. (See the chapter on "Links to Watergate.") Other increasing speculation about Richard Nixon centers upon his close ties to various men who have been associated in some way with organized crime operatives of the Mafia — ties that include some of the men who were closest to him: Murray Chotiner; Charles Colson; and Bebe Rebozo. In the spring of 1976, a heavily documented article by Howard Kohn, "The Hughes-Nixon-Lansky Connection," detailed some of these previously reported Nixon associations with men connected in various ways to syndicate members, including Mafia operatives of syndicate boss Meyer Lansky.[10]

Drew Pearson, the late columnist and his then-assistant Jack Anderson, detailed in 1959 some of the syndicate associations of Murray Chotiner, who had served as Nixon's campaign manager and closest aide since the beginning of Nixon's now-notorious political career. Pearson discovered that Murray Chotiner and his brother had handled the legal defense of syndicate members in 221 Mafia prosecutions during the same three year period in which Nixon moved from Congressman to Senator to Vice Presidential nominee — all under the political management of Murray Chotiner.[11]

Pearson and Anderson later reported that Richard Nixon had earlier received substantial support for his first campaign (for the House of Representatives in 1946) from the powerful (and notoriously brutal) leader of the Los Angeles Mafia, Mickey Cohen. Pearson and Anderson disclosed that, "The cost of this campaign was partly offset by none other than Mickey Cohen, notorious underworld czar, who got to know Chotiner when Nixon rented headquarters in a building owned by Mickey."[12] Pearson and Anderson also later disclosed that Mafia boss Cohen had told them that he had also raised close to $20,000 for the earliest Nixon campaign, during a banquet with his closest syndicate gambling operatives — a banquet which Cohen claimed Nixon and Chotiner had attended.[13] This would have been the single largest contribution to Nixon's first campaign.

In mid-1973, just before the Watergate scandal became the preeminent news story of the next year and a half, Jack Nelson and Bill Hazlitt of the *Los Angeles Times* produced a highly detailed account of the kind of Nixon relationships that now intrigue some critics of the Warren Commission — especially those who believe that organized crime elements may have been behind the Kennedy murder. The *Los Angeles Times* article, "The White House, the Teamsters and the Mafia," included a quote from an FBI man who stated that, "This whole thing of the Teamsters and the mob and the White House is one of the scariest things I've ever seen . . . We don't know what to expect out of the Justice Department."[14] The article contained accounts of several Teamster-Mafia criminal cases, in which officials of the Nixon Administration had intervened on behalf of those interests.[15]

In 1974, when the White House transcripts of some of Nixon's secret tape recordings were publicly released during the Watergate investigation, many observers were astonished to discover that President Nixon, H.R. Haldeman, and John Dean, had discussed the possible use of the Mafia in attempting to "launder" the secret Watergate hush money. This discussion had occurred during the climactic March 21, 1973 Oval Office conversation in which Dean warned Nixon that the "cancer on the Presidency" caused by Watergate was beginning to destroy them all. Interestingly, Nixon voiced not the slightest objection to the possible use of the Mafia during the discussion of the "laundering" process:

> *Dean:* Well, first of all, there is the problem of the continued blackmail [by E. Howard Hunt and the Watergate burglars] . . . It will cost money. It is dangerous. People around

here are not pros at this sort of thing. This
is the sort of thing Mafia people can do:
washing money, getting clean money, and
things like that. We just don't know about
those things, because we are not criminals
and not used to dealing in that business.
Nixon: That's right.
Dean: It is a tough thing to know how to do.
Nixon: Maybe it takes a gang to do that.[16]

Later, during a further discussion about laundering
the Watergate blackmail payments, Nixon and Dean
had returned to the subject of using the syndicate,
possibly in Las Vegas:
Dean: You can get a $100,000 out of a
bank, and it all comes in serialized bills . . .
and that means you have to go to Vegas
with it or a bookmaker in New York City.
Nixon: Is there any other money hanging
around?[17]

In late October, 1973, the *Washington Post* traced
the passage of 900 shares of stolen IBM stock through
Bebe Rebozo's Key Biscayne Bank in Florida.[18] What
brought the matter to the attention of federal investigators was the fact that the IBM stock had been
stolen from E. F. Hutton and Company by four well-
known Mafia figures.[19] The *Washington Post* further
reported that a professional insurance investigator had
submitted a deposition stating that he had personally
informed Rebozo that the stock was stolen — shortly
before President Nixon's closest associate went ahead
and cashed a large amount of it.[20]

In an earlier and somewhat more publicized account,
the *Washington Post* has reported on the extremely
unusual circumstances of a pardon granted by President Nixon in December of 1972 to a top leader of
the New Jersey Mafia, Angelo "Gyp" DeCarlo.[21]
DeCarlo, widely credited by federal authorities with
being a leading Mafia contact for gangland executions,

received the clemency after the White House (through John Ehrlichman and John Dean) "expedited" the handling of the case. The *Post* reported that various lawyers in the Justice Department regarded DeCarlo's clemency as one of the most mysterious cases in the Department's history. One Justice Department official, who refused to be indentified, stated, "This is Gyp DeCarlo. He is a very bad guy, with a history of political connections . . . something or someone just had to give that thing a push . . . who?"[22] Angelo DeCarlo and his agents were notorious for the brutal methods they used in syndicate activities in New Jersey, including the use of meathooks and disembowelment in either torturing or murdering their victims.

Also, in early December of 1973, the *Washington Post* disclosed that acting on behalf of President Nixon, Charles Colson had intervened on behalf of a man associated with a powerful New York Mafia leader, then facing prosecution for extortion in a Teamster scandal.[23] The *Post* reported that Colson had written "Watch for this. *Do all possible*" on a memorandum concerning the prosecution. In the article, the *Post* reported that Colson had also personally intervened in another Justice Department matter and had "arranged" for the early parole of a key convicted Teamster leader in Miami.[24]

Interestingly, perhaps the most overlooked or ignored allegation made by the late Martha Mitchell during the Watergate scandal involved what she claimed was some unknown relationship between Richard M. Nixon and the Mafia — a relationship that she presumably heard about through her husband, John Mitchell. Mrs. Mitchell's strange comments came in September, 1973, at the height of growing speculation that she may have had significant knowledge pertaining to the Watergate conspiracy.

On September 10, 1973, in an article titled "How Much Does Martha Know?", *Newsweek* reported that Mrs. Mitchell had told a reporter that Nixon "planned the whole goddamn thing." *Newsweek* reported that she had spoken in "an undertone of desperation."[25]

Days later, Martha Mitchell called UPI reporter Helen Thomas and again indicated that the President was a direct party to the Watergate cover-up. However, in this late night conversation, Mrs. Mitchell made a further charge about the President: "Nixon is involved with the Mafia. The Mafia was involved in his reelection [campaign]." On September 24, 1973, briefly noting her allegation about Nixon and the Mafia, *Newsweek* reported that Mitchell family associates had recently claimed that Martha had had "a series of unpredictable and sometimes violent outbursts at home." *Newsweek* further reported that John Mitchell had stated, "You think the media would understand and leave Martha alone. It's obvious to anyone who knows her that she's a sick woman."[26]

In a little-known development that will be detailed in the chapter on "The Links to Watergate," Richard M. Nixon himself had been present at a Bottler's Convention in Dallas on the very morning of the Kennedy assassination, and three months later had incorrectly told the FBI that "the only time" he had been in Dallas in 1963 "was two days prior to the assassination." Nixon was then being questioned about Marina Oswald's allegation that her husband Lee had once planned to kill Nixon.

In a lengthy interview with *Village Voice* reporter Dick Russell in February of 1976 (published by *Argosy* magazine), Charles Colson stated;

> I've heard one theory that there is no Howard Hughes, that it's really a headquarters of the Mafia's operation; that they owned Bebe Rebozo, they got their hooks into Nixon early, and, of course, that ties into the overlap of the CIA and the Mob . . . Don't say that's my theory, but I've heard it expounded as a possibility and, of course, it is.[27]

Four months before the Colson interview, former

President Nixon had made his first publicized appearance outside of his San Clemente retreat. Nixon appeared at the notorious La Costa Country Club for a golf tournament run by controversial Teamster boss Frank Fitzsimmons. As the *New York Times*, *Newsweek*, and other news organizations noted, La Costa is widely reported to be a prime gathering place for well-known syndicate figures. Among those playing in the early October, 1975, golf tournament — along with Nixon and Fitzsimmons — were Anthony Provenzano (recently linked to the "disappearance" of James R. Hoffa); Allen Dorfman (a notorious Teamster executive); and Jack Presser (the son of a top Cleveland Teamster). A couple of other men present at the tournament had hidden their faces from photographers, and were never identified.

Gerald R. Ford

Future President Gerald Ford had served as one of the seven members of the Warren Commission in 1963-64. Congressman Ford, then House Minority Leader as well, had been the single most active Warren Commission member, attending the actual questioning of more official Commission witnesses (70 out of 94) than any other member.[28]

Although Ford expressed some degree of discontent

over the way the FBI and CIA were responding to the Commission's investigation, he has, through the years, been a firm defender of the Commission findings. According to a Commission transcript first reported by writer Tad Szulc in September, 1975, during the course of the 1964 investigation, "Ford provoked a near uproar in the panel when, on June 4, 1964, he charged that outside forces were trying to pressure the Commission to decide in advance that Oswald was a solitary assassin."[29] Whatever doubts Ford may have had about the pressures being exerted on the Commission by "outside forces," he became one of the strongest advocates within the Commission for adopting the controversial "single-bullet theory." According to Edward J. Epstein's detailed account of the Commission's proceedings, Gerald Ford made an unsuccessful attempt to have the Warren Commission describe the "single-bullet theory" as "compelling evidence," in the Commission's Report.[30] Other Warren Commission members, led by Senator Richard Russell and Representative Hale Boggs, rejected Ford's recommendation of the word "compelling."

In 1964 and 1965, Ford wrote two published defenses of the Warren Commission findings: one, a magazine article that Ford wrote for *Life* shortly before the Warren Report was released (a Ford action which angered several of his Commission colleagues) and secondly, a 1965 book for Simon and Schuster, *Portrait of the Assassin*. The Ford book was primarily written by Ford crony and former campaign aide Jack Stiles.

In the book, which even many strong defenders of the Warren Commission viewed as poorly done, Ford and Stiles set forth a compendium of the most damaging testimony about Oswald's alleged mental instability. Ford and Stiles indicated that Oswald's reported marital troubles with his estranged wife Marina (including his alleged impotence) were major facts behind his "decision" to assassinate President Kennedy. Ford and Stiles claimed to have compiled "strong evidence that Lee Oswald's mind turned to murder whenever he wanted to impress Marina."

Ford's use (and allegedly slanted "editing") of a highly classified transcript of a tape-recorded Warren Commission meeting later became the subject of criticism by both critics of the Warren Commission and certain members of Congress. The transcript Ford used in his book was of a secret "emergency" Warren Commission meeting of January 22, 1964, at which various rumors of Oswald's FBI and/or CIA connections were first discussed. The actual transcript of the session was not released until 1974, when leading Warren Commission critic Harold Weisberg secured it following his filing of a Freedom of Information suit. When Weisberg, a former Senate investigator, finally received and analyzed the transcript, it became apparent that Gerald Ford had indeed heavily and quite selectively edited the excerpts used in his book.[31]

During Ford's Vice Presidential confirmation hearings before House and Senate panels in late 1973, his use of the secret transcript became a minor issue — an issue to which Ford responded under oath with an inaccurate answer. Ford was questioned by Senator Howard Cannon, Chairman of the Senate Rules Committee, as to whether he had violated the "constraints" and confidentiality of the Warren Commission by releasing and publishing parts of the Commission proceedings. Ford, whose use of the highly classified January 22, 1964 Commission transcript as a central part of his book, inaccurately responded to Senator Cannon's question by stating under oath that "We wrote the book, but we did not use in that book any material other than the material that was in the 26 volumes of testimony and exhibits that were subsequently made public and sold to the public generally."[32] This was, of course, untrue.

While some of the Warren Commission critics cite Ford's sworn response as evidence of perjury by him, little attention has been focused on the matter.

In late May, 1976, shortly after the Church Senate

Intelligence Committee voted to turn over the findings of its re-investigation of the Kennedy assassination to the new Senate Intelligence Oversight Committee, President Ford surprised some observers by making his most impassioned defense of the Warren Commission findings to date. While it had previously been thought that even Ford had once been wary of the extent of cooperation given to the Warren Commission by the FBI and CIA, Ford now seemed to be digging his heels into an even stronger defense of the Commission's work. On May 30, 1976, the *Washington Post* reported that during an interview in the Oval Office on May 29th, Ford had stated that he not only still firmly believed the Warren Commission conclusions, but also believed the Commission "got full cooperation of all federal agencies at that time."[33] Ford indicated that he saw no reason to question the performance of either agency in investigating the Kennedy murder.[34]

Nelson A. Rockefeller

In early 1975, Vice President Nelson Rockefeller was appointed by President Gerald Ford to head a new Commission (popularly known as the Rockefeller Commission) to investigate recent disclosures of CIA abuses (including domestic spying crimes) that had primarily come to light as the result of a major investigative article by Seymour M. Hersh of the *New York Times* on December 22, 1974.[35] To serve in the crucial position of Executive Director of the new Commission, Rockefeller appointed Iowa lawyer David W. Belin, a former Counsel to the Warren Commission. In previous years, Belin had stoutly defended the findings of the Warren Commission, emerging as the most publicly outspoken defender of its conclusion of a single assassin.

In 1973, Belin wrote a book, *November 22, 1963: You Are the Jury*, in which he defended the Warren Report as an historic, "unshakeable" document. Soon after Rockefeller and Belin (and the other Rockefeller Commission members, several of whose ties to the intelligence community were the subject of heavy criticism) began their work, the *New York Times* reported that the Rockefeller group would also investigate charges that the CIA was involved in the Kennedy assassination.[36] While few observers ever really expected the Rockefeller Commission to actually re-investigate the Dallas murder in any substantive manner, the final Report of the Commission surprised many, due to both the brevity and vagueness of its conclusions. The Rockefeller Report was in fact subsequently viewed as an embarrassment to both President Ford (who for a time urged that it be withheld) and Nelson Rockefeller himself.

In a brief eighteen-page section on the Kennedy assassination, the Report concentrated on knocking down several vaguely defined charges that the CIA had directly coordinated the actual assassination.[37] The Report devoted little or no attention to the mass of serious documented evidence set forth by the legitimate critics of the Warren Commission. In one of several noteworthy instances, the Rockefeller Commission Report set forth some information regarding a defector to the United States who had been mysteriously imprisoned and abused by the CIA. The Report stated that the defector had been held "in solitary confinement under spartan living conditions" for three years.[38] What Nelson Rockefeller's Commission and its Executive Director, David Belin, did not report, however, was who this unnamed defector is.

On March 28, 1976, Jack Nelson of the *Los Angeles Times* finally disclosed that the defector was Yuri Nosencho, the Russian intelligence official who had escaped to the United States and had disclosed that the Russian KGB file on Lee Oswald had identified him as a possible "sleeper agent" used by "American intelligence."[39] (See further reference to Yuri Nosencho under the chapter on "The Intelligence Connections.") As the *Los Angeles Times* article made clear, the Rockefeller-Belin group had suppressed the knowledge of who this defector actually was, as well as his knowledge of the Russian KGB file on Oswald.

In another instance, the Rockefeller Commission was accused of "deliberately distorting and suppressing" part of the testimony of the former President of the American Academy of Forensic Sciences as to the nature of President Kennedy's head and neck wounds. Dr. Cyril Wecht, the Pittsburgh coroner regarded by many as the leading forensics expert in the nation, publicly accused the Rockefeller Commission of deliberately editing his testimony about the President's wounds in a misleading way.[40] Wecht demanded that a full transcript of his Rockefeller Commission testimony be released, a request that Rockefeller and Belin refused on the grounds that Commission proceedings were confidential. While Vice President Rockefeller subsequently continued to defend the Commission's Report as "outstanding, first rate," David Belin later sought to disassociate himself from the Report's section on the Kennedy assassination, insisting that he had little to do with that particular area of the Rockefeller probe.

Justice Lewis Powell

Supreme Court Justice Lewis W. Powell, appointed to the Supreme Court by President Nixon in late October, 1971, has been a strong defender of the Warren Commission for many years.

Lewis Powell had, in fact, as president-elect of the ABA, served as a legal observer for the actual Warren Commission sessions, assigned to protect the dead Oswald's legal interests as well as those of other figures.

Powell also emerged in those early days of 1964 as a particularly bitter opponent of Mark Lane, who was then already raising questions about the lack of solid evidence and testimony implicating Oswald. Lane, acting as a legal adviser to Oswald's mother, became involved in several early disagreements with the Warren Commission members and staff and voiced doubts as to the thoroughness of their continuing investigation. While Lane's actions and demeanor have on more than a few occasions struck various people as abrasive, Lewis Powell took particular offense over Lane's efforts.

A declassified document from the internal files of the Warren Commission, first reported by Robert Sam Anson in 1975 in his book, *They've Killed The President!*, reveals the extent of Powell's anger over Mark Lane's actions. On April 17, 1964, the future Supreme Court Justice wrote a letter to J. Lee Rankin, the General Counsel to the Warren Commission, chastising Lane's recent actions and asking if "there isn't some way the Bar can take disciplinary action against Lane."[41] Despite Powell's recommendation, no such "disciplinary" action was ever taken. As a result of Powell's involvement in various Warren Commission activities, some Senate sources believe a voluntary Powell disqualification would likely occur in the event that any matters arising from the Congress' re-investigation of the Kennedy murder reach the Supreme Court. Depending upon the extent of such issues as possible CIA or FBI involvement, or perhaps possible claims of executive privilege (or constitutional questions relating to national security), the Supreme Court may potentially play some role in any re-investigation.

Senator Edward M. Kennedy

Senator Edward M. Kennedy, the sole survivor of the Kennedy brothers, was for many years a public defender of the Warren Commission's conclusion that Lee Oswald was the lone assassin. Like his brother Robert before him, Ted Kennedy seemed to have little heart to engage in any review or re-examination of the shattering event that ended John Kennedy's life and permanently changed their own lives as well. While various close aides of the Kennedy brothers have often-times expressed strong disbelief over some of the Warren Commission's findings (including Frank

Mankiewicz, Arthur Schlesinger, Richard Goodwin, and Adam Walinsky), whatever doubts that Robert and Ted Kennedy may have had about the Dallas murder were kept tightly within the Kennedy family circle. Sources close to the Kennedy family report that the subject is still exceedingly difficult for the family to discuss, with the intervening thirteen years having done little to ease its associated emotional pains.

Though little attention has been focused on it, several sources report that Edward Kennedy (and his wife Joan and other family members) were for a while fearful on the afternoon of the assassination that the shooting in Dallas may have been part of some kind of coup or takeover plot by unknown right-wing domestic forces. This suspicion by various members of the Kennedy circle, in the hours immediately following the shooting, was particularly fueled by several occurrences. Right after the tragic news reached Washington, virtually the entire phone system for the nation's capital went out of order. As has been reported several times, a panic-stricken Ted Kennedy quickly left the Senate chamber (where he had been presiding) and was forced to go door to door through a Washington neighborhood in search of a working telephone, to place a call for further details of the Dallas shooting.

Concerned over the safety of his wife Joan, Kennedy and an aide, Milton Gwirtzman, raced to meet her at the downtown hairdresser where she had been that morning. When Kennedy explained to her that there was no way to telephone for further details, saying "All the phones are gone," Joan Kennedy fearfully remarked. "There must be some national reason."[42]

According to William Manchester's detailed account of the assassination, *The Death of a President*, Ted and Joan Kennedy "began to wonder whether the failure of the [phone] system could be more than an accident."[43] Shortly thereafter, with still no word from Dallas of whether the President was alive or dead, the Kennedy family had another scare, first disclosed by Manchester in 1967. The Secret Service agent who had been in charge of rushing young Caroline Kennedy back to the White House from a school outing, reported back that he had been mysteriously tailed at high speeds by a man in a green sedan. Manchester wrote of Secret Service agent Tom Wells' apprehension: "Perhaps his fear of a coup was being vindicated at this very moment; perhaps the strange sedan was part of it."[44]

In 1975, Senator Edward Kennedy began to express what some students of the Warren Commission believe to be a subtle evolution of his views on the assassination. For the first time in thirteen years, Kennedy voiced public criticism (though moderate in tone) of the Warren Commission's investigation and expressed some doubt as to its thoroughness. In an unprecedented interview with Hays Gorey of *Time* magazine, Senator Kennedy (in late November, 1975) said that while he remains "fundamentally satisfied" with the Warren Commission findings, "There were things that should have been done differently. There were mistakes made."[45] Additionally, Ted Kennedy sought to make clear that the Kennedy family would not stand in the way of any re-investigation of the Dallas murder. As demands for a re-opening of the Kennedy case began to mount in 1975, Senator Kennedy approved the drafting of a new form letter to be sent to people who wrote him urging a new investigation. In the form letter, Kennedy stated that in the event that Congressional or Justice Department investigators decided to re-open the case, "I do not believe that their judgment should be influenced by any feelings or discomfort by any member of my family."[46]

Walter Mondale

Walter Mondale, the respected former Senator now serving as Vice President, has also become a strong skeptic about the Commission's findings. Like Senator Schweiker, Mondale originally arrived at these doubts while serving on the Church Senate Intelligence Committee. In 1975, Mondale became the first member of the Church Committee to disclose the CIA's creation of a secret assassination planning group in the early 1960s, a group that designed what the CIA referred to as the "Executive Action capability." According to the Senate Committee's complex "Report on Alleged Assassination Plots Involving Foreign Leaders":

> "Executive Action" was a CIA euphemism, defined as a project for research into developing means for overthrowing foreign political leaders, including a "capability to perform assassinations."[47]

In an interview in mid-May, 1976, as the Church Committee was ending its investigations, Mondale cautioned:

> There is some evidence that we have not seen everything. For example, we've just come across some files in the FBI with an assassination heading that we did not know about, and even though there had been a request for nearly fifteen months to the

Bureau for all files relating to that issue...
Our staff, in doing its work in the Kennedy
assassination, and looking at the records of
the files we had received, came across
reference to another file or files we didn't
have."[48]

Speaking of the CIA and FBI "cooperation" with
the Warren Commission, Walter Mondale stated, "I
think the record will show that there were some
very grievous inadequacies on the part of those
Agencies."[49] Mondale also went on to say that the
Senate Committee had uncovered several "quite
significant" leads relating to the Committee's examination of various aspects of the Kennedy assassination.[50]

Senator Richard Schweiker

Senator Richard Schweiker, the moderate Republican from Pennsylvania, has emerged as the key Senate proponent of the re-opening of the Kennedy assassination case. Schweiker originally became concerned over the Warren Commission findings during his work on the Church Senate Intelligence Committee. Senator Schweiker evolved into a committed critic of the Warren Commission findings and urged his colleagues on the Church Committee to undertake a review of the FBI and CIA role in investigating the President's murder.

In the fall, 1975, following a continuing string of new revelations about the assassination and Lee Oswald and Jack Ruby, the Church Committee established an informal, two-man subcommittee consisting of Senator Gary Hart of Colorado and Senator Schweiker to review the FBI and CIA role in the Warren Commission's investigation. By late 1975, Schweiker was devoting a large amount of his time to the new inquiry and had committed the resources of his personal Senate staff to the probe as well. "Just getting grounded in the mass of assassination evidence took several months, but we finally began to formulate the various finite areas of doubt and the mysterious trails that led away from each of them," Schweiker said in late 1975.

In the late spring of 1976, the Church Committee voted almost unanimously to turn the initial findings of the Schweiker-Hart inquiry over to the newly created permanent Senate Intelligence Oversight Committee. Senator Schweiker has been quoted widely for having predicted that "The Warren Commission Report is going to collapse like a house of cards." Most observers credit the Senate Intelligence Committee Report on the Kennedy Assassination — prepared under the direction of the Schweiker-Hart subcommittee — as one of the most significant documents on the case to emerge in thirteen years.

Congressman Thomas N. Downing

Rep. Thomas Downing, a veteran conservative Democrat from Newport News, Virginia, has in the last two years become the leading force in the U.S. House of Representatives in working for the reopening of the Kennedy assassination case by Congress. Due in large part to the intense efforts of Congressman Downing, in fall, 1976 the House finally voted by an overwhelming margin to create a Select Committee to reinvestigate the case. Rep. Downing himself was selected as Chairman of the Committee.

Downing originally became interested in the Kennedy case when he viewed a screening of the famous Zapruder film of the assassination, produced by Robert Groden, a film expert who has specialized in photographic evidence of the assassination. Downing later sponsored numerous screenings of the Zapruder film for other Congressmen and Congressional staffers.

Representative Downing has stated that he does in fact believe there was a conspiracy behind the President's assassination, and that it was carried out by a well-organized group of conspirators. Downing announced in 1976 that he would not run for another term in the House, and thus his Chairmanship of the Select Committee on Assassinations ended in early January of 1977.

Congressman Henry Gonzalez

Henry Gonzalez, like Thomas Downing, has served as a Democratic Congressman for many years. Gonzalez, a moderate and highly respected Representative from Texas was traveling with the Presidential entourage in Dallas and was an actual witness to the 1963 assassination.

Gonzalez has sponsored a House resolution calling for the re-investigation of not only the JFK case, but of the Robert Kennedy and Martin Luther King assassinations and the attempted assassination of George Wallace as well.

Gonzalez has stated on several occasions that he believes there is a possibility that various participants in the Watergate conspiracy may have possibly been connected in some way to events surrounding the Dallas assassination. Gonzalez has spoken of the mysterious assortment of Cuban exile operatives linked to both cases.

In 1973, Congressman Gonzalez had the Congressional Research Service of the Library of Congress begin research on several aspects of the Kennedy case.

Congressman Don Edwards

Representative Don Edwards, the widely respected liberal from California who played a key role in the televised impeachment hearings of the House Judiciary Committee in 1974, has also become identified with the growing number of Congressional supporters of a new investigation into the Dallas murder.

Edwards, himself a former FBI agent, has focused new attention on the role of J. Edgar Hoover and the FBI in suppressing and in fact destroying crucial assassination evidence in 1963 and 1964.

In hearings before the Constitutional Rights Subcommittee chaired by Representative Edwards in fall, 1975, key FBI personnel confirmed that Hoover's top aides had indeed ordered the secret destruction of a letter that Lee Oswald had personally delivered to the Dallas FBI office a few days before the assassination. FBI personnel admitted under oath that the destruction of the letter (ordered by the Hoover circle) was within hours after Jack Ruby murdered Oswald. The Edwards Subcommittee hearings also produced for the first time an official FBI confirmation that the FBI had contacted Jack Ruby on at least seven occasions for use as an FBI informant — including during the period that Ruby visited organized crime figures in Havana, Cuba, in 1959. This information had never been made available to the Warren Commission. In the early summer of 1976, Congressman Edwards told a small group of Congressmen that, "There's not much question that both the FBI and CIA are somewhere behind this cover-up. I hate to think what it is they are covering up — or who they are covering for."

Senator Howard Baker

Senate Minority leader Howard Baker, the moderate Republican from Tennessee, and former member of the Ervin Watergate Committee as well as the Church Intelligence Committee, has become a strong advocate of reopening the Kennedy assassination probe. Senator Baker is reported to have long harbored various suspicions relating to the assassination, and conducted a lengthy investigation into various Cuban exile activities during the Ervin Committee probe — activities that many Warren Commission critics believe may relate to the Kennedy assassination. In a CBS interview on May 23, 1976, Senator Baker voiced strong misgivings over the extent of CIA and FBI information turned over to the Warren Commission:

> I don't think the Warren Commission [was] privy to all the facts, for instance, it did not know even of the 56 attempts by the CIA on Fidel Castro's life and apparently did not know of Castro's threat in public, saying look, you're trying to kill me and I

know it. If you don't stop, no American leader is going to be safe. I have no record evidence that the Warren Commission ever considered that.[51]

Senator Baker went on to recommend strongly a continuation of the assassination probe begun by Senators Schweiker and Hart, stating:

> I think that Gary Hart and Dick Schweiker did a great job, a monumental undertaking, and I think just as clearly that the new intelligence oversight committee ought to decide how to pursue the matter, it certainly should not be dropped. I have no information that would indicate that the Warren Commission is wrong, or that Oswald was an agent, or did not act on his own. All I have is a basket of loose ends that Hart and Schweiker have produced, and I think they've got to be examined.[52]

Senator Gary Hart

Gary Hart the freshman Democratic Senator from Colorado, was appointed by the Church Senate Intelligence Committee in late 1975 to head a special subcommittee (along with Senator Richard Schweiker) to review and re-investigate the role of the CIA and FBI in the original Kennedy assassination investigation. Hart and Schweiker's subcommittee work grew steadily — and their task became more complex — as the Senate probe stretched on into 1976.

Senator Hart was at first highly reluctant to become involved in the case, leaving the main thrust of the probe to Senator Schweiker, but Hart subsequently began to exercise a major role in the spring of 1976. On May 1, 1976, saying "I don't think you can see the things I have seen and sit on it," Hart disclosed that he would recommend a full reopening of the Kennedy case by a new Senate Committee. Among the points that should be re-investigated, Hart said, were "Who Oswald really was — who did he know? What affiliation did he have in the Cuban network? Was his public identification with the left wing a cover for a connection with the anti-Castro right wing?"[53]

Senator Hart went on to state that he personally believed that Oswald was "sophisticated" enough to have operated as a "double agent." Equally important, Hart stated that evidence would show that top officials of both the CIA and FBI made "a conscious decision to withhold evidence from the Warren Commission."[54]

Richard A. Sprague

In September, 1976, the newly created House Select Committee on Assassinations chose former

Pennsylvania prosecutor Richard A. Sprague to head its investigation of the John F. Kennedy and the Martin Luther King assassinations. Upon being selected as Staff Director of the new Committee, Sprague noted that "No living person is beyond the reach of this Committee's mandate, no document being held by any agency of government is beyond our reach."

During his years as the First Assistant District Attorney of Philadelphia County, Pennsylvania, Sprague, now 51, had compiled one of the nation's most impressive prosecutorial records. The Commonwealth of Pennsylvania's own statistical records note during Richard Sprague's service as Prosecuting Attorney in more than 10,000 criminal trials, including hundreds of murder cases, 60 of which were first degree murder cases, he obtained the death penalty more than twenty times.

Sprague had come to national attention in the early 1970s during his successful prosecution of a murder conspiracy headed by the President of the United Mine Workers, W. A. "Tony" Boyle. Boyle and several lieutenants were charged with authorizing and carrying out the brutal murders of UMW President Joseph Yablonski, Boyle's chief union opponent, as well as Yablonski's wife and daughter. While Sprague had at first encountered great difficulty in linking the actual Yablonski killers to higher-ups, his methodic and time-consuming investigation of the case finally led to a breaking open of the larger murder conspiracy, and a series of convictions.

1. Robert Sam Anson, *They've Killed the President!* (New York: Bantam Books, Inc., 1975), p. 4.
2. *Senate Intelligence Committee Final Report*, Volume 6, 1976, p. 182.
3. Ibid.
4. *Senate Intelligence Committee Report on Foreign Assassinations*, pp. 74-85.
5. CBS Reports Inquiry, *"The American Assassins,"* Part II, Dan Rather, November 26, 1975.
6. Ibid.
7. *Senate Intelligence Committee Report*, Volume 6, 1976, pp. 175-176.
8. "A Matter of Reasonable Doubt," *Life*, November 25, 1966.
9. Ibid.
10. "The Hughes-Nixon-Lansky Connection: The Secret Alliances of the CIA," Howard Kohn, *Rolling Stone*, May 20, 1976.
11. Drew Pearson and Jack Anderson, *U.S.A.-Second Class Power* (New York: Simon and Schuster, 1958), pp. 281-282.
12. Ibid.
13. "The Hughes-Nixon-Lansky Connection: The Secret Alliances of the CIA," Howard Kohn, *Rolling Stone*, May 20, 1976.
14. "The White House, the Teamsters and the Mafia," Jack Nelson and Bill Hazlitt, *Los Angeles Times*, *Miami Herald*, June 3, 1973.
15. Ibid.
16. *The White House Transcripts*, *New York Times* edition (New York: The Viking Press, 1973), p. 146.
17. Ibid., p. 173.
18. *Washington Post*, October 25, 1973.
19. Ibid.
20. Ibid.
21. *Washington Post*, April 2, 1973.
22. Ibid.
23. *Washington Post*, December 2, 1973.
24. Ibid.
25. *Newsweek*, September 10, 1973.
26. Ibid., September 24, 1973.
27. *Argosy*, March 1976, "Interview with Charles W. Colson.
28. Meagher, *Accessories After The Fact*, p. 30.
29. *Washington Star*, Tad Szulc, September 19, 1975.
30. Epstein, *Inquest*, pp. 149-150.
31. Harold Weisberg, *Whitewash IV: JFK Assassination Transcript* (Frederick, Maryland: Harold Weisberg, 1974), pp. 124-130.

32. Senate Rules Committee, Confirmation Hearings on Ford Nomination as Vice President, November 5, 1973, pp. 89-94.
33. *Washington Post*, May 30, 1976.
34. Ibid.
35. *New York Times*, December 22, 1974.
36. Ibid., March 8, 1975.
37. *Report to the President by the Commission on CIA Activities within the United States*, 1975, pp. 251-269.
38. Ibid., p. 170.
39. *Los Angeles Times*, March 28, 1976.
40. *Saturday Evening Post*, September 1975.
41. Anson, *They've Killed the President!*, p. 73; Declassified correspondence from Lewis W. Powell to J. Lee Rankin, April 17, 1964, Mark Lane file (National Archives, Washington, D.C.).
42. William Manchester, *The Death of a President* (New York: Harper and Row, 1967), p. 199.
43. Ibid.
44. Ibid., pp. 203-204.
45. *Time*, November 24, 1975.
46. Senator Edward M. Kennedy correspondence with constituent, June 2, 1975.
47. *Senate Intelligence Committee Report on Foreign Assassinations*, p. 182.
48. "Face The Nation," CBS, Interview with Sen. Walter Mondale, May 16, 1976.
49. Ibid.
50. Ibid.
51. "Face The Nation," CBS, Interview with Senator Howard Baker, May 23, 1976.
52. Ibid.
53. *Denver Post*, May 2, 1976.
54. Ibid.

CHAPTER FOUR

Plots to Kill Castro

"We have found concrete evidence of at least eight plots involving the CIA to assassinate Fidel Castro," concluded the Senate Intelligence Committee in late November, 1975.[1] The Senate Committee's Report on Foreign Assassination Plots went on to state:

> Although some of the assassination plots did not advance beyond the stage of planning and preparation, one plot, involving the use of underworld figures, reportedly twice progressed to the point of sending poison pills to Cuba and dispatching teams to commit the deed.[2]

Yet after conducting an eight-month investigation of these secret CIA-Mafia efforts to assassinate Fidel Castro (an investigation triggered by a *New York*

Times disclosure by Seymour Hersh on March 10, 1975) the Senate Intelligence Committee would finally conclude, "The origin of the plot is uncertain."[3] As the Senate Committee laboriously pieced together the remaining records available on the CIA-Mafia assassination-conspiring, and as they took extensive testimony from those past participants who were still living, the early history of the plot began to emerge. Some time during the fall of 1960, the Deputy Director for Plans of the CIA, Richard Bissell, ordered the CIA's Director of the Office of Security, Sheffield Edwards, to devise a plan to murder Fidel Castro.[4] Sheffield Edwards then assigned a deputy of his, the Chief of the Operational Support Division of the Office of Security, to assist him in planning the assassination conspiracy; this deputy has never been named publicly.[5]

At that early point in the assassination planning, according to the Senate Intelligence Committee findings, the testimony of those involved already began to conflict in a serious way. All of those involved agree that Edwards and his Deputy (the CIA Support Chief) recruited Robert Maheu, a former FBI agent and top consultant to mystery billionaire Howard Hughes, to coordinate the actual logistics of the assassination plot.[6] And all of those involved also agree that the next man brought into the assassination conspiracy was Mafia leader John Roselli, the former Al Capone gang member, then in Las Vegas. However, the testimony differs at that point as to who first wanted Roselli to join the plot. Robert Maheu has testified that the CIA Support Chief asked him to recruit Roselli for the plot.[7] But the CIA Support Chief insisted in his testimony that it was Howard Hughes' aide Maheu who suggested involving Roselli.[8] Maheu further testified that he was not even aware that Roselli was a powerful syndicate figure, but merely knew him as a man "who could get things done."[9]

It is at this same early planning stage of the CIA-Mafia assassination plotting that the testimony of those involved once again diverges. CIA official Edwards, his deputy the Support Chief, and Robert Maheu all claim that when Maheu first recruited John Roselli, he told the Mafia leader that he was acting as "the representative of businessmen with interests in Cuba," rather than as an operative of the CIA.[10] However, Roselli testified that he was made fully aware of the fact that Maheu was acting on behalf of the CIA.[11]

In any event, according to the Senate Report, Roselli, Maheu, and the CIA Support Chief subsequently met at the Plaza Hotel in New York on September 14, 1960 to begin setting up the assassination squad.[12] Within ten days, the three men had conducted a second planning session, this time in Miami.[13] While there, according to the Senate findings, "Roselli introduced Maheu to two individuals on whom he intended to rely — Chicago Mafia leader Sam Giancana, and Florida Mafia leader Santos Trafficante."[14] According to the Senate Report on the plots, "Maheu recalled that it was Giancana's job to locate someone in Castro's entourage who could accomplish the assassination," and that Giancana and Maheu began meeting "almost daily" over "a substantial period of time" to plan the assassination.[14a]

One of the more ominous early occurrences relating to this CIA-Mafia conspiring is provided by the Senate Intelligence Committee's effort to establish who in the CIA actually "authorized" the plotting. The Senate Committee disclosed that both CIA Deputy Director for Plans Richard Bissell and CIA Office of Security Director Sheffield Edwards had testified that they had received direct authorization for the assassination planning from CIA Director Allen Dulles (who would later serve as a member of the Warren Commission) and his Deputy Director,

General Charles Cabell.[15] Bissell and Edwards claimed that Dulles had given his approval for the plot "in the latter part of September" of 1960.[16] However, as the Senate Committee concluded, the assassination conspiracy had by that time already been set in motion — without any authorization from the Director. The Senate Committee's Final Report noted:

> It is clear, then, that even if Dulles was informed about the use of underworld figures to assassinate Castro, subordinate Agency officials had previously decided to take steps toward arranging for the killing of Castro, including discussing it with organized crime leaders.[17]

Just short of sixteen years after that assassination conspiracy of the Mafia and CIA came into being, the *Washington Post* disclosed some information — indeed, some incredible information — which the Senate Intelligence Committee had come across months earlier: the fact that one of the key Mafia leaders involved, John Roselli himself, had notified the federal government that some of the other Mafia figures involved (specifically Santos Trafficante) had later gone on to plan and carry out the assassination of President John F. Kennedy, on November 22, 1963.[18] Roselli had further told the government that Fidel Castro may have been involved with these Mafia men in planning the assassination.[19]

As will be seen in forthcoming pages, John Roselli had first notified the government of his belief that his fellow Mafia assassination planners had murdered President Kennedy (and then had Jack Ruby murder Lee Harvey Oswald) in early 1967.[20] More incredibly, as will also be seen, Roselli himself was found murdered on August 7, 1976, only a few weeks after he had provided new details about his allegations to investigators of the Senate Intelligence Committee.

And, perhaps fittingly, it was with the discovery of former CIA-Mafia assassination coordinator John Roselli's decomposed body in a 55-gallon oil drum floating off the coast of Miami that touched off perhaps the most serious renewed interest in the Kennedy assassination in over twelve years. Within three weeks the *Washington Post* would reveal Roselli's past allegations about the murder of President Kennedy, and the whole issue would become the focus of efforts which would soon thereafter result in a long-awaited vote by the U.S. Congress to reopen the entire Kennedy assassination case.

With the mysterious death of John Roselli (who was murdered through an apparent combination of being stabbed, strangled, and dismembered), the Kennedy assassination question became more pressing perhaps than ever before. In an unprecedented editorial on August 12, 1976, the *Washington Post* pointed out the deadly mysteries surrounding the Mafia-CIA relationship or alliance, and went on to ask:

> Is it really, as the sophisticated wisdom goes, "paranoid" on our part to brood about the suggestive and possibly monstrous interconnections between all these facts and to wonder why they are not the subject of intense press and government scrutiny. What accounts for the general indifference in high places? [21]

With the murder of Senate witness John Roselli in the late summer of 1976, and increasing speculation over the equally brutal murder of his CIA-Mafia assassination-planning colleague, Sam Giancana, days before he was to appear before the same Senate group in June, 1975, the CIA-Mafia relationship and its offshoots once again became the central area of interest for most assassination investigators. A review of that mysterious relationship provides the backdrop against which today's various "conspiracy scenarios" now seem to emerge.

The Senate Intelligence Committee's Final Report on the CIA-Mafia conspiracies against Fidel Castro disclosed that the CIA Support Chief involved in the assassination plot had stated that the Agency had first considered "a gangland-style killing" in which Castro would be shot to death.[22] However, the Senate Report stated, "Giancana reportedly opposed the idea."[23] Instead, the Senate investigators discovered, the Chicago Mafia leader said that he had a better idea. The Senate Report noted: "There is some evidence that Giancana or Roselli originated the idea of depositing a poison pill in Castro's drink to give the [assassin] a chance to escape."[24]

In any event, by early 1961 the CIA Technical Services Division had devised a deadly poison which could be administered in capsules, which would cause death in about two days (thus leaving plenty of time for an assassin to escape) and would, of course, be untraceable. As the Senate Committee noted, the first attempt to assassinate Castro through the use of this poison was timed to coincide with the Bay of Pigs invasion:

> The record clearly establishes that the pills were given to a Cuban for delivery to the Island some time prior to the Bay of Pigs invasion in mid-April 1961. There are discrepancies in the record, however, concerning whether one or two attempts were made during that period, and the precise date on which the passage[s] occurred.[25]

The CIA apparently believed that the assassination of Castro would virtually insure the success of the planned invasion of the Island by the Agency's Cuban exile forces. In 1973, the actual coordinator of the CIA Bay of Pigs invasion, E. Howard Hunt, disclosed that he had personally recommended an assassination attempt as part of the invasion plan.[26] The future Watergate conspirator had served as the CIA's Chief of Political Action for the invasion, and has stated that he submitted a memorandum (to CIA official Richard Bissell and his Deputy, Tracy Barnes) in which he recommended: "1. Assassinate Castro before or coincident with the invasion (a task for Cuban patriots.)"[27] Hunt has stated further that CIA official Tracy Barnes subsequently informed him that his assassination proposal had been placed "in the hands of a special group."[28] As will be seen in a forthcoming section (see reference to Manuel Artime on p. 513) E. Howard Hunt's closest Bay of Pigs associate and long-time friend, Manuel Artime, using a CIA code name "B-1" was involved in a 1965 CIA assassination plot against Castro.[29]

For reasons which the Senate Intelligence Committee could not fully determine during their investigation in 1975, the CIA-Mafia poisoning plot against Castro (at the time of the Bay of Pigs) did not reach fruition. However, the Senate Committee did establish that the CIA-Mafia conspirators did pass the poison pills to a Cuban operative close to Fidel Castro. The Committee concluded that the CIA poison (described by Maheu as "five or six gelatin capsules filled with a liquid") was passed from the CIA to Maheu and from Maheu to Roselli, and from Roselli to a Cuban-exile leader, in March or April, 1961.[30]

Mafia leader John Roselli testified that the capsules were passed to him in Miami at a meeting during which:

> . . . [Maheu] opened his briefcase and dumped a whole lot of money on his lap . . . and also came up with the capsules and he explained how they were going to be used. As far as I can remember, they couldn't be used in boiling soups and things like that, but they could be used in water

or otherwise, but they couldn't last forever.[31]

The Senate Committee established that the Cuban who was assigned to accomplish the placing of the poison in Castro's food or drink was "a leading figure in the Cuban exile movement," who had been brought into the CIA-Mafia assassination plot by Santos Trafficante, the Florida organized crime leader.[32] As will be seen, Trafficante has long served as the closest associate of Meyer Lansky, who is regarded by most organized crime authorities as perhaps the most powerful Syndicate leader in the nation. The Senate Report noted that the CIA itself had concluded that the Cuban-exile leader involved in the plot was probably "receiving funds" from Trafficante and other racketeers who were interested in obtaining "gambling, prostitution, and dope monopolies" in Cuba after Castro would be assassinated.[33]

The Discovery of the Assassination Conspiracies

One of the key aspects of the CIA-Mafia assassination conspiracies that was pursued by the Senate Intelligence Committee relates to the question of who had knowledge of them, and when. The Senate Committee concluded that the overwhelming bulk of the evidence and testimony obtained during the Committee's investigation indicated that the CIA-Mafia plots were concealed from CIA Director John McCone as well as from President Kennedy himself. As will be seen, the Senate Committee concluded (as did the CIA itself during an internal investigation in early 1967) that the CIA officials who coordinated the secret assassination conspiracies had concealed the existence of the CIA-Mafia plots from President

Kennedy and his brother, Attorney General Robert F. Kennedy, until May of 1962. And more ominously, according to both the CIA and the Senate Committee, when these same CIA officials informed Attorney General Robert F. Kennedy of the plots on May 7 1962, they told him their contact with the Mafia had been ended — when in fact it was actually being increased and reactivated.

The Senate Committee noted that the cast of characters in the secret CIA plot had changed somewhat in 1961 and 1962. John McCone replaced Allen Dulles as Director of the CIA in November, 1961.[34] It was also in November of 1961 that CIA official Richard Bissell assigned a new CIA man, William Harvey, to coordinate the assassination plots with the Mafia.[35] Then in February, 1962, Richard Bissell had been replaced (as CIA Deputy Director for Plans) by Richard Helms. According to the Senate Committee, Helms thereafter assumed control over the secret assassination-conspiring with the Mafia.[36]

Acting under the authorization of Richard Helms, CIA official William Harvey again contacted Mafia leader John Roselli in April, 1962, to begin planning another assassination effort against Castro. According to the Senate Report and the CIA's own 1967 report on the plots, Helms and Harvey at this point decided to exclude Howard Hughes' aide Robert Maheu and Chicago Mafia leader Sam Giancana from any future participation in the assassination plots.[37] Instead, they chose to rely on Mafia leaders John Roselli and Santos Trafficante to continue the plots. According to the Senate Intelligence Report:

> Harvey told Roselli to maintain his Cuban contacts, but not to deal with Maheu or Giancana, whom he had decided were "untrustworthy" and "surplus."[38]

The Senate Committee established that Harvey, Roselli, and the CIA Support Chief then met in New

York on April 8, 1962, to set up the next assassination plan.[39] The Committee reported that, "A notation made during that time in the files of the [CIA] Technical Services Division indicates that four poison pills were given to the Support Chief on April 18, 1962."[40] On April 21, 1962 these newest poison capsules were then passed by CIA official Harvey to Mafia leader Roselli, who testified that Harvey told him these capsules "would work anywhere and at any time with anything."[41]

It was during this same period, in early 1962, that CIA officials Richard Helms and William Harvey decided — according to their own testimony — to conceal any knowledge of this renewed CIA-Mafia assassination plotting from CIA Director John McCone. In his Senate Committee testimony of June 13, 1975, Richard Helms stated:

> . . . I was enormously busy with a lot of other things.
>
> . . . I guess I must have thought to myself, well this is going to look peculiar to him and I doubt very much this is going to go any place, but if it does, then that is time enough to bring him in the picture.[42]

Helms went on to state, "It was a Mafia connection and Mr. McCone was new to the organization and this was, you know, not a very savory effort."[43] CIA official William Harvey, however, provided considerably more detailed reasons for not informing CIA Director McCone of the continuing CIA-Mafia conspiracies being run by Helms and himself. In his 1975 Senate testimony, Harvey, who died in 1976 from a reported heart attack, provided one of the most startling new pieces of information to emerge from the Senate investigation.

Harvey testified that he and Helms did not tell Director McCone of the plot because they had not had time to "assess the individuals involved and determine actually the problem we faced . . . of this government being blackmailed [by those involved]. . ."[44] Harvey disclosed a whole new area of information which Helms had somehow failed to mention during his own Senate testimony. Harvey testified:

> There was a fairly detailed discussion between myself and Helms as to whether or not the Director should at that time be briefed concerning this. For a variety of reasons which were tossed back and forth, we agreed it was not necessary or advisable to brief him at that time.
>
> . . . we faced . . . the possible problem — and it was a very, or it appeared to be, and in my opinion, was, at that time, a very real possibility of this government being blackmailed either by Cubans for political purposes or by figures in organized crime for their own self protection or aggrandizement, which as it turned out, did not happen, but at that time was a very pregnant possibility.[45]

According to the Senate Intelligence Committee, the testimony of the various CIA officials involved, and the documentary records of both the CIA and FBI, Attorney General Robert F. Kennedy was told about the CIA-Mafia assassination conspiracies during a meeting with CIA officials on May 7, 1962.[46] This meeting had been requested by Robert Kennedy after he learned that the CIA was asking the FBI to block the prosecution of a case involving Robert Maheu, which had involved an illegal wiretap.[47] During his work as the key CIA-Mafia assassination coordinator, Maheu had (as a favor to Sam Giancana) hired another detective to wiretap the Chicago Mafia leader's girlfriend, whom Giancana apparently suspected of disloyalty.[48] The detective had been arrested, and Maheu had also subsequently been charged.[49] In early April, 1962, the CIA officials involved in the secret assassination plots requested the FBI to block Maheu's wiretap prosecution on the following grounds:

> . . . Prosecution of Maheu undoubtedly would lead to exposure of most sensitive information relating to the abortive Cuban invasion in April 1961 and would result in most damaging embarrassment to the U.S. government.[50]

In an effort to determine what that "most sensitive information" about the "Cuban invasion" was, Attorney General Robert Kennedy ordered CIA official Richard Helms to give him a briefing on it in early May, 1962. The briefing of the Attorney General was conducted on May 7 by CIA officials Sheffield Edwards (an original architect of the CIA-Mafia plots) and Lawrence Houston, the Agency's General Counsel.[51] And, according to all available evidence, it was at that meeting that CIA officials extended their cover-up of the continuing assassination conspiracies to the Attorney General, as they had earlier done to CIA Director McCone himself. Despite the fact that a new batch of poisoned pills had been delivered from William Harvey to John Roselli and a Cuban exile leader less than three weeks earlier, and despite the fact that the CIA men were then also providing rifles and other equipment for use in trying to assassinate Castro through the use of gunmen, CIA officials Edwards and Houston told Robert Kennedy that the CIA-Mafia plots had been ended.[52] Houston has testified that he mistakenly told Kennedy that it was his "understanding that the assassination plan aimed at Castro had been terminated completely."[53] Edwards likewise told the Attorney General that the assassination conspiracies had ended a year earlier, in May, 1961.[54]

Thus, as the internal CIA Inspector General's Report concluded in 1967 (in a key passage which the Senate Intelligence Committee affirmed in 1975), the CIA officials involved (specifically Sheffield Edwards) deliberately misled Robert Kennedy:

> The Attorney General was not told that the gambling syndicate [assassination]operation had already been reactivated, nor, as far as we know, was he ever told that CIA had a continuing involvement with U.S. gangster elements.[55]

Even upon being misled into thinking that the CIA-Mafia assassination plot had been "terminated completely" a good deal earlier, Attorney General Kennedy was greatly disturbed by the matter, according to CIA General Counsel Houston. Houston told the Senate Committee, "If you have seen Mr. Kennedy's eyes get steely and his jaw set and his voice get low and precise, you get a definite feeling of unhappiness."[56] Houston further stated that Robert Kennedy had also angrily remarked: "I trust that if you ever try to do business with organized crime again — with gangsters — you will let the Attorney General know."[57] Edwards, in his Senate testimony, confirmed Houston's account, saying that Kennedy had concluded the meeting by stating, "I want you to let me know about these things."[58]

Both the Senate Intelligence Committee and the CIA (in their highly secret Inspector General's Report prepared in 1967 at the order of President Johnson) established that CIA official Sheffield Edwards had then carried this cover-up of the continuing CIA-Mafia plots even further. The Senate Committee and the CIA established that Edwards had prepared a fraudulent internal memorandum for the files, a week later, which also deceptively stated that the CIA had terminated the conspiracies.[59] In his Senate testimony, William Harvey admitted that the internal CIA memorandum (of May 14, 1962) "was not true, and Colonel Edwards knew it was not true."[60]

The Senate Intelligence Committee unsuccessfully

sought to re-interview Edwards regarding the false memo but was prohibited from doing so by his physician who stated he had a long-term illness. Edwards however died several months later in 1975.

Finally, according to the Senate Intelligence Committee Report, when Richard Helms was "questioned about the fact that the Attorney General had been told that the operation had been terminated when in fact it was continuing," Helms testified:

> I am not able to tell you whether this operation was ongoing, whether it really had been stopped, whether it had been fairly stopped, whether there was fun and games going on between the officers involved as to, we will create a fiction that it stopped or go ahead with it. I just don't recall any of those things at all. . .[61]

The "fun and games going on between the officers involved" in the secret assassination plots were in fact increasing in both pace and seriousness at that point. While the Senate Intelligence Committee's evidence clearly indicates that Attorney General Robert Kennedy and his brother, the President, finally learned of the CIA-Mafia assassination apparatus about fifteen months after they took office, the same evidence establishes that the assassination conspiracies continued for at least nine months after the Attorney General was told they were "completely terminated," in early May of 1962.[62]

By then, the level of sophistication of the murder plots was growing considerably, with rifles, two-way radios, and explosives being furnished by the CIA officials involved to John Roselli, who in turn was passing the equipment on to the Cuban exiles involved. At one point CIA agent William Harvey and an Agency colleague coordinated the transfer of rifles, handguns, and other equipment to the Cuban exile leader involved, through the use of a rented U-Haul truck in Miami.[64] According to the Senate Intelligence Committee, John Roselli and the CIA Support Chief watched the transfer from the sidelines, across the street.[65] According to the Senate Report, Roselli informed Harvey that the latest batch of poison pills (and guns) "had arrived in Cuba" some time in May.[66] This latest delivery apparently was carried out at virtually the same time Robert Kennedy was misled to believe the plots had been terminated. While it would be interesting to determine exactly when in May, 1962 this delivery was made (in relation to the meeting on May 7th, when RFK was told that the plots had been ended) such a determination cannot be made. At the time of his Senate testimony, on June 24, 1975, Roselli was not asked for the specific date of this delivery.

In any event, the CIA-Mafia assassination plots were then also widening to involve additional militant Cuban exiles during this same period. Again, Florida Mafia leader Santos Trafficante was the man in charge of lining up exile talent. Several weeks after the CIA's briefing of Attorney General Kennedy, according to the Senate findings, Roselli reported new information on the plots to his fellow conspirators at the CIA. On June 21, Roselli told William Harvey that the Cuban exile leader whom they had recruited "had dispatched a three-man team to Cuba."[67] The Senate Committee noted:

> The [CIA] Inspector General's report described the team's mission as "vague" and conjectured that the team would kill Castro or recruit others to do the job, using the poison pills if the opportunity arose.[68]

A little over six weeks later, according to the Senate Committee investigation, CIA conspirator William Harvey was once again made explicitly aware of the strong opposition of CIA Director John McCone to any assassination plotting by the Agency. And, once again, Harvey ignored or "countermanded" his employer's — the Director of the CIA — orders. According to the Senate Report, on August 11, 1962, Director McCone personally informed Harvey that committing assassination was something in which the CIA should not and could not become involved.[69] McCone voiced his opposition to assassination following a brief discussion of it which he learned had occurred during a high level meeting on Cuba, on August 10, 1962.[70] On the following day, McCone strongly stated his belief that "the subject [of assassination] . . . is highly improper. I do not think it should be discussed. It is not an action that should ever be condoned."[71] Also on August 11th, McCone specifically made these views known to William Harvey. In his own Senate testimony, Harvey admitted that McCone had told him that day "if I got myself involved in something like this, I might end up getting myself excommunicated."[72]

Less than four weeks later, however, CIA official Harvey was once again secretly meeting with Mafia leader John Roselli in Miami. Harvey and Roselli conferred about the sending of another Cuban exile team of assassins to Cuba, as well as the status of the CIA poison already on the Island. According to the Senate Report (as well as the CIA's own findings and Harvey's own Senate testimony) these latest CIA-Mafia assassination meetings were conducted toward the middle of September:

> Harvey met Roselli in Miami on September 7 and 11, 1962. The Cuban was reported to be preparing to send in another three-man team to penetrate Castro's body guard. Harvey was told that the pills, referred to as "the medicine," were still "safe" in Cuba.[73]

The exact date when the secret CIA-Mafia assassination conspiracies finally ended remains the subject of considerable speculation. While mid-February of 1963 was set forth by the Senate Intelligence Committee as the likely point at which the conspiracies were terminated, several Senators from the Committee (and a larger number of staff members) are known to feel that the point of termination remains clouded. In setting forth 110 pages in their final Report on these Cuban assassination plots, the Senate Committee devoted only one paragraph to covering the reported termination of the conspiracies.[74] The Committee stated that CIA official "Harvey terminated the operation in mid-February 1963 at a meeting with Roselli in Los Angeles, it was agreed that Roselli would taper off his communications with the Cubans."[75]

Columnist Jack Anderson, who disclosed the first (though at that point officially unconfirmed) details about the CIA-Mafia conspiracies in January 1971, has maintained that the murder plots continued until March of 1963.[76] And, as Anderson has acknowledged, John Roselli had served as a primary source for his columns on the murder plots.

Additionally, as the Senate Intelligence Committee has pointed out, William Harvey and John Roselli are now known to have met with each other as late as June of 1963.[77] According to the CIA, Harvey later stated that the occasion for their meeting then was only for the purpose of having dinner, and that the assassination conspiring had ended over three months earlier.[78]

1. *Senate Intelligence Committee Report on Foreign Assassinations*, p. 27.
2. Ibid.
3. Ibid., p. 74.
4. Ibid.
5. Ibid.
6. Ibid.
7. Ibid., p. 75.
8. Ibid.
9. Ibid.
10. Ibid.
11. Ibid.
12. Ibid., p. 76.
13. Ibid.
14. Ibid., p. 77.
14a. Ibid.
15. Ibid., pp. 94-96.
16. Ibid.
17. Ibid., p. 97.
18. *Senate Intelligence Committee Report on the Kennedy Assassination*, pp. 80-86; *Washington Post*, August 22, 1976; Jack Anderson column, September 7, 1976.
19. Ibid.
20. Ibid.
21. *Washington Post*, August 12, 1976.
22. *Senate Intelligence Committee Report on Foreign Assassinations*, p. 80.
23. Ibid.
24. Ibid.
25. Ibid.
26. E. Howard Hunt, *Give Us This Day* (New York: Popular Library edition, 1973), p. 38.
27. Ibid., pp. 23, 38.
28. Ibid., p. 38.
29. *Senate Intelligence Committee Report on Foreign Assassinations*, pp. 89-90.
30. Ibid., pp. 81-82.
31. Ibid.
32. Ibid.
33. Ibid.
34. Ibid., p. 102.
35. Ibid.
36. Ibid.
37. Ibid., p. 83.
38. Ibid.
39. Ibid., p. 84.
40. Ibid.

41. Ibid.
42. Ibid., p. 103.
43. Ibid.
44. Ibid., p. 102.
45. Ibid.
46. Ibid., pp. 131-132.
47. Ibid.
48. Ibid., pp. 77-79.
49. Ibid.
50. Ibid., pp. 131-132.
51. Ibid.
52. Ibid., pp. 84, 132.
53. Ibid., p. 132.
54. Ibid.
55. Ibid., p. 133.
56. Ibid.
57. Ibid.
58. Ibid.
59. Ibid., pp. 132-134.
60. Ibid., p. 134.
61. Ibid.
62. Ibid., pp. 84, 132-135.
63. Ibid., pp. 83-84.
64. Ibid.
65. Ibid.
66. Ibid.
67. Ibid.
68. Ibid.
69. Ibid., p. 105.
70. Ibid.
71. Ibid., p. 166.
72. Ibid., p. 105.
73. Ibid., p. 84.
74. Ibid.
75. Ibid.
76. Jack Anderson columns, January 18, 1971, September 7, 1976.
77. *Senate Intelligence Committee Report on Foreign Assassinations*, p. 104.
78. Ibid.

CHAPTER FIVE

The Intelligence Community

With the Senate Intelligence Committee's documentation in 1975 of the CIA-Mafia assassination conspiracies against Castro, and the mounting speculation by several sources that those plots may have in some way been responsible for the subsequent murder of President Kennedy, more and more attention is being focused on the darker aspects of CIA activities.

As will be seen, in the early 1960s various CIA officials voiced recurring worry and suspicion over the fact that various "underworld" assassins and "black operatives" used by the Agency were sometimes defiantly independent, or indeed "out of control."[1] As noted earlier, William Harvey, a CIA coordinator of the CIA-Mafia conspiracies, later testified that he had been deeply concerned over the "possibility of this government being blackmailed" by either the Mafia leaders or Cuban exiles involved in the secret plots.[2]

As will be seen, the Senate Intelligence Committee (as well as the Rockefeller Commission) had an exceedingly difficult time even in establishing the basic outlines of some of the activities of the assassination operatives employed by the CIA.

One of the more telling — and more ominous — examples of this quagmire was provided by information supplied by a man quite familiar with CIA assassination attempts: Fidel Castro. In July, 1975, the Cuban Premier assembled an extensive compilation of information pertaining to what he claimed were at least twenty-four CIA assassination plots against him.[3] Included in Castro's report were such items as the identification of several Cuban exiles captured during the alleged attempts; affidavits executed by them; and detailed information about the sophisticated rifles and other weapons taken during the alleged captures. According to Castro, these plots occurred during the same period as the CIA-Mafia assassination plots which were later documented by the Senate Committee.

This lengthy report was forwarded to the Senate Intelligence Committee by Senator George McGovern after returning from a trip to Cuba to confer with Castro.[4] In early August, the Senate Committee turned over a copy to the CIA for its evaluation of the twenty-four alleged assassination attempts,[5] which Castro claimed had reached their peak in the early 1960s, but had continued as late as 1971.[6]

In any event, the CIA's eventual reply, supplied to the Senate Committee in late fall, 1975, was, in the words of a senior Committee staff member, "an exercise in semantics worthy of S. I. Hayakawa." Another former Senate Intelligence staffer has called the fourteen-page CIA response "a classic . . . the best illustration of their [the CIA's] ignorance of what their worst operatives were doing." The Senate Committee, in their final report on CIA-sponsored foreign assassination attempts, published the CIA's official summation which was prepared in response to the Castro report:

> In summary of the . . . incidents described in Castro's Report, the files reviewed indicated that CIA had no involvement in 15 of the cases: i.e., never had any contact with the individuals mentioned or was not in contact with them at the time of the alleged incidents. In the remaining nine cases, CIA had operational relationships with some of the individuals mentioned but not for the purpose of assassination.[7]

It is obvious that the Agency's response indicated that it indeed had had a relationship with some of the Cuban exiles that Castro claimed were trying to murder him in an unstated number of the first fifteen cases cited; and further, that in the remaining nine cases, the Agency had actually employed some of the operatives whom Castro captured, but not — according to the CIA — for the assassination attempts in which Castro says they were apprehended. Indeed, the Agency has had a hard time keeping track of the violent Cuban exile operatives it employed.

With the disclosures, in 1975-76, of the CIA's working relationship with the Mafia during the early 1960s, new attention has been focused on other areas of their past involvements.

The Mafia-CIA relationship seems to date back as far as World War II, when the CIA's predecessor, the OSS (Office of Strategic Services), and the Office of Naval Intelligence secretly recruited top Mafia leaders Lucky Luciano, Frank Costello, and Meyer Lansky to aid the Allied cause. In what is regarded as the definitive history of the OSS, R. Harris Smith provides the following account of what has come to be known as "Operation Underworld" in intelligence circles:

> . . . OSS responsibilities for Italian espionage were preempted by the Office of Naval Intelligence through an arrangement with

the American Mafia. The criminal syndicate agreed to direct clandestine operations on the Island of Sicily in return for the parole of Mafia chief "Lucky" Luciano. [The "deal" was arranged by Assistant New York District Attorney Murray Gurfein, who became an OSS colonel in Europe later in the war.][8]

In June, 1976, a large body of new information about the wartime activities of the OSS became available. Many years after it was first prepared, the Official War Report of the Office of Strategic Services was finally declassified and released. Historian Anthony Cave Brown, who edited it for publication, has written:

> The Sicilian OSS project was initiated by Earl Brennan, a former State Department consular official, Republican member of the New Hampshire legislature, and in 1943 Chief of Secret Intelligence/Washington. While on U.S. diplomatic business in Canada, he had encountered the chiefs of the Italian Mafia, who had been banished from Italy by Mussolini.[9]

The noted historian also detailed the increasing concern, later expressed by OSS officials in Washington, over OSS involvement with organized crime figures:

> There was also some concern that OSS was recruiting Mafiosi and, on a smaller scale, hit men from the ranks of Murder, Inc., and the Philadelphia "Purple Gang." Some [Operational Group] leaders engaged in black marketing on a large scale and as one OSS training officer for OGs [Operational Groups] would recall, the OGs consisted of

"tough little boys from New York and Chicago, with a few live hoods mixed in . . ." By 1945, these groups were considered to be so dangerous that OGs returning from operations were, on the orders of the Allied High Command, confined to a castle near Spczia until they were either returned home or were sent back into the field.[10]

During the Sicilian campaign, OSS operatives formed a close working relationship with factions of the powerful Mafia on that island, a relationship which the *Official War Report of the OSS* indicates created internal controversy within the Service:

> The [Secret Intelligence/Italy staff] took strenuous exception to [Counterintelligence] criticism of the close relations built up by Secret Intelligence during and after the Sicilian campaign with such native groups as the renegade Mafia.[11]

In addition to using Lucky Luciano, the American Mafia leader as the "liaison" to the Mafia in Sicily and Italy, the Office of Naval Intelligence had also employed Luciano and his deputy, Meyer Lansky, for domestic service. The Mafia leaders were asked to set up a network of underworld contacts to act as informers against potential German sabotage on the East Coast, particularly on the New York docks.[12] A key associate of Lansky and Luciano, Joseph "Socks" Lanza, was the key contact for setting up the "Operation Underworld" effort, and in dealing with the federal authorities.[13] Frank Costello, another of their top Mafia associates, was also involved in the operation. Of Lanza's dealings with Naval Intelligence, Luciano was later quoted as having said, "Socks was rehearsed by Costello and Lansky right to the last syllable."[14]

On the day the war in Europe ended, May 8, 1945, Luciano's attorneys submitted a petition for executive clemency to Governor Thomas E. Dewey of New York, who'd been aware of the Mafia-OSS involvement in "Operation Underworld."[15] Several months later, on January 3, 1946, the most notorious Mafia leader in the nation received his clemency and was soon deported.[16] Dewey noted, "Luciano's aid was sought by the Armed Services in inducing others to provide information concerning possible enemy attacks. It appears that he cooperated in such efforts, though the actual value of the information provided is not clear."[17] The Kefauver Senate Committee later discovered that most of the official federal files on the underworld operation were missing, but concluded that Dewey's pardon of Luciano had been issued "at the urgent request of Naval Intelligence." Murray Gurfein, the Assistant District Attorney in New York who played a central role in the Mafia involvement, was subsequently appointed to a federal judgeship by President Nixon in 1971.

The CIA and Mafia were involved with each other in a number of other projects. Author Alfred W. McCoy has provided a detailed account of how the CIA recruited various Mafia figures to "put down" a series of leftist labor strikes in Marseilles during the years 1947 to 1950.[18] These strikes had seriously impeded the flow of American war materials through Marseilles for the French forces then fighting in Vietnam.

During the early 1970s, McCoy, as well as columnist Jack Anderson and the *New York Times*, disclosed hard information, regarding CIA involvement in the heroin trade in South Vietnam, Thailand, Cambodia, and Laos through the Agency's Asian mercenary operatives. Former South Vietnamese Premier Ky was reported to be involved with both CIA elements and Corsican Mafia operatives in the drug trade. On August 30, 1971, the *New York Times* reported that the Director of Customs in South Vietnam had stated that he "believed that planes of the South Vietnamese Air Force were the principal carriers" of heroin into the South Vietnam region.[19] In July, 1971, the NBC Nightly News reported that "extremely reliable sources" had disclosed that South Vietnamese President Thieu and Vice President Ky were financing their respective political campaigns through involvement in the Asian narcotics trade.[20] Santos Trafficante, one of the CIA-Mafia assassination coordinators, is frequently reported to be a central figure in the Southeast Asian heroin trade.

In an interview with George Crile in the summer of 1976, Lucien Conein, who had headed CIA operations in Vietnam during the early 1960s, freely spoke of his close relationship with the deadly Corsican Mafia during his service there.[21] As recently as October, 1976, *Time* magazine reported that past CIA involvement with another key Asian heroin producer, Burmese General Tuan Hsi-wen, seemed likely.[22]

As the CIA-Mafia assassination conspiracies against Fidel Castro first became the subject of investigation by the Senate in early 1975, still other information on that strange liaison surfaced. In February, Hugh Sidey, of *Time* magazine, reported that President Lyndon Johnson privately "called the CIA 'Murder Incorporated' because he believed that the CIA had gone ahead and killed South Vietnam President Ngo Dinh Diem against Kennedy's wishes. He had a further notion that the CIA was somehow linked with the Mafia."[23] A month earlier, *Time* also reported:

> . . . FBI agents once discovered that a Manhattan-based CIA man was in close touch with a Pittsburgh Mafia Chief [John LaRocca] who was being probed by the FBI. The FBI protested so vehemently that the CIA operative was sent to Italy until FBI tempers cooled.[24]

In June, 1975, *Time* disclosed that New York Mafia figures James Plumeri and Salvatore "Sally Burns" Granello had been recruited by the CIA in 1960 or 1961 to aid in the logistical planning of the Bay of Pigs invasion.[25] The two Mafia leaders had been confident of re-establishing their casino operations in Havana, if the Cuban invasion succeeded. Some time after their involvement with the CIA, both Plumeri and Granello were victims of presumed gangland executions.[26] Granello, a member of the Mafia family headed by the late Vito Genovese, was found stuffed in the trunk of a rented car in Manhattan on October 6, 1970. The former CIA collaborator had been shot in the head four times, in a murder which police attributed to an internal Mafia dispute.

Retired Air Force Colonel L. Fletcher Prouty, formerly a top liaison officer to the CIA, has perhaps provided one of the clearer explanations of the mysterious CIA-Mafia links:

> To understand how it works, you have to think of CIA and organized crime as two huge concentric circles spread all over the world. Inevitably, in some places, the circles overlap.[27]

As will be seen, apart from the strange entanglements of the CIA and the Mafia, there are numerous other intelligence strands that run through various areas of evidence relating to the assassination of President Kennedy. Complicated, sensitive, and in frequent cases overlapping, these intelligence connections are of course prime areas for further investigation as the Kennedy case reopens.

Raymond Rocca

Raymond Rocca, a key CIA official for many years, served as the CIA "case officer" or man in charge of handling all inquiries and issues relating to President Kennedy's assassination. Rocca acted in this capacity until late December, 1974, when he was forced into retirement (along with CIA Counterintelligence Chief James Angleton) for reported involvement in the CIA's illegal domestic spying program, first revealed by Seymour Hersh in *The New York Times* on December 22, 1974.[28]

Rocca had been a key deputy to Angleton and had worked with then Deputy Director for Plans, Richard Helms, as CIA liaison to the Warren Commission. Many serious questions have been raised as to the extent of CIA "cooperation" given to the Commission. The extent of Rocca's involvement in handling the CIA's files on the Kennedy assassination (and all inquiries related to it) was underscored in the spring of 1976 when the CIA released 1,500 pages of previously classified documents on the assassination, in response to pending Freedom of Information suits by Warren Commission critics Harold Weisberg, Bernard Fensterwald, Jr. and others.

Among the documents was a heavily-censored twenty-seven-page memorandum that Raymond Rocca had prepared for the Rockefeller Commission in late 1974 or early 1975, which had been forwarded to David Belin at the Commission on May 30, 1975. 30, 1975.

In the memo, over eight pages of which have been withheld, Rocca outlined various allegations and testimony regarding Lee Harvey Oswald's possible involvement with Cuban conspirators, particularly pro-Castro Cubans.[29] While the CIA did not officially endorse the findings of the Rocca memo, the memorandum obviously met with the general approval of the Agency prior to its transmission to the Rockefeller Commission. On the letter of transmission from the Agency to David Belin, the CIA noted that "the attached review represents the research and analysis of an individual officer. It has not been fully researched and verified and does not necessarily represent the position of this Agency."[30]

James Angleton

James J. Angleton, the CIA's mysterious (and sometimes eccentric) Chief of Counterintelligence, handled matters relating to the Kennedy assassination for over ten years. And, like his Deputy, Raymond Rocca, James Angleton was forced into retirement in late 1974 as a result of his involvement in the CIA's illegal "Operation Chaos," a secret domestic spying program that had been greatly enlarged under the Nixon Administration.

Angleton had handled several controversial CIA matters relating to the assassination, such as the mysterious series of CIA photographs taken in Mexico City in September and October, 1963, in which a man identified by the CIA as Lee Harvey Oswald turned out not to be Oswald at all.[31] (See further reference to these mysterious CIA photographs in the chapter on "The Second Oswald.")

The extent of James Angleton's involvement in the CIA's end of the assassination investigation first became underscored in 1974, when Senator Howard Baker (R.-Tenn.) released some information that he had originally secured while serving on the Senate Watergate Committee. Senator Baker disclosed that he had come across at least two CIA "dossiers" indicating that the Agency may have been involved in domestic affairs.[32] He disclosed that one of these CIA files, on Warren Commission critic Bernard Fensterwald, Jr.,[33] contained copies of several high-level internal CIA memos which clearly showed that James Angleton was the key CIA official in dealing with matters related to the Kennedy assassination.

In a memo dated January 13, 1969, to FBI Director J. Edgar Hoover, Angleton noted that Fensterwald was setting up a Washington-based Committee to Investigate Assassinations. In this confidential memo, Angleton noted that "Fensterwald, who said he was setting up an office which would open in a week, left the Senate earlier this week after twelve years as counsel for several committees."[34] Angleton went on to request that Hoover run some kind of vaguely defined identification check on Fensterwald and three other Warren Commission critics associated with him. Other segments of the memo were deleted prior to its release.[35]

In late February, 1976, James Angleton was also linked to the mysterious circumstances surrounding a reported "relationship" between President Kennedy and Mary Meyer, an attractive Georgetown artist. In a story first disclosed by the *Washington Post*, and later confirmed by *Newsweek*, the Kennedy-Meyer friendship was set forth in some detail.[36] Mary Meyer had at the time been a sister-in-law of Ben Bradlee, the Executive Editor of the *Washington Post* and a close friend of President Kennedy. According to the *Washington Post* story, JFK's relationship with Mary Meyer had continued right up to the time of his death. In 1964, the year after the assassination, Mary Meyer was mysteriously shot to death in Georgetown, the victim of a possible attempted robbery, a murder which has never been solved.[37] However, more interestingly, the *Post* reported that shortly after her demise, Mary Meyer's personal diary was taken from her home by James Angleton, a friend of the Meyer family. Sometime following Ms. Meyer's murder on October 12, 1964, according to the *Washington Post*'s information, James Angleton took her diary to CIA headquarters in nearby Langley, Virginia, where he destroyed it.[38]

While several sources have confirmed the details of the Kennedy-Meyer relationship — the second such Kennedy affair revealed in recent years — exact details behind Angleton's involvement have not yet become known. Angleton has refused any comment on his role in retrieving and destroying the Meyer diary.

While little is known of James Angleton's early CIA career, it has been reported that he played a key role in OSS activities in Italy and Sicily during World War II. Although it is not presently known if Angleton was aware of or involved in the OSS-Mafia operations, this appears strongly possible. Angleton had served as second-in-command for the OSS in Italy, an area that he knew well because of his personal ownership of a subsidiary of the National Cash Register Company in Milan.[39]

During an appearance before the Senate Intelligence Committee in February, 1976, Angleton testified that he had been unaware of the CIA-Mafia assassination conspiracies against Castro in the early 1960s, but admitted that he had been aware that his CIA colleague, William Harvey, had been meeting with members of the Mafia during that period.[40] It is not presently known if Angleton knew that John Roselli, Sam Giancana, and Santos Trafficante were the specific Mafia leaders Harvey was working with.

In June, 1976, new information became available regarding Angleton's key role in dealing with the Warren Commission investigation. The Senate Intelligence Committee reported that at a meeting in late December of 1963, Angleton had requested that he be allowed to take over CIA responsibility for dealing with the Warren Commission probe. The Senate Committee's Final Report noted that, "Angleton suggested that his own Counterintelligence Division take over the investigation and [Richard] Helms acceded to this suggestion."[41] Thereafter, Angleton's staff became responsible for all CIA dealings with the Commission.

The Senate Committee further disclosed that James Angleton had also had a valuable source of information from within the Warren Commission itself:

> It is important to note that Mr. Angleton testified he was often in contact with [Allen] Dulles after the latter had left the Agency. Angleton testified that Dulles consulted with him before agreeing to President Johnson's request that he be on the Commission and that he was in frequent contact with Dulles. Angleton has also indicated that he and Dulles informally discussed the progress of the Commission's investigation and that Dulles consulted with him about what further investigation the CIA could do . . .[42]

William Harvey

CIA official William Harvey, a 250-pound gravel-voiced ex-FBI agent, was the CIA field coordinator for its secret conspiracies to assassinate Fidel Castro, which lasted from November, 1961, to sometime in the spring or summer of 1963, when the plots were reportedly ended.[43] Harvey, a tough, confident, and sometimes abusive man, met regularly with John Roselli, Santos Trafficante, Sam Giancana, Robert Maheu, and a militant anti-Castro Cuban exile leader during this time.[44] And, as will be seen, Harvey has freely admitted that he and CIA Deputy Director for Plans Richard Helms deliberately concealed the existence of the CIA's involvement with the Mafia from higher authorities — specifically, from CIA Director John McCone.[45]

William Harvey had also apparently advocated CIA involvement with the Mafia in projects other than assassinations. According to the Senate Intelligence Committee Report on the CIA-Mafia plots, General Edward Lansdale and his close associate, William Harvey, had unsuccessfully sought approval from the Kennedy Administration for a plan to involve Mafia elements in other actions against Cuba.

General Lansdale, who in later years reportedly cultivated a close relationship with the Corsican Mafia during his controversial service in Vietnam, had been in charge of "Operation Mongoose," a covert action program designed to undermine the Castro regime through a wide variety of clandestine methods.

"Operation Mongoose" was the key program being coordinated by the "Special Group Augmented," a secret Cuban policy group that included Attorney General Robert F. Kennedy, CIA Director John McCone, as well as McGeorge Bundy, Alexis Johnson, and occasionally Dean Rusk and Robert McNamara.

In January, 1962, General Lansdale submitted a proposed program to the Special Group Augmented (SGA) that included an operation that would have involved planning for the "defection of top Cuban government officials."[46] According to a CIA memorandum of January 24, 1962, prepared with the assistance of Cuban Affairs Specialist William Harvey, the agency suggested use of "crime syndicates" as intermediaries for these possible defections.[47]

On February 20, 1962, General Lansdale and his CIA associates submitted a "six phase plan" for carrying out his proposed actions against the Castro regime. One operation called for "attacks on the cadre of the regime, including key leaders."[48] The secret Lansdale proposal stated that "Gangster elements might provide the best recruitment potential for actions against [Cuban] police — G2 [intelligence] officials."[49]

According to the Senate Intelligence Committee Report, "Lansdale conceded that his proposal to recruit gangster elements for attacks on 'key leaders' contemplated the targeted killing of individuals . . ."[50] However, the Senate Committee reports that the SGA, under the leadership of Robert F. Kennedy, refused to approve the Lansdale-CIA plan:

> Lansdale's 33 plans were never approved for implementation by the SGA . . . the SGA tabled Lansdale's six phase plan all together in February, 1962, and directed him to plan for and conduct an intelligence collection plan only.[51]

Interestingly, the CIA-Mafia assassination conspiracies being coordinated by William Harvey and other CIA officials were in high gear at that same time. Since the assassination plots were then being concealed from higher authority, as Harvey and Richard Helms later testified, Harvey was free of the SGA restraints that he so despised.

The Senate Intelligence Committee Report noted that the highly independent Harvey had grown increasingly irritated over the constraints placed upon his recommendations to the SGA and had complained to CIA Director McCone (on April 10, 1962) about the SGA advance approval required for all major Cuban operations.[52] Harvey also complained of the "excruciating detail" required by the SGA "control process," which he claimed was "restrictive" and "stultifying."[53]

The abrasive Harvey's penchant for independent initiative and what some would call his resentment of taking orders from non-Agency officials, later resulted in his eventual decline in the government and strongly negative image. John McCone, the Director of the CIA during that period, later remarked, "When you take a plant supervisor and make him President of the Company, it doesn't always work out."[54]

An even more negative assessment of William Harvey had been made by McCone's predecessor as CIA Director, Allen Dulles: "That fellow Harvey is a conspiratorial cop. The only trouble is, I can't tell if he is more conspiratorial or cop."[55] Similar misgivings about Harvey were voiced by SGA member McGeorge Bundy, who reportedly told a CIA official, "Your friend [Harvey] doesn't inspire confidence."[56]

By the time of his transfer to another CIA assignment in the early summer of 1963, William Harvey had become a bitter critic of President Kennedy, and an even more bitter opponent of Attorney General Robert F. Kennedy.

Harvey and the Attorney General had by then been involved in a highly acrimonious disagreement that had occurred during the Cuban Missile Crisis of October, 1962. At the height of the historic Soviet-American nuclear confrontation, Harvey had dispatched ten different covert teams to Cuba to provide intelligence reports on the missiles, and stand by for other covert action. In a detailed examination for the *Washington Post* of William Harvey's checkered career, David C. Martin disclosed that Harvey's superiors, including Attorney General Robert F. Kennedy, had been angered and astonished by this unauthorized action.[57] Martin has written that CIA Director John McCone ordered the immediate cancellation of the Harvey orders, but that by then, three of the secret teams had gone too far into Cuba to be contacted to return home.[58]

Other members of the SGA Cuban policy group have recalled Robert Kennedy's extreme anger over the possibility that Harvey's unauthorized agent teams might upset the intensively delicate negotiations then being conducted by President Kennedy and himself in an attempt to negotiate a settlement with Soviet Premier Khrushchev. The Senate Intelligence Committee provided a brief account of the Harvey-Kennedy confrontation:

> Harvey testified that he had a "confrontation" with Robert Kennedy at the height of the Missile Crisis concerning Harvey's order that agent teams be sent into Cuba to support any conventional U.S. Military operation that might occur. Harvey stated that Robert Kennedy "took a great deal of exception" to this order, and, as a result McCone ordered Harvey to stop the agent operation . . . McCone's assistant at the time similarly described this incident and stated that, although Harvey had to get guidance from top officials during the missile crisis, Harvey "earned another black mark as not being fully under control."[59]

The Senate Intelligence Committee disclosed that William Harvey was busy with another Cuban operation during this same period. Though the CIA — specifically, officials Sheffield Edwards and Lawrence Houston — had finally informed Attorney General Robert Kennedy (on May 7, 1962) about the past existence of the CIA-Mafia assassination conspiracies, the two officials mistakenly told Kennedy that the plots had been "terminated."[60] Actually, as the Senate Intelligence Committee established, William Harvey and the other CIA men then still running the assassination attempts were actually stepping up the pace of the plots.[61] The Senate Committee disclosed portions of an internal CIA report, prepared in 1967, which reached the conclusion that:

> The Attorney General was not told that the gambling syndicate [assassination] operation had already been reactivated, nor, as far as we know, was he ever told that CIA had a continuing involvement with U.S. gangster elements.[62]

The exact date that the secret conspiracies with the Mafia ended has never been established. William Harvey testified that he had made a "tentative decision" to terminate the plots by the fall of 1962.[63] However, Harvey further testified that he "may have deferred" the decision for "a period of a few weeks."[64]

The Senate Intelligence Committee and the CIA have concluded that the best available evidence indicates that the CIA-Mafia plots had ended sometime in February of 1963.[65] Columnist Jack Anderson, who first disclosed authoritative details about the plots in January, 1971, maintains that the secret plots didn't end until the March of 1963.[66]

Additionally, the Senate Intelligence Committee disclosed that William Harvey met with assassination coordinator John Roselli, the Mafia leader as late as June, 1963,[67] and a CIA Report which states that this Harvey-Roselli meeting in June was actually "a farewell dinner before Harvey went on another assignment."[68]

Harvey had indeed finally been reassigned to a different position in the spring of 1963; reportedly, to the CIA station in Rome.[69] Italy was, ironically, the nation in which the earliest Mafia involvement with American intelligence (the OSS) had begun, twenty years earlier.

By this time, William Harvey had become an unwanted and basically an untrusted CIA man, in the view of top officials in the Kennedy Administration. A former member of the SGA Cuban policy group later recalled that Harvey "hated Bobby Kennedy's guts with a purple passion."[70] In his authoritative account of Harvey's work for the CIA, David C. Martin states:

> Some attributed the appointment [to the Rome CIA station] to a desire to get Harvey out of the country as soon as possible, never mind where . . . He would never again be allowed near an operation in which the brothers Kennedy were likely to have an active interest.[71]

In the fall of 1976, several months after Harvey died of a reported heart attack in Indianapolis, David Martin reported that Harvey's widow had stated that her husband had told her never to discuss his past activities. Mrs. Harvey said that "up to his last breath he told me never to talk to anyone"[72] Mrs. Harvey also disclosed that her home had been the subject of two mysterious attempted break-ins after his death. Harvey's widow went on to say, "They're after his papers. But I burned everything."[73]

Richard Helms

Richard Helms served as the CIA's Deputy Director for Plans (DDP) during the early 1960s and went on to become Director of the CIA in 1966. As the CIA's key executive dealing with the Warren Commission, and in conducting the CIA's own investigation of President Kennedy's murder, Richard Helms' role is a very central one to any review of the Kennedy case.

Helms, a confident man of patrician demeanor, has been a central fixture of the Washington political establishment for a decade and a half. However, when Helms announced the end of his public career in early November, 1976, retiring from his final position as Ambassador to Iran, his long career seemed to have ended in dismal disarray. Worse yet, Richard Helms' personal honesty and professionalism had been brought to a low from which few saw any rise. By then, the Justice Department was reviewing a virtual ream of Helms' testimony before several House and Senate Committees and Subcommittees for a final determination as to whether or not the former CIA Director would be indicted for perjury. The Justice Department and FBI were reviewing the circumstances of a domestic burglary (in Fairfax, Virginia) personally authorized by Helms, a crime which the Justice Department had earlier declined to indict him for on largely technical grounds. Several former CIA colleagues by then had stated that his Senate Intelligence Committee testimony on the existence of the CIA-Mafia assassination conspiracies aimed against

Castro seemed to be strewn with inaccuracies and misstatements; and the general consensus of Senate Intelligence Committee sources seemed to concur with the judgment of those former colleagues. Further, a subcommittee of that same Senate Committee by then had issued a lengthy report documenting the serious mistakes and sins of omission attributable to Richard Helms and his closest aides during their work with the Warren Commission. And, perhaps worst of all, the belief that "the man was as good as his word" had been rendered "inoperative" in Helms' case.

People no longer seemed to trust the former CIA Director to any appreciable degree. Part of this latter-day negative reaction was, of course, an overreaction, fostered by a dawning realization that too much trust had been placed in Dick Helms for too many years. But a larger part of the same negativism was based upon the cold face of the emerging record.

Various Warren Commission critics have long cited the central role Helms played in the CIA's virtual noncompliance with the Warren Commission request for CIA assistance in investigating Jack Ruby and his associates.[74]

After waiting nine weeks for Helms' response to a lengthy investigative memorandum, given to him on March 12, 1964, the Warren Commission reaffirmed their request for a reply by sending a second, more urgent, communication to him regarding the need for information on Lee Harvey Oswald's killer. In his letter to Helms of May 19, 1964, Commission General Counsel J. Lee Rankin noted that: "This Commission is nearing the end of its investigation," and asked for a CIA response to the Commission's two-month-old request, "in the near future."[75]

While the Warren Commission may have finally expected a prompt reply from Deputy Director for Plans Helms, no such response was forthcoming. The Commission's request for CIA assistance and information pertaining to "the Ruby Detail" would not be answered until well over twelve weeks later.

Finally, on September 19, 1964 — over six months after the original Commission request was made to Helms, and well over three months after the request had been strongly restated — the Commission received a reply from Helms' assistant, Thomas Karamessines.[76] The very brief response simply stated:

> ... An examination of Central Intelligence Agency files has produced no information on Jack Ruby or his activities. The Central Intelligence Agency has no indication that Ruby or Lee Harvey Oswald ever knew each other, were associated, or might have been connected in any manner.[76a]

As noted earlier, even had the Helms staff come up with a more substantive response, it would have been of little use — because the Warren Commission Report (issued September 24, 1964) was already then being set in type.

Interestingly, a CIA "Memorandum for the Record" obtained under the provisions of the Freedom of Information Act in June, 1976, sheds further light on Helms' apparent attitude toward the Warren Commission during that period. Coincidentally, the newly-declassified CIA document consists of an internal memorandum for the CIA's files, regarding the same March 12, 1964 meeting with the Warren Commission staff, during which Helms had first been given the request for information on Jack Ruby.

The CIA memorandum (portions of which are still being withheld by the Agency) notes that Richard Helms, his aides, and the Warren Commission staff had discussed various phases of the assassination investigation, with emphasis on the activities of Lee Harvey Oswald and Jack Ruby.[77] A central point of the meeting, according to the CIA memorandum, related to the Warren Commission's desire to investigate allegations that Oswald had somehow been employed by the CIA. As the Agency's own internal memorandum reveals, the CIA — specifically, Richard Helms — apparently felt little or no obligation to respond to the Commission's effort to establish the facts (or lack of facts) relating to this area. The CIA memorandum states:

> [Warren Commission Assistant Counsel] Willens noted that Mrs. Oswald had introduced a statement to the effect that she suspected her son to be a CIA agent. Mr. Willens asked whether in fact Oswald had been a CIA agent. Mr. Helms replied that he had not been. Mr. Willens then asked if there were any way of proving this. Mr. Helms first remarked that in him and [deletion] the Commission had the two Clandestine Services officers who certainly would know whether or not Oswald had been an agent for CIA in the Soviet Union. He then said that the Commission would have to take his word for the fact Oswald had not been an agent. Mr. Rankin interjected the view that the Commission had not adopted this procedure with other agencies and wondered whether there was not some way to clarify this point more effectively for the Commission.[77a]

Helms, long regarded as perhaps the most adept and skillful witness to appear before the various House and Senate Committees whose legislative jurisdictions extend to national security affairs, was extensively questioned by the Senate Intelligence Committee during their probe of the secret CIA-Mafia assassination conspiracies of the early 1960s. As the highest level Agency official who had been involved in the plots at the time of their discovery by Robert F. Kennedy in May, 1962, Helms would be a key witness during the 1975 Senate investigation.

By then it had become known that former CIA Director John McCone would testify that his Deputy, Richard Helms, had concealed the existence of the CIA-Mafia conspiracies from him for many months. By then, it also became known that a secret 1967 CIA report on the assassination plots, prepared under Helms' direction, had been the Agency's most closely guarded secret for over eight years. While Richard Helms was then widely believed to be "on the spot" in the words of the *New York Times*, the full extent of the apparent strain that he was under finally became evident in early 1975.

Following an afternoon session of testimony by Helms, former CBS News correspondent Daniel Schorr pressed the ex-spy chief as to his exact knowledge of the Mafia's involvement with the CIA in planning to murder Fidel Castro. When queried by Schorr about the Agency's dealings with professional killers, Helms seemed to come undone, exploding in a stream of obscenities in front of a number of reporters, shouting "Killer Schorr! Killer Schorr! You goddamn bastard! You - - - ! " The normally unflappable Helms continued his public tirade with further obscenities. Though the *New York Times*, *Washington Post* and other news organizations spared Helms the embarrassment of repeating the sexual epithets he had shouted at Daniel Schorr, the widely reported outburst took many observers in Washington by surprise.

The full extent to which the Senate Intelligence Committee was pressing Helms for information about the CIA-Mafia assassination plots, as well as the CIA's role in the investigation of the assassination, later became known with the release of the Committee's various reports.

What was also revealed was the extent to which the somewhat defiant Helms *modus operandi* (found so unmanageable by the Warren Commission) had persisted over the years, changing little if any in the sheer imperiousness of its assertions:

> *Sen. Morgan:* . . . You were charged with furnishing the Warren Commission information from the CIA, information that you thought was relevant?
> *Mr. Helms:* No, sir, I was instructed to reply to inquiries from the Warren Commission for information from the Agency. I was not asked to initiate any particular thing.
> *Sen. Morgan:* . . . in other words if you weren't asked for it, you didn't give it.
> *Mr. Helms:* That's right, sir.[78]

One of the most significant facts to emerge from the extensive testimony the hearings Senate Intelligence Committee is that Richard Helms and William Harvey (whom Helms had personally approved as the Agency field coordinator for the secret CIA-Mafia assassination plots) concealed the existence of these murder plans from Helms' immediate superior, CIA Director John McCone. It was not until mid-August of 1963, over five months after the plots allegedly ended, that Helms finally told McCone of their past existence.[79]

In setting forth the testimony of former Director McCone, the Senate Intelligence Report noted:

> McCone testified that he was not aware of the plots to assassinate Castro which took place during the years in which he was DCI, and that he did not authorize those plots. He testified that he was not briefed about the assassination plots by Dulles, Bissell, Helms, or anyone else when he succeeded Dulles as Director in November, 1961. And that if he had ever been asked about the plots, he would have disapproved.[80]

Richard Bissell, who preceded Richard Helms as Deputy Director for Plans, and who had been an original architect of the CIA assassination involvement with the Mafia, testified that McCone had indeed not been told of the plots against Castro.[81] William Harvey, who coordinated them from 1962 to mid-1963, also affirmed that McCone had not been apprised of the conspiracies being run by Helms and himself.[82] Harvey also testified that the decision to conceal knowledge of the murder plots from Director McCone was a decision personally made by Richard Helms.

In his own Senate testimony, Helms stated that he "didn't recall" whether or not he had ever told Director McCone about the secret plots. While at some points suggesting that he may have dutifully informed McCone of the Agency's involvement with Maheu, Trafficante, Roselli, and Giancana, Helms finally admitted (under sharp questioning) that he had "apparently" never told McCone what was going on: "No, it isn't my impression that I told him, at least I don't have any impression, unfortunately."[83]

Helms went on to testify that at first he "didn't recall that Mr. McCone was not informed."[84] However, according to Helms:

> . . . When I was told that there was evidence that he wasn't informed, I was trying to scratch my head as to why I didn't tell him at the time and my surmises are the best I can come up with. I am really surprised I did not discuss it with him at the time.[85]

While Helms may have been "trying to scratch [his] head," another key CIA official suggested a pretty good reason why he kept McCone in the dark. And ironically, the CIA man who made this suggestion to the Senate Committee was Richard Helms' own Special Assistant, George McManus, assigned by Helms to Cuban Affairs. According to the Senate Intelligence Report, McManus stated:

> George McManus, Helms' Special Assistant for Cuba during the relevant period . . . gave his opinion that if McCone had been asked to approve an assassination, he "would have reacted violently, immediately."

The Senate Report quotes two reasons given by George McManus as to why he was convinced Director McCone would have reacted in this manner:

> (1) McCone had a great love for the President of the United States and he sort of looked at him as an older son or a brother, a very protective sense he had about the President, President Kennedy, and McCone would have immediately said, Jesus, this is a no win ball game.
> (2) Second, as an individual, he would have found it morally reprehensible.[87]

Even more damaging to Richard Helms, two other key CIA officials testified that McCone had (on at least one occasion) conveyed his absolute opposition to any consideration of assassination conspiring. The Senate Committee noted that when a government official once raised the idea of trying to assassinate Castro during an August 10, 1962 meeting on Cuba that McCone attended, the CIA Director had fiercely objected, stating that such an idea was "completely out of bounds" and unacceptable under any circumstances.[88]

The next day, August 11, 1962, or possibly the day after that (according to Director McCone's Executive Assistant) Deputy Director for Plans Richard Helms was specifically told of McCone's strong opposition to such an idea. According to the testimony of Walter Elder, McCone's top aide:

> I told Mr. Helms that Mr. McCone had expressed his feeling . . . that assassination could not be condoned and would not be

approved . . . Mr. Helms responded, "I understand." The point is that I made Mr. Helms aware of the strength of Mr. McCone's opposition to assassination. I know that Mr. Helms could not have been under any misapprehension about Mr. McCone's feeling about this conversation.[89]

When informed of Elder's testimony, Helms told the Senate Committee that "I do not have any recollection of such a conversation . . . let me say that in not recalling this conversation, I very seriously doubt that it ever took place."[90] Unfortunately, while Helms was apparently suggesting that McCone's former top assistant was lying, another key witness was basically corroborating Walter Elder's account.

William Harvey told the Senate Committee that he had also heard from Director McCone shortly after that August 10, 1962 meeting. Harvey revealed that on the very day after the August 10th meeting, CIA Director McCone told him that the thought of trying to assassinate Castro was unacceptable, and further, that "If I got myself involved in something like this, I might end up getting myself excommunicated."[91]

William Harvey provided other testimony (on June 25, 1975) that may eventually be viewed as the most damaging to Richard Helms. Harvey told the Senate Committee of some previously unknown information regarding why he and Helms decided not to inform Director John McCone of the CIA-Mafia assassination plots.

About two weeks before this Harvey testimony, Helms told the Senate Committee that one reason he may have concealed the conspiracies from Director John McCone was because:

> I was enormously busy with a lot of other things . . . I guess I must have thought to myself, well this is going to look peculiar to him . . .

> It was a Mafia connection . . . and this was, you know, not a very savory effort.[92]

Days later, on June 25, 1975, William Harvey revealed some other information indicating exactly how unsavory the "effort" was, and some other reasons why he and Helms had concealed the plots from McCone — reasons which Helms had apparently neglected to mention in his own Senate testimony.

Harvey told the Senate Committee:

> There was a fairly detailed discussion between myself and Helms as to whether or not the Director should . . . be briefed . . . we agreed that it was not necessary or advisable . . .
>
> There were several reasons for this.
>
> . . . including the possible problem — and it was a very, or it appeared to be, and in my opinion was, at that time, a very real possibility — of this government being blackmailed either by [anti-Castro] Cubans for political purposes or by figures in organized crime for their own self-protection or aggrandizement . . . [93]

Senate Intelligence Committee sources have confirmed that Harvey's remarks about possible Mafia or Cuban exile blackmail, stemming from their knowledge of (and involvement in) the CIA assassination plots against Castro, created a stir within the Committee at that time. Press speculation about various aspects of the Mafia's involvement in the CIA plots was then at an early high point, due to the brutal murder of assassination coordinator Sam Giancana on June 20, 1975, five days before Harvey's testimony.

Under intensive questioning about the plots during his own Senate testimony, Richard Helms at one point remarked "I am having a very difficult time . . . before this Committee, because there is something in here that doesn't come together, even to me, I am sorry to say."[94]

According to the assessment of a substantially large number of former Senate Intelligence Committee members and staff, Republicans and Democrats alike, a good deal of evidence indicates that the "something" that "doesn't come together" seems to be the testimony of Richard Helms himself.

"UNGUIDED MISSILES"

QJ/WIN is the CIA code name for its agent who served as a top assassination specialist during the early 1960s, according to the Senate Intelligence Committee.[95] The actual identity of QJ/WIN has never been revealed, and remains one of the Agency's most closely held secrets.

QJ/WIN was the key agent or "asset" involved in the highly secret "Executive Action" assassination planning apparatus set up by the CIA in 1961. This secret program was only partially investigated by the Senate Intelligence Committee in 1975-76 due to what Committee staff members have termed the "reluctance" of the Agency to provide it with full details. According to the Senate Committee Report:

203

> Sometime in early 1961, [Richard] Bissell instructed Harvey, who was then Chief of a CIA foreign intelligence staff, to establish an "Executive Action capability," which would include research into a capability to assassinate foreign leaders.[96]

The Senate Committee Report notes that this assassination "capability" was established after the CIA-Mafia assassination plots against Castro had already begun, and further, that Bissell, Harvey, and Richard Helms state that it was never actually put to use.[97] Noting that "Executive Action" was "a CIA euphemism," the Senate Committee stated that the secret program's intended purpose was to establish a "capability to perform assassinations."[98] The Senate Committee disclosed that the assassination planning operation was given a second CIA code name of ZR/RIFLE.[99] The existence of the early 1960s' "Executive Action" program was first disclosed by Senate Intelligence Committee member Walter Mondale, the future Vice President, in spring, 1975.

According to the Senate investigation, agent QJ/WIN was "placed under Harvey's supervision for the ZR/RIFLE project."[100] The mysterious QJ/WIN was, according to the Senate Committee Report, "a foreign citizen with a criminal background recruited in Europe."[101] Under questioning by the Senate Intelligence Committee, former CIA Director Richard Helms admitted having had detailed knowledge of QJ/WIN's activities, and stated, "If you needed somebody to carry out murder, I guess you had [this] man who might be prepared to carry it out."[102]

The Senate Committee disclosed that agent QJ/WIN's special area of expertise related to various groups of professional assassins and hired killers who operated out of several places in Europe:

> Harvey used QJ/WIN to spot "individuals with criminal and underworld connections

in Europe for possible multi-purpose use."
For example, QJ/WIN reported that a
potential asset in the Middle East was "the
leader of a gambling syndicate," with "an
available pool of assassins."[103]

Ominously, the Senate
investigation determined
that CIA agent QJ/WIN
and an equally dangerous
CIA operative code named
WI/ROGUE, later began
formulating assassination
plans on their own, and
were subsequently regarded as somewhat "out
of control" by their
Agency superiors. According to the Senate
Intelligence Committee Report, this disturbing chain
of events was set in motion in 1960:

In the Fall of 1960, two CIA officials were
asked to assassinate [Patrice] Lumumba
[of the Congo]. Poisons were sent to the
Congo and some exploratory steps were
taken toward gaining access to Lumumba.
Subsequently, in early 1961, Lumumba
was killed by Congolese rivals.[104]

The Senate Intelligence Report further notes:

Michael Mulroney, a senior CIA officer in
the Directorate for Plans, testified that in
October 1960 he had been asked by Richard
Bissell to go to the Congo to carry out the
assassination of Lumumba. Mulroney said
that he refused to participate in an assassination operation, but proceeded to the
Congo . . . [105]

Upon his arrival in the Congo, CIA official Michael Mulroney "was joined by QJ/WIN," according to the Senate Committee.[106] While Mulroney testified that he himself did not become involved in the Lumumba assassination plan, it is clear that Mulroney had knowledge of the plot being developed by his CIA superiors.[107] In his Senate testimony of September 11, 1975, Mulroney was asked about the nature of the mysterious QJ/WIN's activities:

> *Mulroney:* I would say that he would not be a man of many scruples.
> *Question:* So he was a man capable of doing anything.
> *Mulroney:* I would think so, yes.
> *Question:* And that would include assassination?
> *Mulroney:* I would think so.[108]

The Senate Committee noted that the CIA's instructions for agent QJ/WIN's mission in the Congo had been cabled from Agency headquarters in Washington to Leopoldville, in the Congo, on November 2, 1960.[109] According to the cable sent to the CIA station in Leopoldville, "This dispatch should be reduced to cryptic necessary notes and destroyed after the first reading."[110] Soon thereafter, according to the Senate Report, "QJ/WIN had begun implementing a plan to 'pierce both Congolese and UN guards' to enter Lumumba's residence."[111] An abduction of the Congo leader was being considered then as part of the assassination plan.

It was in December of 1960 that QJ/WIN became involved with WI/ROGUE, another assassination specialist.[112] According to the Senate Intelligence Committee, WI/ROGUE was an "essentially stateless" soldier of fortune, and "a forger and a former bank robber."[113] The Senate Committee noted:

> The CIA sent him to the Congo after providing him with plastic surgery and a toupee so that Europeans traveling in the Congo would not recognize him. The CIA characterized WI/ROGUE as a man who "learned quickly and carried out any assignment without regard to danger."[114]

In August 1975, Victor Hedgman, a CIA official who worked closely with operative WI/ROGUE told the Senate Committee:

> I had difficulty controlling him in that he was not a professional intelligence officer as such. He seemed to act on his own without seeking guidance of authority . . . I found he was rather an unguided missile . . . the kind of man that could get you in trouble before you knew you were in trouble.[115]

The Senate Intelligence Committee established that on December 14, 1960, WI/ROGUE had attempted "to recruit QJ/WIN for an execution squad" that was

207

not authorized by the two agents' CIA superiors.[116] As the Senate Committee noted, the available CIA cable indicated that "WI/ROGUE's attempt to form an execution squad was an unauthorized, maverick action . . ."[117]

The Senate Committee released portions of the secret CIA cable (sent to CIA Director Allen Dulles) in which WI/ROGUE's approach to QJ/WIN had been outlined. As the cable indicates, WI/ROGUE later denied trying to establish this assassination team:

> QJ/WIN REPORTED WI/ROGUE HAD OFFERED HIM THREE HUNDRED DOLLARS PER MONTH TO PARTICIPATE IN INTEL NET AND BE MEMBER "EXECUTION SQUAD." WHEN QJ/WIN SAID HE NOT INTERESTED, WI/ROGUE ADDED THERE WOULD BE BONUSES FOR SPECIAL JOBS. UNDER QJ/WIN'S QUESTIONING, WI/ROGUE LATER SAID HE WORKED FOR [AMERICAN] SERVICE.
>
> WI/ROGUE DID NOT ADMIT TO HAVING TRIED RECRUIT HIM [QJ/WIN]. WHEN [STATION OFFICER] TRIED TO LEARN WHETHER WI/ROGUE HAD MADE APPROACH LATTER CLAIMED HAD TAKEN NO STEPS. [STATION OFFICER] WAS UNABLE [TO] CONTRADICT, AS DID NOT WISH [TO] REVEAL QJ/WIN CONNECTION [WITH THE CIA].[118]

Thus, as can be seen, the Senate evidence indicates that one of the CIA's top assassination operatives on one occasion tried to recruit another professional killer for a secret unauthorized assassination team — a potential recruit who was already secretly serving as a CIA assassin.

The Senate Intelligence Committee reported that neither of these two dangerous CIA agents, QJ/WIN or WI/ROGUE, ever actually carried out any assassination for the CIA — according to the available evidence supplied by the Agency.

The Senate Report also noted that after William Harvey took over the ongoing coordination of the secret CIA-Mafia assassination plots against Castro in April, 1962, he "ran it as one aspect of [the] ZR/RIFLE" program created by the "Executive Action" plan.[119]

Though the Senate Committee found no evidence that QJ/WIN (or WI/ROGUE) had become involved in these later CIA-Mafia conspiracies, the Committee found little information available on their subsequent activities. Neither man was available for questioning by the Senate Committee and their present whereabouts are presumably unknown . . . except, very likely, to the CIA.

CIA/SUPPORT CHIEF

The Chief of the CIA's Operational Support Division of the Office of Security — who served as the Agency's key coordinator in recruiting Robert Maheu, John Roselli, Sam Giancana, and other organized crime figures to assassinate Castro — has never officially been identified. No government source has ever released the Support Chief's name and there has never been any official confirmation of his identity. The Senate Intelligence Committee never disclosed who he was, and instead referred to him only as the CIA Support Chief.

The long-time lack of any official confirmation of who the CIA Support Chief was has long been of interest to many observers. The Support Chief had served as the key CIA contact with Mafia leaders Roselli, Trafficante and Giancana, from late 1960 until at least April of 1962.[120] There is a clear conflict, however, between the sworn Senate testimony of the CIA Support Chief and former Howard Hughes aide Robert Maheu regarding whose idea it was to recruit the Mafia for the plan. According to his testimony of May 30, 1975, the Support Chief maintains that it was Robert Maheu "who raised the idea of using Roselli" and the Mafia for the secret plots.[121] Yet, according to Maheu's testimony of July 29, 1975, it was actually the CIA Support Chief who suggested making contact with Roselli and the Syndicate.[122] Thus, one of the earliest and most significant questions regarding the long chronology of CIA-Mafia assassination conspiring remains highly clouded.

The Support Chief is now the only CIA coordinator of the CIA-Mafia plots still alive. Though former CIA executives Richard Helms and Richard Bissell (who were both involved in the plots) are still living, the deaths of CIA men Sheffield Edwards (in 1975) and William Harvey (in 1976) leave the Support Chief as the only living Agency official who worked on the actual coordination and logistics of the plots with the Mafia and Maheu.

The mysterious murders of Sam Giancana in 1975 and John Roselli in 1976, as well as the 1976 death of billionaire Howard Hughes, have also reduced the circle of those who had direct knowledge of the plots.

The first identification of the CIA Support Chief came in January, 1971, when columnist Jack Anderson disclosed details about the inner workings of the CIA-Mafia assassination plots. While their existence was not officially confirmed until four years later, Anderson reported substantial details about their operations in that early column, which had been based in part on an even earlier column by his late colleague, Drew Pearson, from 1967. On January 18, 1971, Anderson named the key CIA official allegedly involved with William Harvey, Robert Maheu, and John Roselli.[123] However, the *Washington Post* and some other newspapers in which Anderson was syndicated deleted the controversial disclosures in the column when it first appeared.[124]

When the Senate Intelligence Committee Report was finally issued in November of 1975, this four-year-old column was essentially confirmed in virtually every aspect, and the Senate Report made repeated reference to the unidentified "Support Chief, or Chief of the Operational Support Division of the Office of Security."[125]

However, the Report briefly noted that the conspirators used "code names" during their early planning sessions, and that Sam Giancana's code name had been "Sam Gold," and the CIA Support Chief's had been "Jim Olds."[126] John Roselli had used the name "John Rawlston."[127]

The whole question of who the Support Chief actually was seemed to be finally resolved when Robert Maheu held a press conference to discuss his involvement in the plots. The Senate Report disclosed that, "The Operational Support Chief had served as Maheu's case officer since the Agency first began using Maheu's services . . ."[128] In his 1975 press conference, Maheu stated:

> I was approached by my project officer. . . (who was then a member of the CIA) and as I said previously, had been assigned to me as my project officer asked me if, in connection with a planned invasion in Cuba, I would contact a Mr. John Roselli in Los

211

Angeles, asking if Mr. Roselli would be inclined to help in a program for removing Mr. Castro from the scene or eliminating him in connection with the invasion of Cuba.[129]

In addition to the inconsistencies as to who originated the idea of bringing the Mafia in on the project, Committee sources have expressed doubts about the veracity of "the Support Chief's" sworn testimony on other points as well, and have expressed consternation over the difficulty of establishing when exactly his role in the plots ended, as well as the part he played in the delivery of some unidentified rifles and other equipment to the Mafia-associated Cuban exile leader some time during April or May, 1962.[130]

George De Mohrenschildt

George De Mohrenschildt, a Dallas oil engineer, and his wife Jeanne were close friends of Lee Harvey Oswald and his wife, Marina, and became key witnesses before the Warren Commission. Many students of the Kennedy assassination believe De Mohrenschildt has, in all likelihood, intelligence connections. De Mohrenschildt himself has stated that he worked as an Allied Intelligence agent during World War II.[131]

Interestingly, George and Jeanne De Mohrenschildt undertook a "long walking vacation" in 1960, which ended in Guatemala City in April, 1961. Guatemala City, as is now widely known, served as the key CIA training center and staging area for the planning of the Bay of Pigs invasion. E. Howard Hunt, the top Watergate conspirator, has publicly acknowledged his work for the CIA there during the planning stages. The Warren Commission Report stated that De Mohrenschildt "and his wife made an 8-month hike from the United States-Mexican border to Panama over primitive jungle trails." A lengthy film and complete log was prepared by De Mohrenschildt and a report of the trip was made to "the United States Government."[132] Many observers have pointed out that the CIA would seem to be the logical recipient of De Mohrenschildt's "report" on this trip, but thus far, this has never been conformed officially.

The De Mohrenschildts have also figured prominently in speculation that some of Oswald's Dallas friends (particularly in the conservative, anti-Communist White Russian community) were associated with the CIA. George De Mohrenschildt and his mysterious background will likely become a central focus of the reinvestigation of the Kennedy murder, particularly in view of his close association with Lee Harvey Oswald. De Mohrenschildt's former son-in-law told the Warren Commission that the two men were very close and that "whatever his [De Mohrenschildt's] suggestions were, Lee grabbed them and took them, whether it was what time to go to bed or where to stay."[133] The wealthy and sophisticated De Mohrenschildt and his associations with oil industry executives and international financiers remain the subject of intense interest to the various critics of the Warren Commission. Many observers believe that De Mohrenschildt, a man with strong conservative leanings and whose close friendship with Oswald is well documented, provides reasonable evidence that Oswald's true political stance was right-wing rather than left-wing.

In any event, De Mohrenschildt is indeed one of the more intriguing Oswald associates. Still living in Dallas, De Mohrenschildt refuses any comment relating to the assassination.

Michael and Ruth Paine

Michael and Ruth Paine were a young married couple who lived in a Dallas suburb and were (like the De Mohrenschildts) close personal friends of Lee and Marina Oswald. It was Michael and Ruth Paine who had taken Marina Oswald into their home after she left Lee, following a marital dispute. It was at the Paine's house, in their small garage, that Oswald supposedly stored his rifle in 1963. And the Warren Commission concluded that Oswald had retrieved his rifle from the Paine's garage on the night before the assassination, smuggling it into the Texas School Book Depository the next morning, disguised as "curtain rods."

Michael and Ruth Paine emerged as key witnesses for the Warren Commission. Ruth Paine's testimony provided at least two interesting points which have become the subjects of continuing interest. First, she told the Warren Commission that the rifle which was found in the Texas School Book Depository, and with which the Warren Commission concluded that Oswald shot Kennedy, was different in appearance from the rifle Oswald owned and stored in her garage. Mrs. Paine raised some question as to whether they were different rifles, testifying that the sling on the rifle in her garage looked quite different from the alleged sling on rifle found in the Depository building.[134]

In the second place, Ruth Paine raised a question regarding Oswald's possible contact with the Dallas FBI — a question which was never answered until 12 years later, in early 1976. In this instance, she told the Warren Commission that Lee Harvey Oswald had told her that he had visited the Dallas FBI office a few days before the assassination, and had delivered some kind of message there.[135] Marina Oswald had also testified that Oswald said he had visited the Dallas FBI office shortly before the assassination. But the Warren Commission (and, of course, Hoover's FBI) had ignored their testimony and had never investigated its various implications.

Long-time Warren Commission critic Sylvia Meagher, author of the definitive work *Accessories After the Fact*, raised questions about this testimony for many years.[136] It was not until 1975, however, that the mysterious circumstances of Oswald's visit to the FBI office were revealed, and Ruth Paine's testimony was finally substantiated. In 1975, it was disclosed that Oswald had indeed delivered a secret letter to the Dallas FBI — a letter which was reportedly threatening in nature — and which was secretly destroyed two days after the assassination, presumably with at least the concurrence of J. Edgar Hoover.

In early 1976, Michael and Ruth Paine became the central focus of yet another mysterious disclosure of long-suppressed assassination evidence. On February 11, 1976, due largely to the invensive investigative research done by Warren Commission scholar Kevin Walsh, the National Archives declassified a key page of Warren Commission Document 206, which had previously been withheld from the public. On this page, which appeared to be based directly upon the log of an FBI wiretap, it was disclosed that a mysterious conversation had been "overheard" during a telephone call placed between Michael Paine's office and his home, very likely between Paine and his wife Ruth. The Commission document (page 66) reports that a "Confidential Informant" who "overheard" the Paine's telephone call

> . . . advised that the male voice was heard to comment that he felt sure that LEE HARVEY OSWALD had killed the President but did not feel OSWALD was responsible, and further stated, "We both know who is responsible."[137]

What the mysterious basis of this remark by Oswald's close friend was, cannot presently be determined. Nor can it be determined what the Warren Commission and the FBI did with the information, other than classify it and thus withhold it from public disclosure. Incredulously, it was later reported in the spring of 1976, that a Dallas telephone repair man had been the "Confidential Informant" who had "overheard" the call.

In spring, 1975, as investigators for the Church Senate Intelligence Committee began to review the circumstances behind the mass of classified FBI and CIA Warren Commission Documents still locked up in the National Archives, they were interested to find that a large number of the withheld classified Documents were directly related to Michael and Ruth Paine and their relatives. Efforts to secure the release of some of these Paine documents from the CIA (through the Freedom of Information Act) have thus far been unsuccessful. The focus of these secret classified files on the Paines still has not been determined.

Marilyn Dorothy Murret

Marilyn Murret, Lee Harvey Oswald's cousin, first housed the Oswald family when they moved to New Orleans after returning from the USSR. Marilyn Murret had lived in Japan during the same period that Lee Harvey Oswald had served in the U-2 program at the CIA base at Atsugi, Japan. It is not known if they visited each other during this time.

Marilyn Murret, strangely enough, seems to have possible connections to a CIA-affiliated group. This information first came to light accidently, due to a mistake in the filing of classified documents at the National Archives. Inadvertently, the first page of classified Warren Commission Document 1080 was released to a Commission critic. This document, an FBI report dated May 22, 1964, was titled "Marilyn Dorothea Murret," and set forth FBI information on Oswald's cousin Marilyn. This FBI information dealt with another Bureau report that stated that "Murret was linked in some manner with the ... apparatus of Professor Harold Isaacs."[138] This page details the background of Professor Harold Isaacs, stating that the former *Newsweek* and *Christian Science Monitor* correspondent was now serving "as research associate at the Center for International Studies at MIT." The FBI report said that a secretary at MIT had stated that "the Center for International Studies is endowed to a great extent by the United States Government. She stated that much of Isaacs' work takes him away from MIT and consists of international travel and concentration on study in India."[139]

It has long been reported that the CIA is the government agency that helps fund the Center for International Studies and some of its personnel. In 1964, in their authoritative book on the CIA, *The Invisible Government*, David Wise and Thomas B. Ross reported, ". . . the MIT Center, which was set up with CIA money in 1950, has adopted many of the practices in effect at the CIA headquarters in Virginia. An armed guard watches over the door and the participating academicians must show badges on entering and leaving."[140]

The exact extent of other classified information regarding Marilyn Murret and her reported links to Professor Isaacs and/or the CIA is not presently known.

William Reily

William Reily, of the William Reily Coffee Company, was the man who first employed "pro-Castro" Lee Harvey Oswald when Oswald moved from Dallas to New Orleans in 1963. William Reily, it turns out, was at that time a financial supporter of the "Free Cuba Committee," sometimes also referred to as the "Crusade to Free Cuba Committee." The "Free Cuba

Committee" was a militant right-wing anti-Castro group with solid connections to the CIA.[141] The "Free Cuba Committee" was one of the anti-Castro exile groups that was merged into the "Cuban Revolutionary Council," which was the large anti-Castro organization coordinated by the CIA. As will be seen in other chapters, the "Free Cuba Committee" figures prominently in various activities involving both CIA-connected and Mafia-connected Cuban exiles. The information that Oswald's first New Orleans employer, William Reily, was a contributor to the anti-Castro group was set forth in Milton Brener's 1969 book, *The Garrison Case: A Study in the Abuse of Power*.[142]

Alexi Davison

Air Force Captain Alexi Davison, M.D., served as the official doctor at the American Embassy in Moscow during the period when Lee Harvey Oswald was living in Russia.

During 1962, Oswald had repeated contact in Moscow with the American Embassy regarding passport and visa matters and travel plans. It was then that Oswald and his Russian wife Marina came into contact with Captain Alexi Davison at the Embassy. There are records to show that during a visit to the Embassy to arrange for passage back to the U.S.,

Oswald and his wife agreed to have Marina undergo a physical examination by Dr. Davison.[143] Not only did Davison examine Marina, according to Warren Commission testimony, he also suggested that Oswald and his wife look up his mother in Atlanta, Georgia, if they were ever in that area.[144] Oswald obviously took Alexi Davison's suggestion seriously, as Davison's mother's name was indeed listed in the personal notebook that was found amid Oswald's possessions after the assassination.[145]

What makes Oswald's contacts with Dr. Davison in Moscow so significant in the eyes of various assassination scholars revolves around just who and what Alexi Davison was. Just five months after the Oswalds left Moscow and returned to America, Alexi Davison was identified by the Soviet Union as a key operative in the single most important CIA espionage network ever uncovered inside Russia. In this now-famous episode, the Russians announced the arrest of Colonel Oleg Penkovskiy, a high-level Soviet intelligence official, and charged him with being a spy for the American CIA and for British Intelligence.[146] The "Penkovskiy Affair" became one of the two or three biggest espionage cases in Soviet-American history. Barely five months after the Russians arrested Col. Penkovskiy, he was convicted of spying and treason and was executed.[147] The Russian government named American Dr. Alexi Davison — Oswald's friendly Embassy acquaintance — as one of the CIA's key contacts and couriers for Col. Penkovskiy.[148]

The Russians stated that Davison's phone number had been found on Col. Penkovskiy at the time of his arrest, and that Davison had also been seen retrieving some of the famous "Penkovskiy Papers" at a CIA intelligence "drop" in Moscow.[149]

On May 6, 1963, at the height of the Penkovskiy affair, Alexi Davison left the USSR and returned to the United States.[150] In 1966, with the publication of *The Penkovskiy Papers*, it was reported that among the secret information that Col. Penkovskiy had passed to the CIA, was classified data on Soviet missiles which had been of significant use to the American government during the 1962 Cuban Missile Crisis.[151] In early 1976, former CIA executive Victor Marchetti disclosed that the CIA had, in effect, also helped to arrange *The Penkovskiy Papers* for publication in the United States.

Beyond the intriguing Oswald contact with Alexi Davison at the American Embassy in Moscow, and Davison's subsequent role in the historic Penkovskiy spying for the CIA, there remains one further piece of information which may possibly be of some significance. When Lee Harvey Oswald and his wife finally returned to the United States, they did in fact make a stopover in Atlanta, Georgia, before going on to Dallas.[152] Whether Oswald made any contact with Alexi Davison's mother there, as Dr. Davison had suggested in Moscow, is not known. Perhaps Oswald's Atlanta stopover was a coincidence; however, it has been established that several faster nonstop flights to Dallas were available that same day — flights that Oswald chose not to make.

The intriguing facts behind the Oswald-Davison contact are expected to be one of the areas of renewed investigation. Alexi Davison is now practicing medicine in Atlanta, Georgia.

Richard E. Snyder

Richard Snyder, an American Embassy official in Moscow, also had contact with Lee Harvey Oswald. Snyder served as Second Secretary at the Embassy and has long been suspected of being an American intelligence operative, most likely of the CIA. Richard

Snyder had in fact previously served as an intelligence officer for the State Department.[153] Informed sources report that Snyder definitely did serve in an "intelligence capacity" at the Embassy during this period.

Snyder was the Embassy official with whom Lee Oswald conferred with at the Embassy following his decision to "renounce" his American citizenship.[154] According to the Warren Commission Report, Oswald told Snyder that he was not only renouncing his US citizenship, but would also turn over to the Russians any information he had regarding his Marine training in a U-2 radar unit.[155] According to his own testimony, Snyder asked Oswald to return to the Embassy two days later to further discuss his citizenship. The Warren Commission stated that Oswald did not return for the second meeting.[156]

Yuri Nosencho

Yuri Nosencho was a top Soviet Intelligence official who "defected" to the United States only two months after the assassination of President Kennedy. His defection was regarded as one of the most significant American intelligence "coups" in many years.

Nosencho, upon his arrival in the United States,

indicated his willingness to provide the CIA with full knowledge of his role as a Russian intelligence officer. As things developed, Yuri Nosencho would soon become a central focus of one of the most intriguing areas of information relating to the assassination.

Nosencho not only had had access to the Russian KGB file on Lee Harvey Oswald, he had also brought an actual copy of it with him when he "escaped" from Russia. The secret "Nosencho File," as it was known, became a subject of consuming interest to CIA officials in Washington. And it was only in the spring of 1975, thirteen years after the assassination, that the contents of this KGB file on Oswald became public.

In early 1975, Daniel Schorr of CBS News disclosed that the KGB's "Oswald file," brought over by Yuri Nosencho, had several startling points to it. In an FBI report on the file, it is revealed that the Russians had given some consideration to using Oswald for various unknown purposes, but that they finally decided he was too "unstable."[157]

The FBI file goes on to state, in what was to become the single most important disclosure from Nosencho that "Nosencho commented that the possibility that Oswald might be a 'sleeper agent' for American intelligence had been considered by the KGB . . ."[158] The exact basis for the Russians' suspicion of the possibility that Lee Harvey Oswald was a CIA agent cannot of course be fully determined.[159] However, most knowledgeable sources agree that the Soviets must have had Oswald under intensive surveillance and would have had some knowledge of Oswald's contact with Alexi Davison at the American Embassy (see preceding profile of Dr. Davison) and other Oswald contacts.

Yuri Nosencho's copy of Oswald's KGB file, it turns out, did not sit well with American CIA officials. Some CIA analysts regarded it as a possible fabrication and began to wonder if Nosencho's "defection" was a possible "set-up" to get the Russians "off the hook" vis-a-vis the Kennedy assassination.[160] Former CIA Counterintelligence Chief James Angleton was particularly suspicious of the Nosencho file and is reliably reported to view the whole episode as "a definite set-up."

While several CIA officials were perhaps disturbed that the KGB regarded Oswald as a possible CIA "sleeper agent," recent information has shown exactly how disturbed they were. In 1975, the Rockefeller Commission (in their final Report) set forth a brief account of an unidentified defector who had been abused and imprisoned by the CIA, and had been held "in solitary confinement under spartan living conditions" by the Agency for three years.[161] What the Rockefeller Commission did not disclose, however, was the identity of this unnamed defector. It was not until March 28, 1976, almost a year later, that Jack Nelson of the *Los Angeles Times* disclosed that the defector mysteriously abused and imprisoned by the CIA was in fact Yuri Nosencho.[162] Apparently the CIA had been able to persuade the Rockefeller Commission to keep Nosencho's identity secret. Daniel Schorr was in the process of determining whether the abused defector and Yuri Nosencho were one and the same when he was suspended from reporting by CBS for his role in leaking the House Intelligence Committee Report. Thus, it was not until the *Los Angeles Times* disclosure (in March, 1976) that the information was confirmed. According to Senate sources, Yuri Nosencho was later released from his unusual imprisonment by the CIA and is now reported to be living freely (though under periodic surveillance) in the Washington area, where he uses a new identity given him by the federal government.

Guy Banister

Guy Banister, who ran a mysterious detective agency in New Orleans in 1963, was formerly in charge of the FBI office in Chicago.

The late Guy Banister was one of the central targets of Jim Garrison, former New Orleans District Attorney, during his investigation of the Dallas assassination.[163] However, Garrison, as will be seen, was not the first person to have investigated Guy Banister's possible connection to the assassination.

The mysterious Banister was also the subject of brief interest by both the FBI and the Warren Commission in the days immediately following the assassination. Ex-FBI Agent Banister was one of the better-known private investigators in New Orleans, and he was known for his various contacts with both right-wing groups as well as Mafia operatives. Banister ran his detective agency in New Orleans at 531 Lafayette Street, the side entrance of the mysterious 544 Camp Street Building, which housed the anti-Castro "Cuban Revolutionary Council."[164]

The "Cuban Revolutionary Council," known as the CRC, was the umbrella group of various anti-Castro exiles that had been formed at the urging of the CIA in the early 1960s.[166] In an effort to consolidate the far-flung network of Cuban militants, the CIA had assigned E. Howard Hunt and Bernard Barker, the future Watergate conspirators, to create the CRC.[166] Both Hunt and Barker have spoken of their deep involvement with the CRC. In *The Invisible Govern-*

ment, David Wise and Thomas Ross wrote that, ". . . by the end of May, 1960, five exile groups had been organized as a revolutionary frente, or front . . . At a meeting in New York, the CIA promised financial support to the newly formed frente . . . The CIA began pumping what eventually became millions of dollars into the frente and its successor, the Cuban Revolutionary Council. The CIA funds were deposited in a Miami bank . . ."[167]

In addition to the fact that the CRC and Guy Banister both conducted their operations from the same Camp Street building, there is also a solid connection between Lee Harvey Oswald and the same premises. The Warren Commission established that Oswald had given "544 Camp Street" as the address for his "Fair Play for Cuba Committee" and that address had been printed on his "Hands Off Cuba" literature in 1963. Whether Oswald ever actually had or shared an office at that address is something the Warren Commission never clarified. Most Commission critics concede that while the strange web of mysterious associations revolving around the Camp Street building is crucial, the same web has proved exceedingly difficult to untangle.

A typical example was provided shortly after Guy Banister's death. Jim Garrison reported that Banister's widow found a large stack of Oswald's "Fair Play for Cuba" literature in her husband's office while she was gathering up his effects. Thus, another Oswald-Banister connection is possible.

Another possible link between Oswald and Banister was the late David Ferrie. It is now widely know that Ferrie worked as a private detective with Guy Banister at the Camp Street building. Ferrie, like Banister, was an active partisan in anti-Castro activities, and was then also working as an investigator for New Orleans Mafia leader Carlos Marcello. Further, David Ferrie had been a participant in the CIA's Bay of Pigs operation in early 1961. (See further reference to David Ferrie in the chapter on "The New Orleans Probe.")

On April 25, 1967, the *New Orleans States Item* reported that Guy Banister had also served as a munitions supplier for the Bay of Pigs advance planning.[168]

Guy Banister's professional investigative career, ironically enough, had begun in the FBI. Banister served as the Special Agent in Charge (SAC) of the Chicago FBI office during the 1940s,[169] and his work in that office provides another interesting association: one of his colleagues in the Chicago FBI office had been Robert Maheu, who later left the FBI in the 1950s. Robert Maheu later became the chief go-between and planner for the CIA and Mafia during their murder plots against Fidel Castro in the early 1960s.[170] Maheu subsequently emerged as a chief object of interest during the Church Senate Intelligence Committee probe into the secret CIA-Mafia assassination apparatus.[171] The extent of the Banister-Maheu relationship is not presently known.

Both the Warren Commission and the FBI briefly investigated Guy Banister and the Camp Street operation immediately after the assassination. Several hours after Kennedy was shot, an employee of Guy Banister, Jack Martin, reported to the New Orleans Police Department that he suspected that David Ferrie was involved in the assassination.[172] Martin told the authorities that he thought that Ferrie had trained Oswald with a telescopic rifle. Though the FBI did look into the charges, they dropped any further investigative work after Martin retracted his story.[173] Some critics point out that Martin's retraction would have been a wise decision at the time, in view of Ferrie's well-known connections with the violent New Orleans Mafia.[174] As the preceding shows, a second reading of the mysterious (and very solid) pieces of information about Guy Banister is necessary to understand the significance of his connections.

William G. Gaudet

William Gaudet is a retired CIA operative who now lives quietly in Waveland, Mississippi, just outside of New Orleans. He is the subject of an intriguing piece of assassination evidence that has only become available in the past two years.

The story dates back to Lee Harvey Oswald's mysterious trip to Mexico City in September, 1963, which became a central focus of Warren Commission probing, and which remains highly mysterious to this day. Even defenders of the Warren Commission findings concede that Oswald's stay in Mexico City, two months before the assassination, is still a matter of insufficient clarity.

Interestingly, the Warren Commission listed the names of all the people in New Orleans who had received Mexican travel visas on the same day that Oswald got his — except for one. The Warren Commission withheld the identity of the person who had received a visa immediately before Oswald received his.[175] This name was not made available to the public for over eleven years, and even then it was only accidentally disclosed. In 1975, an FBI report was inadvertently declassified, and the identity of the man who got his visa ahead of Oswald was finally revealed: William George Gaudet,

Gaudet listed his occupation as a correspondent for a Costa Rican newsletter, the "Latin American Traveller."[176] What makes William Gaudet's previously classified identity so intriguing is that Gaudet himself had admitted to the authorities that he had long been an operative of the CIA.[177] Gaudet had stated that he had worked for the CIA in Latin America in the 1940's, 1950s and 1960s.[178] In a May 13, 1975 taped interview with Bernard Fensterwald, Gaudet disclosed that he had also been present once when Lee Harvey Oswald handed out his "Fair Play for Cuba" literature outside the International Trade Mart in New Orleans.[179]

Gaudet also stated that it had only been a "coincidence" that he had obtained his Mexican visa immediately before Oswald received his, on the same day in 1963. Gaudet stated that there was nothing further to these two separate instances in which he and Oswald crossed paths, other than coincidence.

However, in a further piece of strange, related information, another Warren Commission document indicates that William Gaudet volunteered information to the FBI in 1963 regarding Jack Ruby's presence in New Orleans at an art store. This brief reference to Gaudet is in addition to the long-classified document referring to his mysterious presence at the Mexican visa office right ahead of Oswald.

This other document on Gaudet consists of an FBI report from November 27, 1963, just five days after the President's murder, in which a New Orleans FBI official stated that William Gaudet had called the New Orleans FBI office after Lee Harvey Oswald had been murdered to "advise that he had heard Jack Ruby from Dallas, Texas, had purchased paintings from one Lorenzo Borenstein."[180] The New Orleans FBI office subsequently contacted Borenstein, who confirmed that he knew Ruby and had in fact sold him several paintings in the summer of 1959.[181]

As can be seen, the strange web of information relating to William Gaudet is quite intriguing. Gaudet (by his own admission) worked for the CIA; he also crossed paths with Oswald on two separate documented occasions; and he also subsequently supplied the FBI with new information on Jack Ruby's presence in New Orleans.

Further details about what work William Gaudet was performing for the CIA during this period are not presently available. In the case of Lee Harvey Oswald and William Gaudet, the previously-classified FBI report adds one more case to a growing list of strange instances — instances in which CIA operatives seemed to be traveling in the same apparent path as the alleged assassin of President Kennedy . . . and in this instance, the assassin of the assassin.

Otto Otepka

Otto Otepka, who is now retired and living in a Washington suburb, was the highly controversial Chief Security Officer of the State Department in the late 1950s and early 1960s. In a highly melodramatic series of events, he was dismissed from the State Department at least on the pretext of having given classified material to the Senate Subcommittee on Internal Security.

Otepka's connection, if any, with the events surrounding President Kennedy's death are purely circumstantial but nevertheless intriguing. By what appears to be complete coincidence, on the very day after Oswald was granted a new passport by the State Department in June of 1963, Secretary of State Dean Rusk ordered that Chief Security Officer Otepka be removed from office. Not only did Rusk order that Otepka be locked out of his office, he also had his office safe drilled open and the contents removed. Only a number of years later was it discovered that the only non-routine material in the safe was a half-finished study on American "defectors," including none other than Lee Harvey Oswald.[182]

According to Otepka, he had ordered the study because of the State Department's inability to sort out the so-called American defectors, who had gone to either the USSR or Red China.[183] Neither the CIA nor the military intelligence people would tell the State Department which of the "defectors" were genuine and which were U.S. agents. For their own purposes, State was attempting to make an independent evaluation.

When asked whether Lee Harvey Oswald was one of ours or one of theirs, Otepka barked, "We had not made up our minds when my safe was drilled and we were thrown out of the office." To this day he doesn't know.[184]

Under subpoena, he might provide significant information to the Congressional investigating committee.

Francis Gary Powers

Gary Powers, the American U-2 pilot shot down over Russia in 1960, has also supplied some interesting information regarding Lee Harvey Oswald. In 1970, in a detailed book on his secret U-2 missions for the CIA, Powers stated that he suspected Oswald may have supplied secret U-2 data to the Russians — data that allegedly resulted in Powers being shot down. Powers recounted in his book, *Operation Overflight*, how Lee Oswald had "renounced" his American citizenship at the American Embassy in Moscow on October 31, 1959:

> During the course of the conversation he mentioned that he had already offered to tell the Russians everything he knew about the Marine Corps and his specialty, radar operation . . . . . Six months later my U-2 was shot down.[185]

Gary Powers wrote that he suspected that Oswald had learned enough secret information about the U-2's "height finding" radar gear and radio codes to enable the Soviets to shoot it down.[186] It should be recalled that Oswald served as a U-2 radar operator at the CIA base at Atsugi, Japan and other bases during his hitch with the Marines from 1956 to 1959; and that when he got to the Soviet Union he *said* he was going to give them information about the U-2 program. Powers, who is now working as a helicopter weatherman for a California radio station, states that he has no proof of his suspicions but suggests that such proof may exist in various information withheld by the CIA.

John H. Bowen, alias Albert Osborne

John H. Bowen was a self-described "mission-

ary" who traveled widely throughout the world, using what turned out to be a false identity. John Bowen also rode from Texas to Mexico City on September 26, 1963 on the same bus on which Lee Harvey Oswald was riding. Oswald was making the mysterious trip to Mexico City which still remains one of the central focuses of the various Kennedy assassination investigators.

Because Bowen made the same bus trip to Mexico as Oswald, the FBI sought him out for questioning after the assassination. The FBI's efforts to locate Bowen, however, proved difficult. The FBI finally tracked down a man named Albert Osborne — and Osborne seemed to possess very detailed (though sometimes hazy) information about John Bowen. Finally, after three different interviews by the FBI, "Missionary" Albert Osborne admitted to the FBI men that he was in fact John Bowen, using an alias.[187] Needless to say, the FBI was both irritated and puzzled over John Bowen's use of the secret identity of Albert Osborne.

In an effort to learn more about Osborne-Bowen, General Counsel J. Lee Rankin wrote a letter (classified as Secret) to J. Edgar Hoover on April 24, 1964, in which he outlined the Commission's request that Osborne (Bowen) be made available for further questioning:

> Contact is to be maintained with the Mexican authorities to ascertain whether Albert Alexander Osborne, also known as John Howard Bowen, will be available on reasonably short notice should the Commission decide to request his voluntary or involun-

tary appearance for the taking of testimony.[188]

During the subsequent investigation of Osborne (Bowen) it was established that he had traveled widely as a "missionary," particularly in Latin America. However, Osborne gave no explanation for his use of a false identity in his work. Nor was he ever prosecuted for lying to the FBI on the occasion of their first three interrogations, despite an available Federal statute.

Osborne, who appeared to be in his mid-fifties but claimed to be much older, continued his travels after he returned from the Mexican bus trip of September, 1963. On October 10, Osborne applied for a Canadian passport while visiting New Orleans. On November 13, nine days before the assassination, Osborne embarked on another one-man "missionary tour," heading for Spain and Italy. While some Warren Commission critics sought to determine how Osborne financed his expensive (and almost continuous) travels, no explanation as to his means of support was ever made public.

In the last several years, reports that Osborne (Bowen) was an intelligence operative (possibly of the CIA) have steadily grown. Interestingly, the Warren Commission also discovered that the exact details of who else traveled with Oswald and Osborne on the bus to Mexico were not available. While a partial baggage list from the bus was entered as evidence, the actual passenger list (or "passenger manifest") was never found. Thus a full determination as to who rode on the bus with Oswald was never possible. On March 19, 1964, the manager of the bus terminal involved stated that the original passenger list had been "borrowed by investigators of the Mexican government soon after the assassination." Five days later, on March 24, the same manager disclosed that a duplicate list had also been borrowed by "unidentified investigators" of the Mexican government. The

Mexican government disputed this claim, however, and the actual list was never produced.[189]

The first member of the Warren Commission to publicly voice doubt as to the Commission's conclusions cited this bus trip as a key reason for his suspicion. In mid-January of 1970, the *Washington Post* reported that Senator Richard Russell indicated that he now believed that there had in fact been a secret conspiracy behind the Kennedy assassination.[190] Senator Russell, who had also served in the important position of Chairman of the Senate CIA Oversight Subcommittee, said of Oswald: "I think someone else worked with him." Russell further stated, "There were too many things . . . some of the trips he made to Mexico City and a number of discrepancies in the evidence, or as to his means of transportation, the luggage he had and whether or not anyone was with him — caused me to doubt that he planned it all by himself."[191] (See further reference to the late Senator Russell's suspicions in the chapter on "The Warren Commission.")

Further details about Albert Osborne, alias John Bowen, and his "missionary" travels are not currently available. In his FBI testimony, Osborne denied any relationship with Oswald. It is hoped that Bowen-Osborne's connections will be explored in considerably greater depth in the reinvestigation of the case.

General Charles T. Cabell

Air Force General Charles Cabell served as Deputy Director of the CIA under Allen Dulles, and as Acting Director of the CIA during the Bay of Pigs invasion while Dulles was out of the country. According

 to the Senate Intelligence Committee Report in late 1975, as Deputy Director of the CIA General Cabell had also been a party to the secret CIA-Mafia assassination conspiracies against Fidel Castro.[192] According to the Senate investigation, CIA Director Dulles and Deputy Director Cabell had authorized the CIA-Mafia plots during "the latter part of September, of 1960."[193] According to a secret CIA Inspector General's Report noted by the Senate Intelligence Committee, "With Bissell present, Edwards briefed the Director [Dulles] and the DDCI (Cabell) on the existence of an [assassination] plan involving members of the syndicate."[194] Days later, during the week of September 25th, Robert Maheu, the CIA Support Chief, and Mafia leaders John Roselli, Sam Giancana, and Santos Trafficante met in Miami to set up the secret assassination plans, according to the Senate Committee.[195] General Cabell was later replaced as Deputy Director of the CIA by President Kennedy in April, 1962, due to what Kennedy believed was Cabell's poor performance during the Bay of Pigs invasion and planning.

While Kennedy had been greatly angered over what he believed was the astonishingly negligent invasion planning, he had rejected the advice of some aides to dismiss the CIA and military officials on whom he placed the blame. Pierre Salinger recalled the President remarking, "We really blew this one. How could that crowd at CIA and the Pentagon be this wrong?"[196] Still, as Salinger recalls, Kennedy decided to wait a "decent interval" before replacing the top CIA officials. JFK's former Press Secretary remembers the President stating, "If I'm going to knock some heads together, now isn't the time to do it with everybody looking down the barrel at us."[197]

While Deputy CIA Director Cabell's role in the secret CIA-Mafia assassination conspiracies was revealed in late 1975, the General had been the subject of an even more startling allegation about assasinations two years earlier. On September 16, 1973, the *Washington Post* reported:

> New Orleans District Attorney Jim Garrison, as late as March 1971, was preparing to accuse another person of conspiring to assassinate President John F. Kennedy. Garrison's intended defendant this time was the late Air Force General Charles Cabell, former deputy director of the Central Intelligence Agency . . . [198]

The *Post* reported that only limited details were available about the controversial District Attorney's latest conspiracy theory, but noted that General Cabell's brother, Earl Cabell, had been Mayor of Dallas at the time of the assassination.[199] The *Post* reported that Earl Cabell was aware of Garrison's suspicions that he or his brother may have been involved in the assassination, and had said of Garrison: "He's nuttier than a fruit cake."[200] The *Washington Post* account also stated that Garrison had told a former aide about his suspicions of what he claimed were General Cabell's "mysterious" movements in New Orleans in November of 1963.[201] Garrison reportedly believed that President Kennedy's decision to remove Cabell as Deputy Director of the CIA — and replace other CIA officials as well — had played a part in what Garrison claimed was the eventual assassination conspiracy. As far as is known, however, Garrison never pursued these allegations any further.

General Charles Cabell died of a heart ailment on May 25, 1971, in a Fort Myers clinic. During his retirement, Cabell served as a consultant to Howard

Hughes, in the Hughes Aircraft Corporation, and as a board member of Air America, a CIA proprietary firm. Cabell reportedly worked closely with Robert Maheu during that period.

A longtime colleague of General Cabell, E. Howard Hunt, once described him as "A short, rather aggressive man, Cabell came to CIA with no prior background in covert intelligence, much less in propaganda or political-action operations."[202] Hunt had first worked with Charles Cabell in 1954, during the famous CIA covert operation that led to the overthrow of the Guatemalan government of leftist Jacobo Arbenz.[203] Hunt had served as the CIA's Chief of Political Action for the Guatemalan operation, with General Cabell as his coordinating superior.[204] Frank Wisner, a former top CIA official who committed suicide in 1966, also served as a coordinator of the operation.[205]

E. Howard Hunt had also worked closely with Deputy Director Cabell during the 1961 Bay of Pigs invasion, in which Hunt played a leading role, once again as Chief of Political Action.[206]

During the Bay of Pigs, General Cabell (then serving as Acting CIA Director due to Allen Dulles' absence from the country) had a confrontation with President Kennedy over the issue of air cover for the floundering invasion. Despite assurances that additional air strikes against Cuba would not be necessary — assurances that Kennedy had exacted from Dulles, Cabell, and other CIA higher-ups — Agency officials requested further air strikes against the island as the CIA's Cuban exile force was being driven back by Castro's large army.

In their award-winning account of CIA activities, *The Invisible Government*, David Wise and Thomas B. Ross reported the details surrounding this Kennedy-Cabell confrontation. After Kennedy first refused the air cover request, "Bissell and General Charles T. Cabell, the CIA's Deputy Director, hurried to the State Department to appeal to Secretary of State

Dean Rusk."[207] Soon thereafter, "From his office in the State Department, Rusk telephoned Kennedy at Glen Ora. He told him that Cabell and Bissell were there and believed the [air] strike should go ahead as planned. The President said no."[208] Hours later, according to Wise and Ross, after midnight, Cabell made a final plea to President Kennedy to order American air cover for the retreating Cuban exile force:

> At 4 o'clock a.m. Cabell could stand it no longer. He decided to appeal again to Rusk.
> Cabell drove through the darkened capital to Rusk's hotel. In Rusk's apartment, he again expressed his fears . . . Despite the hour, the Secretary of State called the President once more . . . This time Cabell did speak directly to him. In answer to the CIA official's pleadings, the President's reply was still negative.[209]

Interestingly, while General Charles Cabell's knowledge of the CIA-Mafia assassination conspiracies was set forth by the Senate Intelligence Committee, there are few specifics available about his exact role. This lack of detailed information regarding Cabell's involvement in the plots was apparently due to a rather strange decision of future CIA Director Richard Helms.

The first official accounting of these plots had been secretly prepared in April and May of 1967, at the direction of President Johnson, who had ordered CIA Director Richard Helms to have the CIA Inspector General prepare a detailed report on the plots.[210] According to the Senate Intelligence Committee Report on the Kennedy Assassination, Johnson had ordered the secret CIA report prepared because he was then suspicious that the CIA-Mafia plots may have somehow led to the assassination of John F. Kennedy.[211]

In any event, for reasons that the Senate Intelligence Committee were unable to establish, General Cabell was never interviewed during the preparation of the CIA Inspector General's Report. Even though CIA-Mafia assassination coordinators William Harvey and Sheffield Edwards were extensively questioned for the report, former Deputy CIA Director Charles Cabell was never contacted.

Thus, without a Cabell interview in 1967, and with his death in May, 1971, only limited information on Cabell's role in the plots was available to the Senate Intelligence Committee in 1975 and 1976. An attorney who served on the Senate Committee and worked extensively on their investigation, later commented, "There just wasn't much information around on Cabell . . . very, very little."

Jack Crichton

Jack Crichton is a wealthy Dallas oilman who volunteered his services to the Dallas Police Department as a translator for Russian-born Marina Oswald shortly after the assassination.[212] Jack Crichton translated for Marina during her initial questioning by the Dallas authorities in the crucial hours immediately after her husband Lee had been arrested.[213] While Crichton's role as interpreter on that day is mentioned in at least two Warren Commission documents, the exact details of how he became involved in assisting the Dallas police are unclear. Interestingly, Jack Crichton was, by his own admission, a former Army Intelligence operative.[214]

Crichton was also a prominent Dallas oilman whose conservative political activities were well-known throughout Dallas. Crichton had in fact once been a GOP gubernatorial candidate in Texas. At the present time, Crichton is still active in various business activities in the Dallas area.

1. *Senate Intelligence Committee Report on Foreign Assassinations*, pp. 48, 102.
2. Ibid., p. 102.
3. *Washington Post*, July 31, 1975.
4. *Senate Intelligence Committee Report on Foreign Assassinations*, p. 71.
5. Ibid.
6. *Washington Post*, July 31, 1975.
7. *Senate Intelligence Committee Report on Foreign Assassinations*, p. 71.
8. R. Harris Smith, *OSS: The Secret History of America's First Central Intelligence Agency* (New York: Delta Books Edition, 1973), p. 86.
9. Anthony Cave Brown, editor, *The Secret War Report Of The OSS* (New York: Berkley Publishing Corp., 1976), p. 190.
10. Ibid., p. 209.
11. Ibid., p. 217.
12. Martin A. Gosch and Richard Hammer, *The Last Testament of Lucky Luciano* (New York: Dell Publishing Company Inc., 1976) pp. 262-277.
13. Nicholas Gage, *Mafia, U. S. A.* (New York: Dell Publishing Company Inc., 1973), pp. 144-148.
14. Gosch and Hammer, *The Last Testament of Lucky Luciano*, p. 263.
15. Ibid., pp. 275-276.
16. Ibid.
17. Ibid.
18. Alfred W. McCoy, Cathleen B. Read, and Leonard P. Adams III, *The Politics Of Heroin In Southeast Asia* (New York: Harper Colophon Books Edition, 1973).
19. *New York Times*, August 30, 1971.

20. *NBC Nightly News*, July 15, 1971; McCoy, Read, and Adams, *The Politics of Heroin In Southeast Asia*, p. 189.
21. *Washington Post*, June 13, 1966.
22. *Time*, October 11, 1976.
23. Ibid., February 10, 1975.
24. Ibid., January 13, 1975.
25. Ibid., June 9, 1975.
26. Ibid.
27. Anson; *"They've Killed The President!"* p. 297.
28. *New York Times*, December 22, 1974.
29. "30 May 1975" CIA memorandum to David W. Belin, Rockefeller Commission, declassified: Spring, 1976.
30. Ibid.
31. Warren Commission Document 631.
32. *New York Times*, January 17, 1975.
33. Ibid.
34. "13 January 1969" CIA memorandum from Chief of Counterintelligence James Angleton to FBI Director J. Edgar Hoover, "Subject: Garrison and the Kennedy Assassination: Bernard Fensterwald et al."
35. Ibid.
36. *Washington Post*, February 23, 1976.
37. Ibid.
38. Ibid.
39. Brown, *The Secret War Report of the OSS*, p. 204.
40. *Senate Intelligence Committee Report on the Kennedy Assassination*, p. 69.
41. Ibid., p. 31.
42. Ibid., p. 69.
43. *Senate Intelligence Committee Report on Foreign Assassinations*, pp. 74-85.
44. Ibid.
45. Ibid., pp. 102, 134.
46. Ibid., p. 143.
47. Ibid.
48. Ibid.
49. Ibid.
50. Ibid., p. 144.
51. Ibid.
52. Ibid., p. 145.
53. Ibid.
54. *Washington Post*, October 10, 1976.
55. Ibid.
56. Ibid.
57. Ibid.
58. Ibid.
59. *Senate Intelligence Committee Report on Foreign Assassinations*, p. 148.

60. Ibid., pp. 132-133.
61. Ibid., pp. 83-84.
62. Ibid., p. 133.
63. Ibid., p. 105.
64. Ibid.
65. Ibid., pp. 84-85.
66. Jack Anderson column, January 18, 1971, September 7, 1976.
67. *Senate Intelligence Committee Report on Foreign Assassinations*, p. 104.
68. Ibid.
69. *Washington Post*, October 10, 1976.
70. Ibid.
71. Ibid.
72. Ibid.
73. Ibid.
74. Warren Commission Exhibit 2980.
75. May 19, 1964 Warren Commission letter from General Counsel J. Lee Rankin to CIA Deputy Director for Plans Richard Helms.
76. Warren Commission Exhibit 2980.
76a. September 19, 1964 CIA memorandum from Thomas Karamessines to Warren Commission General Counsel J. Lee Rankin, "Information Concerning Jack Ruby (aka Jack Rubenstein) and His Activities."
77. March 12, 1964 CIA Memorandum For The Record, "Subject: Meeting with the Warren Commission."
77a. Ibid.
78. Testimony of Richard Helms, July 17, 1975; *Senate Intelligence Committee Report on the Kennedy Assassination*, p. 70.
79. *Senate Intelligence Committee Report on Foreign Assassinations*, pp. 107-108.
80. Ibid., pp. 99-100.
81. Ibid., p. 100.
82. Ibid., p. 102.
83. Ibid., p. 100.
84. Ibid., p. 101.
85. Ibid.
86. Ibid.
87. Ibid.
88. Ibid., p. 164.
89. Ibid., p. 106.
90. Ibid.
91. Ibid., p. 105.
92. Ibid., p. 103.
93. Ibid., p. 102.
94. Ibid., p. 103.
95. *Senate Intelligence Committee Report on Foreign*

Assassinations, pp. 37, 43-47, 182.
96. Ibid., p. 181.
97. Ibid.
98. Ibid., p. 182.
99. Ibid.
100. Ibid.
101. Ibid., p. 43.
102. Ibid., p. 142.
103. Ibid.
104. Ibid., p. 4.
105. Ibid., p. 37.
106. Ibid.
107. Ibid.
108. Ibid., p. 43.
109. Ibid.
110. Ibid.
111. Ibid., p. 44.
112. Ibid., p. 45.
113. Ibid.
114. Ibid., p. 46.
115. Ibid., p. 48.
116. Ibid., p. 47.
117. Ibid., p. 48.
118. Ibid., pp. 46-47.
119. Ibid., p. 182.
120. Ibid., pp. 74-75, 80-84.
121. Ibid., p. 75.
122. Ibid.
123. Jack Anderson column, January 18, 1971.
124. Ibid.
125. *Senate Intelligence Committee Report on Foreign Assassinations*, pp. 74-84.
126. Ibid., p. 77.
127. Ibid., p. 76.
128. Ibid., p. 75.
129. CBS Reports Inquiry, "The American Assassins," Part Two, Dan Rather, November 26, 1975.
130. *Senate Intelligence Committee Report on Foreign Assassinations*, p. 84.
131. Warren Commission Volume 9, p. 183.
132. Warren Commission Report, p. 262.
133. Warren Commission Volume 9, p. 96.
134. Warren Commission Volume 3, p. 25.
135. Warren Commission Volume 1, p. 57; Warren Commission Volume 3, p. 18.
136. Meagher, *Accessories After The Fact*, p. 216.
137. Warren Commission Document 206, p. 66.
138. Warren Commission Document 942, FBI report.
139. Warren Commission Documents 1080, 942.

140. David Wise and Thomas B. Ross, *The Invisible Government* (New York: Vintage Books Edition, 1974), p. 20.
141. Ibid., p. 27.
142. Milton Brener, *The Garrison Case: A Study in the Abuse of Power* (New York: Clarkson N. Potter, 1969), p. 47.
143. Warren Commission Documents 235, 409,87(SS) 569.
144. Ibid.
145. Warren Commission Exhibit 18; Warren Commission Volume 16, p. 50.
146. *The Penkovskiy Papers* (New York: Avon Books, 1966), p. 24.
147. Ibid., p. 359.
148. Ibid., pp. 360, 366.
149. Ibid., pp. 366-367.
150. Ibid., p. 359.
151. Ibid., p. 357.
152. Warren Commission Volume 16, p. 616; Warren Commission Volume 18, p. 16.
153. Warren Commission Report, pp. 617-618.
154. Ibid.
155. Ibid.
156. Ibid.
157. *Los Angeles Times*, Jack Nelson, March 28, 1976.
158. Ibid.
159. Ibid.
160. Ibid.
161. *Rockefeller Commission Final Report*, p. 170.
162. *Los Angeles Times*, Jack Nelson, March 28, 1976.
163. Harold Weisberg, *Oswald In New Orleans* (New York: Canyon Books, 1967), pp. 326-348.
164. Ibid.
165. Wise and Ross, *The Invisible Government*, pp. 20, 27.
166. Hunt, *Give Us This Day*, pp. 40-50, 182-189.
167. Wise and Ross, *The Invisible Government*, pp. 20, 27.
168. *New Orleans States-Item*, April 25, 1967.
169. "The Garrison Commission on the Assassination of President Kennedy," William Turner, *Ramparts*, January, 1968.
170. *Senate Intelligence Committee Report on Foreign Assassinations*, pp. 74-85.
171. Ibid.
172. New Orleans Police Report Item #K-126-34-63; FBI File #89-69, New Orleans Office; Warren Commission Document 75.
173. Ibid.
174. "The Mafia, The CIA, And The Kennedy Assassination," Milton Viorst, *The Washingtonian*, November 1975.
175. Warren Commission Documents 75, 588, 613, 652.

176. Ibid.; Taped interview with William Gaudet, May 13, 1975.
177. Warren Commission Documents 75, 588, 613, 652.
178. Ibid.
179. Taped interview with William Gaudet, May 13, 1975.
180. Warren Commission Exhibit 2880; Warren Commission Volume 26, pp. 337-338.
181. Ibid.
182. Interview with Otto Otepka, Summer of 1971.
183. Ibid.
184. Ibid.
185. Francis Gary Powers, *Operation Overflight* (New York: Holt, Rhinehart, Winston, 1970), pp. 357-359.
186. Ibid.
187. April 24, 1964 letter from Warren Commission General Counsel J. Lee Rankin to FBI Director J. Edgar Hoover; Warren Commission Volume 24, pp. 623-624.
188. Ibid.
189. Warren Commission Volume 24, p. 624.
190. *Washington Post*, January 19, 1970.
191. Ibid.
192. *Senate Intelligence Committee Report on Foreign Assassinations*, pp. 91-98.
193. Ibid., pp. 94, 98.
194. Ibid., p. 98.
195. Ibid., p. 97.
196. Salinger, *With Kennedy*, p. 148.
197. Ibid., p. 154.
198. *Washington Post*, September 16, 1973.
199. Ibid.
200. Ibid.
201. Ibid.
202. E. Howard Hunt, *Undercover* (New York: Berkley Publishing Corporation, 1974), p. 93.
203. Ibid., pp. 96-100, 115.
204. Wise and Ross, *The Invisible Government*, p. 172; Hunt, *Undercover*, pp. 96-100.
205. Ibid.
206. Hunt, *Give Us This Day*, pp. 23, 38-41.
207. Wise and Ross, *The Invisible Government*, p. 21.
208. Ibid.
209. Ibid., p. 22.
210. *Senate Intelligence Committee Report on the Kennedy Assassination*, pp. 85-86.
211. Ibid.
212. Warren Commission Document 386; Warren Commission Volume 9, pp. 102, 106.
213. Ibid.
214. Ibid.

CHAPTER SIX

Hoover's FBI

"The thing you've got to remember about the [Warren Commission] investigation," a former staff counsel recently remarked, "is that we produced conclusions which were only as good as the material the FBI submitted to us. Like you say — I'll admit it — the FBI did our investigating. Period."

And that was the problem, as the Church Committee concluded in their June, 1976 report. The Warren Commission had been totally reliant on the investigative reports and functions of J. Edgar Hoover's FBI. As the Committee reported, Hoover had been so strongly supportive of the FBI's almost instant finding of a "lone leftist assassin" that he vehemently urged President Johnson not to appoint the actual Warren Commission. For J. Edgar Hoover, the assassination was an open and shut case within three days after it occurred, and the investigation was, for all intents and purposes, just about over with.

Yet now, over thirteen years later, the investigation — for the FBI — is only just beginning. And this time, as the Church Committee probe indicated in late 1975 and early 1976, the FBI itself is a suspect of sorts, with numerous documented instances of the Bureau's cover-up of information on both Lee Harvey Oswald and Jack Ruby. The main question, as the Church Committee admittedly left open, is "Why?"

What kind of cover-up and for what reasons?

There is no doubt J. Edgar Hoover knew a lot more about the assassination than he was telling. That, coupled with his virtually unchallengeable power in the nation's capital, provided the wall (indeed the stonewall) which now must be carefully dismantled in order to establish the truth about the President's murder.

The Church Committee was surprised to discover that Hoover had ordered secret dossiers prepared on the members of the Warren Commission. While Hoover's penchant for keeping files on politicians was well-known, the disclosure of these dossiers had a chilling effect on most observers.

About two years ago, a former Hoover friend who became somewhat fearful of the FBI's tactics offered a vivid interpretation of Hoover's power. Former Chairman of the House Judiciary Committee Emanuel Celler recalled:

> The source of his power derived from the fact that he was the head of an agency that in turn had tremendous power, power of surveillance, power of control over the lives and destinies of every man in the nation. He had a dossier on every member of Congress and every member of the Senate . . . He had no right to have such dossiers. But he had them, no question about it.[1]

Upon entering office, the Kennedy brothers actively sought to curb many of the already burgeoning excesses and abuses of the freewheeling *modus operandi* of J. Edgar Hoover. As Kennedy aide Kenneth O'Donnell has said, "It just gets back to the crux of one thing — Bobby is the boss, and for the first time in Hoover's life he can't go over the boss's head."[2]

The Kennedys' relationship with the aging FBI Director soon grew beyond coldness and acrimony towards outright bitterness and contempt. While JFK initially viewed keeping Hoover as a prudent political decision, by late 1962 he had begun to lay plans for a post-Hoover Federal Bureau of Investigation. William Hundley, then head of the Justice Department's organized crime section (and a criminal lawyer for former Attorney General John Mitchell during Watergate) has recalled:

> I am convinced that the thing that finally destroyed their relationship was that Bobby mentioned to too many people who complained to him about Hoover that, "Look, just wait," and we all got the message that they were going to retire him after Jack got re-elected and Hoover hit seventy. And it got back to him.[3]

David Powers, one of President Kennedy's closest associates, gives a slightly milder account of the plans to "dump" Hoover: ". . . the word would not be dumped. The President would never, never use that word . . . maybe that could have been what he was talking to him about that three weeks before the assassination when he saw him."[4]

O'Donnell and Powers surprisingly disclosed that President Kennedy and Director Hoover met with each other only a mere handful of times during the Kennedy Presidency, excluding purely ceremonial occasions.[5] O'Donnell recalls roughly only five such Kennedy-Hoover meetings: one during the Bay of

Pigs episode; one when Hoover apprised JFK of information pertaining to the anti-Castro CIA-Mafia assassination plots; one during the early civil rights crisis at the University of Mississippi; and perhaps two other meetings during 1963, and speaks of "the distance" between the two men. O'Donnell has noted, "I think Bobby perhaps got along with Hoover better than the President did."[6] David Powers believes that the question of Hoover's retirement may well have been the subject of an "off-record lunch" between Kennedy and Hoover shortly before the assassination. Powers states, "He [Hoover] had a long lunch with the President and Bobby [on October 31st] and, as you know, three weeks later we went to Dallas."[7]

J. Edgar Hoover

FBI Director J. Edgar Hoover, is now coming under increasing scrutiny for his actions — and inactions — in the wake of the assassination. Due to the fact that the Commission decided not to set up an independent investigatory staff, Hoover and his top aides were directly responsible for most of the Commission's investigative work, and though deeply involved in virtually every aspect of the Dallas inquiry, engaged in withholding of information from the Warren Commission relating to many crucial areas.

On June 23, 1976, the Church Senate Intelligence Committee released its long-awaited Report on The Investigation of the Assassination of President John F. Kennedy: Performance of the Intelligence Agencies. This Report, which was the culmination of a year-and-a-half-long probe of the investigation, placed heavy criticism on J. Edgar Hoover and his top FBI aides, and disclosed new documentary evidence relating to Hoover's firm judgment — made within two days of the assassination — that Lee Harvey Oswald was a lone assassin, and that the FBI had all the evidence it needed to prove it. The Report noted that Hoover didn't believe there was any real need to investigate further and had discounted the possibility of any kind of conspiracy.

The Church Committee disclosed a previously secret Hoover memo regarding a discussion he had had with LBJ aide Walter Jenkins several hours after Jack Ruby murdered Oswald. The November 24, 1963, memo stated that, "The thing I am most concerned about, and so is Mr. Katzenbach, is having something issued so we can convince the public that Oswald is the real assassin."[8] Five days later, on November 29, 1963, in another secret memo released by the Church Committee, Hoover told his top aides, including Clyde Tolson, Cartha DeLoach, and William Sullivan, that he was opposing President Johnson's proposed plan to set up an independent commission to investigate the Kennedy murder: "The President stated he wanted to get by just with my file and my report. I told him I thought it would be very bad to have a rash of investigations. He then indicated the only way to stop it is to appoint a high-level committee to evaluate my report and tell the House and Senate not to go ahead with the investigation. I stated that would be a three-ring circus."[9]

The Church Committee investigators, directed by Senators Richard Schweiker and Gary Hart, also received evidence that Hoover himself had leaked a copy of the initial FBI assassination report to the press — a report that set forth Hoover's conclusions that Oswald had acted alone and which stated that there was an absence of any evidence of conspiracy. Hoover's Assistant FBI Director, William Sullivan, told the Church Committee that Hoover had leaked the secret FBI report about ten days after the President's murder to "blunt the drive for an independent investigation of the assassination."[10]

The Church report also revealed that Hoover's penchant for compiling secret dossiers on the personal backgrounds, such as the sexual and drinking habits, of various FBI targets, also extended as far as members of the Warren Commission:

> After the Warren Commission had been established, each time Hoover received word that a particular person was being considered for the Commission staff, he asked "what the Bureau had" on the individual. Although derogatory information pertaining to both Commission members and staff was brought to Mr. Hoover's attention, the Bureau has informed the Committee staff that there is no documentary evidence which indicates that such information was disseminated while the Warren Commission was in session.[11]

Hoover's desire to compile damaging "derogatory information" about the members of the Warren Commission and its staff had continued even after the Commission ended its investigation. The Church report disclosed:

> On September 29, 1964, Mr. Hoover, after reading a *Washington Post* article captioned "Praise is Voiced for Staff Engaged in Warren Report," directed that the Bureau's files on the eighty-four staff members listed in the article "be checked." On October 2, 1964,

the Director was informed that "Bureau files contained derogatory information concerning the following individuals and their relatives."[12]

What other sins of commission or omission, if any, were committed by J. Edgar Hoover in relation to the investigation of the death of President Kennedy will have to await the re-investigation of the murder — presumably a re-investigation in which the FBI will *not* play the role of chief investigator.

James Hosty

James Hosty was the Special Agent in Dallas assigned to handle the FBI's "internal security" case of Lee Harvey Oswald. Hosty had interviewed Marina Oswald during the month before the assassination and had spent considerable time on the Oswald "case." Several hours after JFK's death, questions began to arise about FBI Agent Hosty's exact relationship to Lee and Marina Oswald. His immediate FBI superior, Gordon Shanklin, asked Dallas Police Chief Jesse Curry not to disclose that Hosty had had previous dealings with Oswald.[13] Chief Curry agreed to "sit on" the information, and in fact, he never disclosed Shanklin's request until late 1975, when the *New York Times* broke the story.[14]

Just hours after the assassination, Hosty became embroiled in another incident relating to Oswald. When Hosty entered the Dallas police room where suspect Oswald was being interrogated, Oswald jumped from his seat, pounded his fists on the table, and accused Hosty of twice accosting his wife Marina in a threatening manner.[15] (Marina Oswald later told the Warren Commission that FBI men had in fact intimidated her in the months before the assassination, during their probe of Oswald's "pro-Castro" activities.[16])

The FBI's attempts to cover up Hosty's previous dealings with Oswald shifted into even higher gear following his murder by Ruby, who had been contacted on at least nine occasions by the Dallas FBI for service as a possible informant.[17] One of the FBI's more pressing problems was Oswald's personal notebook, confiscated on the day of the assassination, in which he had written FBI Agent James Hosty's name, address, telephone number and auto license number.[18] However, when the FBI Director authorized turning the notebook over to the Warren Commission, the page with the information about Hosty was missing. The FBI did not tell the Warren Commission of that notebook entry. Fortunately, however, rumors began circulating in the press that Hosty's name had indeed been in Oswald's notebook; and finally, on February 11, 1964, the FBI informed the Commission about the missing page.[19] On that day, the FBI sent a "supplemental report" to the Warren Commission admitting that Hosty's name had been excised from Oswald's notebook. No explanation was given for the action.[20]

It was not until August, 1975, that the single most important incident involving Hosty and Oswald was finally uncovered. On August 31, 1975, the *Dallas Time Herald* disclosed the now-famous story of how Lee Harvey Oswald had delivered a secret note addressed to James Hosty at the Dallas FBI office a few days before the assassination — a note that the FBI secretly destroyed two hours after Oswald was murdered.[21] Although Agent Hosty immediately denied the *Dallas Times Herald* story, by Tom Johnson, a former top aide to President Johnson, the incident was later confirmed by the FBI, and is currently still being investigated for possible criminal prosecution by the Justice Department. When first questioned by the *Times Herald*, Hosty stated, "I don't know anything about that ... I don't know what you're talking about ... I think I'm right, so, I'll just go along and take orders."[22] Subsequently, it was revealed that it had been James Hosty himself who destroyed the secret Oswald note, on the orders of FBI superiors, by flushing it down a toilet in the FBI office.[23]

Though he has now admitted his role in the affair, and may eventually face prosecution, Special Agent Hosty is still with the FBI, working in the Kansas City office.

Gordon Shanklin

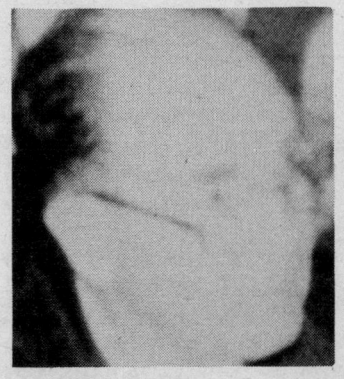

Gordon Shanklin, as Special Agent-in-Charge of the Dallas FBI office at the time of the assassination, was James Hosty's superior and had been involved in the mysterious post-assassination actions involving Hosty and the FBI. Only recently has he retired from the FBI, after a lifetime of service.

During subcommittee hearings chaired by Representative Don Edwards in

October of 1975, Agent James Hosty testified under oath that it was Gordon Shanklin who passed the orders to him to destroy the secret Oswald note.[24] Shanklin, under oath, denied this. Thus, it is clear that either FBI agent Hosty or FBI agent Shanklin perjured himself. A strong consensus of Warren Commission critics believes that Hosty was telling the truth. Norman Kempster, the *Washington Star* reporter who extensively covered that Edwards investigation, pointed out the inherent contradictions in the version of events set forth by Gordon Shanklin. Kempster, now with the *Los Angeles Times*, wrote:

> Somebody lied to the FBI investigators this year about a twelve-year cover-up in the Bureau's Dallas field office of a letter written by Lee Harvey Oswald just a few days before the murder of President John F. Kennedy. That seems to be the one uncontroverted fact that emerged from the first full-scale Congressional hearing to examine the role played by the FBI in the Warren Commission investigation of the November 22, 1963 assassination.[25]

Warren C. deBrueys

Warren deBrueys was the FBI Special Agent in New Orleans assigned to report on various political groups, and Commission critics have long suspected him of having had some connection with Lee Harvey Oswald, when Oswald lived in New Orleans in the

months preceding the assassination.

It was not until late 1975, however, that a substantive charge along these lines was made against deBrueys.

A known FBI informer in New Orleans named Orest Pena, whose allegations were first publicized by CBS News reporters Dan Rather and Bruce Hall, stated that he had seen FBI Agent Warren deBrueys and Lee Oswald meeting together on "numerous occasions" in New Orleans.[26] In an interview for CBS, which was broadcast on November 26, 1975, Orest Pena said that he, himself, was then serving as an informant for deBrueys. Pena charged that he'd seen deBrueys and Oswald meeting together in a Greek restaurant in the French Quarter of New Orleans.[27] While Warren deBrueys told CBS that he did have repeated contact with Pena, he denied having had any contact with Oswald: "I have never seen Lee Harvey Oswald at any time in my life personally, or — nor have I talked to him by telephone knowingly. I've had absolutely no contact, no personal knowledge, firsthand contact with Lee Harvey Oswald . . . He was not my informant, and I have no information whatsoever that he had ever been an informant for the FBI."[28]

Orest Pena made another serious charge against Warren deBrueys. Pena had been questioned by the Warren Commission in 1964, and he had been asked about an allegation that Lee Harvey Oswald had met with several men in Pena's New Orleans bar on a number of occasions. Pena testified that this was untrue. However, he later changed his testimony, saying he had been scared; and admitted seeing Oswald in his bar. In his CBS interview, Pena stated that Warren deBrueys had "threatened" him into giving false information to the Warren Commission: "About ten days before I came — went to the — to testify at the Warren Commission, could be less than ten days, and he [Warren deBrueys] came and he called me from behind the bar and said he wanted to talk to me . . . He told me he was very, very nervous, very nervous; and he told me, 'If you ever talk anything about me, I will get rid — get rid of your ass.' Just in those words."[29] deBrueys denied Pena's charge and stated that he had never made such a threat.[30]

Interestingly, FBI informant Orest Pena had been active in Cuban exile activities in New Orleans, and had of course been a Bureau source on what was happening in the different exile groups.[31] Pena had particularly been involved with the New Orleans branch of the Cuban Revolutionary Council, the largest of the Cuban exile groups established by the CIA during the planning of the Bay of Pigs invasion.[32]

Pena had worked closely with Sergio Arcacha Smith, the director of the Council in New Orleans, and Smith's close associate, David Ferrie.[33]

Interestingly, Orest Pena had charged that FBI Agent Warren deBrueys was involved with the New Orleans Cuban Revolutionary Council, and had been a participant in various Council meetings.[34] While deBrueys might have been assigned by the FBI to investigate or infiltrate the right-wing Cuban exile group, Orest Pena told the Warren Commission that deBrueys had participated in the Council meetings on his own, and further that the other members all knew that he was an FBI employee.[35]

If Orest Pena's account is true, it would mean that Agent deBrueys was actually participating in the same Cuban exile activities and meetings as David Ferrie, the mysterious figure who helped coordinate the Council in New Orleans.

Warren deBrueys currently serves as the Special Agent-in-Charge (SAC) of the highly-coveted FBI Office in Puerto Rico.

Jack Ruby

Among the more interesting connections of the man who silenced Lee Oswald (many of which are covered in other chapters), was a connection to the Dallas FBI office. And it is this relationship between Jack Ruby and the Dallas FBI that was one of the more closely-guarded secrets of both the Warren Commission and the FBI. It was not until ten years after the Kennedy assassination that the existence of this Ruby-FBI relationship first became public. Just two years ago, the National Archives declassified a letter from J. Edgar Hoover to Warren Commission General Counsel J. Lee Rankin, dated February 27, 1964, in which he told the Commission of some new information about Jack Ruby, FBI information that "was obtained through a search of all files in the Dallas office wherein references to Jack Ruby appeared":

> For your information, Ruby was contacted by an Agent of the Dallas Office on March 11, 1959 in view of his position as a night club operator who might have knowledge of the criminal element in Dallas. He was advised of the Bureau's jurisdiction in criminal matters, and he expressed a willingness to furnish information along these lines. He was subsequently contacted on eight occasions between March 11, 1959 and October 2, 1959, but he furnished no information whatever and further contacts

with him were discontinued. Ruby was never paid any money, and he was never at any time an informant of this Bureau."[36]

The declassified FBI documents identify Dallas FBI Agent Charles W. Flynn as the Agent who established these contacts with Ruby.[37] Flynn, who is reportedly still working for the FBI, has never been reached for possible comment on his dealings with Ruby. Although the FBI still denies that Ruby was a Bureau informant, the fact that he was contacted on at least nine occasions during a seven-month period in 1959 by the Dallas FBI, suggests that he was indeed an informant. Most federal and state law enforcement personnel who are aware of these contacts believe that their mere frequency suggests quite a bit more to the relationship than Hoover was admitting. Interestingly, these FBI contacts occurred during the same months in which Ruby made at least two trips to Havana, Cuba — trips which the Warren Commission was only able to investigate in a limited way.[38] The Commission established that Ruby travelled to Cuba in 1959 to visit his close friend, Lewis McWillie, who paid Ruby's travel expenses.[39] Sixteen years later, in 1975, the Church Senate Intelligence Committee disclosed that Mafia leader Santos Trafficante, an employer of Lewis McWillie, had been the key Mafia figure used by the CIA in 1960 to try to assassinate Fidel Castro, in a plot that also involved Chicago Mafia leader Sam Giancana and John Roselli.[40]

John Quigley

John Quigley was another FBI Special Agent in the Bureau's New Orleans office who had contact with Lee Oswald on at least one occasion. In the summer of 1963, during the same period that Oswald organized his mysterious "Fair Play for Cuba Committee," he was involved in a brief fist fight in New Orleans with a leading anti-Castro Cuban exile leader, a fist fight which landed him in jail. Upon being arrested, according to New Orleans police records, Oswald immediately requested that the FBI be contacted and that he be allowed to meet with an FBI representative. In response to this somewhat unusual request, Special Agent John Quigley showed up at the station to confer with Oswald.[41] Quigley's report shed little light on Oswald's request to see someone from the New Orleans FBI; according to the report, Oswald never explained why he made the request.[42] Quigley also reported that Oswald talked mainly about his activities with the "Fair Play for Cuba Committee" during the course of their hour-and-a-half discussion.[43] Little else is known about the episode.

John Fain

John Fain, an FBI Special Agent working out of the Fort Worth, Texas office in 1962, was also involved in investigating Oswald. On August 15, 1962, John Fain and another FBI man interviewed Oswald near his home in Fort Worth.[44] Some Commission critics have voiced suspicions over the exact circumstances of this meeting, and suggest that Oswald may have been serving as an FBI informant at that time. An FBI report on the meeting — a report which was not mentioned by the Warren Commission Report — stated "Oswald agreed to report to the FBI any information concerning contacts or attempted contacts by Soviets under suspicious circumstances . . ."[45] According to Fain's account of his meeting, he and his FBI colleague had parked their car near Oswald's home, and had approached him as he walked down the street.[46] Then, according to Fain, they asked Oswald if they could talk to him in their car. Fain stated that "we felt if we talked to him there in the car informally, he would better cooperate with us."[47] Agent Fain also stated: "Actually he invited us in when we stopped him. He said, you come in the house?' And I said, 'Well, we will just talk here. We will be alone to ourselves and we will be informal, and just fine.' So he got in the car."[48]

Some Commission critics have pointed out that the Agents' refusal to speak with Oswald in his house and their preference for talking to him in their car seems to indicate a desire to avoid being overheard. The fact that Oswald apparently offered to provide information to the FBI during the same meeting raises further suspicion in the eyes of many critics regarding Oswald's exact relations or status with the FBI.

While no solid evidence has yet emerged indicating that Lee Harvey Oswald ever actually worked for the FBI, allegations that he was connected with the Bureau, possibly as an informant, have steadily increased over the years. Interestingly, his brother, Robert Oswald, has inadvertently set forth an account which might conceivably indicate how his brother's possible interest in the FBI began:

> One of his [Lee's] favorite [television] programs was "I Led Three Lives," the story of Herbert Philbrick, the FBI informant who posed as a Communist spy. In the early 1950s, Lee watched that show every week without fail. When I left to join the Marines, he was still watching the re-runs.[48a]

Clyde Tolson

Clyde Tolson served as Assistant Director of the FBI and was Director Hoover's single closest friend and associate. Clyde Tolson, who in later years reportedly grew even more erratic and senile than Hoover, was Hoover's top aide in dealing with the Warren Commission. Senate Intelligence Committee sources report that Tolson was instrumental in preparing the secret "derogatory dossiers" on the members of the Warren Commission and its staff that Hoover had ordered. On December 3, 1975, Senator

 Richard Schweiker of the Senate Intelligence Committee disclosed a startling and previously secret memo written by Cartha DeLoach, Hoover's third closest aide, and sent to Clyde Tolson on April 4, 1967. In this memo (the full contents of which have thus far not been released by the Senate Committee), DeLoach told Tolson that President Johnson's close aide, Marvin Watson, had informed him that President Johnson "was now convinced" that the CIA had been involved in the Kennedy assassination.[49] Tolson, who died in 1975, was never questioned about his knowledge of President Johnson's belief.

William Walter

William Walter worked as an FBI security code clerk in the New Orleans FBI office from 1961 to 1966. A strong defender of the Warren Commission findings, Walter has ironically provided two separate pieces of information which throw those same findings into question. Walter, who is no longer with the FBI, has stated that he is "very sure" that Lee Oswald was at the very least an informant for the New Orleans FBI,[50] and that he is "positive" that Oswald's name was on the FBI Security Index File during the period Walter worked in New Orleans, an allegation which the FBI sent out a teletype messate to all its offices

 five days before the assassination, warning of a reported conspiracy "to assassinate President Kennedy on his proposed trip to Dallas, Texas, November 22-23, 1963." The FBI has firmly denied that such a message was ever transmitted. But Walter has stated, most recently in a CBS interview with Dan Rather, that he personally saw the message on the FBI teletype and took the exact wording down in his notes. In his notes, which have been turned over to the Justice Department for investigation, Walter indicated that the alleged FBI teletype stated that "a militant revolutionary group" was to be involved in the reported assassination plot in Dallas.[51] He further stated that he immediately notified the Special Agent-in-Charge of the New Orleans office of the teletype message. Harry Maynard, the FBI man who then held that position, has denied Walter's allegation. While the FBI still strongly denies Walter's story about the teletype warning, the Justice Department is currently reviewing the matter for a final determination as to what was sent or not sent over the FBI wire service.[52]

1. Ovid Demaris, *The Director* (New York: Harper's Magazine Press, 1975), p. 186.
2. Ibid., p. 185.
3. Ibid., p. 147.
4. Ibid., p. 177.
5. Ibid., pp. 175, 191.
6. Ibid., p. 191.
7. Ibid., p. 175.
8. *Senate Intelligence Committee Report on the Kennedy Assassination*, p. 33.
9. Ibid., p. 34.

10. Ibid., p. 35.
11. Ibid., p. 47.
12. Ibid., p. 53.
13. *New York Times*, September 2, 1975.
14. Ibid.
15. Warren Commission Report, p. 548.
16. Warren Commission Volume 1, pp. 79-80.
17. Letter from FBI Director J. Edgar Hoover to Warren Commission General Counsel J. Lee Rankin, February 27, 1964; Warren Commission Document 1052.
18. Warren Commission Report, pp. 304-305.
19. Warren Commission Exhibit 833, p. 15; Warren Commission Volume 5, p. 112.
20. Ibid.
21. *Dallas Times Herald*, August 31, 1975.
22. Ibid.
23. Constitutional Rights Subcommittee Hearings, December, 1975, House Judiciary Committee.
24. Ibid.
25. *Washington Star*, October 22, 1975.
26. *CBS Reports Inquiry*, "The American Assassins," Part Two, November 26, 1975.
27. Ibid.
28. Ibid.
29. Ibid.
30. Ibid.
31. Warren Commission Volume 2, pp. 353-362.
32. Hunt, *Give Us This Day*, pp. 40-50, 182-189; Wise and Ross, *The Invisible Government*, pp. 20, 27.
33. Warren Commission Volume 2 pp. 357-358; Weisberg,
34. Ibid.
35. Ibid.
36. Letter from FBI Director J. Edgar Hoover to Warren Commission General Counsel J. Lee Rankin, February 27, 1964; Warren Commission Document 1052.
37. Ibid.
38. Warren Commission Report, pp. 707-708; Warren Commission Exhibits 1442 and 1443.
39. Ibid.
40. *Senate Intelligence Committee Report on Foreign Assassinations*, pp. 74-85.
41. Warren Commission Volume 4, p. 437; Warren Commission Volume 17, pp. 757-762.
42. Ibid.
43. Ibid.
44. Warren Commission Volume 4, p. 420; *Washington Star*, October 8, 1975.
45. *Washington Star*, October 8, 1975.

46. Warren Commission Volume 4, p. 420.
47. Ibid.
48. Ibid.
48a. Oswald, *Lee*, p. 47.
49. *Senate Intelligence Committee Report*, Volume 6, p. 182.
50. *CBS Reports Inquiry*, "The American Assassins," Part Two, November 26, 1975.
51. *Washington Post*, October 1, 1975.
52. Ibid.

CHAPTER SEVEN

The Mafia Connection

With an almost incomprehensible yearly income pegged by federal authorities as somewhere between fifty and eighty billion dollars, and a subterranean infrastructure that extends into the highest echelons of politics, finance, and world trade, the organized crime empire in the United States — the Mafia or National Crime Syndicate — has grown in power in leaps and bounds since the days in the 1950s when Robert Kennedy labeled it "the enemy within." Exercising an increasingly open and somewhat more "respectable" role in virtually every facet of American society, the Mafia has in fact steadily grown into a crime confederation which — according to Senate and House committees and the Justice Department — now exceeds even the most conservative estimates of its manipulative hammerlock on a wide range of activities in America.

"The American system of ours, call it Americanism, call it capitalism, call it what you like, gives each and every one of us a great opportunity if we only seize it with both hands and make the most of it." These ironic words of Mafia leader Al Capone were frequently quoted by Attorney General Robert F. Kennedy during his efforts to organize a federal assault on organized crime in the early 1960s.[1]

It was of course under Robert Kennedy's leadership that the massive investigative resources of the federal bureaucracy were targeted against the Mafia, or as RFK called it, the "private government of organized crime."[2]

Upon becoming Attorney General, Robert Kennedy increased the organized crime section of the Justice Department by four hundred per cent, and initiated a "hit list" of important Mafia leaders to be targeted for prosecution.[3] The list began at 40, but by the time he resigned as Attorney General, months after his brother's death, it had grown to 2,300.[4]

In 1964, Robert Kennedy set forth a summary of progress that had been made during his tenure at Justice:

> The statistics for cases involving organized crime give some indication of our activity. For the first six months of 1963, we secured indictments of 171 racketeering figures, compared with 24 for the same period three years ago. In 1963, the number of convictions was 160; three years before it was 35.
>
> Organized crime cases have been in large part responsible for sharp increases in the

work figures for the entire Criminal Division. In 1962 Criminal Division attorneys spent 809 days in court and 7,369 days in the field. Two years prior, the figures were 283 days in court and 1,963 days in the field.[5]

As the figures indicate, the Kennedy Administration briskly and quite substantively enlarged the federal effort against organized crime, which had dwindled substantially during the Eisenhower Administration. While there had been a mere nineteen Mafia indictments during the last year of the Eisenhower-Nixon Administration, there were 687 such indictments during the last year of the Kennedy-Johnson Administration.[6]

In late April, 1976, the Senate Intelligence Committee released a report which contained some new figures indicating the extent to which the government's activities against organized crime had been drastically limited during the Eisenhower years. While noting that there had been a significant upsurge during the Truman Administration of federal efforts against the Mafia — primarily as a result of the Kefauver Committee probe of 1950 and 1951 — they stated that this progress had been largely reduced during the Eisenhower Administration.[7]

The Senate report noted that "the Eisenhower Administration . . . consistently declined to provide special funds for racketeer work" for the IRS Intelligence Division, which had become a crucial arm of the federal effort.[8] Al Capone and other top Mafia leaders had been successfully prosecuted on tax charges as a result of earlier IRS anti-racketeering work. The Senate Intelligence report stated that, "In contrast to 10,041 racketeer cases investigated in FY 1953, by FY 1955 total racketeer cases developed had declined to 1,039; by FY 1960, to 125."[9]

With the startling testimony of Mafia figure Joe Valachi in 1963 (the highest-ranking organized crime informant ever to become a federal witness against the mob) the efforts of the Kennedy Administration reached a new peak. As Robert Kennedy later noted, "For the first time an insider, a knowledgeable member of the racketeering hierarchy, [had] broken the underworld's code of silence."[10]

The Kennedy Justice Department soon was able to document the long-rumored existence of "the Commission," the secret governing body of the Mafia's far-flung organized crime syndicate, which consisted (according to RFK) of "between nine and twelve active members."[11] In setting forth the activities of the Justice Department during this period, RFK said:

> We know that in the past two years at least three carefully planned Commission meetings had to be called off because the leaders learned that we had uncovered their well-concealed plans and meeting places.[12]

The commitment of John and Robert Kennedy to combat organized crime had of course preceded by several years their successful quest for the Presidency. It had been during Senator John F. Kennedy's service on the McClellan Committee (of which Robert Kennedy was Chief Counsel) that the Kennedy interest in fighting syndicate crime began. It was during the extended McClellan Committee investigation that Robert Kennedy had recruited some of the key people who would later serve as top officials in the Kennedy White House. As staff investigators for the McClellan Senate probe of the Mafia, Robert Kennedy assembled his former college roommate, Kenneth P. O'Donnell, an investigative reporter from the West Coast, Pierre Salinger, as well as two investigators who were later to head the organized crime probes of the Kennedy Justice Department, Walter Sheridan and Carmine Bellino. O'Donnell recalls that the McClellan effort "evolved into the biggest Committee operation in the history of Washington." Salinger has told of one case in which the Senate committee faced the prospect of implicating a powerful Democratic political figure in

Indiana, something which the Democratic members of the committee may have preferred to avoid. However, Salinger recalls that Senator John F. Kennedy ordered him to proceed with that area of the investigation, stating, "Go back and build the best case against him that you can. We have only one rule around here. If they're crooks, we don't wound 'em, we kill 'em."[13]

By the early 1960s, the national and worldwide power of the Mafia's organized network had increased more quickly and comprehensively than even the Kefauver and McClellan Committees had predicted. As will be seen, the penetration of the American political process by organized crime had been one of the Mafia's high-priority target areas. In a commentary in mid-October of 1976, CBS News correspondent Eric Sevareid pointed out the increasingly ominous rate at which the Mafia expanded its activities in the United States:

> Government can organize beautifully to eliminate millions of gangsters thousands of miles away — the Nazis for example — but cannot eliminate a few thousand living right here. The Mafia has thrived since it was exported here from Sicily 90 years ago. Police catch them. Then the case is lost or diluted in the courts. The cherished rights of due process, designed to protect individual citizens against the arbitrary of Government, protect the Mafia. But are they individual citizens or are they in fact a separate Government, an enemy government?
>
> A case can be made that the Mafia constitutes not only a separate government, but a separate society . . . [14]

Ralph J. Salerno, one of the nation's leading authorities on organized crime activities later became widely quoted for his prediction that, "Organized crime will one day put a man in the White House. And he won't even know it until they hand him the bill." As will be seen, a more serious body of information may relate not to the question of organized crime putting a man in the White House, but instead, organized crime taking a man out.

Jack Ruby

In the years since the assassination, various Warren Commission critics have assembled extensive material relating to Jack Ruby's ties to numerous Mafia figures and syndicate activity. Much of this information was either largely ignored or completely overlooked at the time of the Warren probe. As will be seen, the mysterious murderer of Lee Harvey Oswald was actually involved in a string of significant Mafia cases, dating back as far as 1939. While various investigators for the Warren Commission — inexperienced or unschooled in the structure and operations of organized crime — may have missed the import, magnitude, and trail of Ruby's various Mafia connections, those same connections are now clearly visible to the present day observer.

In February of 1960, at a time when the McClellan Senate Committee investigation of organized crime had already made him a national figure as well known as his brother, Robert F. Kennedy's first book, *The Enemy Within*, was published. It quickly became a highly praised best seller, an account of organized crime and Teamster corruption that still ranks as a definitive work in the field. The *New York Times* said, "Mr. Kennedy exposed himself and his family to terrible danger for three years . . . an example of courage that calls for more imitation if we are to delay our surrender to the mob."

While RFK had no way of knowing it at the time, one of the key episodes in the book — relating to the rise of Jimmy Hoffa and his Mafia associates — involved the man who later silenced the young assassin accused of shooting his brother. As Robert Kennedy stated, Teamster leader Hoffa had early designs to extend his influence nationwide with the help of the syndicate:

> For him, the key to the entire Midwest was Chicago. He needed a powerful ally there — and he found his man in Paul Dorfman. Dorfman, our testimony showed, was a big operator — a major figure in the Chicago underworld who also knew his way around in certain labor and political circles.
>
> . . . Dorfman took over as head of the Chicago Waste Handler's Union in 1939 after its founder and secretary-treasurer was murdered . . .
>
> Hoffa made a trade with Dorfman. In return for an introduction to the Chicago underworld, the Committee found, Hoffa turned over to him and his family the gigantic Central Conference of Teamsters Welfare Fund insurance.[15]

The front page of the *Chicago Daily Tribune* of December 9, 1939, contained the earliest account of the shooting of the Chicago Waste Handler's Union founder, Leon Cooke, an account never mentioned by the Warren Report. The *Tribune* article, complete with banner headline, "Attorney Shot; Union Row," reported that Cooke had been shot in the back the night before and that another union official, John Martin, was being sought as his assailant.[16] It also noted that Cooke was an alleged bootlegger whose handling of the union finances was under investigation.[17]

According to the report, "Much of the information was obtained from Jack Rubinstein [Ruby], secretary of the union ... Rubinstein was absent at the time of the shooting."[18] Beneath a photograph of Jack Ruby — wearing a dark hat and suit similar to the ones he wore as he murdered Lee Harvey Oswald twenty-two years later — the *Tribune* noted, "Jack Rubinstein ... was seized for questioning."[19] While Ruby's associate, John Martin, was later convicted for the Leon Cooke murder, which had led to Paul Dorfman's takeover of the union and subsequent power in establishing the Hoffa empire, the Warren Report never cited Ruby's exact relationship to the episode in evaluating his associations.

Seven years after the Cooke slaying, Jack Rubinstein had changed his name to Ruby and had moved to Dallas, Texas. In his testimony of June 7, 1964, Ruby briefly mentioned that "I was with the union back in Chicago and I left the union when I found out the notorious organization had moved in there."[20] Ruby went on: ". . . my background ... isn't so terribly spotted — I have never been a criminal — I have never been in jail ... I am not a gangster ... I had a very rough start in life, but anything I have done, I at least tried to do it in good taste."[21]

In 1947, the same year in which Ruby was setting up the "Silver Spur," a nightclub in Dallas, the Police Department in that city became the target of a large-scale bribery conspiracy by the Chicago Mafia — an organized crime case later termed "classic" by the Kefauver Committee in its investigation of the Mafia.

Interestingly, the key Mafia figure involved, a man named Paul Jones, was a close associate of Jack Ruby. In their *Third Interim Report*, the Kefauver Senate Committee stated:

> Some indication of how modern crime syndicates operate and how they open new territory is apparent from the facts described . . . elsewhere in this report in relation to the extraordinary testimony of Lt. George Butler of the Police Department of Dallas, Texas. Lieutenant Butler was approached by a member of the Chicago mob by the name of Paul Jones . . . Jones stated that he was an advance agent of the Chicago crime syndicate and was prepared to offer the District Attorney and the Sheriff $1,000 a week each or a twelve and a half percent cut on the profit if the syndicate were permitted to operate in Dallas under "complete protection." Jones also stated that syndicate operations were conducted by local people who "front" for the Chicago mob.[22]

During this incident (which received national attention at the time) officers of the Dallas Police Department, including Lieutenant Butler and Sheriff Guthrie, secretly tape recorded the bribery offers made by Chicago Mafia "advance agent" Paul Jones. The two Chicago mob leaders during that period were of course Sam Giancana (the future CIA assassination coordinator) and Tony "Big Tuna" Accardo, who still runs the Mafia in that city.

Chicago Mafia man Paul Jones was a close associate of Jack Ruby, according to plentiful, yet mostly ignored, Warren Commission documentation. Warren Commission Exhibit 1184 shows that Ruby had first met Jones through two mutual friends: Paul "Needle Nose" Labriola and Jim Weinberg.[23] Both men were well-known in Chicago as syndicate associates of Sam Giancana. A few years after introducing Ruby to Paul Jones, "Needle Nose" Labriola and Jim Weinberg were both executed in a Mafia murder that received considerable attention. Organized crime reporter Ovid Demaris has written of the case, in which the two men were found — with their heads partially severed — in the trunk of a car in 1954.[24]

As noted earlier, the Chicago Mafia's attempt to buy "complete protection" from the Dallas Police Department was later exposed through secret tape recordings that the police made of Paul Jones' discussions. The Kefauver Senate Committee commended the Dallas PD for their work in the case. Interestingly, the Dallas Sheriff during that period, Steve Guthrie, informed the Warren Commission that Jack Ruby had himself been involved with Paul Jones in the bribery conspiracy plan of the Giancana-Accardo mob. According to the Warren Report, Sheriff Guthrie stated that Jones and his Chicago associates "frequently mentioned that Ruby would operate a 'fabulous' restaurant as a front for gambling activities."[25]

The Warren Commission, however, concluded that Sheriff Guthrie's account was "difficult to accept."[26] The Commission stated that Lieutenant George Butler, who also handled the Jones case, didn't remember Jack Ruby being involved.[27] The Commission cited an FBI report of December 9, 1963, in which Butler had said Ruby was not a part of the Chicago Mafia bribery conspiracy.[28] However, the Commission apparently ignored the fact that a Chicago newspaperman, Mort Newman, had earlier written that Butler disclosed that "Jack Ruby came to Dallas from . . . Chicago in the late 1940s and was involved in an attempt to bribe Sheriff Steve Guthrie."[29] Thus, there seems to be a clear discrepancy in Butler's account. Beyond that, Sheriff Guthrie might be expected to have had the clearer impression of exactly who it was from the Giancana-Accardo mob that was involved in the attempt to bribe him. But the Warren Commission disagreed.

The Commission also cited the twenty-two secret tape recordings that were made of Paul Jones by the Dallas Police, concluding that:

> . . . 22 recordings of the conversations between Guthrie, Butler and Jones not only failed to mention Ruby, but indicate that Jones was to bring from outside the Dallas area, only one confederate, who was not to be Jewish.[30]

The way in which the secret tape recordings were reviewed for the Warren Commission establishes even further questions about the entire episode. The recordings, it turned out, were obtained from Lieutenant Butler himself, who had them stored in his home, for reasons that are unclear.[31] To review the recordings, the FBI assigned a single agent who listened to the twenty-two hours of tape without preparing a transcript of any kind.[32] Instead, the FBI man simply prepared a brief FBI report stating that Jack Ruby or Rubinstein's name was not mentioned on any of the tapes.[33] After the FBI began the tape review, it was discovered that one of the tapes was missing, containing Recording Numbers Eight and Seventeen.[34] The missing tape has never been found.

While the Warren Commission used Lieutenant Butler's denial that Ruby had been involved in the Chicago Mafia bribery plan to rebut the testimony of Sheriff Guthrie, still more questions have been raised about Butler's veracity. According to another little-noticed Warren Commission Exhibit, two other Dallas Police officers disclosed that Butler had approached them after Ruby murdered Oswald to give them some "important" information: namely, that young Lee Oswald was Jack Ruby's illegitimate son.[35] Despite the wild Butler story, the Warren Report concluded that Butler was a highly credible witness. As various Commission critics have pointed out, Butler had also been assigned to the ill-fated transfer of Oswald on the morning of November 24th.[36]

Whether Jack Ruby was indeed involved with his Chicago Mafia friend, Paul Jones, in this bribery scheme, their relationship continued during subsequent years. According to Warren Commission documentation, Jones once approached Ruby's brother, Hymie Ruby, to participate in a liquor smuggling operation.[37] Ruby's brother stated that he declined the offer.[38]

When one of Jones' lieutenants was later arrested for smuggling opium (and possibly heroin) into the United States from Mexico, both Jack and Hymie Ruby were questioned during the investigation.[39]

Interestingly, Giancana-Accardo mob member Paul Jones was also once convicted of the crime that his friend Jack Ruby became famous for: murdering a state witness. This killing was later reviewed by both the Kefauver Senate Committee as well as the McClellan Committee.[40] Although Paul Jones later spent considerable time in prison, he was a free man by the early 1960s, and in fact saw Ruby less than ten days before the Kennedy assassination.[41]

While no evidence turned up that either Ruby brother had been directly involved in the Paul Jones narcotics case, Jack Ruby was later linked to another Mafia drug operation. Almost seven years before the assassination of President John F. Kennedy, according to a lengthy FBI report, an informant for the Federal Narcotics Bureau and the Los Angeles Police Department identified Jack Ruby as a key figure in "a large narcotics set-up operating between Mexico, Texas and the East."[42] On March 13, 1956, the informant, Mrs. James "Bunny" Breen, notified the L.A. police that her husband James (also an informant) was missing, and that she feared this narcotics ring had murdered him.[43]

On March 13, 1956, Mrs. Breen further stated that her husband had originally "made connections" with the "large Texas-Mexico narcotics set-up" through Ruby.[44] She told the police, "In some fashion James got the O.K. to operate through Jack Ruby of Dallas."[45] Little else is known of the Breen episode or the extent to which the authorities followed up on these allegations about Ruby. If the 1956 information was accurate, Ruby would of course be importantly involved with the Mafia — since the syndicate then controlled (and still does) the narcotics operations of that key region.

While the preceding areas of information pertaining to Jack Ruby's "alleged" ties to the Mafia (both in Chicago and Dallas) are considerable, there is another area of information even more ominous, and highly substantive. It concerns Jack Ruby's close involvement with two known Mafia assassins whose relationship with Oswald's killer was almost entirely overlooked by the Warren Commission. As will be seen, these two Chicago hit men are credited with being early proponents of the use of poison as a useful tool for the syndicate's professional killers.

Ruby's close association with these two Chicago Mafia figures — Dave Yaras and Lenny Patrick — first came to the attention of the Warren Commission when Jack Ruby's sister, Eva Rubinstein Grant, gave her testimony. Eva Grant told the Commission about Ruby's "tough" old days in Chicago, and stated that two of his closest friends had been Dave Yaras and Lenny Patrick.[46] As will be seen later, the Commission had incorrectly put down the name of Dave Yaras as "Dave Yeres," thus possibly missing the significance of the Yaras record during their subsequent probing.[47]

However, the FBI subsequently interviewed Dave Yaras, who confirmed his close friendship with Ruby as well as their mutual friendship with Lenny Patrick.[48] The FBI never asked Yaras about his own Mafia connections, but did ask him whether he thought Ruby was connected with the syndicate. Yaras, as one might guess, stated that he doubted that Ruby had such connections.[49] This was the kind of testimony that the Warren Commission would later refer to in concluding that while Ruby may have had limited contact with "minor criminal" figures, he was not involved with organized crime. This view was classically expressed by General Counsel J. Lee Rankin during a January 27, 1964 Commission session. Rankin told Commission members that Ruby had some links to "the minor underworld," but that "it isn't apparent that any of the important people in the underworld would have given him any consideration at all as far as being a part of it." [50]

Despite what Rankin and other Commission members wished to believe, Ruby's connections were not minor; Ruby's close association with Dave Yaras and Lenny Patrick illustrate that all too clearly.

Jack Ruby's two friends had been arrested and indicted together for the famous syndicate murder of James M. Ragen, the owner of the Continental Press Service in Chicago, the key wire service used to operate the Mafia's nationwide betting network.[51] Ragen had earlier taken over the racing wire from Moses Annenberg, the well-known syndicate figure who had been sent to prison earlier. Ragen had become a key target of the Chicago Mafia during their successful effort to expand various gambling activities.

Ruby's friends, Yaras and Patrick, were accused of carrying out the execution of James Ragen, who had been shot repeatedly as he walked down a Chicago street on his way to a business meeting, on behalf of the leadership of the Chicago mob.[52] Ragen's bullet-riddled body had been rushed to a hospital, where he managed to survive in guarded condition, and was provided round the clock police protection. Despite the police protection, James Ragen died three months later.

The Ragen autopsy revealed that he had been poisoned through the use of a large dose of mercury toxin. The prosecution of Ruby's two associates, Dave Yaras and Lenny Patrick, was subsequently obstructed by the brutal murder of the state's key witness against them.[53] Additionally, the Chicago Police Captain who had played the leading role in the

Yaras-Patrick case was also murdered shortly thereafter, the victim of a carefully-executed syndicate hit.[54] When the Kefauver Senate Committee later brought its own investigation to Chicago, in part to reinvestigate the Ragen murder (then regarded as a landmark syndicate event) yet another key witness in the case was brutally shot to death.

Dave Yaras was later a target of the McClellan Senate Committee investigation of organized crime, then under the direction of Chief Counsel Robert F. Kennedy. The McClellan Committee heard testimony that Yaras had played a significant role in the establishment of the Mafia's gambling empire in Havana, Cuba, then under the control of syndicate leader Meyer Lansky, and his close associate, Cuban dictator Fulgencio Batista,[55] and that Yaras was involved with the corruption-ridden Teamster Local 320, in Miami.[56]

In later years, Yaras extended his influence in the Mafia and became even more notorious both in Chicago and in Miami. In January and February of 1962, Dave Yaras was one of several important Mafia figures overheard by an electronic eavesdropping device installed in a Mafia hang-out by the FBI.[57] The FBI bugging, conducted in Miami, recorded a conversation between Yaras and Jackie Cerone, another member of the powerful Giancana-Accardo Chicago mob.[58] The 1962 FBI transcript revealed that the Yaras-Cerone conversation centered upon murdering another man:

> *Yaras:* I wish . . . we were hitting him now, right now. We could have hit him the other night. We went to prowl the house . . .
>
> *Cerone:* Yeah, that would have been a perfect spot to rub him out . . .
>
> *Yaras:* Leave it to us. As soon as he walks in the . . . door, BOOM! We'll hit him with

an . . . ax or something. He won't get away from us.[59]

As will be seen in forthcoming profiles of other Mafia figures — some of whom were or are the most powerful in the nation — Jack Ruby's mysterious connections travel to the heart of organized crime.

That Ruby himself was a man with a violent and dangerous streak was something that even the Warren Commission chose not to ignore. But instead of admitting his role as a long-time heavy of sorts in organized crime, the Commission chose to portray the exact opposite: a lightweight, somewhat crazy, crum bum whose only offenses could be attributed to disorganized crime — the acts of an emotionally upset loner.

Yet, Jack Ruby's own Warren Commission testimony seems to portray a man whose use of violence was far from irrational; the testimony indeed seems to indicate a characteristically cool, deliberate, and well-planned course of attack whenever Ruby struck:

> Well, in running a — in my business, when you get somebody a — it's a very exciting business. One particular night a man pulled a knife on me and I took a pistol and hit him on the head in that altercation.[60]

At another point, Ruby described another one of his "altercations":

> This man threatened to kill me and was going to go for his gun . . . he was causing a nuisance in the vicinity of the club . . . a little boy of Italian descent . . . and I knew he had a car and he said "I'm going to get my pistol . . . " so I got my pistol and I cornered him and I called him by his name and I called him a name, and I said, "You're going to kill me, you so and so?"[61]

One of the few "light moments" that had occurred during Ruby's testimony before the Warren Commission (aside from borrowing Chief Justice Earl Warren's glasses to try and read some papers) came when FBI agent Bell Herndon noticed something about one of Ruby's hands:

> *Herndon:* I notice you have one finger cut off on that hand. What happened there, Mr. Ruby?
>
> *Ruby:* Oh, running a nightclub you get involved in various altercations.[62]

Exactly why and how Ruby came to be involved in his final "altercation" with the accused assassin of President Kennedy — and on whose behalf — was an area in which the Warren Commission turned in one of their poorest performances. As noted earlier, three years after the Warren Commission ended its work, a previously secret handwritten note from Jack Ruby to one of his attorneys ("Joe, you should know this. [Ruby lawyer] Tom Howard told me to say I shot Oswald so that Caroline and Mrs. Kennedy wouldn't have to come to Dallas to testify. OK?") would shatter the very foundations of Ruby's lengthy Warren Commission testimony.[63]

Strangely enough, Ruby himself had raised what may now be one of the final ironies of his own testimony. Midway through his appearance on June 7, 1964, when once again telling how he had acted only out of his love for "our beloved President" and his widow, Ruby broke down and started crying, in an apparent outburst of spontaneous emotion. Telling of a televised eulogy of Kennedy that he said he had watched, the tearful Ruby said: "I must be a great actor, I tell you that."[64]

That unfortunately seems to be a possibility that the Warren Commission never seriously considered.

Lewis McWillie

Another target of increasing attention by critics of the Warren Commission and various Senate investigators, Lewis McWillie was one of Jack Ruby's two or three closest friends.[65]

The Warren Commission established that Ruby visited McWillie in Havana, Cuba, sometime in early 1959.[66] Ruby's sister testified that Ruby and McWillie discussed various black-market smuggling deals, centering on Cuba, including one that was to involve over 800 jeeps.[67] Other testimony links Ruby and McWillie to Cuban gun-running operations.

In one instance, the Warren Commission did solidly establish that McWillie asked Ruby to arrange for the delivery of some pistols to him in Las Vegas, about nine months prior to the assassination.[68] Senate investigators believe the Ruby-McWillie relationship is one of the more compelling examples of potential areas of conspiracy that were insufficiently investigated by the Warren Commission. The Commission in fact had never followed through with an original staff decision to call McWillie as a witness to testify about Ruby's Cuban associations and reported Mafia connections.

Of particular interest to some Senate investigators is a March 26, 1964, FBI memo that clearly indicates that Ruby's close associate McWillie was also a close associate of the most powerful organized crime leaders in the nation — including Santos Trafficante, the man who the CIA used, along with Sam Giancana and Robert Maheu, to set up the secret CIA-Mafia assassination apparatus aimed at Fidel Castro.[69] Excerpts from the March, 1964 FBI report:

> . . . McWillie was a member of the "so-called gambling syndicate" operating in the Dallas area . . . As of May, 1960, McWillie was pit boss at the Riviera Casino, Havana, Cuba. Report reflects that it would appear McWillie consolidated his syndicate connections through his association in Havana, Cuba, with Santos Trafficante, well-known syndicate member, for Tampa, Florida; Meyer and Jake Lansky; Dino Cellini and others who were members of or associates of "the syndicate."
>
> . . . He left Dallas and went to Havana, Cuba, where he was known to associate with nationally known gambling characters such as Willie Bischoff, also known as Lefty Clark, Jake Lansky, Trafficante, and others.[70]

During his Warren Commission testimony in June of 1964, Jack Ruby spoke of his closeness to Lewis McWillie, stating that "I called him frequently . . . I idolized McWillie. He is a pretty nice boy, and I happened to be idolizing him."[71] Ruby stated that, "I always thought a lot of him . . . I have a great fondness for him."[72]

Speaking of the time when he had planned to ship some guns to McWillie in Havana, Ruby testified that, "He called me or sent me a letter . . . He wanted some four little Cobra guns — big shipment."[73] Ruby continued, "That was the only relationship I had of any . . . person from Havana, Cuba."[74]

Jim Braden

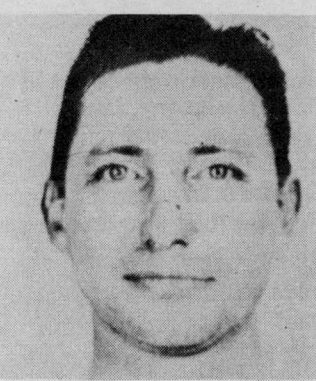

Jim Braden is the central character involved in one of the more incredible areas of evidence that was not available to the Warren investigation. Braden is the main character in one of the most significant books on the Kennedy case, *Legacy of Doubt*, by Peter Noyes. According to Noyes and other investigators, Braden is believed by federal authorities to be presently serving as a "personal courier" for syndicate leader Meyer Lansky.[75]

Jim Braden, incredibly enough, had actually been stopped and held for questioning at the scene of the Dallas assassination shortly after the shots were fired.[76] Braden was picked up by Dallas Police Deputy C.L. Lewis, for "acting suspiciously."[77] He was released after an hour and was later given only minimal attention by the FBI and Warren Commission as a "bystander" at the scene of the murder.[78]

Due to the fact that the Dallas police didn't fingerprint Braden or run a make on him to check his background, Jim Braden's actual identity never became available to the Warren Commission or the FBI. Braden had actually changed his identity — by legally changing his name — only a few weeks prior to the assassination.

Jim Braden's real name had been Eugene Hale Brading. However, on September 10, 1963, Brading had received a new driver's license in California under his new legal name of "Jim Braden" and had been arrested and identified only under that name.[79] Thus

Jim Braden's real background as Eugene Hale Brading was never available to federal investigators.

The investigators were not aware it actually consisted of a long criminal record and heavy involvement with many powerful organized crime figures across the nation. Brading had in fact been associated with top Mafia leaders in virtually every national crime syndicate jurisdiction.[80] Peter Noyes has compiled a mass of federal, state, and local law enforcement files covering Braden's involvement with Mafia figures stretching over a twenty-year period.

In addition, it turns out, Braden also had some other startling connections which were also never discovered by the Warren Commission. Jim Braden had visited the same Dallas office of the H.L. Hunt Oil Company that Jack Ruby visited on November 21, 1963 — the afternoon before the assassination — and at approximately the same time.[81] Braden was also staying at the Cabana Motel in Dallas — a reported "mob hang-out" that was frequented by Jack Ruby and various Ruby associates.[82] As will be seen later, Jack Ruby visited the Cabana Motel sometime around midnight on the night before the assassination — November 21, 1963 — while Jim Braden was a registered guest there.[83]

Braden also has a possible connection to the late David Ferrie. According to information documented by Peter Noyes, Braden worked out of an office suite — Room 1701 — in the Pere Marquette Building in New Orleans in the fall of 1963, in the weeks immediately preceding the assassination.[84]

During this same period in late 1963, David Ferrie was working for Mafia leader Carlos Marcello on the same floor . . . in the same building . . . just down the hall from Braden — in Room 1707.[85]

In recent years, Jim Braden has been the subject of various tax and gambling investigations in California and Nevada.[86] Until his move to Atlanta, Georgia, in 1975, Braden had lived at the La Costa resort in

California, widely reported to be a prime meeting place for various Mafia and Teamster leaders.

Interestingly, in the spring of 1976, the National Archives disclosed that at least two documents pertaining to the arrest of Jim Braden were missing from the official Archives collection of assassination documents. In a listing of "Records Relating to the Warren Commission Investigation Missing from the Archives" (prepared for the House Subcommittee on Government Information and Individual Rights), the Archives included the following two items: "Records of the Dallas Police and County Sheriff's Office concerning arrests on November 22, 1963," and a "Photograph taken by Philip Willis in Dealey Plaza showing man being arrested or under arrest near the Dal Tex Building . . . "[86a]

Lawrence V. Meyers

Lawrence V. Meyers and his brother Edward, two New York businessmen, are another subject of increasing interest by various investigators of the Kennedy assassination. Lawrence Meyers was a personal friend and associate of Jack Ruby.[87]

In the last several years, an impressive and quite ominous amount of information has been compiled regarding the Lawrence Meyers-Jack Ruby relationship, and what appear to be highly possible links to Mafia figure Jim Braden, as well as David Ferrie, the mysterious private investigator and pilot for New Orleans Mafia leader Carlos Marcello.

Lawrence Meyers was briefly examined by the Warren Commission in late August, 1964, as the final draft of the Warren Report was being finished.[88] Meyers testified that he had known Jack Ruby for at least five or six years and had visited him in Dallas repeatedly over the years.[89]

Due to the fact that Meyers had been a close friend of Ruby's for so many years, the Warren Commission sought to determine how much knowledge Meyers had about Ruby's background and associations. When asked by Commission counsel Burt Griffin whether Ruby had ever talked about "his associations with underworld characters — hoodlums," Lawrence Meyers had replied: "Many times. Generalities . . . nothing specific . . . just dropping names of so-called important people that he met or had known."[90] When asked if he knew whether Ruby had "been a part of any gambling organization," Meyers had requested to go off-the-record for his response.[91] The Commission transcript (from August 24, 1964) notes that upon going back on the record, Commission counsel Griffin stated that Meyers had only discussed Ruby's reported use of his nightclub strippers as prostitutes, during the off-the-record exchange.[92]

An FBI report of December 12, 1963, contains the following account of a late-night meeting that Lawrence Meyers had with Jack Ruby on the night before the Kennedy assassination:

> [Meyers] advised that on November 20, 1963, he flew to Dallas, Texas, where on the night of November 20, 1963, he stayed at the Ramada Motel and checked into the Cabana Motel on the morning of November 21, 1963. He stated he pursued his normal business affairs that date and in the evening following dinner he went to Jack Ruby's Carousel Club. Mr. Meyers stated that on this trip to Dallas he was accompanied by Miss Jean West whom he had known casually in Chicago. He described Miss West as a "rather dumb, but accommodating broad." He further pointed out that his association with Miss West is not known to members of his family or to his business associates. When he and Miss West arrived at the Carousel Club he introduced her to . . . Jack Ruby, and Ruby joined them at their table . . . [93]

The FBI report goes on to set forth the circumstances of another "get together" of Ruby and Meyers later that same night, November 21, 1963:

> Meyers advised that he and Miss West remained at the Carousel Club for approximately one hour, returning to the motel at

> about 11:00 PM. Mr. Meyers stated that while at the Carousel Club he had invited Ruby to join him at the Cabana Motel for a drink with him and his brother, Edward Meyers, and Edward's wife, who were attending a [Bottler's] convention in Dallas. He said that shortly thereafter Jack Ruby came to the motel where he was introduced to his brother and his wife. Ruby remained at the motel for only a few minutes before he left, saying that he had to return to his club.[94]

Braden was also staying at the Cabana Motel at this same time. Thus, late on the night before the assassination, Ruby met with Lawrence Meyers at the same motel in Dallas where Braden was staying. As noted before, Braden had told the authorities that he was in Dallas on "oil business," including a meeting with Lamar Hunt, the son of oil billionaire H. L. Hunt.[95] Thus, a second possible Ruby-Braden connection arises, in addition to their having both been at the H.L. Hunt offices in Dallas, sometime earlier that same afternoon, as previously detailed.

Lawrence Meyers was queried about his late-night meeting with Ruby on the eve of the assassination during his brief Warren Commission appearance. Meyers stated that during his visit to Ruby's Carousel Club at about 9 o'clock that night, he had told Ruby to "meet me at the Cabana Motel at 11 o'clock that evening."[96] Meyers further stated that Ruby had arrived at the Cabana between 11:30 and midnight.[97] Interestingly, Commission counsel Griffin had asked Meyers where he had been in between the time he left Ruby's club and when he met him around midnight.[98] Meyers answered that he didn't recall where he had been, but assumed that he had been having dinner somewhere in Dallas, although "I haven't got the vaguest recollection of where I had dinner that night."[99]

It is interesting to note that Ruby's contact with the Cabana Motel is one of the areas of inquiry in which the Warren Commission had unsuccessfully sought information from the CIA; specifically, Deputy Director for Plans Richard Helms had delayed for several months before responding to the lengthy Commission request of March 12, 1964 regarding information on Ruby and his associates.[100] And then, the CIA had finally sent a brief response, devoid of any information, that arrived at the Commission offices as the Warren Report was already being set in type.[101] In their request to the CIA for information on the Cabana Motel — a place "frequented by Ruby in Dallas" — the Commission included reference to it under a sub-section heading that read: "The following groups and places seem significant in looking for ties between Ruby and others who might have been interested in the assassination of President Kennedy."[102] Senate investigators regard the CIA's response — or "nonresponse" — to this request as one of the most serious breaches in the assassination investigation.

Ominously, Lawrence Meyer's "woman friend," Miss Jean West, who accompanied him to his two November 21 meetings with Ruby, also apparently had another mysterious friend: David W. Ferrie, the mysterious man associated with Mafia leader Carlos Marcello. Ferrie's connection to Jean West was first uncovered during Jim Garrison's abortive investigation of Ferrie in 1967. Garrison discovered that on September 24, 1963 (the same day that Lee Oswald had left New Orleans to make his now-famous trip to Mexico City) David Ferrie had made a long-distance phone call to Chicago. According to the Bell Telephone records subpoenaed by Garrison, the Ferrie call went to the Chicago phone number WH-4-4970.[103]

Incredibly enough, WH-4-4970 was the Chicago phone number of Jean Aese West, Lawrence Meyer's companion. This information regarding West's phone number was set forth in Warren Commission Exhibit 2350, which contained a reference to a call from

Meyers to her at that same number.[104] Meyers' phone records had been briefly examined due to his close association with Ruby.[105]

Garrison had originally been interested in the David Ferrie call to Miss West because it had been made on the same day (September 24) that Lee Harvey Oswald had left on his mysterious ten-day visit to Mexico City. Interestingly, Lawrence Meyers' brother, Edward Meyers, had also made a recent trip to Mexico City. A December 6, 1963 FBI report states that Ed Meyers left New York "on November 8, 1963, and went to Mexico City. He returned from Mexico City to Dallas, Texas, on the 18th of November . . . "[106] The FBI report further notes that on the night of November 21, "Edward Meyers was unable to have dinner with his brother, but did meet his brother at . . . the Cabana Motel about midnight . . . [where] Lawrence Meyers introduced Edward Meyers to Jack Ruby."

The convention that Ed Meyers was attending in Dallas, for the American Bottlers of Carbonated Beverages, was the same gathering that former Vice President Richard Nixon was also attending. Nixon was then handling legal work for Pepsi Cola, as a member of the New York law firm of Mudge, Rose, Guthrie, and Alexander. Meyers, as the December 6, 1963 FBI report notes, was the owner of a Pepsi Cola distributing company in New York, the Queens Beverage Company.[107]

Lawrence Meyers also spoke with Jack Ruby on the night before Ruby murdered Lee Harvey Oswald. In his Warren Commission testimony, Meyers confirmed that Ruby had called him around "9 or 10 o'clock" on the night of November 23, 1963. Meyers stated that they talked for about twenty minutes, during which time Ruby expressed his sadness over the assassination.[108]

The next day, upon hearing that his friend Ruby had shot Oswald to death, Meyers decided not to contact the authorities. According to a December 12, 1963 FBI report:

Meyers stated that . . . he debated whether or not to contact the Dallas Police concerning his recent association with Ruby, but decided that in light of the apparent hectic activities then ensuing at the police station it would be better if he did not do so.[109]

David W. Ferrie

David Ferrie was a mysterious private investigator and pilot active in anti-Castro activities in New Orleans, who was at one time or another investigated by the FBI, Secret Service, Warren Commission, CIA, and Jim Garrison, in connection with the assassination.

The late David Ferrie is today once again a prime focus of various Kennedy assassination investigators, including those active in both the House and Senate. Ferrie was known to associates as a master of intrigue, an active homosexual with a formidable academic background and outspoken right-wing political views. An FBI report summarizing an interview with David Ferrie noted that Ferrie had admitted "being publicly and privately" vitriolic toward President Kennedy, and had said on occasion such things as, "He ought to be shot."[110] While clearly a man with varied connections, David Ferrie's strongest connections — indeed his working connections — were with the leadership of the

Mafia, in particular Carlos Marcello, the New Orleans Mafia boss widely believed to be the second or third most powerful Mafia leader in the nation. And it is Ferrie's work for the Mafia that provides the most substantive information concerning his possible role in the assassination.

David Ferrie had been a suspect in the President's assassination as early as the day of the actual shooting. At that time, Ferrie was working with New Orleans private investigator Guy Banister, who also had Mafia connections as well as an equally active involvement in anti-Castro Cuban exile activities. As covered previously (see section on Guy Banister in chapter on "The Intelligence Community"), detective Banister's office, in which Ferrie worked, was located in a small building which also had housed the New Orleans branch of the Cuban Revolutionary Council, an anti-Castro group which had originally been financed and coordinated by the CIA during the Bay of Pigs.[111] It had also been this same building, at 544 Camp Street in New Orleans, that Lee Oswald had originally printed as his address on the "Fair Play for Cuba Committee" literature which he distributed.[112]

In any event, shortly after the assassination on the afternoon of November 22, 1963, an employee of Guy Banister named Jack S. Martin, contacted the New Orleans Police Department and the FBI, and told the authorities that he had some information linking his colleagues David Ferrie and Guy Banister to the assassination.[113]

Jack Martin claimed that Ferrie had been involved with Lee Harvey Oswald and had been active in the actual planning of the Kennedy assassination. Thus it was due to Martin's allegations that David Ferrie first came to the attention of Federal investigators. However, this attention was to be short-lived. Almost as soon as Martin made his allegations, he reportedly retracted them, saying that he had made it all up and had been drinking too much. With this retraction in hand, the FBI and Secret Service dropped David Ferrie as a suspect and ended any further investigation into his possible involvement. Before Jack Martin retracted his story, however, the FBI did conduct a lengthy interview with Ferrie. Interestingly, over thirty pages of the November 25, 1963 FBI-Ferrie interview have never been released, and are locked up with the other classified files from the assassination in the National Archives.[114]

Strangely, in the spring of 1976, the National Archives disclosed that an "Original Statement of David W. Ferrie transcribed in [Warren] Commission Document 205" was missing from the official Archives collection of assassination documents.[115]

It was not until New Orleans District Attorney Jim Garrison began his controversial investigation, some time in 1967, that David Ferrie's possible involvement in the Kennedy murder once again came into focus. Garrison, who had briefly investigated Ferrie in the days immediately after the assassination, now charged Ferrie with being an integral figure in what he announced was a complex conspiracy behind the Kennedy killing, a conspiracy that had allegedly taken shape in New Orleans. According to Garrison, Ferrie was assigned, among other things, to transport the actual assassins out of Texas in a private plane, following the shooting.

During the course of his bizarre and ill-fated investigation, District Attorney Garrison stated that:

> A number of the men who killed the President were former employees of the CIA involved in its anti-Castro underground activities in the New Orleans area . . . The CIA knows their identity. So do I.[116]

In mid-February of 1967 Garrison had placed David Ferrie under protective custody at his request. On February 22, 1967, the day after he was released from custody, David Ferrie was found dead in his New Orleans apartment. Jim Garrison's leading suspect would never stand trial. The New Orleans Coroner's office concluded that Ferrie had died from a cerebral hemorrhage caused by a ruptured blood vessel.[117] In a press conference called shortly after Ferrie's death, District Attorney Garrison stated that his suspect would be shown to have been "one of history's most interesting individuals."

During Garrison's subsequent unsuccessful prosecution of wealthy New Orleans businessman Clay Shaw, the District Attorney sought to connect David Ferrie to Lee Harvey Oswald and connect them in turn to a large group of assassination conspirators. Garrison noted that Oswald, Ferrie, and various anti-Castro Cubans connected to the CIA had all been traced to the building at 544 Camp Street, where Ferrie worked out of Guy Banister's office and where Oswald listed his address on his "Fair Play for Cuba Committee" literature.

Garrison also offered the testimony of various witnesses (several of whom were of highly dubious veracity) who linked Oswald, Ferrie, and Shaw to the alleged assassination conspiracy. While much of Garrison's controversial case fell flat — largely due to Ferrie's untimely death, according to Garrison — Garrison had established at least a few interesting points.

Perhaps most interesting was a detail that was not confirmed until years later. In 1975, former CIA executive Victor Marchetti revealed that former CIA Director Richard Helms had privately admitted that some of Garrison's chief suspects had indeed once worked for the CIA. Victor Marchetti had served as the Executive Assistant to the Deputy Director of the CIA and had subsequently been the author of the definitive work, *The CIA and the Cult of Intelligence.*[118]

In 1975, Marchetti stated that during the course of several high-level CIA staff meetings in January and February of 1969, CIA Director Helms had disclosed that both David Ferrie and Clay Shaw, and at least one of Garrison's Cuban exile suspects, had indeed once worked for the CIA.[119] Marchetti further stated that Helms repeatedly voiced worry over Garrison's prosecution of Clay Shaw and instructed his top aides (including CIA General Counsel Lawrence Houston and Helms' Deputy Thomas Karamessines) to "do all we can to help Shaw" during his trial.[120] Marchetti also states that Helms spoke of "other meetings" that were being held regarding Garrison's investigation.[121] While Marchetti's disclosure in no way establishes that any of these former CIA men were involved in the assassination, it does show that Garrison was at least correct in identifying them as former CIA operatives.

David Ferrie's possible relationship with Lee Harvey Oswald had also been the subject of some Warren Commission testimony by a witness whom the Commission had regarded as highly reliable. This testimony, by a friend and former high school classmate of Oswald named Edward Voebel, was never pursued by the Commission either.

Edward Voebel told the Warren Commission that he had gotten Oswald interested in the Civil Air Patrol several years back, and that Oswald had gone to CAP training sessions with him in New Orleans.[122] It has been established that pilot David Ferrie was serving as a Civil Air Patrol instructor in New Orleans during the same period, reportedly using his position to establish homosexual contacts with adolescent boys. In any event, when Edward Voebel was asked by the Warren Commission if he remembered who had headed the CAP unit during that period, he answered: "I think it was Captain Ferrie."[123]

In another account, contained in a Louisiana police report dated November 27, 1963, it was disclosed that "Voebel stated that he believed Oswald attended a party (not sure) at the home of David Ferrie (Captain) right after the members of the CAPC received their stripes."[124]

It is his close association with the Mafia — and New Orleans Mafia leader Carlos Marcello in particular —

that proves to be perhaps the most interesting aspect of David Ferrie's activities. His Mafia links were not fully pursued by Jim Garrison in 1967, but were subsequently explored more thoroughly by Los Angeles investigator Peter Noyes, the author of *Legacy of Doubt*.[125] In his 1973 book, the former CBS producer set forth a large new body of documented evidence regarding David Ferrie's work with the Mafia in 1963.[126] It had previously been known that Ferrie had been working as a private investigator and pilot for Mafioso Marcello during that period ... work which dated back further than 1963, however. According to an investigative report in *Look* magazine in late 1969, David Ferrie had secretly flown Marcello back into the United States following Marcello's famous deportation by Attorney General Robert Kennedy in 1961.[127] Marcello's efforts secretly to re-enter the United States met with failure (according to the *Los Angeles Times*) when U.S. authorities discovered his identity and once again detained him.[128]

Several months after this incident (according to a federal informer's report cited by Ed Reid, the respected organized crime reporter) Marcello told a group of his top Mafia associates that plans were then being made to assassinate John F. Kennedy.[129] (See further reference to Carlos Marcello later in this chapter.)

David Ferrie's involvement with Marcello subsequently became more pronounced, with yet even more chilling implications. In the past several years, dating back to the Garrison investigation, Ferrie's contacts with Carlos Marcello on the very day of the assassination have been documented. At the very moment of the murder, Ferrie was in Federal Court in New Orleans, at the side of Carlos Marcello, during some legal proceedings relating to a perjury charge against the mob leader. Ferrie had told the FBI of this court appearance with Marcello when he was questioned by the Bureau on November 25, 1963.[130]

Under further questioning by the New Orleans

police immediately after the assassination, Ferrie also stated that he had driven over a thousand miles on the night of the assassination (and early morning hours of November 23) to go goose hunting in Texas.[131] Under subsequent questioning by the authorities, David Ferrie's "goose hunting" companions disclosed that they had later decided against hunting and had subsequently gone to a skating rink where David Ferrie waited two hours at a telephone booth before receiving a call he was expecting.[132]

As pointed out in the 1969 *Look* magazine article, Ferrie's "goose hunting" companions refused to answer any questions about the trip when they were questioned by the authorities shortly after the assassination. According to the *Look* report, it was not until an attorney on the payroll of Carlos Marcello showed up to represent Ferrie's friends that they agreed to respond to questioning.[133] It should again be remembered in this sequence of events (which are admittedly confusing, although well documented) that Ferrie was then under brief investigation due to allegations that he had been involved with Oswald in the assassination — allegations made to the FBI and New Orleans Police Department by his colleague, Jack Martin, who subsequently reportedly retracted his information.

In the past several years Peter Noyes has uncovered substantial new information regarding David Ferrie's activities in 1963. Noyes in fact has uncovered documented evidence which shows that in the three-month period before the assassination, Ferrie worked out of the same floor of offices in a New Orleans building which were also being used by Jim Braden. Noyes has documented that just ten weeks before the November assassination, David Ferrie was working out of *Room 1707* of the Pere Marquette Building in New Orleans (in an office used by a top attorney for Mafia leader Marcello) at the same time that Mafia figure Jim Braden was working out of *Room 1701*.[134] Noyes established that in one official parole office document relating to ex-convict Braden, the alleged Mafia courier had even given his address as *Room 1706* in the Pere Marquette Building, which would have been right next door to David Ferrie in *Room 1707*.[135]

It was apparently through his Mafia involvement that David Ferrie also became heavily involved with various right-wing anti-Castro Cuban militants. It has been noted through the years (most recently in the Church Senate Intelligence Committee Report) that the Mafia and various anti-Castro Cubans had fashioned a close relationship — particularly in the Miami, Florida area — after the fall of Cuba to Fidel Castro. As the Church Committee disclosed, top Mafia figures Sam Giancana and Santos Trafficante had been used by the CIA to recruit Cuban exiles for involvement in assassination plots against Castro.[136] David Ferrie had been involved to a still unknown extent in the CIA's abortive Bay of Pigs invasion in April, 1961, apparently as a pilot for clandestine landings inside Cuba. Ferrie himself often spoke of having made a landing somewhere within the island on the very night of the invasion.[137] Three months later, in July 1961, according to a New Orleans Police Department report, David Ferrie had become involved with Cuban exile leader Sergio Arcacha Smith, the head of the Cuban Revolutionary Democratic Front.[138] The Cuban Revolutionary Democratic Front, according to various intelligence sources, was closely affiliated with the CIA, particularly during the Bay of Pigs. E. Howard Hunt, the top Watergate conspirator and former Executive Assistant to CIA Director Allen Dulles, has himself written of the CIA's close involvement with the Cuban Revolutionary Democratic Front, which later became a key part of the larger CIA-coordinated Cuban Revolutionary Council.[139]

According to several reports, David Ferrie was later

involved in training militant anti-Castro Cuban exiles (with CIA assistance) at a secret training camp across Lake Pontchartrain in Louisiana in 1962.[140] This training operation also was reportedly conducted with some degree of cooperation from organized crime figures in Louisiana.[141]

In a mysterious episode that the members of the Warren Commission themselves expressed puzzlement over, Lee Harvey Oswald had once offered to secretly train anti-Castro Cubans in Louisiana for use in clandestine guerrilla warfare. According to the Warren Commission, Oswald made this offer to Cuban exile leader Carlos Bringuier in the summer of 1963 in New Orleans.[142] Bringuier testified that he had rejected Oswald's offer when he found out that Oswald was a "pro-Castro" activist.

While there are several other areas of information relating to David Ferrie's involvement with anti-Castro Cuban exiles, perhaps the most striking example of the mysterious and violent world of Ferrie and his Cuban associates is provided by the late Eladio del Valle. Eladio del Valle was a wealthy former Cuban Congressman during the Batista regime who had later become a well-known organizer of anti-Castro Cuban exiles in Miami. Eladio del Valle had been an associate of David Ferrie and had reportedly financed some of Ferrie's activities through a group formed by del Valle, the "Anti-Communist Civilian and Armed Forces." Three days before David Ferrie's death on February 22, 1967, investigators from New Orleans District Attorney Garrison's office made an attempt to locate Ferrie's associate, Eladio del Valle, in Miami. Garrison's men were seeking to question the wealthy Cuban exile about the extent of his association with Ferrie. District Attorney Garrison's attorneys, and the Miami Police Department, however, were unable to locate del Valle until the early morning hours of February 23rd, about 12 hours after David Ferrie was found dead in New Orleans. In Miami, at 1:34 a.m. on the 23rd, Miami Police Officer

J. W. Hammon discovered the badly mutilated body of Eladio del Valle in a Miami parking lot.[143] Ferrie's friend had been shot in the heart at point blank range and had also had his skull split open, apparently with an ax. Police reported that del Valle had also apparently been tortured prior to the actual killing.[144]

Whatever information Eladio del Valle possessed about David Ferrie's activities died with him just hours after the mysterious Ferrie had himself been found dead. The Miami police have never solved the murder.

With the death of David W. Ferrie in 1967, the man who most Warren Commission critics view as a prime assassination suspect became even more of a mystery than he had been in life. As can be seen from the preceding information, Ferrie's chain of associations — particularly his possible links to both Lee Oswald and Jim Braden — are as solid as they are mysterious.

Interestingly, an episode relating to a morals charge against David Ferrie has provided an indication of the powerful political forces with which Ferrie was allied — political forces allied with Carlos Marcello.

Ferrie had been suspended as a pilot by his employer, Eastern Airlines, in the early 1960s, due to a homosexual incident. Ferrie subsequently filed suit against Eastern in an attempt to retain his job, and the case stretched on into the spring of 1963. Representing Ferrie in the case was G. Wray Gill, who served as Carlos Marcello's top criminal lawyer.

An internal Eastern Airlines legal memorandum, dated May 2, 1963, disclosed that Eastern's lawyers had been approached by two U.S. Congressmen who expressed their interest in Ferrie's behalf.[145] According to the Eastern Airlines lawyer who wrote the memorandum:

This afternoon I talked with both Congressmen Morrison and Long from Louisiana in regard to Captain Ferrie. Both men expressed their great affection and admiration for Mr. Gill . . . They stated they merely wanted to express to Eastern their interest in the Ferrie case and to explore the possibility of a compromise.[146]

The May 2, 1963 Eastern memorandum goes on to note:

I explained to the Congressmen that Captain Ferrie's case had received serious consideration by many of the top management officials of Eastern . . . I also explained that . . . Eastern would be willing to accept a resignation so that Captain Ferrie would not have a black mark against him.

The Congressmen indicated that they did not believe that Captain Ferrie and Mr. Gill would be interested in a resignation as a compromise.[147]

Despite the pressure from the two Louisiana Congressmen, Eastern Airlines subsequently fired Ferrie, as a result of the homosexual incident.

Carlos Marcello

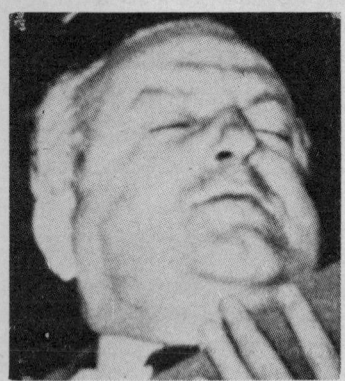

Carlos Marcello is recognized by most Federal law enforcement authorities as either the second or third most powerful Mafia leader in the United States, surpassed in power and influence only by Meyer Lansky, and perhaps the Gambino family of New York. Carlos Marcello is known to have made at least one direct threat to have President Kennedy assassinated, and his employment of David Ferrie and others adds a further dimension to Marcello's possible connection with the events of Dallas.

Marcello, known as "The Little Man" in syndicate circles (due to his diminutive height of 5'4"), had long controlled most organized crime activities in the Gulf states, with a personal empire that extends through Texas and most southern and border states. Marcello's own base of operations is headquartered in New Orleans, Louisiana, and his political and organized crime control in the State of Louisiana is widely regarded as near total. Carlos Marcello's organized crime income — in the State of Louisiana alone — is estimated to be over one billion dollars a year. This astonishing figure has been set forth by both the New Orleans Crime Commission, and organized crime authority Ed Reid. [148]

Carlos Marcello, now 66, was born in Tunis, North Africa in 1910, of Silician parents who later immigrated to the United States. Confusion still exists as to Marcello's original name — sometimes given as Calogero Minacori, other times as Calorso Minicari —

and the circumstances of his subsequent entry into the United States later resulted in extensive legal problems for him during the Kennedy Administration.

Marcello, along with his close associates James Hoffa and Sam Giancana, was also a key target of investigations coordinated by John and Robert Kennedy, probes first conducted in the Senate and subsequently by the Department of Justice during the Kennedy Administration. Carlos Marcello's Mafia empire, particularly his heavy involvement in the world-wide narcotics trade, had long been the subject of various investigative efforts. The McClellan Senate Committee had identified Marcello's New Orleans operations as the key distribution point for heroin shipments coming into the United States.[149] With the influx of vast sums of money for the narcotics trade coming into New Orleans, Carlos Marcello fashioned himself a "broker's position" for dealing with the heroin operations of other crime syndicates.

Instrumental in helping set up the Marcello narcotics empire, according to federal investigators, was Santos Trafficante, the Florida Mafia leader who was recruited by the CIA, Sam Giancana, John Roselli, and Howard Hughes' aide, Robert Maheu, who coordinated the CIA's assassination attempts against Fidel Castro during 1960 to 1963.[150] The Church Committee determined that Santos Trafficante had provided the services of militant Cuban exiles, who were on his Mafia payroll, in these CIA assassination plots.[151]

In 1970, Aaron Kohn, the Director of the New Orleans Crime Commission, noted that Carlos Marcello's Louisiana empire "had corrupt collusion of public officials at every critical level — including police, sheriffs, justices of the peace, prosecutors, mayors, governors, state legislators, and at least one member of Congress." While a top aide to Robert Kennedy described Carlos Marcello as "the perfect embodiment of the American Mafia," the story told by Carlos Marcello himself is quite different:

All I ever hear is "Mafia boss" or "Cosa Nostra boss." I don't know what they're talking about. Sure, I used to be involved in the rackets; I don't deny that. I know a lot of guys around the country who've been in the rackets. But the Mafia — I don't know a thing about it . . . I've never heard of anything like that in Louisiana . . . I wouldn't know a Mafia or a Cosa Nostra from a Congolese tribesman.[152]

In a rare interview with organized crime writer Michael Dorman five years ago, Marcello maintained that various investigators, particularly Congressional investigators, were always trying to "crucify" him:

People take one little piece of true information, twist it around, add a lot of bullshit and come up with some charges that don't even resemble the truth.[153]

Apparently Carlos Marcello had always had problems with "bullshit" evidence produced during literally dozens of different investigations of him. First arrested at the ripe age of nineteen for bank robbery, Marcello had managed somehow to evade imprisonment until about a year later, when he was sentenced to prison for assault and robbery. After serving just four years of his original lengthy sentence, Marcello was back out on the streets, where he subsequently managed to escape convictions on later charges of further robbery, assault and Federal income tax evasion. In 1938, however, at the age of twenty-eight, Marcello was back to prison for a year, for selling twenty-three pounds of marijuana.

Several years later, Carlos Marcello was given his first opportunity to break into the real world of organized crime. As with so many other top Mafia leaders who went on to amass their own empires, Marcello owed his start to one man: Meyer Lansky.

It was "organized crime wizard" Lansky who set Marcello up in the rackets in the seamy Algiers section of New Orleans. According to Organized crime reporter Hank Messick:

> Lansky gave Marcello a franchise for the Algiers section, allowing him to keep two-thirds of the slot machine profits. By 1940 he had 250 machines in operation.[154]

Marcello had later joined with Meyer Lansky and their mutual close friend and associate, Santos Trafficante, in establishing Marcello's extensive holdings (in gambling, prostitution and, of course, narcotics) on the island of Cuba during the corrupt Batista regime. Harry Anslinger, the former director of the Federal Bureau of Narcotics, had told, in a confidential report he provided to the Cuban Ambassador during that period, of the plans that Marcello and Lucky Luciano were developing for Cuba:

> The report stated that Marcello had already become friendly with a number of high Cuban officials through the lavish use of expensive gifts. Luciano had developed a fullfledged plan which envisaged the Caribbean as his center of operations . . . Cuba was to become the center of all international narcotics operations.[155]

While it has never been established how Marcello first came into contact with David Ferrie, they apparently first met during early 1961, when Ferrie was working with Cuban exile leaders involved in the CIA's Bay of Pigs invasion. It was, of course, during this period that the mysterious amalgamation of Cuban exiles, CIA officials, and powerful Mafia leaders all came together in the unsuccessful attempts to topple Fidel Castro either through invasion or assassination. The first known Marcello-Ferrie contact occurred about two months after the Bay of Pigs invasion.

In this early episode, Carlos Marcello used the services of David Ferrie to pilot an airplane out of Guatemala. It all began when the Justice Department ordered Marcello's immediate deportation from the United States on April 4, 1961, two weeks before the Bay of Pigs invasion.

The actual Marcello deportation — which he later described as a "kidnapping" — was personally coordinated by Robert F. Kennedy and his aides. As Marcello was walking along the street, federal agents quickly approached him, arrested and handcuffed him, and then drove him to a waiting jet liner, in which he was flown, as the only passenger on board, to Guatemala. He was not allowed to pack a bag, call his lawyer or even call his wife. It was the most publicized deportation of a Mafia gangster since Lucky Luciano had been expelled from America in the late 1940s.

Two months later, in June of 1961, Carlos Marcello returned to the United States to begin a new and successful legal battle against his deportation. He made his way back into this country by flying up from Guatemala in a private plane. According to federal investigators, the pilot Marcello employed for this flight home was David Ferrie. Years later, both *Look* magazine and the *Los Angeles Times* set forth this Marcello-Ferrie episode during their coverage of Marcello's organized crime activities in New Orleans.[156]

Marcello's questionable deportation, at the hands of his powerful enemies, the Kennedy brothers, was something that enraged the Mafia leader almost beyond words. Friends and associates of Marcello, who has remained in the United States to this day, stated that Marcello spoke of little else for weeks.

Marcello's hatred toward President Kennedy and his brother had intensified by 1962.

Marcello's threat on both their lives was first publicly disclosed in 1969 by Ed Reid, who had earlier co-authored (with Ovid Demaris) the respected Mafia account, *The Green Felt Jungle*.[157] According to Reid's account, which is based on a federal informant's report sent to the Justice Department, Mafia leader Marcello told a highly secret gathering of his closest aides in September of 1962 that plans were being developed to assassinate President Kennedy and that Robert Kennedy might be assassinated also.[158] Carlos Marcello made this threat during a meeting held in a secret bungalow located somewhere on Churchill Farms, a 6,000-acre swamp owned by Marcello on the outskirts of New Orleans.[159]

Ed Reid reports that an enraged Carlos Marcello informed his top Mafia operatives that President Kennedy and Attorney General Kennedy had finally gone too far in their investigations of organized crime. According to Reid's account of the Churchill Farms meeting, Marcello invoked a centuries-old Sicilian death threat against the Kennedy brothers saying, "Livarsi na petra di la scarpa!" which means "Take the stone out of my shoe!" Marcello then reportedly stated — in words chillingly similar to those of his close friend Jimmy Hoffa in an earlier threat — "Don't worry about that little Bobby son of a bitch. He's going to be taken care of."[160] Marcello reportedly further stated that President Kennedy himself would first be assassinated, in a plan to which Marcello was already apparently giving considerable thought:

> . . . the conversation at Churchill Farms also made clear that Marcello had begun to plan a move. He had, for example, already thought of using a "nut" to do the job.[161]

While other details pertaining to Carlos Marcello's reported discussion about having President Kennedy assassinated are not presently available, investigator Ed Reid reports that Marcello seemed to be quite serious in making the threat against the President. This author has written, "No one at the meeting had any doubt about Marcello's intentions . . . Marcello did not joke about such things."[162]

There can also be little doubt that Carlos Marcello was a man quite capable of bringing together the necessary mob expertise (meaning professional assassins) to attempt such a project. Not only was Marcello in a powerful enough position perhaps to draw upon the assassination-planning experience of his associates Santos Trafficante and Sam Giancana, the same men whose resources the CIA had used in trying to assassinate Castro, Marcello himself was, of course, no stranger to having people killed. In 1973, a highly reliable account was furnished regarding Carlos Marcello's handling of his enemies.

In that year, the Justice Department unveiled the single most important Mafia operative to become a federal informant since Joe Valachi a decade earlier. Vincent Teresa had been the third most powerful leader of the New England Mafia, which stretches through six states and includes, according to Teresa, a pool of roughly twelve professional killers.[163]

Vincent Teresa, whose testimony has now led to the indictment and conviction of several high-level Mafia members, has told of several important murders — or "hits" carried out by the New England Mafia's hit men. Teresa notes, "Our assassins had done the same thing for other mobs," including, of course, Carlos Marcello:

> I know they were sent to New Orleans to handle a job for Carlos Marcello, the boss down in Louisiana. I don't know who the target was, but I know they had a contract down there.[164]

One of the key questions that arises in regard to

the reported discussion by Carlos Marcello at Churchill Farms in September, 1962, about having President Kennedy murdered, is whether Marcello's private investigator and pilot, David Ferrie, was present at the meeting. Based upon information contained in an FBI report some four days after the Kennedy assassination, and in light of the kind of activities that Ferrie undertook for Marcello, there seems to be a strong chance that Ferrie was indeed present at the meeting. In an FBI report dated November 26th, 1963, which contained the results of an interview conducted with Ferrie the day before, the FBI stated that Ferrie had informed them that he had been employed by Carlos Marcello's top criminal attorney "since March, 1962." The FBI report goes on to state:

> He [Ferrie] said that since the end of August, 1963, and up until November 22, 1963 he has been working on a case involving CARLOS MARCELLO who was charged in Federal Court in connection with a fradulent birth certificate . . .
>
> He stated that on November 9 and November 16, 1963 he was at Churchill [Farms], which is a farm owned by CARLOS MARCELLO, mapping strategy in connection with MARCELLO'S trial. He informed that on November 11, 1963 he was in New Orleans, during the entire day and did not leave the city.
>
> FERRIE stated that from October 11 to October 18, 1963 he was in Guatemala and again from October 30, 1963 to November 1, 1963, he was in Guatemala in connection with investigation of the MARCELLO case.
>
> FERRIE said that prior to a very recent trip he was last in the state of Texas in August, 1962.[165]

The FBI report notes that Ferrie placed at least six telephone calls to Carlos Marcello's top lawyer during the immediate three-day period following the Kennedy assassination.[166] As noted earlier, David Ferrie was at that point driving straight through from New Orleans to Houston on what he claimed was a goose hunting vacation.[167] The November 26th FBI report states that Ferrie claimed that his first several telephone calls late the night of the assassination (or in the early morning hours of November 23rd) were to let Carlos Marcello and his lawyer know that he "had left New Orleans and was on a vacation trip."[168]

The FBI report notes that Ferrie had returned from Houston to New Orleans on November 24, 1963, after hearing news reports that he was a suspect wanted for questioning in regard to the Dallas assassination.[169] According to the report, Ferrie then consulted with Marcello's top lawyer, G. Wray Gill, in the Pere Marquette Building in New Orleans, and then "surrendered" himself to District Attorney Jim Garrison's office late on the afternoon of November 25, 1963.

While Garrison pursued David Ferrie several years later as a "leading suspect" in what Garrison alleged was a massive conspiracy behind the Presidential assassination, the links between David Ferrie and Carlos Marcello and other top Mafia figures — including Jim Braden — have only begun to receive more serious attention in recent years.

In the immediate years following the Kennedy assassination, Carlos Marcello's close relationship with Florida Mafia leader Santos Trafficante became even more apparent. Santos Trafficante was the top Mafia leader selected by the CIA to plan the assassination of Fidel Castro. According to the Church Committee, "Cosa Nostra Chieftain" Trafficante (using the code name "Joe") worked with Mafia figures John Roselli, Sam Giancana, and Robert Maheu in the assassination conspiracies against Castro from late 1960 to mid-1963.[170]

In late 1966, Santos Trafficante and Carlos Marcello

were involved in a famous Mafia incident that still puzzles Federal organized crime investigators. On September 22, 1966, New York police officers inadvertently became aware of a meeting of several Mafia members in an Italian restaurant, La Stella, on Long Island. When the New York Police Department dispatched several officers to the restaurant to cover the meeting, they quickly discovered that they had come upon the largest and most powerful assemblage of Mafia leaders since the notorious Apalachin meeting of a decade earlier.

Among those dining at a table reserved by Carlos Marcello, in addition to Marcello himself, were CIA-Mafia assassination coordinator Santos Trafficante; New York Mafia "boss of bosses" Carlos Gambino; Thomas "Tommy Ryan" Eboli (the head of the Vito Genovese mob); Mafia boss Joseph Columbo, and several others. The New York police placed each of the powerful Mafia leaders under arrest — ironically for "consorting with known criminals" — and the incident became an historic footnote in organized crime history. As might be expected, the charges filed against the men didn't stick, and they were back out on the streets shortly thereafter.

Despite several hundred hours of probing by state and federal investigators, the purpose of the high level Mafia meeting has still never been determined. Investigators have noted that of the five top Mafia bosses discovered at the restaurant, only Carlos Marcello and Santos Trafficante have fared well in the years since. For the other three men, life was either about to become highly troublesome or very short. On June 28, 1971, Marcello and Trafficante's dining companion Joe Columbo was shot to death in downtown New York City. Later that same year, the powerful Carlos Gambino (after having lost a bid in the U.S. Supreme Court to nullify a deportation order) became subject to immediate deportation as soon as his "ill health" permitted enforcement of the ruling. On July 16, 1972, Thomas "Tommy Ryan" Eboli was also found brutally shot to death in New York.

Several years after the famous "La Stella raid" of 1966, Carlos Marcello offered his own version of the New York restaurant meeting, denying there was any sinister intent to it:

> . . . I decided to see some of my old friends — so we all got together for lunch. Sure, some of these fellows had been in the rackets . . . But, if they're in the Mafia, I don't know a damned thing about that. This was strictly a social gathering; that's all there was to it . . . What's the matter with some old friends getting together for lunch?[171]

Carlos Marcello is now still thriving in New Orleans, reportedly in excellent health.

Santos Trafficante Jr.

Santos Trafficante Jr. is one of the half-dozen most powerful Mafia leaders in the United States, with an organized crime empire that extends through most of Florida (with headquarters in Tampa) and which exercises what federal narcotics experts believe is perhaps the dominant role in the world-wide heroin trade. Santos Trafficante Jr., and his late father, were regarded as key architects of the Mafia's present-day international narcotics operations.

As will be seen, Santos Trafficante Jr., now 61, is also reliably reported to have made a threat on the life of President Kennedy — saying "He is going to be hit" — a threat which was subsequently reported to the Miami FBI. However, perhaps the most important aspect of Trafficante's threat, which reportedly occurred during September of 1962, is provided by Trafficante's previous background: from late 1960 until at least September 11, 1962, Santos Trafficante was serving as a top coordinator of the secret CIA-Mafia assassination conspiracies against Fidel Castro.[172]

Trafficante's involvement in the CIA-Mafia assassination conspiracies was first officially documented by the Church Committee in November, 1975,[173] when it disclosed that these secret plots had been mounted with the knowledge and authorization of CIA Deputy Director for Plans Richard Helms. It was also shown that Helms withheld knowledge of the plots from CIA Director John McCone, as well as President Kennedy and Attorney General Robert F. Kennedy.[174]

The Senate Intelligence Committee stated that Santos Trafficante was involved in the CIA-Mafia plots from the beginning, with Mafioso John Roselli introducing him to organizer Robert Maheu sometime in late September or early October of 1960.[175] The Senate Committee Report noted:

> Roselli introduced Maheu to two individuals on whom Roselli intended to rely: "Sam Gold," who would serve as a "back-up man," or "key" man, and "Joe," who "Gold" said would serve as a courier to Cuba and make arrangements there.[176]

The Senate Committee reported that "Sam Gold" was in fact Chicago Mafia leader Sam Giancana, and "Joe" was in fact Florida Mafia leader Santos Trafficante.

The CIA's use of Trafficante in its Mafia-allied plots against Castro was primarily a result of Trafficante's well-known status as a leading Mafia figure in Havana, Cuba, prior to the Castro take-over. Alfred W. McCoy, the author of the highly respected analysis, *The Politics of Heroin in Southeast Asia*, has provided the following account of Trafficante's pre-Castro Havana activities:

> Santo Jr.'s official position in Havana was that of manager of the Sans Souci Casino, but he was far more important than his title indicates. As his father's financial representative, and ultimately Meyer Lansky's, Santo Jr. controlled much of Havana's tourist industry and became quite close to the pre-Castro dictator Fulgencio Batista. Moreover, it was reportedly his responsibility to receive the bulk shipments of heroin from Europe and forward them through Florida to New York and other urban centers, where their distribution was assisted by local Mafia bosses.[177]

In any event, Trafficante was the man selected by the Mafia and CIA to arrange the logistics of the attempts to poison Fidel Castro in late March or early April of 1961, just before the Bay of Pigs. The Senate Intelligence Committee Report states:

> ...Roselli told the Support Chief that Trafficante believed a certain leading figure in the Cuban exile movement might be able to accomplish the [Castro] assassination. The Inspector General's Report suggests that this Cuban may have been receiving funds from Trafficante and other racketeers interested in securing "gambling, prostitution, and

dope monopolies" in Cuba after the overthrow of Castro.[178]

The Senate Report notes that Trafficante was present when the CIA's highly sophisticated and non-traceable poison capsules were passed from the Central Intelligence Agency to the Mafia and in turn to Trafficante's top Cuban exile operative.[179] According to the Report, "The money and pills were delivered at a meeting between Maheu, Roselli, Trafficante, and the Cuban at the Fontainebleau Hotel in Miami."[180] The Senate Report set forth the testimony of John Roselli regarding this key meeting, at which (according to Roselli) Robert Maheu delivered the assassination devices. Interestingly, Roselli's testimony of June 24, 1975, was given before the Senate Intelligence Committee just four days after his assassination-planning colleague, Sam Giancana, was found shot to death in his Chicago home. John Roselli himself was found brutally murdered (apparently through a combination of being stabbed, strangled, and dismembered) a little over a year later in the summer of 1976.

Santos Trafficante was never called to testify by the Senate Intelligence Committee, and thus was the only living principal in the CIA-Mafia plots whose testimony was never heard. The Senate Committee stated that Trafficante was believed to be out of the country at the time — reportedly in Costa Rica — and was thus beyond the reach of subpoena. Santos Trafficante's reported statement in September of 1962, that President Kennedy "is going to be hit" was not publicly known at the time of the Senate Intelligence Committee's investigation of 1975 and early 1976, although other information about various "hits" attributed to him was known.

Perhaps the best illustration of Trafficante's enormous standing in the national crime syndicate — and the most vivid evidence of his authority as an organizer of high-level Mafia murder — came in late 1957. Following the decline of New York Mafia leader

Frank Costello in the mid-1950's, an epic struggle for control of the Mafia's governing board, "The Commission," was set in motion between the two most violent Mafia leaders in the nation: the wildly vicious Vito Genovese and the even more violent Albert Anastasia, the actual leader of "Murder Incorporated," the Syndicate's group of professional killers. Most organized crime experts forecast an imminent inner-Syndicate war of enormous proportions. Both Anastasia and Genovese reportedly voiced fears of being "set up" by the other in a Mob killing.

On October 25, 1957, Albert Anastasia agreed to confer with Santos Trafficante at the Park Sheraton Hotel in New York. Among the matters discussed by the two Mafia bosses were Anastasia's plans to run a casino in Havana that would have competed with casinos being run by Meyer Lansky and Trafficante.[181] An hour after Trafficante checked out of the Park Sheraton that morning, Albert Anastasia was approached by two men in the hotel barber shop and was literally blown out of a barber's chair by a long volley of point blank pistol shots.

While Santos Trafficante was never indicted for the murder of Albert Anastasia, organized crime experts almost universally credit Trafficante with the "set-up" of the hit. Fred J. Cook, the veteran investigative journalist, has written of the significance of the Anastasia murder and the end it brought to his freewheeling "Murder Incorporated":

> In retrospect, it can be seen that the slaying of Albert Anastasia was an event of such pivotal importance that the repercussions, continuing to the present day, have changed the face and lifestyle of the . . . Mafia.
>
> . . . It proclaimed . . . the end of the rule of order and the licensing of unauthorized murder as an instrument of change.[182]

After successfully planning and carrying out the Mob assassination of Anastasia — himself the most skillful and heavily-guarded Mafia executioner in the nation — Trafficante may perhaps have regarded the assassination of Fidel Castro as just another "job."

The account of Santos Trafficante's reported threat against President Kennedy was first set forth publicly in May of 1976 in a lengthy article by George Crile for the *Washington Post*.[183] Crile, who has conducted extensive research into the mysterious intrigues of the Cuban exile community, and who is collaborating with former Watergate burglars Bernard Barker and Eugenio Martinez on a forthcoming book, set forth the account of José Aleman.

Aleman was a well-known and wealthy Cuban activist who had been a prime catalyst behind efforts to overthrow the corrupt Batista regime. José Aleman had at one time owned the Miami Stadium and the Tradewinds Motel, a gathering place for many Cuban exile militants.[184] Aleman had long been regarded as a reliable source of information within the Cuban community by various law-enforcement authorities, including the FBI.

According to the account of José Aleman provided to Crile, Santos Trafficante sent an emissary to see Aleman some time in September, 1962, in order to set up a meeting. During their subsequent meeting, Trafficante discussed arranging a $1.5 million loan to Aleman.[185] Aleman states that a Trafficante associate had earlier informed him that the loan was to be arranged through the Teamsters Union, and that it had "already been cleared by Jimmy Hoffa himself."[186]

According to Aleman's account of his September 1962 meeting with Trafficante, the Florida Mafia leader discoursed on a wide variety of subjects; Trafficante "spoke almost poetically about Democracy and civil liberties." Then Trafficante turned to the subject of the Kennedys, accusing President Kennedy and his brother, the Attorney General, of various offenses. Speaking of President Kennedy, Trafficante reportedly stated:

> Have you seen how his brother is hitting Hoffa, a man who is a worker, who is not a millionaire, a friend of the blue collars? He doesn't know that this kind of encounter is very delicate. Mark my word, this man Kennedy is in trouble, and he will get what is coming to him.[187]

José Aleman states that at that point he told Trafficante that he disagreed, interjecting that he thought President Kennedy would be re-elected. It was then, according to Aleman, that Trafficante stated, "No, José he is going to be hit."[188]

Aleman states that he reported the details of this meeting with Santos Trafficante to the FBI shortly thereafter, but that the Bureau seemed uninterested in the threat. Aleman further states that he began to meet with Trafficante on frequent occasions after that first meeting, and that he always reported the substance of these meetings to two FBI men to whom he was close: Agents George Davis and Paul Scranton.[189] On one occasion Trafficante introduced Aleman to Philadelphia Mafia leader Angelo Bruno. According to George Crile's account, Aleman states that by the summer of 1963, "I advised the FBI in long conversations that I thought something was going to happen . . . I was telling them to be careful."[190] The FBI never apparently gave any credence to his information about Trafficante until several hours after President Kennedy was shot to death on November 22, 1963. Then, according to Aleman:

> Two agents came out to see me. They wanted to know more and more. I finally had to tell them he [Santos Trafficante]

didn't say he was going to do it. He just said
Kennedy was going to get hit.[191]

Aleman further claimed that the FBI agents requested him to keep his account of the Trafficante meeting confidential, which Aleman says he did. Journalist George Crile reports that FBI men Paul Scranton and George Davis both acknowledge their "frequent contact" with Aleman, but that both FBI men refuse any comment regarding Aleman's reported discussions with Trafficante. According to Crile, Scranton declined to discuss the alleged Trafficante threat, saying, "I wouldn't want to do anything to embarrass the Bureau."[192]

Needless to say, José Aleman's account of Santos Trafficante's reported statement about President Kennedy being assassinated could be cleared up during the official re-opening of the Kennedy case. Obviously the testimony of FBI agents Scranton and Davis, as well as a review of related FBI files would provide a firm basis in probing the episode.

Interestingly, at the same time as the alleged Trafficante threat, Trafficante was preparing another "three-man team" of Cuban exile assassins to try to kill Fidel Castro in Cuba. José Aleman has said that his meeting with Trafficante occurred sometime in September of 1962.[193] According to the Senate Intelligence Committee Report, a top Cuban exile leader employed by Trafficante was meeting with CIA official William Harvey and Mafia leader John Roselli during that same period: September, 1962. The Senate Report stated:

> Harvey met Roselli in Miami on Sept. 7 and 11, 1962. The Cuban was reported to be preparing to send in another three-man team to penetrate Castro's bodyguard. Harvey was told that the pills, referred to as "the medicine" were still "safe" in Cuba.[194]

The Senate Report noted that "According to FBI memoranda dated Dec. 21, 1960, and Jan. 18, 1961, the Cuban was associated with anti-Castro activities financed by United States racketeers, including Santos Trafficante, who hoped to secure illegal monopolies in the event of Castro's overthrow."[195]

Incredibly enough, these areas of information pertaining to Trafficante only scratch the surface of information that may relate to Kennedy's assassination. As was noted earlier, Lewis McWillie, a close associate and trusted employee of Santos Trafficante's, happened to have been one of Jack Ruby's closest friends. And in fact, Ruby had visited Lewis McWillie during two 1959 trips to Havana, according to the Warren Report. The Warren Commission said Ruby "idolized" McWillie, who was the manager of the Tropicana Casino in Havana, owned by Trafficante and Meyer Lansky.[196]

While Trafficante's secret role as a top CIA-Mafia assassination coordinator would not be disclosed until 1975, the close relationship between Santos Trafficante and Lewis McWillie — and between Lewis McWillie and Jack Ruby — was set forth by the Warren Commission eleven years earlier. According to a March 26, 1964 memorandum for the Warren Commission, prepared by the FBI:

> . . . it would appear McWillie solidified his Syndicate connections through his association in Havana Cuba with Santos Trafficante, well-known syndicate member, for Tampa Florida; Meyer and Jake Lansky; Dino Cellini and others who were members of or associates of "the syndicate".
>
> . . . He left Dallas and went to Havana Cuba, where he was known to associate with nationally known gambling characters such as Willie Bischoff, also known as Lefty Clark, Jake Lansky, Trafficante, and others.[197]

In addition to setting forth other details of the Ruby-McWillie relationship, the Warren Commission noted that the two men had discussed a plan to ship a gun through the mail a few weeks before the assassination, and that Ruby subsequently did in fact ship a pistol to McWillie.[198] The Warren Commission, however, never fully investigated the gun shipment, and McWillie was never called before the Commission as a witness.

In spring, 1976, a newly-declassified CIA document added a highly significant new area of information pertaining to Santos Trafficante and the Kennedy assassination. While the Trafficante-McWillie and McWillie-Ruby relationships have been previously documented, the new document declassified by the CIA in April 1976 raised the even more incredible spectre that Santos Trafficante and Jack Ruby may not only have had a close mutual friend in Lewis McWillie but also may actually have known each other.

This information was set forth in a previously secret CIA memorandum that had been prepared on November 28, 1963, less than a week after the assassination of President Kennedy. In the declassified document, which was sent to McGeorge Bundy at the White House, to U. Alexis Johnson at the State Department, and to the FBI, the CIA disclosed the following information:

> On 26 November 1963, a British journalist named John Wilson, and also known as Wilson-Hudson, gave information to the American Embassy in London which indicated that an "American gangster-type named Ruby" visited Cuba around 1959. Wilson himself was working in Cuba at that time and was jailed by Castro before he was deported.
>
> In prison in Cuba, Wilson says he met an American gangster-gambler named Santos

who could not return to the U.S.A. because there were several indictments outstanding against him. Instead he preferred to live in relative luxury in a Cuban prison. While Santos was in prison, Wilson says, Santos was visited frequently by an American gangster type named Ruby. His story is being followed up. Wilson says he had once testified about Castro activities before the Eastland Committee of the U.S. Senate, sometime in 1959 or 1960.[199]

As with so many other recently declassified Kennedy assassination documents, this one raises chilling possibilities. Key aspects of this information supplied by British journalist Wilson-Hudson definitely seem to mesh with other known facts: Santos Trafficante did indeed conduct his operations out of a Havana prison cell in the months after the overthrow of the Batista government by Castroite forces; Trafficante did indeed face legal charges back in the United States; and perhaps more importantly, Jack Ruby did indeed make at least two known trips to Havana, Cuba in late 1959, where he visited his close friend Lewis McWillie — the top Trafficante gambling aide.[200] In addition, the Warren Commission noted that Ruby may well have made other trips to Cuba during later periods.

However, the Warren Commission itself (with the exception of member Allen Dulles) was never privy to the secret CIA-Mafia assassination conspiracies that had involved Santos Trafficante, and thus had no inkling of the possible significance of the CIA memorandum regarding John Wilson-Hudson's information about a gangster named "Santos" meeting a gangster named "Ruby" in his Havana prison cell. Likewise, the reported Trafficante threat against President Kennedy — and the Wilson-Hudson CIA document — were unknown to the Senate Intelligence Committee before the Committee's investigative staff ended its work in early 1976. Santos Trafficante, is presently reported to be visiting Syndicate friends somewhere in Costa Rica.

Howard Hughes and Robert Maheu

With the death of Howard Hughes on April 5, 1976, there came the inevitable outpouring of news stories by the national press about the mystery billionaire's financial intrigues and his eccentric, reclusive, and often ruthless personal activities. There were also endless stories about his large web of associations with both elected public officials and the CIA, as well as organized crime figures. The press focused a great deal of attention on the mysterious and direct connections of Howard Hughes to such things as a secret $100,000 cash payment to President Richard Nixon through his close friend, Bebe Rebozo; the Hughes involvement in the top-secret CIA project of raising a sunken Soviet submarine from the bottom of the ocean in "Project Jennifer"; the involvement of former Hughes executive Robert Maheu in other CIA activities; and the close relationship between Hughes and various Mafia leaders whose Las Vegas gambling operations often interlocked with his own.

Surprisingly however, even with the mass of detailed news accounts of the death of the "phantom billionaire" and the long reviews of his checkered career (notably in cover stories in both *Time* and *Newsweek*) an important part of the Howard Hughes story was left out.

Perhaps the reason for the omission was the fact that initial confirmation of this information had come in a widely overlooked footnote on page 75 of the Senate Intelligence Committee's Report on Alleged Assassination Plots Involving Foreign Leaders.

Very simply, it can now be established that billionaire Howard Hughes was a direct party to and indeed an indirect sponsor of the top secret CIA-Mafia assassination conspiracies of late 1960 to mid-1963, targeted against Fidel Castro.[201]

Hughes' connection to these plots began in late 1960, when, according to the Senate Report, "The CIA took steps to enlist members of the criminal underworld with gambling syndicate contacts to aid in assassinating Castro."[202] While the Senate Committee noted that "the origin of the plot is uncertain," the crucial coordinating role of Hughes' top consultant, Robert Maheu, was set forth in detail in the Committee's Report, which states that the small group of top CIA officials who set them in motion "decided to rely on Robert A. Maheu to recruit someone 'tough enough' to handle the job."[203] Within a few short months, Maheu had recruited at least three top Mafia leaders who did indeed seem "tough enough" to handle the job: Sam Giancana of Chicago, John Roselli of Chicago and Las Vegas, and Santos Trafficante of Florida.[204] As noted earlier, these conspiracies were concealed from both President Kennedy and CIA director John McCone by CIA officials working in the Agency's Plans Directorate under Richard Helms, and Office of Security, under Sheffield Edwards.[205]

While the details of these conspiracies against Fidel Castro were finally set forth by the Senate Intelligence Committee in 1975, the story of Howard Hughes' involvement had already begun leaking out the previous year. In the spring of 1974, Robert Maheu gave extensive testimony in Federal Court regarding his past activities as Howard Hughes' "right-hand man." Maheu was then suing Hughes for 17.5 million dollars in a defamation of character suit which Maheu subsequently won. During his testimony in mid-May of 1974, Maheu stated that he had been involved in a "very sensitive assignment" for the CIA in Miami during 1960 and 1961.[206] According to the *Los Angeles Times*, "Maheu testified he had been asked by the U.S. government to recruit the services of Johnny Roselli, alleged underworld figure," in connection with this CIA assignment:[207]

> Three years ago, Roselli sought a reduction in his prison sentence in the Friars Club card cheating case on the grounds that he had worked with Maheu in a CIA mission to assassinate Cuban Premier Fidel Castro in the early 1960s.[208]

In his testimony, Maheu quoted Hughes as saying he also had known Roselli for many years, and it was Roselli who helped "grease the way for Hughes' original entry onto the Las Vegas scene."[209] While Maheu did not admit in Federal Court that his "sensitive assignment" for the CIA had been as field coordinator for CIA-Mafia conspiracies against Castro, he did disclose that he had informed Howard Hughes of the "assignment."[210]

Finally, in November of 1975, after a lengthy investigation of the CIA's foreign assassination conspiracies, the Senate Intelligence Committee set forth the findings of their complex probe. And it was then, in a brief footnote, that the involvement of Howard Hughes, through Robert Maheu, was finally confirmed. According to the Senate Report:

Maheu told the committee that at that time, Hughes was becoming an important client, and that devoting time to the CIA's assassination plot was hindering his work for Hughes. He testified that shortly before the election in November 1960, while he was in Miami working on the assassination project, Hughes phoned and asked him to return to the West Coast. Maheu testified that, since he did "not want to lose" Hughes as a client, he "definitely told him that the project was on behalf of the United States Government, that it included plans to dispose of Mr. Castro in connection with a pending invasion."[211]

Not only did Howard Hughes provide continuing authorization for Maheu to coordinate the conspiracy between the CIA and the Mafia during the early 1960s, he subsequently sought to involve himself in an even deeper relationship with the CIA. According to Maheu, his mysterious employer once instructed him to set up a secret CIA-Howard Hughes link, which could be used to shield Hughes from scrutiny by any other investigative or regulatory agency. Maheu has stated:

> Mr. Hughes suggested I try to work out some kind of arrangement with the CIA whereby either he or the Hughes Tool Company could become a front for this intelligence agency.
> He pointed out that if he ever became involved with the Government — a regulatory body or investigative agency — he thought it would be very beneficial to him . . .
> I told him I couldn't believe what he was telling me, and under no circumstances would I assist him.[212]

While Robert Maheu stated that "under no circumstances" would he "assist" Howard Hughes in establishing a secret relationship with the CIA, the available public record suggests otherwise. Not only did Robert Maheu through his previous CIA associations actually become Hughes' liaison to the CIA, he also went on to handle other jobs for the CIA on his own. One such example came to light in February, 1976, when the House Intelligence Committee Report was published in the *Village Voice* after being obtained by Daniel Schorr of CBS News. The Report revealed that Robert Maheu had been involved in another of the CIA's more questionable operations:

> Taxpayers monies were spent to provide heads of state with female companions and to pay people with questionable reputations to make pornographic movies for blackmail [against heads of state]. . . .
> One of these was titled "Happy Days," with Mr. Robert Maheu as casting director, make-up man, camera man and director.[213]

Though Maheu claims to have been disturbed over Hughes' desire to "become a front" for the CIA, there is strong documentary evidence that Maheu himself shared that desire. And, once again, relevant information dates back to the CIA-Mafia-Maheu assassination plot. In September, 1975, the Senate Intelligence Committee heard the testimony in executive session of Joseph Shimon, a close friend of John Roselli and Sam Giancana. Shimon testified that he had accompanied Giancana and Roselli to Miami shortly before the Bay of Pigs invasion in early 1961, and had been present when CIA officials passed the non-traceable poison pills to Roselli and Giancana for use in murdering Fidel Castro.[214]

Shimon told the Senate Committee that Maheu indicated to him that he was letting John Roselli handle the details of the proposed Castro assassination. Shimon testified that Maheu told him, "Johnny's going to handle everything, this is Johnny's contract."[215] In his Senate testimony of September 20, 1975, (most of which has never been publicly released) Joseph Shimon also states that Giancana had told him that Robert Maheu was using his involvement in the CIA-Mafia plot to further his own purposes, and that "Maheu's conning the hell out of the CIA."[216]

Maheu's role in the CIA-Mafia plots particularly disturbed Attorney General Robert Kennedy when he first learned of them in May, 1962. The Senate Intelligence Committee set forth the testimony of William Harvey, the CIA's designated coordinator for the plots, regarding his fear that some of the plot's participants might later be able to blackmail the entire government. Harvey testified that he had thought at the time that there was "a very real possibility of this government being blackmailed either by Cubans [exiles] for political purposes or by figures in organized crime for their own self protection . . . "[217] The Committee released portions of a May 10, 1962 memorandum written by J. Edgar Hoover in which he describes a private meeting he had with RFK shortly after the Kennedys found out about the CIA-Mafia plan:

> I expressed great astonishment at this in view of the bad reputation of Maheu . . . The Attorney General shared the same views.[218]

In the same previously-secret Hoover memorandum, the FBI Director quoted Robert Kennedy's fears about the possible power gained by these men by having been involved in this way with the CIA. While William Harvey feared "this government being blackmailed" by the Mafia leaders or Cuban exiles, Robert Kennedy apparently also had Howard Hughes' aide, Robert Maheu, in mind. According to the May 10, 1962

Hoover memorandum, RFK told the FBI Director that there was a possibility that "for these reasons, the CIA was in a position where it could not afford to have any action taken against Giancana and Maheu."[219]

While Maheu's role as a conspirator began to leak out during his 1974 defamation of character suit against Howard Hughes, that same law-suit and trial provided other new information regarding the Hughes-Maheu relationship as well. During the course of his lengthy and highly detailed testimony regarding his work for Hughes over the years, Maheu briefly disclosed that Hughes had once "assigned" him to have President Kennedy "removed" from office, and had subsequently wanted President Johnson removed from the Presidency also. Maheu testified that Hughes had spoken of the possibility of using some kind of "recall movement" to accomplish these two separate Presidential "removals."[220] However, Maheu provided no further details about Hughes' orders to "start recall movements against two Presidents of the United States."[221] At the time of the Hughes-Maheu trial in 1974, Maheu did not identify which "two Presidents" Hughes had wanted removed. However, observers pointed out that there had been only four presidents — Eisenhower, Kennedy, Johnson, and Nixon — in office during the period in which Maheu worked for Hughes, and further, that Hughes' admiration for Eisenhower and strong sustained financial support for Nixon were well known. Additionally, Hughes' anger over JFK's civil rights policies (Hughes was an avowed white supremacist who believed Negroes were "rampant carriers" of germs) was as well known as his apparent desire to see the CIA and Mafia successfully rid Cuba of the leadership of Fidel Castro. In any event, shortly after the 1974 trial, Maheu's attorneys privately confirmed that President Kennedy, and later President Lyndon Johnson, were indeed the two men whom Howard Hughes "assigned" Maheu to remove or "recall" from office.

Hughes' wish to maneuver himself into a position

where he could influence or even control actions and decisions at the highest levels of the American government not only came into play with regard to the Central Intelligence Agency, but also J. Edgar Hoover's FBI. George Allen, a close personal friend of FBI Director Hoover and a former official in the Roosevelt and Truman Administrations, has provided the following account of one of Howard Hughes' other plans:

> I was at La Jolla with Hoover one day when Howard Hughes came to the Del Charro and tried to hire him . . . I talked to him right after his meeting with Hughes and he told me everything they talked about. Hughes wanted him [Hoover] to represent him in Washington. To be his contact man, lobbyist, so to speak . . . He said, "You name the price and I'll pay you anything you like, give you a lifetime contract — any amount of money."
>
> Hoover said, "I appreciate your offer but I'm not interested in any job." But the thing that tickled Hoover was that when Hughes first came in, he looked all around and said, "Is this place bugged?" And Hoover said, "Oh, no, there's no bugs."[222]

During the same trial further details became available about the relationship between Howard Hughes and Johnny Roselli. In the course of lengthy testimony about Hughes' famous acquisition of several Las Vegas hotels and casinos during the late 1960s, Moe Dalitz, one of the former owners of the Desert Inn, said that Howard Hughes' subsequent purchase of the Desert Inn had been accomplished through the involvement of two of Hughes' close associates: Teamster President Jimmy Hoffa and Mafia operative John Roselli. Moe Dalitz, now one of the principal owners of the La Costa resort in California, "is alleged to have had crime syndicate ties dating back to Prohibition days," according to the *Los Angeles Times* and other sources.[223] Dalitz testified that his "old friend" Jimmy Hoffa had been the man who coordinated Hughes' lengthy stay at the Desert Inn several months before the billionaire decided to buy it. Hoffa told Dalitz that the Desert Inn should provide special accomodations for Howard Hughes as a "personal favor" to Hoffa.[224] Dalitz stated that Hoffa said he had "personal reasons" for interceding on behalf of Howard Hughes.[225] When Hughes finally bought the Desert Inn in March, 1967, a one hundred and fifty thousand dollar finder's fee was paid to Edward P. Morgan, a Washington attorney closely associated with Hoffa, Hughes, and Maheu. In turn, Morgan paid fifty thousand dollars to John Roselli, a close associate of Maheu, Hoffa, and Hughes.[226] Howard Hughes' practice of making vast, often secret, political contributions to Congressmen, Senators, Governors, Vice Presidents, and Presidents of both parties has come under increasing attention in recent years. Particular interest has centered around the still highly mysterious payment of at least one hundred thousand dollars in cash from Howard Hughes to President Richard Nixon sometime during 1970-71, with Bebe Rebozo and Hughes employees Richard Danner and Robert Maheu serving as the couriers for the transaction. The Ervin Watergate Committee allocated a massive amount of its investigative time and resources to the "Hughes-Rebozo investigation," but was never able to arrive at any final conclusions as to why, when, or exactly how Hughes made the secret payment to Richard Nixon.[227] This payment, originally disclosed by columnist Jack Anderson, was separate and apart from other sizeable public contributions to Nixon's 1968 and 1972 Presidential campaigns.

The Ervin Watergate Committee's final Report details the strange circumstances of the Hughes-Nixon payments, including the testimony of Robert Maheu's son Peter, himself a former CIA agent:

> Peter Maheu [in his Select Committee staff interview] stated that someone in his father's office gave him a typed sheet of paper to be signed by Richard Nixon acknowledging Nixon's receipt of one hundred thousand dollars from Hughes. Danner told Peter Maheu that Nixon "will never sign it," and Maheu has been unable to find the document.[228]

According to this Report, the payoff to Nixon was eventually accomplished through the delivery of two fifty-thousand-dollar cash bundles:

> The second delivery, according to Maheu, occurred at Rebozo's home in Key Biscayne. Maheu saw the envelope passed from Danner to Rebozo, who opened it but did not count the money. Rebozo then took the envelope, went into another room, and returned in a short time without the envelope. The only conversation was something by Danner to the effect of "Here's the second 50." No one else was present and the three immediately left in Rebozo s car...[229]

Some observers, including Senator Howard Baker, Jack Anderson, writers J. Anthony Lukas and Hank Greenspun, as well as Watergate conspirators James McCord, Charles Colson, and Jeb Magruder, have speculated about the possibility that Howard Hughes was directly involved in the unsolved mysteries of Watergate in a much more direct way than has been previously indicated.

James McCord testified that his fellow Watergate conspirators, E. Howard Hunt and G. Gordon Liddy, had once formulated plans to conduct a break-in of the Las Vegas newspaper office of Hughes' enemy, Hank Greenspun, under the joint authorization and sponsorship of both the Nixon White House and Howard Hughes.[230] Additionally, during the Ervin Committee probe of 1973-74, Senator Baker established that a key Washington "public relations" employee of Hughes, Robert Bennett (who headed a CIA-affiliated P R firm, the Robert Mullen Company), had mysteriously served as the key go-between or "point of contact" for Hunt and Liddy during the immediate two weeks following the Watergate break-in of June 17, 1972.[231] Hunt and Liddy were then both in hiding to avoid questioning and arrest in connection with the break-in.

The mysterious political, intelligence, and organized crime involvements of Howard Hughes and his multi-billion dollar empire have apparently not even ended with his death. On May 6, 1976, a month after his demise, Jack Anderson disclosed that virtually the entire upper echelon of Hughes' top aides were making substantial political contributions to the 1976 political campaigns. Anderson reported that Senator Howard Cannon of Nevada, the powerful Chairman of the Senate Rules Committee, was the key recipient of these contributions from the Hughes empire.[232] Hughes' past efforts to cultivate helpful relationships in the U.S. Senate are now well known. Close to one dozen current members of the Senate received political contributions from him.

Interestingly, a close friend of former President Gerald Ford has provided an illuminating account of how the political intrigues of Howard Hughes may have worked. In 1974, in the Ford biography *Jerry Ford Up Close*, Bud Vestal asked, "Did billionaire Howard Hughes try to buy Jerry Ford a Senate seat?"[233] Vestal, a reporter from Ford's hometown of Grand Rapids, Michigan, who has known him for twenty-five years disclosed that "under most peculiar circumstances" a small "delegation of very conservative Republicans" had once offered Gerald Ford "unlimited campaign funds" if he wanted to run for a U.S. Senate seat from Michigan.[234] According to Vestal, Ford confided to him that the offer was never "generally known,"[235] and that he had later heard that "the people who came to see me allegedly had been urged to do so by some of Howard Hughes' friends."[236]

Sam Giancana

Sam Giancana, the Chicago Mafia leader and coordinator of the anti-Castro CIA-Mafia assassination conspiracies, was found murdered in his home at the age of 67 on June 19, 1975. Giancana had been shot in the face and neck six times by an assailant whom he probably knew. Two weeks later, the Giancana murder weapon was found: a .22 caliber pistol with more than forty holes drilled in the barrel to make its silencer almost completely effective. Police were unable to trace the murder weapon beyond its delivery to a Miami gun dealer by the manufacturer on June 20, 1965, and its subsequent sale to another Florida dealer who later re-sold it. At the time of his murder, the aging Mafia leader's house was under surveillance by at least one Chicago Police Intelligence Division Unit consisting of two to four officers.[237] There are also reliable reports that Giancana was under FBI surveillance as well.

Even though John Roselli, his colleague in the attempts to kill Castro, was not murdered until approximately nine months later, Giancana's murder caused speculation it might somehow be connected to the Kennedy assassination. On December 29, 1975, the *Washington Star* noted:

> It takes a bit more imagination — but no longer strains credulity — to think that Giancana's death may have been related in some bizarre way to the assassination of Kennedy twelve years before.[238]

Sam Giancana had been one of the most notorious Mafia leaders of the 1950s and 1960s, known for the particularly violent ways and means that he had inherited from his former boss, Al Capone. During the Kennedy Administration, Sam "Momo" Giancana had become one of the two or three top targets of Attorney General Robert Kennedy's intensive drive against the Mafia.

Nicholas Gage of the *New York Times*, one of the nation's leading specialists on organized crime, has set forth a typically gruesome account of a syndicate murder carried out by Giancana's men. In this report — supplied by a Mafia informant — of a conversation between Giancana aides James Torello and Fiore Buccieri, the murder of a man identified as William Jackson was set forth:

> *Torello:* Jackson was hung up on that meat hook. He was so . . . heavy he bent it. He was on that thing three days before he croaked.
>
> *Buccieri:* [giggling] Jackie, you shoulda seen the guy. Like an elephant, he was, and when Jimmy hit him . . . that electric prod . . .

> *Torello:* He was floppin' around on that hook, Jackie. We tossed water on him to give the prod a better charge, and he's screaming . . .[239]

During the 1975 Senate probe, reports surfaced that the Committee had uncovered information pertaining to a young woman who had been a close friend of President Kennedy at the same time she was friendly with Mafia leaders Sam Giancana and John Roselli. In December, 1975, the woman, Judith Campbell Exner, called a press conference to announce that she had not only known Giancana and Roselli but had also allegedly been having an affair with President Kennedy during that period. The Senate Committee determined, from an FBI memorandum of February 27, 1962, that Exner had in fact made a series of phone calls to the White House, ostensibly to President Kennedy, during 1961 and 1962. Further reports subsequently surfaced that Judith Exner had been introduced to President Kennedy by their mutual friend, singer Frank Sinatra.

Numerous allegations and rumors quickly spread relating to Judith Exner's reported relationship with Kennedy and Giancana. Some suggested that Giancana had used his close friend Sinatra to "place" a girl near the President for the possible purpose of blackmailing him — presumably into calling off the Attorney General's pursuit of Giancana and other top Mafia leaders. Others suggested that Exner may have been some kind of mysterious liaison between the President and the mob. Still others theorized that the Kennedy Justice Department may somehow have used Exner to spy on Giancana himself. Some observers believe the key piece of information necessary for understanding Exner's role and connections might be supplied by determining whether she met Kennedy before Giancana . . . or Giancana before Kennedy. Robert Sam Anson, who spent considerable time reviewing the many allegations about the Exner episode, has written:

> . . . Judy Exner's recollections of Sam Giancana seem remarkably dim. She puts her first meeting with Giancana — "Moe" or "Mooney" his friends called him — several months after she met Kennedy, and with Roselli well after that. That is not how federal investigators remember it nor even Roselli, who puts the date of his introduction with the lady well before the time she met Kennedy. The point seems trivial until the rumor drifts by that when Judy finally tells all, she will claim that Kennedy recruited her to spy on the Mob. She probably wouldn't have been much of an agent.[240]

There has recently been speculation of an even stranger possibility, relating to a theory that Mafia leader Giancana may have been trying to use Exner (without her knowledge) in a plot to poison President Kennedy. This theory is based on an assumption that Sam Giancana was well aware that some of his close Mafia colleagues, including Santos Trafficante and Carlos Marcello, were reportedly talking about having Kennedy killed, and may have decided to revive his old poisoning skills, which had been unsuccessfully brought to bear in the CIA plots to murder Castro. The Senate Intelligence Committee Report included an FBI memo dated October 18, 1960 which stated that it had been Giancana's original idea to "plant" a girl near Castro for that purpose. According to this memo, which J. Edgar Hoover had sent to Richard Bissell of the CIA, "Giancana claimed that everything [had] been perfected for the killing of Castro and that the 'assassin' had arranged with a girl, not further described, to drop a 'pill' in some drink or food of Castro's."[241]

Though allegations about "the Exner affair" are, in the words of a former Senate investigator, "a dime a dozen, or even cheaper," speculation continues. With the serialization of Judith Exner's memoirs in the *National Enquirer*, both Ms. Exner and her various allegations have become even better known.

Whatever Sam Giancana may have been up to during the Kennedy Administration, it is clear that he remained a central target of it to the very end. Robert Sam Anson has noted:

> If the Mob was employing Judy Campbell [Exner] as a means of blackmailing Kennedy, the attempt failed miserably. The organized crime prosecutions did not stop; if anything, they intensified. Giancana continued to be a special target. In June 1963 . . . Giancana was put under "rough surveillance." Carloads of federal agents were parked outside his house around the clock, seven days a week. They dogged his every step, interviewed his neighbors, followed his family, tailed his friends . . .
>
> . . . Giancana was merely getting a taste of the medicine Robert Kennedy had in store for the whole of organized crime. At the time of his brother's death, Bobby was laying the groundwork for the strongest dose of all: a massive federal assault on the whole of Nevada, a demonstration that if the Mob could be taken on and beaten on its home ground, it could be defeated anywhere.[242]

John Roselli

With the retrieval of Johnny Roselli's decomposed body from a 55-gallon oil drum floating off of Miami on August 7, 1976, the momentum behind reopening the investigation of the Kennedy assassination significantly mounted. The feeling increased that the CIA-Mafia attempts against Castro may have led to the subsequent murder of President Kennedy, and, in the opinion of many observers, the brutal and as yet unsolved murder of a second coordinator of those plots pushed "the realm of coincidence" too far.

With the *Washington Post* disclosure two weeks later that John Roselli had secretly informed the government that he believed that some of his former associates had gone on to murder President Kennedy — possibly with help from Fidel Castro -- the entire Kennedy case was transformed.[243] Within weeks, the House of Representatives voted overwhelmingly to reopen the Kennedy assassination investigation, under a select committee headed by Congressman Thomas Downing of Virginia.

A year earlier, members and staff of the Senate Intelligence Committee had been angered when the FBI — under the specific orders of Director Clarence Kelley — had refused to investigate the murder of Roselli's assassination-planning colleague, Sam Giancana. Giancana was murdered in June, 1975, days before he was to appear before the Senate Committee and while he reportedly was under round-the-clock surveillance by the FBI and Chicago police. With the unsolved murder of a scheduled Senate witness and the FBI's refusal to investigate that murder, despite a Senate request to do so, a certain bitterness arose between the two.

Upon Roselli's disappearance in late July, 1976, and the recovery of his mutilated body about ten days later, the Senate Intelligence Committee again asked the FBI and Justice Department to investigate not only the Roselli murder, but any possible connection to the earlier Giancana murder.[244] By this time, it had already been disclosed that Roselli had testified several months earlier about the possible connection of the CIA-Mafia assassination apparatus to the murder of President Kennedy. On August 11, 1976, the Associated Press reported that a Senate Intelligence Committee spokesman "confirmed that Roselli had made a secret appearance in April before Senate investigators probing the assassination of President Kennedy."[245]

However, later that same day, FBI Director Clarence Kelley announced after conferring with Attorney General Edward Levi that the FBI was refusing to investigate the Roselli murder because "There is no jurisdiction, at least that we know of."[246] Kelley stated that there appeared to be no grounds for the Bureau to investigate the murder of the Senate witness, despite the Senate Committee's request. As might be expected, Senate Committee sources were outraged over Kelley's pronouncement. It has long been known that the FBI can easily set forth a legal rationale to justify extending its federal jurisdiction into virtually any criminal case, particularly a murder. This was easily accomplished during both the Patty Hearst and James Hoffa kidnapping cases.

The temporary FBI refusal to investigate the murder of a second CIA-Mafia assassination coordinator — one who had told the Senate Committee that his colleagues may have gone on to kill the President of the United States — raised what must still be regarded as quite serious questions. While the full details about the FBI-Senate Committee conflict have yet to be fully reported, some information has emerged. Informed Senate sources report that immediately after Kelley's refusal to order the FBI into the investigation, a series of discussions were held among many Senate Committee members and staff. One of the suggested courses of action involved notifying the Justice Department and the FBI of a press conference to be held by various Committee members.

Under the proposed action — which was discarded soon after Attorney General Levi's decision to overrule the FBI's refusal — the press conference was to serve as a public accounting of information concerning FBI resistance to the Senate Committee's request. According to informed Senate sources, the press conference was to have included specific charges that the FBI was doing as little as possible to cooperate with the Senate investigation, and — in the nature of hardball statements — that the FBI's refusal to intervene in the Roselli matter "raised further questions" about the FBI's questionable performance in investigating the Kennedy assassination, as set forth by the Senate Intelligence Committee Report on the assassination, in late June.

While this potential course of action was finally unnecessary, the episode provides a telling look at some of the pressures which have already been manifested in the effort to reinvestigate the Presidential assassination.

With Roselli's murder and the escalating interest in what he knew or may have known about Mafia, Cuban, or CIA involvement in the assassination, new interest has focused on his background. Roselli, known as Don Giovanni to his Mafia colleagues, had been the actual Don or Capo Mafioso for Las Vegas since the late 1950s.

Roselli was a central figure in a famous organized crime case which resulted in a temporary blow to the Al Capone mob in Chicago, of which he was a key member. During his Kefauver Senate Committee testimony in the early 1950s, Roselli admitted being associated with Capone, and working for Capone's brutal top aide, Frank "The Enforcer" Nitti. On March 18, 1943, Roselli, Nitti, and other Capone mob leaders were indicted for conspiracy, extortion, and mail fraud in connection with the extorting of two and one-half million dollars from several top Hollywood movie studios. Roselli, who had once worked as an "associate producer" with Robert T. Cain Productions, had been one of Capone's strong-arm men in threatening the Hollywood studio bosses.

Capone aide Frank Nitti committed suicide during the prosecution of the case, and Roselli was subsequently convicted and sentenced to ten years in prison (a third of which he served) and fined $10,000. The chief prosecution witness against Roselli and his co-defendants, Willie Bioff, was later murdered when his car was blown up in Arizona, where he had become a close friend of Senator Barry Goldwater.[247]

In their early and highly respected account of the Mafia in America, *The Green Felt Jungle*, Ed Reid and Ovid Demaris set forth the following description of "Don Giovanni" Roselli:

> Roselli is definitely of the new school — sharp silk suits, diamond accessories, swanky apartment, busty show girls in full-length minks, big Cadillac, gourmet taste, sportsman, golfer — the best of everything in the best of all possible worlds.
>
> Medium in height, slim, with iron gray hair and sharp features, Roselli is also a quiet man in an ostentatious way. He owns no property, has no visible interests in any hotel-casino, and is unemployed. In fact, he has been unemployed since 1949.[248]

In his Kefauver Committee testimony, as Reid and Demaris have pointed out, John Roselli admitted knowing the following top Mafia leaders:

> Frank Costello, Meyer Lansky, Al Polizzi, Tony Accardo, Lucky Luciano, Mickey Cohen, Bugsy Siegel, Charlie Fischetti, Jack Dragna, Mo Mo Adamo, Phil Kastel, Gene Normile, Joe Sica, Joe Adonis, Augie Pisano, Joe Massei, Tony Gizzo, Frank Nitti, Sam "Golf Bag" Hunt, Moe Sedway, Jack "Machine Gun" McGurn, Bones Remmer, Louis Campagna, Paul "The Waiter" Ricca, Tony Cornero, Black Tony Parmagini, Frank Milano, Willie Moretti, Sam Maceo, and Joseph Profaci.[249]

Aside from possible connections to events surrounding the JFK assassination, the secret relationship between the CIA and the Mafia has raised other important questions. One of the more serious relates to the possibility — or indeed probability — that the gangsters involved may have resultingly been in a position to either blackmail the U.S. government, or at least perhaps receive carte blanche "favors" or immunity from federal authorities. Both Robert F. Kennedy and assassination-coordinator William Harvey spoke of the possibility of blackmail at various times after the secret plots became known in April, 1962.[250]

In a little-noticed footnote in the Senate Intelligence Committee Report on Foreign Assassinations, a substantial amount of information was set forth regarding the ability of Johnny Roselli to receive various forms of "assistance" and occasional immunity from the federal government, with a little help from his former colleagues in the Central Intelligence Agency. As the footnote indicates, this CIA "assistance" continued as late as 1971:

> In May 1966, the FBI threatened to deport Roselli for living in the United States under an assumed name unless he

cooperated in an investigation of the Mafia (Roselli, whose true name is Filippo Saco, was born in Italy and was allegedly brought illegally into the United States while still a child). Roselli contacted [CIA Office of Security Director] Edwards, who informed the FBI that Roselli wanted to "keep square with the Bureau," but was afraid that gangsters might kill him for "talking." After Roselli was arrested for fradulent gambling activities at the Friars Club in Beverly Hills in 1967, he requested Harvey, who had left the Agency, to represent him. Harvey contacted the Agency and suggested that it prevent the prosecution. Roselli was subsequently convicted of violating U.S. interstate gambling laws. In 1971, the CIA approached the Immigration and Naturalization Service, Department of Justice, to "forestall public disclosure of Roselli's past operational activity with CIA" that might occur if deportation proceedings were brought. It was agreed that CIA would be kept informed of developments in that case. The deportation order is presently being litigated in the courts.[251]

The deportation order pending against Roselli was of course later unnecessary. Nine months after the Senate report on the CIA-Mafia plots against Castro, was first published, some unknown party acting in classic Mafia style saw to it that John Roselli was "deported" in a more permanent fashion.

Jimmy Hoffa

Jimmy Hoffa, the controversial and violent President of the Teamsters Union during most of the 1960s, has figured prominently in a large number of areas of evidence pertaining to the assassination of his bitter enemy, President Kennedy. In recent years, a possible Hoffa link has come under increasing attention, as the integral relationship between the Teamsters and the Mafia has become more firmly documented; and as links between Hoffa's lieutenants and Oswald's murderer, Jack Ruby, have become more and more apparent. Of course with James Hoffa's disappearance and presumed murder on July 30, 1975 perhaps a good deal of related information on the Kennedy assassination died with him.

Jimmy Hoffa, as is widely known, spent the better part of the years 1950 to 1964 in a bitter struggle against the efforts of the Kennedy brothers to investigate organized crime and union corruption. It was this struggle between Hoffa and the Kennedys (Bobby in particular) that was later recognized as one of the more dramatic and long-term "feuds" in Washington history. It began in 1957 when the Kennedys began an investigation of Hoffa's key role in the Teamsters-Mafia relationship or alliance. At that time, Senator John F. Kennedy was serving as a member of the McClellan Senate Committee, with Robert Kennedy as the Committee's Chief Counsel.

As Jack and Robert Kennedy assembled an investigative staff of close to a hundred, the clash with

Teamster boss Jimmy Hoffa had already begun. The nationally televised McClellan sessions launched the two Kennedy brothers into national fame, and propelled JFK toward the 1960 Democratic Presidential nomination. Hoffa himself later remarked bitterly, "Who the hell ever heard of the Kennedys before the McClellan Committee?"[252]

"They have the look of Capone's men," Robert Kennedy said of Hoffa's associates at that time. In his subsequent best-selling book, *The Enemy Within*, Robert Kennedy recalled one of his early face-to-face meetings with the controversial Teamster leader:

> I noticed that he was glaring at me across the counsel table with a deep, strange, penetrating expression of intense hatred. I suppose it must have dawned on him about that time that he was going to be the subject of a continuing probe — that we were not playing games . . . There were times when his face seemed completely transfixed with this stare of absolute evilness.[253]

In his own autobiography, written during the months immediately preceding his disappearance and presumed murder, Jimmy Hoffa recounted the circumstances of what he claims developed into a near fist fight between he and Robert Kennedy when they met outside an office hallway:

> . . . when the guy with the big mouth [RFK] crowded me again, I shoved him back into the hallway so hard he almost fell down.[254]

Hoffa told of another confrontation with McClellan Committee Chief Counsel Robert Kennedy, which he claims transpired in a Capitol Hill restaurant:

> . . . somebody grabbed my arm from behind and swung me around.

> It was Robert Kennedy.
> My hands shot out and grabbed him by the front of his jacket and bounced him up against the wall. Hard.[255]

According to Hoffa, he angrily told Kennedy, "I'm only gonna tell you this one time. If you ever put your mitts on me again, I'm gonna break you in half."[256] Hoffa later admitted, "Okay, so I didn't like him. Like him? Hell, I hated the bastard."[257]

By mid-1962, Jimmy Hoffa's threats against the Kennedys had grown increasingly virulent, and, according to several sources, increasingly violent. With John Kennedy in the White House and Robert Kennedy head of the Justice Department, Hoffa's legal problems — and his threats — had grown much more serious. Hoffa had, according to one of his top lieutenants, already begun to formulate a plan to assassinate Robert Kennedy, his most immediate threat. This plan first came to light in 1964, when the episode was disclosed by *Life* Magazine. *Life* reported the information had been supplied to Federal investigators by a former Hoffa lieutenant in Louisiana, Edward Partin, who had also been a key prosecution witness against Hoffa in 1964, when Hoffa was finally convicted of the jury tampering offense for which he was sentenced to eight years in Federal prison. Edward Partin submitted to an independently verified polygraph examination which confirmed the accuracy of the charges he made against Hoffa in *Life* Magazine. According to Partin:

> One day in mid-summer of 1962, in the Teamsters headquarters in Washington, D.C., I was talking with Jimmy Hoffa in his office. We were alone when he asked my help in a scheme to kill Attorney General Robert Kennedy — and he was willing to chance killing Kennedy's kids to do it.
>
> . . . as nearly as I can remember his exact

words, he said: "You know anywhere you can get hold of a plastic bomb?" I told him that, hell, I don't even know what a plastic bomb was and what did he want it for?

He said, "Well, somebody needs to bump that sonofabitch off." I asked what sonofabitch and he said he meant the Attorney General. Then he got to thinking more about it and talking about it. He said, as well as I recall the order of it, "You know I've got a run-down on him . . . His house sits here, like this, and it's not guarded . . ." Jimmy was making a kind of diagram with his fingers and I remember being surprised about the Attorney General's house not being guarded. Then Hoffa said, "He drives alone in a convertible and swims by himself. I've got a .270 rifle with a high power scope on it that shoots a long way without dropping any. It would be easy to get him with that. But I'm leery of it; it's too obvious."

He wasn't quite ready to give up thinking about the rifle, though, because then he asked, "Do you know where I could get a silencer for it?"

But then he went on thinking it out some more, and he said, "What I think should be done, if I can get hold of these plastic bombs, is to get somebody to throw one in his house and the place'll burn after it blows up. You know, the s.o.b. doesn't stay up too late."[258]

According to Ed Partin, Hoffa then stated that "The thing for the person that did it would be to lay low for awhile, and not to try to run off to some place like Puerto Rico."[259]

Partin stated that Hoffa had gone on to say that Robert Kennedy "has so many enemies now they wouldn't know who had done it."[260] Partin further adds that Jimmy Hoffa had a specific idea of where such an assassination should take place: "The ideal set-up would be to catch him somewhere in the South, where it would look like some of the segregation people had done it."[261] Apparently with this last idea, Hoffa was again thinking of using a telescopic rifle for the plan — the rifle that he had earlier suggested could be used to kill Robert Kennedy as he rode in his "convertible."

Partin states that Hoffa's scheme eventually led to his decision to disassociate himself from the Hoffa circle. Partin told of how he had tried to express some objections to Hoffa's proposals:

> By then it was getting home to me, and I guess I said something like, "Yeah, but hasn't he [Kennedy] got kids — kids, and throwing a bomb in his house?" And Hoffa said, "Damn 'em. They're his kids, aren't they?"[262]

Jimmy Hoffa, the Teamsters, and their powerful Mafia associates had by now come under the full force of the Kennedy Administration's "war on organized crime." For the first time since the rapid ascension of the Mafia in the 1920s and 30s to a powerful position in American society, the forces of the Justice Department, FBI, and IRS, were being committed to the fight against the mammoth syndicate. Under the direction of Robert Kennedy, an intensive effort was launched to ferret out Hoffa's criminal activities and associations. This special RFK task force came to be known as the "get-Hoffa squad."

Jimmy Hoffa and his Teamster associates, including his deputy, Frank Fitzsimmons, had consistently maintained that the scandal-ridden Teamsters Union was not connected in any way to the Mafia, a claim that by now had been buried beneath scores of various state and Federal convictions resulting from Teamster-Mafia prosecutions, as well as literally thousands of pages of Congressional testimony. "Some magazine said I control the Mafia," Hoffa noted. "Now, I never heard a more goddamned ridiculous statement in the whole world than that goddamned magazine."[263] In some statements, the glib, fast-talking Hoffa even relied on another RFK adversary — J. Edgar Hoover — to buttress his denial of involvement with the Mafia:

> I don't believe there is any organized crime, period. Don't believe it. Never believed it. I've said it for the last 40 years. Hoover said it! Supposed to be the greatest law enforcement man in America, with the means to find out. He said there was no Mafia, no so-called organized crime . . . That's what he said. That's what Hoover said.[264]

Regardless of what Hoffa and Hoover claimed was an absence of organized crime in America, there was certainly (under the Kennedy Administration) no absence of organized crime indictments and convictions. Under the leadership of John and Robert Kennedy, the Justice Department indicted over one hundred Teamster officials and ninety other Teamster associates, most of whom were underworld figures.

Following on the heels of Hoffa's conviction and his sentencing to eight years in Federal Prison on March 12, 1964, there apparently was another plan set in motion by Hoffa's associates to assassinate Robert Kennedy. As will be seen in a forthcoming section, the assassination plan originated, according to the Justice Department, with Frank Chavez, Hoffa's top lieutenant in Puerto Rico.

While Hoffa had tried as early as 1960 to contribute his considerable political muscle to keep the Kennedy brothers out of the White House, his effort to counter what he called "the Kennedy threat" apparently turned much more "hardball" by 1963. By then, Hoffa's hatred of JFK and RFK had crystallized to the point where the violent Teamster leader claimed "I am convinced that there was a long-range scheme among the Kennedy's to grab the Presidency of the United States and keep it in the family for a whole generation."[265]

Hoffa was of course no stranger to political intrigue. During the 1960 Presidential campaign, the Teamster President had fought John F. Kennedy during both the primary campaign and general election. In an incident that has been recorded by several newsmen over the years, John Connally (then serving as one of Senator Lyndon B. Johnson's top political aides) had tried to work out an arrangement by which Teamster resources would be pooled with the Johnson campaign to keep the 1960 Democratic Presidential nomination away from JFK. Hoffa has written that, "John Connally, one of LBJ's supporters, came to see me and Connally asked for the support of the Teamsters in trying to stop Kennedy."[266] Following Kennedy's nomination, Hoffa's considerable resources were enlisted on behalf of Richard Nixon's campaign. On September 7, 1960 Jimmy Hoffa's national Teamsters Board of Directors voted to oppose Senator Kennedy's candidacy and urge voters to elect Richard Nixon President and Democratic candidates to state office.[267] Hoffa had even gone on a nation wide speaking tour in support of Nixon, and reportedly contributed vast sums of money to his campaign. Former Kennedy Justice Department official and Hoffa biographer Walter Sheridan has reported that the Eisenhower Administration aborted a Federal indictment of Hoffa involving Florida Teamster funds, in reciprocation for Hoffa's campaign efforts.[268] Under the Kennedy Administration, the indictments finally went forward. It is also interesting to note that Hoffa subsequently received a Presidential pardon from Richard Nixon in late 1971.

With the Hoffa-Kennedy war reaching a near-fever pitch in 1963, Hoffa's mind may have increasingly turned toward extreme solutions to his problems. In spring, 1975, *Washington Post* executive editor Ben Bradlee, a close personal friend of JFK, disclosed yet another apparent Hoffa threat; this time from early 1963. According to Bradlee, who has generally discounted the idea of a conspiracy behind the assassination, JFK informed him on February 10, 1963 that the Justice Department had uncovered evidence of a Teamster assassination plot against Attorney General Robert Kennedy.[269] In this instance, according to Bradlee, President Kennedy told him that Hoffa's men had hired "some hoodlum," outfitted him with a silenced weapon, and had sent him to Washington to murder the Attorney General.[270] Bradlee said, "I found this one hard to believe, but the President was obviously serious."[271]

As will be seen in forthcoming sections on Irwin S. Weiner, Barney Baker, Paul Dorfman, Frank Chavez and Leopoldo Ducos, several close associates and "enforcers" who worked for Jimmy Hoffa have been directly linked to Jack Ruby.

Jimmy Hoffa himself had been conducting a private Teamsters meeting in Miami on the morning of November 22, 1963 and was informed of the President's assassination shortly thereafter. Two days later, Hoffa reportedly remarked, "Bobby Kennedy is just another lawyer now."[272] Years later, in his autobiography, Hoffa would perhaps strain credulity when he wrote:

> . . . I'd like to say that I never felt any great animosity toward John Fitzgerald Kennedy . . . So I felt bad along with the rest of the nation when JFK was assassinated in Dallas.[273]

In his interview with Detroit reporter Gerry Stanecki for *Playboy* Magazine, just over a month before he disappeared, Jimmy Hoffa was asked for his views on the Kennedy assassination. When asked why he thought President Kennedy had been assassinated,

Hoffa strangely responded: "Who the hell knows what deals he had? That he didn't keep? Who knows?"[274]

When asked whether he thought that Lee Harvey Oswald had been the President's assassin, the former Teamster boss replied, "Aw, who the hell cares."[275]

Barney Baker

According to Robert Kennedy's 1960 book, *The Enemy Within*, Barney Baker served as Jimmy Hoffa's "roving organizer and ambassador of violence."[276] Baker was indeed widely regarded as one of Hoffa's key lieutenants, particularly in dealing with the Mafia, which Hoffa of course did extensively. Robert Kennedy also wrote that Barney Baker "boasted that he knew such underworld figures as Joe Adonis, Meyer Lansky, the late Benjamin "Bugsy" Siegel, "Trigger Mike" Coppola . . . and others . . . Sometimes the mere threat of his presence in a room was enough to silence men who would otherwise have opposed Hoffa's reign . . . "[277]

Barney Baker, as subsequent though limited investigation by the Warren Commission showed, was also acquainted with Jack Ruby. In fact, Ruby had telephoned Baker in Chicago at least twice in the three-week period immediately preceding the assassination.[278] Ruby later testified that he had called Baker only to inquire about a labor matter regarding his nightclub entertainers.[279]

Many Warren Commission critics view Baker as perhaps as essential Ruby link to the powerful Chicago mob.

Irwin S. Weiner

Irwin S. Weiner was a bondsman for the Teamsters in Chicago who became an integral figure in Jimmy Hoffa's dealings with the Mafia.[280] Weiner, who is well known to organized crime investigators throughout the nation, served as a top Hoffa advisor for many years. Irwin S. Weiner is also one of the men whom Jack Ruby telephoned during the month before the assassination.[281] Although establishing the Ruby-Weiner calls through an examination of Ruby's phone records, the Warren Commission never questioned Ruby about the specifics of his relationship with the top Hoffa henchman. Ruby told the Commission that other calls he made in November of 1963, to such people as Barney Baker and Dusty Miller, "were related not in any way . . . with the underworld," but he never explained the Weiner calls.[282]

Most recently, in 1974, Irwin S. Weiner was indicted by the federal government in connection with the alleged defrauding of a Teamster pension fund of

$1.4 million.[283] While federal investigators believed they had a strong case against the former Hoffa lieutenant, events soon began to intervene against a successful prosecution. Shortly before Weiner was to go on trial, the Government's chief witness was brutally murdered — shotgunned to death as his wife and children stood within feet of him.[284] Weiner was subsequently acquitted.

He has refused to respond to requests for interviews, and is quite abusive to any who attempt to question him about Jack Ruby.

Leopoldo Ramos Ducos

Leopoldo Ducos is another former associate of Jimmy Hoffa who has been linked to an area of evidence pertaining to the Kennedy assassination. While he was the subject of an inquiry made by the Warren Commission to CIA official Richard Helms in February and March of 1964, Ducos more importantly has alleged that Jack Ruby was an associate of other top Hoffa confidantes.

Leopoldo Ducos was appointed as a top official of the Teamsters Union Local in Puerto Rico in early 1962.[285] Hoffa's men had taken control of the independent Hotel and Restaurant Workers Union in San Juan following the firebombing and demolishment of the independent union's headquarters in February, 1962.[286] To head the new Teamsters Local there, along with Ducos, Hoffa had appointed Frank Chavez, a Teamster with a long criminal record, including a charge of attempted murder through the hurling of a firebomb.[287] Interestingly, as will be seen later, Frank Chavez was subsequently identified by the FBI during the course of the Warren investigation as having been involved in an abortive plan to murder Attorney General Robert F. Kennedy.

An FBI Report of December 2, 1963, disclosed that Leopoldo Ramos Ducos had informed the Bureau that the Secretary-Treasurer of the San Juan Teamsters, Maria Del Valle, had informed him on November 26, 1963 that another Puerto Rican Teamster official had told her "We killed Kennedy and the next will be Ramos Ducos."[288] Maria Del Valle identified Teamster organizer Miguel Cruz as the person who had made the strange statement.[289] When the FBI interviewed Del Valle about the allegation, she confirmed that Miguel Cruz had indeed made the threat, and that he had made the statement "at about 5 o'clock p.m.," on the day of the Kennedy assassination.[290]

Ducos apparently took the threat seriously enough to inform the FBI of some additional information. According to the same FBI Report, Ducos stated that his Teamster colleague, Frank Chavez, had previously spoken of a connection of Jack Ruby to the Teamsters — a connection which would of course conflict with the Warren Commission conclusion that there were no such Ruby-Teamster connections. The FBI Report notes that some time during the period from 1960 to March, 1962, Ducos "heard Frank Chavez, Secretary-Treasurer of that Local, mention the name of one Jack Ruby as someone connected with Teamsters Union."[291] The FBI Report further states:

> Sometime in about September, 1961, Frank Chavez told Ramos Ducos that Chavez had an appointment to meet Richard Kavner,

International Vice President of Teamster Union, and Jack Ruby as well as a third Teamster official whose name Ramos Ducos could not recall. The meeting was to be in San Juan, but Ramos Ducos could not furnish any further details.[292]

Ducos' first name, Leopoldo, has also provided another small piece of information that was briefly pursued by the Warren Commission, and remains of interest to the Commission's critics. "Leopoldo" was the name that Cuban exile leader Sylvia Odio claimed was used by a right-wing militant whom she states accompanied Lee Oswald in a visit to her home in September of 1963. (See reference to this Sylvia Odio testimony in the chapter on "The Second Oswald.") In their effort to resolve the Odio matter (which raised a strong possibility that Oswald was working with right-wing anti-Castro exiles shortly before the assassination), the Warren Commission turned to the CIA for help. In a Commission memo of February 24, 1964, sent to CIA Deputy Director for Plans Richard Helms, the Commission staff noted:

> [Ducos] was threatened by a person suggesting that the same group that would kill Ducos had been responsible for getting rid of Kennedy. Name "Leopoldo" has been mentioned by others who claimed that Ruby was associated with an anti-Castro group in the procurement of arms. Name "Leopoldo" also mentioned by a woman in Dallas [Sylvia Odio] who claims she was introduced to a "Leon Oswald," description fitting Lee Harvey Oswald, in October 1963 by anti-Castro Cuban leader.[293]

CIA officials Richard Helms and Thomas Karamessines delayed for over six months before replying to this Warren Commission request, despite a strongly-worded Commission protest of May 19, 1964.[294] And, when the CIA officials finally did respond on September 15, 1964, as the Warren Report was being set in type, the terse reply was virtually devoid of any information.[295]

The present whereabouts of Leopoldo Ramos Ducos is unknown.

Frank Chavez

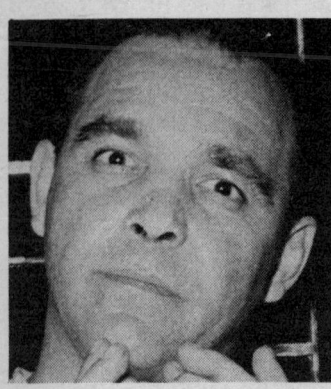

Frank Chavez is the notorious Hoffa lieutenant who figured prominently in the allegation made to the FBI by his colleague, Leopoldo Ducos. Chavez reportedly served as a top Teamster "enforcer," and has long been credited with the first firebombing of the independent union headquarters in Puerto Rico that presaged the Teamsters takeover there in 1962.[295] The exact extent to which the FBI followed up on Leopoldo Ducos' charges that Chavez had been associated with Jack Ruby — and had met with him in September, 1961 — is not presently known. However, it appears that little attention was focused on the area.

Strangely enough, Frank Chavez has been linked to a plot to murder Robert F. Kennedy in February and March of 1964, during the course of the Warren Commission investigation. This information, based upon a series of FBI reports, was first detailed in 1973 by

Walter Sheridan, the former top Justice Department official who had coordinated Attorney General Robert F. Kennedy's efforts to convict Teamster leader Hoffa on various charges. Sheridan, who later wrote what is regarded as the definitive biography of Hoffa, disclosed that Frank Chavez had traveled to New York in March of 1964 for the purpose of killing Robert Kennedy.[297]

Sheridan reports that the FBI determined that Chavez and two accompanying bodyguard associates were heavily armed and had apparently planned the RFK assassination for several weeks.[298] However, according to Sheridan, Teamster President Hoffa had learned of the Chavez assassination plan and had ordered his lieutenant to call it off.[299] Hoffa reportedly told Chavez that killing Robert Kennedy would produce a new storm of investigation, and was unnecessary, with Kennedy leaving the Justice Department to run for the United States Senate.[300]

As Walter Sheridan has noted, Frank Chavez was later murdered by one of his own bodyguards following an internal Teamster dispute. Whether the Warren Commission ever reviewed or investigated Chavez' plot to murder Robert Kennedy in March 1964, is not presently known. Although the episode clearly seems to have fallen within the Commission's scope of interest, particularly in view of Leopoldo Ducos' allegation of a Frank Chavez-Jack Ruby relationship, there are no Commission records presently available indicating that the matter was ever probed.

Al Capone

Al "Scarface" Capone, the most famous and sadistic Mafia leader in American history, and his top deputy Frank Nitti, used to hire assorted teenage boys during the 1920s to run "errands" for the mob on Chicago's West Side. According to an FBI document submitted to the Warren Commission, the teenaged Jack Ruby was one such Capone errand boy.[301] Ruby's close friend from his boyhood years, Barney Ross, told the FBI that he and Ruby were paid by Capone deputy Frank Nitti to run such errands after school.[302] Ross stated that he and young Jack Ruby delivered various envelopes that "did not contain messages or anything of value."[303] Ross further told the FBI that Capone's purpose in employing teenage errand boys was to keep them from "going bad."

Robert McKeown

In late 1975, Robert McKeown, a man whom the Commission had already identified as a Cuban contact of Jack Ruby, was linked to Lee Harvey Oswald himself in some information disclosed by CBS reporter

Dan Rather. The Warren Commission had established that well-known Cuban gun-runner McKeown had been contacted at least twice in 1959 by Jack Ruby.

On the first occasion, Ruby had discussed a proposition to smuggle blackmarket jeeps into Cuba and also plan to help several Cubans escape from the island.[304] McKeown told the Commission that the second time he talked to Ruby, he had offered to pay McKeown $25,000 if he could arrange a "letter of introduction" to Fidel Castro for an unnamed third party.[305] In his own Warren Commission testimony Jack Ruby confirmed that he had indeed discussed the jeep smuggling plan with McKeown, but never spoke of the alleged "letter of introduction" to Castro. McKeown testified that Ruby never followed through on the offer.

On November 25, 1975, in the first of a two-part CBS investigative documentary on the Kennedy assassination, Dan Rather disclosed that McKeown, now elderly and in poor health had revealed to him that he'd once also been contacted by Oswald in an effort to buy several powerful automatic rifles.[306] In the Rather interview, the former gun-runner said he'd been contacted by Oswald and an unidentified Latin companion about buying the rifles just a few weeks before the assassination.[307] McKeown's startling disclosure about Oswald's attempt to obtain rifles was corroborated by a long-time friend who had witnessed McKeown's meeting with Oswald.

McKeown's friend also agreed to be interviewed by CBS and confirmed the story.[308] Both men told Dan Rather that when Oswald was later charged as President Kennedy's assassin, they agreed to "keep" their "mouth shut" out of fear that they might be threatened by other conspirators if they told the authorities of their meeting.[309]

The CBS's disclosure of the Oswald-McKeown contact, when added to the Commission's evidence of the Ruby-McKeown contacts, provides one of the more fertile areas for continuing investigation.

William and Mike McLaney

The McLaney brothers have long been associated with various reported syndicate operations. William McLaney operated for a time out of Lewis McWillie's Tropicana Hotel in Havana, Cuba, which Jack Ruby visited in 1959. Mike McLaney was the owner of the National Casino in Havana at that time, which the Cleveland syndicate had previously run.[310]

On July 31, 1963, the FBI made several arrests during a raid on a house McLaney had rented[311] on the outskirts of New Orleans which was being used as an apparent training center by a group of militant anti-Castro exiles. During that same summer, Lee Oswald was establishing his "Fair Play For Cuba Committee," also in New Orleans. Oswald had, according to the Commission, established contact during July and August with Carlos Bringuier, a leading anti-Castro exile leader who had been associated with some of the same men arrested on the McLaney property.³¹² Their tangled relationships are still under investigation.³¹³

The McLaney brothers' alleged syndicate activities have continued through the years. In late 1973, in sworn testimony before the Senator Henry M. Jackson's Permanent Subcommittee on Investigations, Mike McLaney was accused of trying to arrange for Mafia agents to assassinate the Prime Minister of the Bahamas. In late September, 1973, an important organized crime informer, Louis Mastriana, told the Subcommittee that Mike McLaney, "who represents Meyer Lansky," offered Mastriana $100,000 to assassinate Governor Lynden Pindling of the Bahamas.³¹⁴ Mastrinana testified that, "They came to me and they wanted him dead, they wanted him killed . . . They gave me $10,000 front money" to begin planning the assassination.³¹⁵ Mike McLaney strongly denied the alleged assassination plot during his subsequent testimony before the same Subcommittee, which had turned up strong evidence of various McLaney ties to top Mafia leaders.

Meyer Lansky

Meyer Lansky is said to be the most powerful organized crime leader in the world. The 76-year-old Lansky, who was the original partner of Lucky Luciano and Frank Costello, is credited with being the key architect of the transformation of the underworld into a syndicated, stream-lined, and tightly organized colossus — a transformation that he primarily conceived in the 1930s and 40s.

For years now, Lansky has been termed "the Chairman of the Board" of the national crime syndicate, a man whose influence pervades every aspect of Mafia activity, and whom the *Washington Post* refers to as the long-time "finance minister of the mob."[316]

Lansky's name surfaces repeatedly in any review of events surrounding the Kennedy assassination: he established the first links between the Mafia and American intelligence agencies; he created the syndicate gambling empire in Cuba; his key deputy, Santos Trafficante, was a key coordinator of the CIA-Mafia plots against Castro; and he was connected to several of Jack Ruby's associates — and, as will be seen — possibly to Ruby himself.

Lansky's role in "Operation Underworld," the secret OSS-Naval Intelligence operation that involved the top Mafia leadership, is still an area of considerable speculation. Lansky had helped Lucky Luciano coordinate the Mafia's participation, which resulted in a pardon for the imprisoned Luciano after the war. What Lansky received for his services remains a matter of speculation. Hank Messick, whose books include a biography of Lansky, has written:

> Was Lansky rewarded? No final answer is possible, but he has been strangely immune to prosecution on the Federal level. Twice the [IRS] Intelligence Division has recommended prosecution, and twice the Justice Department has declined. Lansky remains the only top man in the national crime syndicate to escape untouched . . . because of his brains and the troubles of his colleagues, he rules as undisputed chairman of the

board. His personal wealth has been estimated at $300,000,000. If immunity was granted him, the nation has paid high for his secret services during Operation Underworld.[317]

Even before the CIA began planning Castro's assassination Lansky was in favor of such a plan, because he'd been the chief financial victim of Castro's takeover and confiscation of the Syndicate's massive holdings. According to Nicholas Gage, "Lansky was so angry he called a meeting of the Syndicate board and persuaded it to put up a $1 million price on Castro's head. It was partly this bounty that worried U.S. officials when Castro later visited New York for a UN session . . ."[318]

In July, 1971, during an abortive attempt to establish residence in Israel, Meyer Lansky agreed to an interview by reporter Uri Dan of the Israel newspaper *Ma'ariv* — the only interview that Lansky is ever known to have given. Lansky mentioned the persistent reports that he had wanted to assassinate Fidel Castro:

> . . . the climax in that period came when I was recuperating in my home for long months in 1959 and Castro came for his famous visit to the U.S. A reporter phoned my home and asked my wife: "Is it true that your husband gave an order to murder Castro?" I then weighed 117 pounds. My wife answered him: "You'd better ask him if he even has the strength to press the trigger."[319]

By late 1960, the Senate Intelligence Committee reports the CIA had recruited Santos Trafficante, worked closely with CIA officials such as William Trafficante provided the services of militant Cuban exiles who were on his Mafia payroll.[321] Trafficante worked closely with CIA official William Harvey as well as with Robert Maheu and fellow Mafia leaders John Roselli and Sam Giancana.[322]

Meyer Lansky had helped establish the original Meyer Lansky had helped establish the original Trafficante Syndicate in Florida, and had played the leading role in his rise in organized crime. Hank Messick has set forth an account of the time during the 1950s when Trafficante swore a Sicilian oath of allegiance to Lansky in the presence of other Mafia colleagues:

> With an ancient Spanish dagger — none from Sicily was available — Trafficante cut his left wrist, allowed the blood to flow, and wet his right hand in the crimson stream. Then he held up the bloody hand:
>
> "So long as the blood flows in my body," he intoned solemnly, "do I, Santos Trafficante, swear allegiance to the will of Meyer Lansky and the organization he represents. If I violate this oath, may I burn in hell forever."
>
> A written copy of the oath — dictated by [Vincent] Alo over the telephone from New York — was signed by Trafficante in his own blood. [Charles] Tourine witnessed the signature with an X in ink.[323]

While Trafficante's CIA-Mafia involvement was documented by the Senate Committee in late 1975, few anticipated the new wave of allegations that revolved around Trafficante in 1976. Shortly after the brutal murder of John Roselli the *Washington Post*, Jack Anderson, and others reported that Roselli had previously indicated a strong suspicion that Trafficante had planned the assassination of President Kennedy.

Long before these reports surfaced, it was known that Ruby's friend Lewis McWillie was a key operative of both Meyer Lansky and Santos Trafficante. A March 26, 1964 FBI report notes that "McWillie solidified his Syndicate connections through his associations in Havana, Cuba, with Santos Trafficante, well-known Syndicate member, for Tampa, Florida, [and] Meyer and Jake Lansky . . ."[324]

Recently, increasing attention has focused on what may be a direct connection between Meyer Lansky and Jack Ruby himself.

Ruby told the Warren Commission on June 7, 1964 about his 1959 visit to McWillie in Havana, and also spoke of knowing McWillie's bosses. Interestingly enough, McWillie's bosses at that time were Meyer and Jake Lansky. Ruby mysteriously spoke of meeting two brothers who'd owned the Tropicana Casino, which McWillie managed.[325] Ruby said he was unsure of their last name but thought it had been Fox.[326]

It has long been known that Meyer and Jake Lansky were in fact the two key Tropicana owners.[327] The Tropicana had been a cornerstone of their Cuban holdings.[328] Ruby also described "the Fox brothers" as "the greatest that have been expelled from Cuba," and said they were then living in Miami.[329] Meyer and Jake Lansky were known as the most prominent Syndicate men expelled by the Castro government and were in fact then living in Miami. Ruby said he thought one of the "Fox brothers'" first names may have been Martin.[330]

Ruby further testified that one of the "Fox brothers" had later visited him in Dallas, accompanied by Lewis McWillie.[331] Ruby claimed that they had dined at the Dallas airport together.[332] Ruby further testified that Fox and McWillie had also subsequently dropped by his nightclub, where they posed for photographs with him.[333] Ruby later took the photos with him when he visited McWillie in Cuba:

> *Ruby:* One of the Fox brothers came to visit me in Dallas with his wife. They came to the Vegas Club with Mrs. McWillie, and we had taken some pictures, 8 x 10's.
>
> Evidently the Foxes were in exile at that time, because when I went to visit McWillie

371

... they looked through my luggage and they saw a photograph of Mr. Fox and his wife. They didn't interrogate but they went through everything and held me up for hours.

Congressman Ford: Castro employees?

Ruby: Yes; because evidently, in my ignorance, I didn't realize I was bringing a picture that they knew was a bitter enemy.[334]

1. Robert F. Kennedy, *The Pursuit of Justice* (New York: Harper and Row, Perennial Library Edition, 1964), p. 37.
2. Ibid., p. 38.
3. Victor S. Navasky, *Kennedy Justice* (New York: Atheneum Publishers, 1971), pp. 53-55.
4. Ibid., p. 55.
5. Kennedy, *The Pursuit of Justice*, p. 41.
6. "The Mafia, The CIA, and The Kennedy Assassination," Milton Viorst, *The Washingtonian*, November, 1975.
7. Senate Intelligence Committee, *Supplementary Detailed Staff Reports on Intelligence Activities and the Rights of Americans*, 1976, Book III, pp. 869-870.
8. Ibid., p. 870.
9. Ibid.
10. Kennedy, *The Pursuit of Justice*, p. 38.
11. Ibid., p. 39.
12. Ibid.
13. Pierre Salinger, *With Kennedy* (New York: Doubleday and Company, 1966), p. 26.
14. CBS Evening News With Walter Cronkite, Eric Sevareid commentary, October 18, 1976.
15. Kennedy, *The Enemy Within*, p. 87.
16. *Chicago Daily Tribune*, December 9, 1939.
17. Ibid.
18. Ibid.
19. Ibid.
20. Warren Commission Volume 5, p. 200.
21. Ibid., pp. 204-205.
22. *Third Interim Report*, Kefauver Senate Committee, 82nd Congress, 1st Session; cited by Gus Tyler, *Organized Crime in America* (Ann Arbor: University of Michigan Press, 1973), pp. 337-339.

23. Warren Commission Exhibit 1184.
24. Ovid Demaris, *Captive City* (New York: Lyle Stuart, 1969), pp. 5, 17, 169-170.
25. *Warren Commission Report*, Government Printing Office edition, p. 793.
26. Ibid.
27. Ibid.
28. Warren Commission Exhibit 2887.
29. Ibid.
30. *Warren Commission Report*, Government Printing Office edition, p. 793.
31. Warren Commission Exhibit 2416.
32. Ibid.
33. Ibid.
34. Ibid.
35. Warren Commission Exhibit 2249, p. 41.
36. Warren Commission Volume 15, pp. 593-595.
37. Warren Commission Exhibits 1271 and 1798; Warren Commission Volume 22, p. 374; Warren Commission Volume 23, pp. 203-204.
38. Ibid.
39. Ibid.
40. Kefauver Senate Committee Hearings, Part 5, p. 1177; McClellan Senate Committee Hearings, p. 12520.
41. Warren Commission Volume 22, p. 302.
42. Warren Commission Volume 23, p. 369; Warren Commission Exhibit 1761, Item 3.
43. Ibid.
44. Ibid.
45. Ibid.
46. Warren Commission Volume 14, p. 444.
47. Ibid.
48. Warren Commission Volume 22, p. 372.
49. Ibid.
50. January 27, 1964, Warren Commission Session Transcript, p. 209; Weisberg, *Whitewash IV*, p. 118.
51. *Newsweek*, October 9, 1950; Demaris, *Captive City*, p. 130.
52. Ibid.
53. Ibid.
54. Ibid.
55. McClellan Senate Committee Hearings, 85th Congress, pp. 7416, 12520-12522.
56. Ibid.
57. *Life*, May 30, 1969.
58. Ibid.
59. Ibid.
60. Warren Commission Volume 14, p. 545.
61. Ibid., pp. 545-546.

62. Ibid., p. 520.
63. *Newsweek*, March 27, 1967.
64. Warren Commission Volume 5, p. 198.
65. Warren Commission Report, p. 346; Warren Commission Exhibit 1697; Warren Commission Volume 5, p. 201; Warren Commission Volume 23, p. 166.
66. Warren Commission Exhibits 1442, 1443.
67. Warren Commission Report, pp. 345-346.
68. Warren Commission Exhibit 1697; Warren Commission Volume 23, p. 166.
69. "Jack L. Ruby, Lee Harvey Oswald — Victim," FBI Memorandum, March 26, 1964; *Senate Intelligence Committee Report on Foreign Assassinations*, pp. 74-85.
70. Ibid.
71. Warren Commission Volume 5, p. 201.
72. Ibid., p. 202.
73. Ibid.
74. Ibid.
75. Peter Noyes, *Legacy of Doubt* (New York: Pinnacle Books, 1973), pp. 220-221, 240-249.
76. Dallas Police Department, Statement of Jim Braden, November 22, 1963; Warren Commission Documents 385, 401, and 816; Dallas Police Report of Deputy C. L. Lewis, November 22, 1963.
77. Ibid.
78. Ibid.
79. California Department of Motor Vehicles, License Report of Jim Braden, 1963, #H751755; Request for license name change of Eugene Brading (Jim Braden), September 19, 1963.
80. Miami Police Department Arrest Report, Eugene Brading, February 24, 1941; FBI Report on Eugene Brading arrest, August 11, 1951, New York FBI office; Los Angeles Police Department records, 1956 investigation of Arthur Clark, Eugene Brading; Federal Strike Force on Organized Crime, investigative records on Jim Braden, La Costa investigation, 1971 and 1972; Noyes, *Legacy of Doubt*, pp. 39-60, 210-219, 240-249.
81. November 21, 1963 Report of Roger Carroll, Chief Parole Officer, Dallas, Texas; August 2, 1969 letter of Lawrence E. Miggins, Chief Probation Officer, Office of Probation Officer, Southern District of Texas, to author Peter Noyes; Noyes, *Legacy Of Doubt*, pp. 80-82; *Warren Commission Report* (GPO edition) p.333; Warren Commission Exhibit 2980.
82. Dallas Police Report, Statement of Jim Braden, November 22, 1963; Warren Commission Exhibit 2980; Warren Commission Volume 15, pp. 626, 628; Warren Commission Exhibits 2266-2268.

83. Ibid.
84. Federal Parole Records, 1963, Eugene Hale Brading; Leasing and Rental records, Pere Marquette Building, New Orleans, Louisiana, 1963; Noyes, *Legacy Of Doubt*, pp. 157-158.
85. FBI Report of Interview of David W. Ferrie, November 26, 1963, Warren Commission Document 75; Pere Marquette Building Leasing and Rental records, 1963; Noyes, *Legacy of Doubt*, pp. 157-158.
86. Federal Strike Force on Organized Crime, investigative records on Jim Braden, La Costa investigation, 1971 and 1972; Noyes, *Legacy of Doubt*, pp. 240-249.
86a. "National Archives — Security Classification Problems Involving Warren Commission Files and Other Records," Hearings before the House Subcommittee on Government Information, 1975-1976.
87. FBI Report of December 12, 1963, interview with Lawrence V. Meyers; Warren Commission Exhibit 2267.
88. Warren Commission Volume 15, p. 620.
89. Ibid., pp. 622-623.
90. Ibid., p. 637.
91. Ibid.
92. Ibid.
93. FBI Report of December 12, 1963, interview with Lawrence V. Meyers; Warren Commission Exhibit 2267.
94. Ibid.
95. Warren Commission Document 385; November 21, 1963 Report of Roger Carroll, Chief Parole Officer, Dallas, Texas.
96. Warren Commission Volume 15, p. 626.
97. Ibid.
98. Ibid., p. 629.
99. Ibid.
100. Warren Commission Exhibit 2980, Warren Commission Volume 26, pp. 467-473.
101. Ibid.
102. March 12, 1964 Warren Commission request to CIA, "Subject: Jack Ruby — Background, Friends and other Pertinent Information," Warren Commission Exhibit 2980.
103. Bell Telephone Records in New Orleans, September 24, 1963, call from David W. Ferrie (524-0147) to Chicago, Illinois, 312/WH-4-4970, Amount: $3.85.
104. Warren Commission Exhibit 2350.
105. Ibid.
106. Warren Commission Exhibit 2268.
107. Ibid.
108. Warren Commission Volume 15, p. 631.
109. Warren Commission Exhibit 2267.

110. Weisberg, *Oswald In New Orleans*, p. 184.
111. Wise and Ross, *The Invisible Government*, p. 27; Warren Commission Document 87; Anson, *"They've Killed The President!"*, p. 124.
112. Ibid.
113. New Orleans Police Department Report #K-126 34-63; New Orleans FBI # 89-69.
114. Weisberg, *Oswald In New Orleans*, pp. 176-181.
115. "National Archives — Security Classification Problems Involving Warren Commission Files and Other Records," Hearings before the House Subcommittee on Government Information, 1976.
116. *Playboy* Magazine, Interview with Jim Garrison, October 1967.
117. *New Orleans Times - Picayune*, February 26, 1967.
118. Victor Marchetti and John D. Marks, *The CIA and the Cult of Intelligence* (New York: Alfred Knopf Company, 1974).
119. Anson, *"They've Killed The President!,"* pp. 122, 376; Interview with Victor Marchetti, October 7, 1975.
120. Ibid.
121. Ibid.
122. Warren Commission Volume 8, p. 14; Weisberg, *Oswald In New Orleans*, p. 57.
123. Ibid.
124. Warren Commission Volume 22, pp. 826-827.
125. Noyes, *Legacy of Doubt*, pp. 104-140, 157-161.
126. Ibid.
127. "The Persecution of Clay Shaw," Warren Rogers, *LOOK*, August 29, 1969.
128. *Los Angeles Times*, September 4, 1970.
129. Ed Reid, *The Grim Reapers* (Chicago: Henry Regnery Company, 1969), p. 158.
130. Warren Commission Document 75.
131. Edward Jay Epstein, *Counterplot* (New York: Viking Press, 1968), p. 37.
132. "The Garrison Commission on the Assassination of President Kennedy," William Turner, *Ramparts*, January 1968; Warren Commission Document 75.
133. *Look*, August 29, 1969 "The Persecution of Clay Shaw," Warren Rogers.
134. Federal Parole Records, Eugene Hale Brading (Jim Braden); Leasing and Rental records, Pere Marquette Building, New Orleans, Louisiana, 1963; Warren Commission Document 75; Noyes, *Legacy Of Doubt*, pp. 157-158.
135. Ibid.
136. *Senate Intelligence Committee Report on Foreign Assassinations*, pp. 74-85.

137. Rosemary Jones and Jack Wardlaw, *Plot or Politics* (New Orleans: Pelican Books, 1967), p. 72.
138. New Orleans Police Department Report, August 30, 1961.
139. Hunt, *Give Us This Day*, pp. 182-184; Wise and Ross, *The Invisible Government*, pp. 26-27, 41-42.
140. Epstein, *Counterplot*, pp. 36-37; "The Garrison Commission on the Kennedy Assassination," William Turner, *Ramparts*, January 1968.
141. Ibid.
142. Warren Commission Volume 10, pp. 36, 82.
143. Miami Police Department, Homicide Report, February 23, 1967.
144. Ibid.
145. Eastern Airlines legal memorandum, May 2, 1963, "Personal and Confidential, Re: Captain Ferrie."
146. Ibid.
147. Ibid.
148. New Orleans Crime Commission Reports, 1969-1973; Reid, *The Grim Reapers*, p. 153.
149. Senate Committee on Government Operations, *"Organized Crime and Illicit Traffic in Narcotics,"* 88th Congress, pp. 800-801.
150. *Senate Intelligence Committee Report on Foreign Assassinations*, pp. 74-85.
151. Ibid., pp. 80-81.
152. Michael Dorman, *Pay-Off* (New York: David McKay Company Inc., Berkley Medallion Edition, 1973), p. 105.
153. Ibid., p. 111.
154. Messick, *Lansky*, p. 86.
155. Harry J. Anslinger, *The Murderers* (New York: Farrar, Straus and Company, 1961), p. 106.
156. *Los Angeles Times*, September 4, 1970; *Look*, August 26, 1969.
157. Reid, *The Grim Reapers*, pp. 158-159.
158. Ibid.
159. Ibid.
160. Ibid.
161. Ibid.
162. Ibid.
163. Vincent Teresa and Thomas Renner, *My Life In The Mafia* (New York: Doubleday, Fawcett Crest Edition, 1974), pp. 11-16.
164. Ibid., 187.
165. Warren Commission Document 75; FBI Report on David W. Ferrie, New Orleans Office, November 26, 1963.
166. Ibid.
167. Ibid.
168. Ibid.

169. Ibid.
170. *Senate Intelligence Committee Report on Foreign Assassinations*, pp. 74-85.
171. Dorman, *Pay-Off*, p. 106.
172. *Senate Intelligence Committee Report on Foreign Assassinations*, pp. 74-85.
173. Ibid.
174. Ibid., pp. 102, 132-133.
175. Ibid., p. 77
176. Ibid.
177. McCoy, *The Politics of Heroin in Southeast Asia*, p. 27.
178. *Senate Intelligence Committee Report on Foreign Assassinations*, pp. 80-81.
179. Ibid.
180. Ibid.
181. Senate Committee on Government Operations, *"Organized Crime and Illicit Traffic in Narcotics,"* 88th Congress, Part One, pp. 524-525; Part Two, p. 928.
182. Fred J. Cook, *Mafia!* (Greenwich, Connecticut: Fawcett Publications, Inc., 1973), pp. 188-189.
183. *Washington Post*, May 16, 1976.
184. Ibid.
185. Ibid.
186. Ibid.
187. Ibid.
188. Ibid.
189. Ibid.
190. Ibid.
191. Ibid.
192. Ibid.
193. Ibid.
194. *Senate Intelligence Committee Report on Foreign Assassinations*, pp. 83-84.
195. Ibid., p. 124.
196. Warren Commission Report, p. 708; Warren Commission Exhibit 1697; Warren Commission Volume 5, p. 201; Warren Commission Volume 23, p. 266.
197. March 26, 1964 FBI Memorandum, "Jack L. Ruby, Lee Harvey Oswald — Victim."
198. Warren Commission Exhibit 1697; Warren Commission Volume 23, p. 166.
199. CIA Memorandum of November 28, 1963, Document #206-83.
200. *Washington Post*, May 16, 1976; Warren Commission Report p. 708; Warren Commission Volume 5, p. 201; Warren Commission Volume 23, p. 166.
201. *Senate Intelligence Committee Report on Foreign Assassinations*, pp. 74-77.
202. Ibid., p. 74.

203. Ibid.
204. Ibid., pp. 74-85.
205. Ibid., pp. 102, 132-134.
206. *Los Angeles Times*, May 16, 1974.
207. Ibid.
208. Ibid.
209. Ibid.
210. Ibid.
211. *Senate Intelligence Committee Report on Foreign Assassinations*, p. 75.
212. *Los Angeles Times*, May 16, 1974, Robert Maheu testimony, May 15, 1974.
213. "The Report On The CIA That President Ford Doesn't Want You To Read," *The Village Voice*, February 16, 1976, (Final Report of the House Select Committee on Intelligence), p. 72.
214. *Senate Intelligence Committee Report on Foreign Assassinations*, pp. 81-82.
215. Ibid., p. 82.
216. Ibid.
217. Ibid., p. 102.
218. Ibid., p. 133.
219. Ibid.
220. *Los Angeles Times*, May 22, 1974.
221. Ibid., Robert Maheu testimony of May 21, 1974.
222. Demaris, *The Director*, p. 30.
223. *Los Angeles Times*, March 30, 1974.
224. Ibid.
225. Ibid.
226. Ibid., *Senate Intelligence Committee Report on Foreign Assassinations*, pp. 74-85.
227. *Senate Watergate Committee Final Report*, pp. 931-1071.
228. Ibid., p. 953.
229. Ibid., p. 952.
230. J. Anthony Lukas, *Nightmare, The Underside of the Nixon Years* (New York: Viking Press, 1976), pp. 174-177; Senate Watergate Committee, Book One, Testimony of James W. McCord, p. 202.
231. *Senate Watergate Committee Final Report*, p. 1123.
232. Jack Anderson column, May 6, 1976.
233. Bud Vestal, *Jerry Ford Up Close* (New York: Coward, McCann and Geoghegan, Berkley Medallion Edition, 1974), p. 99.
234. Ibid.
235. Ibid.
236. Ibid., p. 100.
237. *Washington Star*, December 29, 1975.
238. Ibid.

239. Nicholas Gage, *Mafia U.S.A.* (New York: Dell Publishing Company edition, 1973), p. 13.
240. *New Times*, January 23, 1976.
241. *Senate Intelligence Committee Report on Foreign Assassinations*, p. 79.
242. *New Times*, January 23, 1976.
243. *Washington Post*, August 22, 1976; Jack Anderson column, September 7, 1976.
244. *Washington Post*, August 11, 1976.
245. Ibid.
246. *Washington Post*, August 12, 1976.
247. Hank Messick, *The Mob In Show Business* (New York: Pyramid Books, 1975), pp. 70-71.
248. Ed Reid and Ovid Demaris, *The Green Felt Jungle* (New York: Trident Press, 1963), p. 224.
249. Ibid., p. 227.
250. *Senate Intelligence Committee Report on Foreign Assassinations*, pp. 102, 132-133.
251. Ibid., p. 85.
252. *Playboy* Magazine, Interview with James R. Hoffa, December, 1975.
253. Robert F. Kennedy, *The Enemy Within* (New York: Harper and Row, 1960), p. 84.
254. James Hoffa and Oscar Fraley, *Hoffa, The Real Story* (New York: Stein and Day, 1975), pp. 86-87.
255. Ibid., pp. 93-94.
256. Ibid., p. 94.
257. Ibid., p. 115.
258. "An Insider's Chilling Story of Hoffa's Savage Kingdom," Edward Partin, *Life*, May 15, 1964.
259. Ibid.
260. Ibid.
261. Ibid.
262. Ibid.
263. *Playboy*, Interview with James R. Hoffa, December, 1975.
264. Ibid.
265. Hoffa and Fraley, *Hoffa, The Real Story*, p. 101.
266. Ibid., p. 149.
267. Walter Sheridan, *The Fall and Rise of Jimmy Hoffa* (New York: Saturday Review Press, 1972), p. 157.
268. Ibid., p. 5.
269. Benjamin C. Bradlee, *Conversations With Kennedy* (New York: W. W. Norton, Pocket Book Edition, 1976), pp. 125-126.
270. Ibid.
271. Ibid.
272. Sheridan, *The Fall and Rise of Jimmy Hoffa*, p. 300.
273. Hoffa and Fraley, *Hoffa, The Real Story*, p. 150.
274. *Playboy*, Interview with James R. Hoffa, December, 1975.

275. Ibid.
276. Kennedy, *The Enemy Within*, p. 60.
277. Ibid., p. 88.
278. Warren Commission Exhibit 2303; Warren Commission Volume 25, p. 247.
279. Warren Commission Volume 5, p. 200.
280. *Time*, August 25, 1975.
281. Warren Commission Exhibit 2303, p. 30; Warren Commission Volume 25, p. 245-247.
282. Warren Commission Volume 5, p. 200.
283. *Time*, August 25, 1975.
284. Ibid.
285. Reid and Demaris, *The Green Felt Jungle*, p. 104.
286. Ibid.
287. Ibid., p. 105.
288. Warren Commission Document 86, volume 2.
289. Ibid.
290. Ibid.
291. Ibid.
292. Ibid.
293. Warren Commission Exhibit 2980; Warren Commission Volume 26, p. 467.
294. Ibid.
295. Ibid.
296. Reid and Demaris, *The Green Felt Jungle*, pp. 104-105.
297. Sheridan, *The Fall and Rise of Jimmy Hoffa*, p. 407.
298. Ibid.
299. Ibid., p. 408.
300. Ibid.
301. Warren Commission Exhibit 1288.
302. Ibid.
303. Ibid.
304. Warren Commission Volume 23, pp. 158-159.
305. Ibid., pp. 159-160.
306. CBS Reports Inquiry, "The American Assassins," Part One, November 25, 1976.
307. Ibid.
308. Ibid.
309. Ibid.
310. *Parade*, Jack Anderson, April 23, 1963.
311. *Washington Post*, August 1, 1963.
312. *Senate Intelligence Committee Report on The Kennedy Assassination*, pp. 12-13.
313. Associated Press, March 4, 1967; Weisberg, *Oswald In New Orleans*, pp. 67-70.
314. "*Organized Crime and Securities: Thefts and Frauds*," Part Two, Permanent Subcommittee On Investigations, Committee On Government Operations, United States Senate, p. 190.

315. Ibid.
316. *Washington Post*, November 19, 1976.
317. Hank Messick, *Secret File* (New York: G.P. Putnam's Sons, 1969), p. 185.
318. Nicholas Gage, *The Mafia Is Not An Equal Opportunity Employer* (New York: Dell Publishing Company, 1971), p. 78.
319. *Ma' ariv*, Israel, Interview with Meyer Lansky, July 5, 1971.
320. *Senate Intelligence Committee Report on Foreign Assassinations*, pp. 74-85.
321. Ibid.
322. Ibid.
323. Hank Messick, *Lansky* (New York: Berkley Medallion Edition, 1971), p. 210.
324. March 26, 1964 FBI memorandum, "Jack L. Ruby, Lee Harvey Oswald — Victim."
325. Warren Commission Volume 5, p. 205.
326. Ibid.
327. McClellan Senate Committee Hearings, p. 12432; Messick, *Lansky*, p. 189; *New York Daily News*, April 23, 1975.
328. Ibid.
329. Warren Commission Volume 5, p.205.
330. Ibid.
331. Ibid., pp. 205-206.
332. Ibid.
333. Ibid., p. 208.
334. Ibid.

CHAPTER EIGHT

The Second Oswald

The possibility that Lee Harvey Oswald was falsely implicated or framed in the assassination of President Kennedy, through the use of an impostor using Oswald's name and identity, provides an aspect of the Kennedy case that is coming under increasing attention. As will be seen, there are numerous sets of Warren Commission testimony and documents which could lend themselves to such an interpretation. It is within the realm of possibility that someone might have impersonated Oswald on several occasions (for instance, during his alleged trip to Mexico City), leaving a trail of damaging pieces of information that may have later falsely implicated Oswald as the Presidential assassin.

While various critics of the Warren Commission have circulated theories of a "second Oswald" for many years, it was not until more than eleven years after the President's murder that such a theory began to receive more serious attention. The new-found credibility of the "second Oswald" came as a result of a stunning disclosure by the *New York Times* in February, 1975.[1]

As noted earlier, the *Times* reported that J. Edgar Hoover himself had become concerned about the possibility of an Oswald impostor — over two and a half years *before* the assassination of President Kennedy. In a memo dated June 3, 1960, Director Hoover set forth information on Lee Harvey Oswald's defection to the Soviet Union and warned the State Department that "there is a possibility that an impostor is using Oswald's birth certificate" in Russia.[2] Hoover's warning was subsequently transmitted through the State Department in two internal Department memos, dated June 10, 1960, and March 31, 1961.[3]

At the time of this *New York Times* disclosure, an ex-Commission counsel called for a reopening of the investigation on the basis of this new information. Former top Warren Commission lawyer David Slawson noted that "the interposition of an impostor, if that happened, is a political act."[4] Significantly, Slawson also said that he thought the CIA, in addition to the FBI, may well have been involved in the suppression of the Hoover memorandum for more than eleven years. Slawson stated:

> It conceivably could have been something related to CIA. I can only speculate now, but a general CIA effort to take out anything that reflected on them may have covered this up.[5]

However, at the time of the 1975 disclosure, another key investigative official had a different theory regarding the cover-up. Richard A. Frank, who was the State Department's liaison to the FBI during the investigation, stated that "when the Oswald file suddenly became the object of the most intensive research and review, Mr. Hoover and his friends in the security operation at State simply made it disappear."[6]

Neither the FBI, the CIA, nor the White House had any comment on the disclosure. However, the whole mysterious episode provided new impetus to theories of a "second Oswald" and provided a firmer basis for speculations that Oswald may have been serving as an agent — possibly of the CIA — during his defection to the Soviet Union. It is believed that these Hoover memos will likely become a key focus during the new investigation.

Robert Sam Anson has noted that for various intelligence operatives skilled in clandestine methods it " . . . would have been relatively easy to use an Oswald look-alike to implicate the real Oswald in the crime . . ."[7] Anson theorizes that the following may have taken place:

> Not the Agency [CIA], but someone close to the Agency familiar with its workings and its weaknesses, discovers a young, former Marine who once served in an intelligence capacity and now works as a government informer. Again a double is used, but this time without Oswald's knowledge. A trail of incriminating clues is left, pointing straight at a pro-Castro activist. When Oswald is arrested and charged with the President's murder, there is no convincing way that either the FBI or CIA can explain that while he was once their man, he is no longer. After November 24,

1963, Oswald himself is in no position to talk. Confronted with such a conundrum, one fraught with peril for the security of the world, the United States government does what is has to do. It left sleeping dogs lie.[8]

As will be seen in forthcoming pages, the CIA is deeply involved in another strange incident directly relating to the possibility of an Oswald impostor. In this episode, the Agency made a series of photographs of a man they identified as Lee Harvey Oswald in Mexico City. As will be seen, the man the CIA identified as Lee Oswald turned out to look nothing like him at all.

Interestingly, hours before his murder by Jack Ruby, Oswald had angrily charged that he was being framed through the use of some fabricated photographs of himself holding the alleged assassination rifle. During his police interrogation, prisoner Oswald was shown the photos allegedly of himself holding his rifle. The photographs subsequently became famous when published in *Life* Magazine days later. While the Dallas authorities made light of Oswald's protestations, the incident is interesting nonetheless. Upon viewing the photographs, Oswald angrily charged:

> That is not a picture of me; it is my face, but my face has been superimposed — the rest of the picture is not me at all, I've never seen it before . . . That small picture is a reduction of the large picture that someone I don't know has made . . . someone took a picture of my face and faked that photograph.[9]

Richard Popkin

Richard Popkin, a Professor of Philosophy and author of the 1966 book, *The Second Oswald*, has been an active researcher of the Kennedy assassination for many years.[10] Professor Popkin was a prime originator of the theory that there may have been more than one assassination conspirator using the name and identity of "Lee Harvey Oswald," and that Oswald may have been set up or framed by others using his identity. While the idea of "a second Oswald" was discounted for years as being too improbable, recent disclosures about sophisticated covers and multiple identities have refocused attention on Professor Popkin's concepts. Although some Warren Commission critics now look askance at some of Popkin's newest assassination research, most critics acknowledge his significant early role in outlining the areas of evidence relating to the theory of "more than one Oswald."

Sylvia Odio

Sylvia Odio was a somewhat wealthy Cuban exile leader in Dallas, who has become one of the single

 most important Warren Commission witnesses, according to most assassination investigators. Sylvia Odio provided the Warren Commission with what the Commission staff itself regarded as strong testimony indicating that Lee Harvey Oswald was secretly in Dallas working with a militant anti-Castro group at the same exact time that the Warren Commission concluded he was on his way from New Orleans to Mexico City, on the bus trip which is still a source of mystery to many observers.

Sylvia Odio (and her sister) testified that Lee Oswald and two Latin men named "Angelo" and "Leopoldo" came to her house in Dallas on the night of September 26, 1963, less than eight weeks before the assassination.[11] Mrs. Odio testified that these two Latin companions of Oswald introduced him using the name "Leon Oswald." Sylvia Odio stated that Oswald and the two men told her that they had just come from New Orleans, and wanted to know if she could finance some anti-Castro operations that they were planning.[12] Mrs. Odio refused their offer.

Mrs. Odio further testified that she received a phone call the next day from "Leopoldo," who told her that "our idea is to introduce him [Oswald] to the underground in Cuba, because he is great, he is kind of nuts." According to Mrs. Odio, "Leopoldo" went on to tell her that "Leon Oswald" had served in the Marine Corps and had been an excellent marksman. Odio testified that "Leopoldo" concluded the call by saying that "Kennedy should have been assassinated after the Bay of Pigs," and that anti-Castro Cubans "should have done that" not only because the President deserved it, but also because, "it is so easy to do it."[13]

Mrs. Odio further told the Warren Commission that she could positively identify Lee Harvey Oswald as the "Leon Oswald" who visited her with the two Latin men. Odio testified that she had fainted as soon as she saw Oswald's photograph on television a few hours after the assassination. Again, her sister backed up her account. Needless to say, members of the Warren Commission were apprehensive over Sylvia Odio's testimony. First of all, the Odio account put Oswald in Dallas in the company of apparently violent anti-Castro operatives (who talked of the need for Kennedy to be murdered) less than two months before the actual assassination. And, as mentioned earlier, "Leon Oswald" and the two men had visited Odio's home in Dallas on the very night the Warren Commission had already concluded Oswald was on his bus trip to Mexico City. If Oswald had indeed been in Odio's home that night, then further credence would have to be given to the possibility that an Oswald impostor was using his identity in Mexico City. And such an impersonation of Oswald in Mexico City would certainly explain the mysterious CIA photographs taken there of a man whom the CIA identified as Oswald, but who turned out to look nothing like Oswald at all.

In August, 1964, as the Warren Commission neared the end of its investigation, General Counsel J. Lee Rankin wrote to FBI Director J. Edgar Hoover, stating that, "It is a matter of some importance to the Commission that Mrs. Odio's allegations either be proved or disproved."[14] Hoover's FBI subsequently secured the testimony of a man named Loran Hall, an anti-Castro exile leader with reported Mafia links who stated that he had been one of the three men who had visited Odio on the night in question, and further stated that Lee Oswald was not one of the other two men.[15] Mrs. Odio strongly denied Loran Hall's account, and was subsequently vindicated when Hall retracted his story on October 2, 1964, and denied being there that night.[16]

For the Warren Commission, the mysterious and

alarming testimony given by Sylvia Odio would not go away. Eleven years after the investigation ended, a key Commission document that had previously been withheld from the public was finally declassified and released. The Warren Commission memo, written by William Coleman and David Slawson, included a section dealing with Sylvia Odio that stated that her veracity and reliability as a witness had been attested to by her various friends and acquaintances. The Coleman/Slawson memorandum stated that, "Mrs. Odio has checked out thoroughly . . . And, with one exception — a layman who speculates that she may have subconscious tendencies to over-dramatize and exaggerate — the evidence is unanimously favorable."[17]

According to sources familar with the innerworkings of the Warren Commission, Counsel Wesley Liebeler was particularly concerned over the strong basis of Odio's testimony. Liebeler and other Commission staffers concluded that Odio's story seemed to include information about Oswald that she couldn't have known without having had some contact with him, or others close to him. According to Edward Epstein's respected account of the Warren Commission investigation, *Inquest*, when Liebeler tried to explain the important unsolved allegations of Odio's testimony to General Counsel J. Lee Rankin, Rankin angrily told him that, "At this stage, we are supposed to be closing doors, not opening them."[18]

Oscar Deslatte

Oscar Deslatte was the Assistant Manager of a Ford Motors car lot in New Orleans who provided one of the more solid and intriguing pieces of information

 on the possible activities of a "second Oswald." Oscar Deslatte informed the federal authorities and the Warren Commission about a man who approached him in January, 1961, on behalf of an anti-Castro group. The man, who used the name "Oswald," wanted to purchase ten Ford trucks for an organization called "Friends of a Democratic Cuba."[19] The interesting thing about this incident is that at that time, Lee Oswald was thousands of miles away in the Soviet Union.

Thus, it must have been a different "Oswald" involved in the proposed truck purchase — another man, using the name Oswald, who also was involved with a Cuban group, and who also operated in New Orleans. In any event, the similarities are intriguing, no matter which theory of Oswald's actions is subscribed to. Interestingly, the "Friends of a Democratic Cuba" was the same right-wing anti-Castro exile group which had been coordinated in part by Guy Banister, the New Orleans private detective who employed David Ferrie and who may have had other connections to Lee Harvey Oswald.[20]

Oscar Deslatte further stated that the man named "Oswald" also suggested that a discount on the trucks be given to the "Friends of a Democratic Cuba," since it was a political organization.[21] While Lee Oswald was supposedly in Russia at this time, it should again be pointed out that J. Edgar Hoover wrote a memo on June 3, 1960, disclosing that the FBI suspected that, "An impostor is using Oswald's birth certificate" in Russia. As previously noted, this startling Hoover memo wasn't made public until 1975.

Albert Bogard

Albert Bogard, another highly credible witness heard by the Warren Commission, also testified about circumstances indicating the possibility of some other person using the identity of "Lee Oswald."

Albert Bogard was a car salesman for a Lincoln-Mercury dealership in Dallas. According to Bogard (whose story was not only backed up by his co-workers but was also confirmed by a successful lie detector test), a man who identified himself as "Lee Oswald" approached Bogard on November 9, 1963 to discuss buying a used car.[22] The man named "Lee Oswald" stated that he didn't have enough money for the car yet but would be receiving "a lot of money in the next two or three weeks."[23] Bogard also said that he accompanied "Lee Oswald" on a test drive of the car during which "Oswald" drove at speeds up to 70 miles per hour. Bogard further stated that "Lee Oswald" was somewhat irritated over the various financing plans available for such cars, and stated that he might go "back to Russia where they treat workers like men."[24]

Despite Bogard's solid and substantiated testimony, evidence seems to indicate that the real Oswald was not the same "Lee Oswald" who met with Bogard. The Warren Commission established that Oswald did not even know how to drive, and further, that Oswald was not in Dallas on the day the incident happened, November 9, 1963.[25]

Thus, in the Bogard account, the possibility is raised that an imposter was using Oswald's identity in Dallas just two weeks before the assassination — an imposter who skillfully utilized knowledge of Oswald's Russian travels during his conversation with the car salesman, and who may have attempted to cleverly implicate the real Oswald by saying he was going to be receiving "a lot of money in the next two or three weeks." Bogard testified that the "Lee Oswald" who approached him was definitely different in appearance from the photographs of the real Lee Harvey Oswald the police showed him following the assassination.

Again, while Albert Bogard's story has been referred to by various Warren Commission critics for years, it has only recently begun to receive serious attention.

Mrs. Lee Dannelly

Mrs. Lee Dannelly, the Assistant Director of the Austin, Texas Selective Service System's Administrative Section, also provided information to the Warren Commission and FBI which indicated that Lee Harvey Oswald was somehow able to be in two places at the same time.

Mrs. Dannelly testified that a man she firmly believed was Lee Harvey Oswald came into her Selective Service office in Austin on September 25, 1963.[26] She stated that she was immediately able to identify Oswald as the man who had visited her office when she saw his picture on television. Mrs. Dannelly stated that Oswald was seeking to upgrade his undesirable discharge from the Marine Corps, and had told her of his hardship in supporting his family in Fort Worth while trying to find decent employment where his undesirable discharge would not affect his hirability.[27]

Despite the fact that Mrs. Dannelly made what she regarded as a positive identification of Lee Harvey Oswald in this instance, and despite the fact that Dannelly was regarded as a reliable witness, her account is distinctly puzzling. The Warren Commission concluded that on the day in question, September 25, 1963, Lee Oswald was several hundred miles away — in New Orleans, preparing to leave for Mexico City.[28] Thus, if Mrs. Dannelly's account is accurate, either Oswald never went from New Orleans to Mexico City (and was impersonated there) or Oswald somehow managed to make a long, mysterious, detour during his Mexico City trip, which the Warren Commission never found out about.

Silvia Duran

Silvia Duran, a young Mexican citizen, served as the Assistant to the Cuban Counsel at the Cuban Embassy in Mexico City in 1963, and provided a key piece of evidence regarding Oswald's mysterious trip to Mexico City in September, 1963.

As mentioned before, both the Warren Commission and its league of critics have focused on Oswald's visit to Mexico as a key area of the assassination investiga-

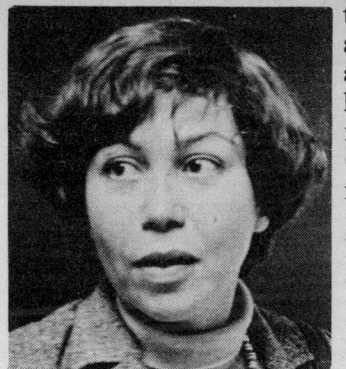

tion. Serious questions about the possibility of an Oswald impersonator have been raised, primarily resulting from the CIA's acknowledged role in the now well-known CIA photography-surveillance operations conducted outside of the Russian and Cuban Embassies in Mexico City.

In this instance, the CIA photographed a man entering and/or leaving one or both of these Embassies and identified the man as "Lee Oswald." As it turned out, the man labeled Oswald in the CIA photographs was not Lee Oswald at all, and looked nothing like him. Thus, a crucial question arises as to whether this other man (whose identity has never been substantiated) was an Oswald impostor — implicating Oswald perhaps by making these visits to the Cuban and Russian Embassies.

In any event, Cuban Embassy employee Silvia Duran is the *only* person who ever positively identified Lee Harvey Oswald as the man who came into the Cuban Embassy on the day the Warren Commission says he did.

Silvia Duran testified that she clearly remembered Oswald's face when she saw his photograph in the newspapers immediately after the assassination. Duran made what she called "a positive identification" of Oswald on the day after the assassination, November 23, 1963, in a sworn deposition with the Deputy Director of the Mexican Federal Security.

Interestingly, that was the last that was ever heard from Silvia Duran. Later, in 1964, a Mexican reporter sought to interview Mrs. Duran in the hope of obtaining further information regarding the reported Oswald visit to the Embassy. Mrs. Duran's husband, however, told the reporter that his wife was not available for any further questioning, stating that she had "suffered a nervous breakdown following her interrogation by the Mexican authorities and had been prohibited by her physician. . . from discussing the matter further."[29]

Informed sources report that investigators of the Senate Intelligence Committee made an effort to locate and interview Silvia Duran in May, 1976, without success.

However, Duran was finally located and questioned early in 1977 by both *Washington Post* reporter Ron Kessler and investigators for the House Committee on Assassinations.

Name and Identity Unknown

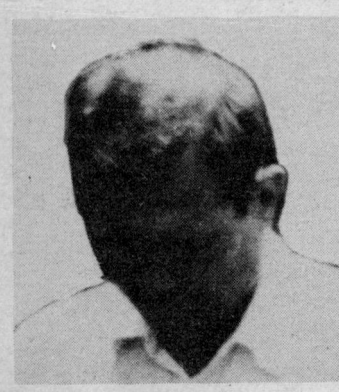

One of the single most mysterious (and in large part unexplained) areas of evidence regarding the possibility of an Oswald impostor is provided by the CIA itself, and also occurred during the period when the Warren Commission said Oswald was in Mexico City.

The incident centers around a highly sophisticated CIA surveillance and photographic operation that was charged with monitoring and photographing people going in and out of the Russian and Cuban Embassies in Mexico City. On October 10, 1963, just six weeks before President Kennedy was shot, the

CIA sent a secret teletype message to the FBI, the State Department, and the Navy. This CIA teletype reported that Lee Oswald had been photographed coming out of the Russian Embassy:

> On 1 October 1963 a reliable and sensitive source in Mexico reported that an American male, who identified himself as Lee OSWALD contacted the Soviet Embassy in Mexico City inquiring whether the Embassy had received any news concerning a telegram which had been sent to Washington. The American was described as approximately 35 years old, with an athletic build, about six feet tall, with a receding hairline."[30]

Needless to say, the "Lee Oswald" described in the CIA teletype was a man whose physical description didn't match the real Lee Harvey Oswald at all; he was only 23 years old and slimly built. Later in the month, the CIA itself was apparently in the process of trying to get the Navy to release its own photograph of Oswald to the Agency for comparison with the Mexican photographs.[31]

But the assassination in Dallas on November 22nd brought the question of the mystery man in the CIA photographs to a head. On the very day of the President's murder, the CIA turned over their secret Mexican photographs to the FBI and it became readily apparent that the man identified as "Lee Oswald" in the CIA photos was not Oswald at all and looked nothing like him. The CIA immediately admitted having made some kind of mistake in the identification of Oswald, and later promised the Warren Commission a full explanation as to the misidentification. Though the CIA did later reluctantly provide some "classified" information regarding its secret photographic operation at the Russian and Cuban Embassies, no full explanation of the mysterious matter was ever provided to the Warren Commission.

929 - 927 A

930 - 927 B

932 - 927 D

933 - 927 E

936-927 H

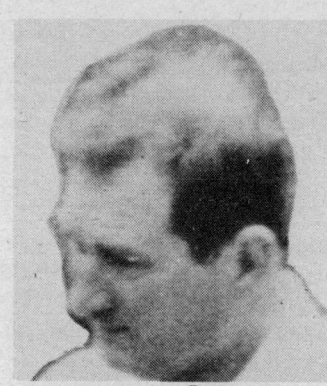

934-927 F

939-927 K

938-927 J

Members of the Warren Commission staff were immediately suspicious of the CIA's misidentification of Oswald and asked the CIA to find out who exactly was the man in its photographs. The CIA subsequently stated that they were unable to identify the man in the photographs whom they had originally stated was Lee Oswald, and the man's name and identity have never been established to this day.

In the past several years, the CIA has been forced (through Freedom of Information lawsuits) to release several other photographs that they had made of the same man at the Russian Embassy. While the CIA has told Senate investigators that it has made further efforts through the years to identify this man, the Agency says it still does not know who he is.

While a strong consensus of investigators believe this incident provides the single most compelling evidence of an Oswald impostor, the mystery surrounding it (and Oswald's entire Mexican trip) has never subsided. The "Lee Oswald" shown in the CIA's October 1963 photographs remains missing and totally unidentified.

Hugh McDonald

Hugh McDonald is another of the assassination researchers who have periodically announced that they have found the "final solution" to the mystery of the Kennedy assassination. McDonald in fact claims to have actually tracked down and interviewed the actual assassin of President Kennedy, a man identified only as "Saul," whom McDonald states was a professional assassin who had been employed by the CIA during the Bay of Pigs invasion.

However, there is something that distinguishes Hugh McDonald from many of the other assassination buffs, namely, his well-known and highly-respected work over a 30-year period as one of the nation's top law enforcement authorities. It is mainly because of McDonald's abundant law enforcement credentials that his recent book, *Appointment in Dallas*, has become the subject of considerable interest as well as a surprise best seller nationwide.

Hugh McDonald's long career began in the military during the 1940's when he was second in command of the nation's largest Military Intelligence School, at Fort McArthur, California. During the 1950s McDonald served as Chief of Police at various times in several California cities, and then went on to become a Security Consultant for billionaire Howard Hughes, working for Hughes Aircraft. During the '60s, Hugh McDonald was a member of the Los Angeles County Sheriff's Department, from which he was retired as Chief of Detectives in 1967. Additionally, he was selected by the Republican National Committee in 1964 to be Chief of Security for Senator Barry Goldwater's Presidential campaign. McDonald is perhaps better known as the inventor of the "Identi-Kit" criminal identification process which is now in standard use by police in many nations. He is also the author of three books, including *The Psychology of Police Interrogation*, which are now standard texts in most police academies throughout the nation.

Hugh McDonald says he first saw the man who he claims later murdered President Kennedy, in late April of 1961.[32] McDonald writes that he first met this professional hit man, "Saul," at CIA headquarters in the office of Herman Kimsey, a ranking CIA official.³³ "Saul" was highly upset over what he felt was a CIA double cross during the Bay of Pigs invasion. McDonald states that it wasn't until 1964, during his security work for Senator Goldwater, that Herman Kimsey explained the full details of "Saul's" role in the Dallas murder during a three-hour conversation with McDonald, and also warned him that his life would be "worthless" if he ever revealed the information. McDonald asked Kimsey if the CIA had been connected with the hiring of "Saul" for the assassination, and says that Kimsey answered:

> "Are you crazy? Of course not! This man was a free lance, open to offers. Someone hired him. That's not the way the Company operates. That's one of the reasons that this story has to be kept quiet. No matter how it came out, the image of the Company would be seriously hurt.... When he ["Saul"] first talked to me about it, he felt there might have been a government connection. You know the rules of the game, Hugh. On a job like that, the less one knows, the better. He finally came to feel that the man who hired him was working for a private group, that that group had strong government connections."³⁵

McDonald, who spent over five years investigating the information given to him by his CIA friend, further writes Kimsey told him that:

> "He [Saul] first met the man who hired him to kill the President in 1961, at the staging camp in Guatemala for the Bay of Pigs invasion. At that time, at least, he felt this man had a connection with the U.S. Government. When he saw him next, it was in Haiti and the meeting took place in a

house that could have been United States Government property of some kind."[36]

McDonald claims that after years of complex dealings with various European intelligence operatives, he finally located "Saul" in London, England in June of 1972, where "Saul" confirmed that he had indeed shot President Kennedy, and that Herman Kimsey's account had been accurate. "Saul" appeared confident that McDonald would be unable to interest any U.S. law enforcement authorities in the information, and he was contemptuous of McDonald for thinking that the conspiracy would ever really be properly investigated. "Saul" explained that Lee Harvey Oswald had been entrapped as the "patsy" or fall guy in the conspiracy, and was to have originally been murdered even sooner after the assassination than he was.[37] McDonald writes that "Saul" provided a graphic description of his shooting of the President, which was carried out with a sophisticated semi-automatic weapon:

> ". . . When I first brought the President's head into my telescopic sight, he was leaning forward at an appreciable angle. My cross hairs were exactly on the back of his skull . . . Just as my gun fired, the President straightened up from his forward position . . . I realized that my first shot was low and to the right. Almost instinctively, I took the bead again on the back of the President's head, and fired. This bullet blew out the right side of his head."[38]

While Hugh McDonald's book has provoked widespread interest, many questions have been raised about various points in the story, including what some critics believe is an inaccurate physical reconstruction of the shooting as described by the alleged assassin, "Saul." Yet McDonald's five-year investigation does indeed remain intriguing. Not only does McDonald have law enforcement credentials, he has offered to turn over his entire file on the matter to Congressional investigators, testify under oath, and submit to a lie detector test.

Interestingly, McDonald also claims that "Saul" was the mysterious and unidentified man whom the CIA photographed in Mexico City, and whom the CIA misidentified as Lee Oswald. McDonald indicates that "Saul" was impersonating Oswald during a visit to the Russian Embassy there and that the use of a "second Oswald" was an integral part of the assassination plan. McDonald states that "Saul" has changed very little in appearance during the thirteen years since the CIA photographs were made.

Unfortunately for McDonald, Herman Kimsey is now dead. Thus the key figure who could have shed light on McDonald's account of the assassination is not available for collaboration of the story. In a recent interview, McDonald claimed that "Saul" is now believed to be somewhere within the United States.

The I.N.S. Inspector

In June, 1976, the Senate Intelligence Committee disclosed that an Inspector of the Immigration and Naturalization Service had informed the Committee of some new information purportedly indicating that Lee Harvey Oswald had been using a second identity as a "Cuban alien" in New Orleans — at a time when the Warren Commission concluded he was living in Texas.

Rather than indicating that someone was impersonating Oswald, the I.N.S. Inspector's testimony raised the possibility that Oswald had himself used another identity — an identity never discovered by the Warren Commission.

The Senate Intelligence Committee disclosed that the I.N.S. Inspector (whom the Committee did not name) had testified that "he is absolutely certain that he interviewed Lee Harvey Oswald in a New Orleans jail cell sometime shortly before his [the Inspector's] April 1, 1963 transfer out of New Orleans."[39] The Senate Committee noted that the Inspector was unsure what name Oswald had been using, but that Oswald was "claiming to be a Cuban alien."[40] The I.N.S. Inspector testified that he had readily ascertained (by interviewing Oswald) that he was not actually a Cuban.[41] The Inspector, whom the Senate Committee staff regarded as highly credible, further testified that he had few other details regarding the encounter.

As the Senate Committee noted, this alleged Oswald presence in New Orleans in February or March of 1963, occurred before Oswald is known to have been in that city.[42] The Warren Commission had concluded that Oswald was then living in Texas.[43]

The Senate Committee further reported that the New Orleans Police Department could find no records pertaining to any arrest under Oswald's name during that period, and had no information on the alleged incident.[44] As will be seen in a forthcoming section, Oswald was later involved in a fistfight with a Cuban exile leader in New Orleans, and was briefly jailed at that time. However, the I.N.S. Inspector testified that the episode he was referring to had occurred several months earlier than that incident.

1. *New York Times*, February 23, 1975.
2. Warren Commission Document 294 B; *New York Times*, February 23, 1975.
3. Ibid.
4. *New York Times*, February 23, 1975.
5. Ibid.
6. Ibid.
7. Anson, *They've Killed the President!* p. 214.
8. Ibid.
9. Meagher, *Accessories After the Fact*, p. 235.
10. Richard H. Popkin, *The Second Oswald* (New York: Avon Library Edition, 1966).
11. Warren Commission Volume 11, pp. 371-372; Warren Commission Exhibit 3147.
12. Ibid.
13. Ibid.
14. Warren Commission Volume 26, p. 595.
15. Warren Commission Report, p. 324.
16. Meagher, *Accessories After the Fact*, p. 387.
17. Memorandum to the Warren Commission from William Coleman and David Slawson, undated.
18. Epstein, *Inquest*, p. 103.
19. Warren Commission Document 75.
20. Anson, *They've Killed The President!*, p. 214.
21. Ibid.
22. Warren Commission Volume 26, p. 577.
23. Warren Commission Volume 10, p. 353.
24. Warren Commission Volume 26, p. 685.
25. Warren Commission Report, p. 298.
26. Warren Commission Volume 24, pp. 729-734.
27. Ibid.
28. Warren Commission Report, pp. 652-653.
29. Warren Commission Document 963.
30. Warren Commission Document 631.
31. Ibid.
32. Hugh McDonald, *Appointment In Dallas* (New York: Hugh McDonald Publishing Corp., 1975), pp. 17-21.
33. Ibid.
34. Ibid., pp. 35-39.
35. Ibid.
36. Ibid., p. 38.
37. Ibid., pp. 155-160, 170.
38. Ibid., pp. 176-177.
39. *Senate Intelligence Committee Report on the Kennedy Assassination*, p. 91.
40. Ibid.
41. Ibid.
42. Ibid.
43. Ibid.
44. Ibid.

CHAPTER NINE

The Dallas Police

The performance of the Dallas Police Department in the aftermath of the Kennedy assassination has long been the subject of intensive criticism. With the mysterious murder of prisoner Lee Harvey Oswald — in front of a roomful of Dallas police officers in the police basement on November 24, 1963 — the role of the Dallas P.D. came under increasing doubts and indeed, suspicion. Such suspicions spread even further with the Warren Commission's documentation of Jack Ruby's close ties to several police officers, something that had been apparent right from the moment that Jack Ruby shoved his pistol into Oswald's stomach on November 24th. Seconds after firing the fatal shot, as he was being wrestled to the floor, Ruby yelled, "You know me, I'm Jack Ruby." As will be seen, Ruby's statement, "You know me," was indeed an understatement.

Jack Ruby

The Warren Commission had this to say about Jack Ruby's relationship with the Dallas Police Department: "Although Chief Curry's estimate that approximately 25 to 50 of the 1,175 men in the Dallas Police Department knew Ruby may be too conservative, the Commission found no evidence of any suspicious relationships between Ruby and any police officer."[1]

Yet, as assassination researcher Sylvia Meagher has noted, "Of the 75 or so policemen who were present when Oswald was killed, at least 40 knew Ruby. If the same proportion — over 50 per cent — is applied to the total police force, Ruby must have known more than 500 of the men."[2] In fact that is roughly what one of Jack Ruby's close friends estimated the correct number to be during a statement he made for the Commission's investigation. Reagan Turman, a prize fighter who had known Ruby for some time, stated that "Ruby was acquainted with at least 75 per cent, or probably 80 per cent, of the police officers of the Dallas Police Department."[3] It is interesting to note that of the 40 Dallas policemen who knew Ruby and who also witnessed him murdering Lee Oswald (40 of the 75 policemen then present) 17 of them were never asked to testify during the Warren Commission investigation.[4]

While the Warren Report only briefly alluded to it, Commission documentation clearly indicates that Jack Ruby's night clubs — particularly his strip joint "Carousel Club" — were well known hangouts for Dallas police officers, with Ruby serving free drinks (and occasionally free whores) for the pleasure of various Dallas cops. While admitting that "I think a lot of the officers knew Ruby," Captain Will Fritz of the Dallas Homicide Division even sought to place some distance between himself and Ruby, stating,

"He seemed to be well-known. It seems a lot of people in town knew him. But I was never in his place . . ."[5]

Among the Dallas police officers who were more than well acquainted with Jack Ruby, in addition to the ones covered in forthcoming pages, were Lieutenants George Butler, George Arnett, R. E. Swain, Erich Kaminski, and J. R. Gilmore; Detectives Eberhardt, Standifer, McGee, Cutchshaw, Lowery, and Harrison; and Officers D. L. Blankenship, E. E. Carlson, Glen Neal, and Truett Walton.[6]

Will Fritz

Captain Will Fritz, the Chief of Homicide for the Dallas Police Department, played a key role in the probe inasmuch as he conducted the lengthy interrogation of Lee Harvey Oswald. Fritz kept no transcription or detailed account of Oswald's answers during the interrogation, and had reportedly decided against taping the lengthy question and answer session. Thus, no official transcript of the interrogation has ever been produced.

Captain Fritz has also been the subject of heavy criticism for his handling of Oswald's ill-fated transfer, which led to his murder in the police basement. While the exact circumstances that enabled Ruby to penetrate the heavily-guarded basement have never been determined, Captain Fritz has been criticized by both defenders and critics of the Warren Report for the poorly coordinated security of this maneuver.

In an episode yet to be fully clarified, which Captain Fritz first disclosed to the Commission in 1964, it became known that he had secretly listened in on a telephone call between the head of the Dallas FBI Office, Gordon Shanklin, and an agent, James Bookhout several hours after the assassination. Shanklin told Bookhout that FBI Agent James Hosty knew Lee Harvey Oswald and had interviewed the alleged assassin on more than one occasion in 1963.[7] According to Captain Fritz, Shanklin told Bookhout to order Hosty into the investigation at once, saying, "I want him in that investigation right now because he knows those people he has been talking to . . ."[8] Fritz told the investigators that he had never before revealed that he'd listened in on this phone call: "I walked out of there . . . I didn't tell them that I even knew what Mr. Shanklin said."[9]

Fritz, now retired from the Dallas Police Force, has steadfastly refused any comment on his actions in the Kennedy case for over twelve years.

In 1976, the National Archives disclosed that a Warren Commission letter, pertaining to the "interrogation of Oswald by [the] Dallas Police Department," written by David Belin to J. Lee Rankin on January 23, 1964,[9a] was one of the items missing from the Commission records in the Archives.

Jack Revill

Jack Revill, who served as a Lieutenant with the Dallas Police Department in 1963, received some

secret FBI information about Lee Oswald from James Hosty within an hour of the assassination. In late 1975, it was revealed that the Revill-Hosty incident had been the subject of a high-level cover-up for over eleven years, involving not only Dallas Police Chief Jesse Curry, Dallas FBI Chief Gordon Shanklin, but possibily Commission Chairman Earl Warren as well.

The story began when James Hosty excitedly ran up to Revill less than an hour after Kennedy was shot and stated with great agitation, "Jack . . . a Communist killed President Kennedy. We know this guy. He is in our Communist file."[10] Hosty said the FBI also "had information that this man was capable . . . of committing this assassination."[11] Soon after, Revill informed police Chief Curry of Hosty's statement; Curry thereafter disclosed this FBI information to the press. Yet later that day, Chief Curry retracted his statement and said that he had been misinformed as to the FBI's information on Oswald.

It was not until over eleven years later, in September, 1975, that the reason for Chief Curry's strange retraction finally came to light when the *Houston Chronicle* disclosed that Curry had sent a letter to Earl Warren in 1964, revealing that Shanklin had told him that "the [FBI] was extremely desirous that I retract my statement to the press."[12] Not only did Curry agree to do it, he further ordered Lt. Revill to remain silent about the FBI information as well.

The entire handling of the Hosty-Revill incident by Curry and Shanklin provides another clear example of the Bureau's pattern of covering up certain information relating to the accused Presidential assassin. Not only did the cover-up involve the Chiefs of both the Dallas P.D. and FBI office, it is evident that Earl Warren himself went along with it by never disclosing Chief Curry's letter. After the *Houston Chronicles* story, Curry confirmed the details of the episode but offered no explanation for his action. Gordon Shanklin refused to comment on the matter.

In 1976, the National Archives disclosed that a Warren Commission letter to Lt. Jack Revill, requesting "records relating to a possible pro-Castro demonstration by Oswald in Dallas" was one of the items missing from the Commission records in the Archives.[12a]

Gerald Hill

Sergeant Gerald Hill, a long-time acquaintance of Jack Ruby,[13] told the Warren Commission that he used to see Ruby at the Carousel Club "once in a while."[14] Hill also stated that he had last spoken with his friend Ruby "six to eight weeks" before the assassination, when Hill says he ran into him when "I was walking by a garage one night."[15] In a set of circumstances that has received little attention, Gerald Hill was the Sergeant in charge of the immediate police search of the Texas School Book Depository, minutes after the shooting in Dealey Plaza.

Sergeant Hill has long been of interest to assassination investigators because he took part in three separate — and very crucial — actions involving the Dallas police on the afternoon of the assassination. Not only was Sergeant Hill in command of the Dallas policemen who found the Oswald rifle and bullet shells on the sixth floor of the Book Depository, he was also one of the first police officers to arrive at the scene of the Tippit shooting, and subsequently was also one of the officers who arrested Lee Harvey Oswald in the Texas Theater by wrestling him to the ground.[16] All three of these police actions occurred within a time span of ninety minutes.

Hill provided the first detailed account of the Tippit incident in an interview with a Dallas radio station not long after the shooting, in which he incorrectly stated that the pistol taken from Oswald during his arrest, which he allegedly used in killing Officer Tippit, had been fired twice. Subsequent examination of Tippit's body revealed that he had actually been shot four times. An excerpt from the Hill radio interview:

> *Interviewer:* What kind of weapon did he use to kill the officer with, Gerry?
>
> *Hill:* A thirty-eight snub nose that was fired twice, and both shots hit the officer in the head.

Following Oswald's capture, Gerry Hill had the Oswald pistol in his possession until later that afternoon. According to Hill's arrest report on Oswald, "I retained this gun in my possession until approximately 3:15 p.m. Friday, November 22, 1963, when in the presence of Officers Carroll and McDonald, I turned the weapon over to Detective T. L. Baker of the Homicide and Robbery Bureau . . . "[17]

Various Warren Commission critics (particularly George O'Toole, the former chief of the CIA's Problem Analysis Branch, and author of *The Assassination*

Tapes) have raised questions about another area of information involving Sergeant Gerald Hill. Hill, along with four other Dallas police officers, had also been present during the transfer of Oswald by car to police headquarters following his arrest in the Texas Theater. According to police reports filed by these officers — which subsequently became key Warren Commission documents — Oswald's wallet was opened during this car ride and was found to contain identification cards made out in the alias of "Alek Hidell." In perhaps its single most important finding, the Commission subsequently concluded this alias was used by Oswald to purchase the mail order rifle allegedly used in the assassination. In an interview with George O'Toole in 1973, Hill recounted his ride to the police station with suspect Oswald:

> As I say, in the car on the way downtown, he was belligerent, he was surly, he wouldn't tell us who he was. We took his billfold out of his pocket, and we found the ID in both names, Oswald and Hidell, that he later was proved to order the gun under. He had library cards and draft cards in one name, and he had identification cards from various organizations in the other name.[18]

Yet in Sergeant Hill's radio interview on the day of the assassination, he provided considerable details about Oswald, but did not mention the alleged alias identification supposedly found in Oswald's wallet:

> The boy that we had apprehended for shooting Officer J.D. Tippit is an employee of the book factory where the shots that killed the President were fired from. He was seen on the floor below the window where the shots were fired some 15 minutes prior to the shooting. He was a former U.S. Marine marksman who defected to Russia

in 1957 and returned to the U.S. approximately a year ago with a Russian bride, I understand . . . he won't admit anything other than he was a Communist. He started screaming "brutality" as soon as we got the cuffs on him . . .[19]

George O'Toole, who has conducted a lengthy probe of the ID cards in Oswald's wallet, has written:

> Hill's radio interview sounded like a preliminary brief for the prosecutor. He related all kinds of incriminating details about Lee Harvey Oswald, but he left out something that he might be expected to emphasize: the discovery of forged credentials in Oswald's possession. Hill made absolutely no mention of finding the "Alek Hidell" identification on Oswald. It seems very strange that in such a detailed account of the arrest, made less than a few hours after the incident, Hill would omit such a significant point.
>
> In the supplementary volumes of the Warren Report, I found the transcript of another broadcast interview with Gerald Hill on November 22, 1963. In this one, the subject of the contents of Oswald's wallet is raised by Hill, who tells the newsman, "The only way we found out what his name was was to remove his billfold and check it ourselves; he wouldn't even tell us what his name was."
>
> Later in the interview a reporter asks, "What was the name in the billfold?" Hill replies, "Lee O-S-W-A-L-D."
>
> And that was all. Hill didn't refer even

obliquely to finding any false identification.[20]

Hill, who is now a lieutenant with the Dallas Police Department, has been generally unavailable for comment on this episode and his other activities of November 22, 1963. However, in a taped interview with George O'Toole in 1973, Officer Hill was asked whether he had ever known Lee Harvey Oswald prior to the assassination. Hill replied negatively, adding that, "He [Oswald] was a statistic as far as we were concerned." Hill further noted, "The only one I knew before was Jack Ruby."[21]

Harry Olsen

While some attention has been focused over the years on Police Officer Harry Olsen and his close friendship with Jack Ruby, the circumstances of their relationship has generally been overlooked. Harry Olsen told the Warren Commission that he had known Jack Ruby for over three years, and that their friendship had developed during the course of weekly visits by Olsen to Ruby's night club.[22] In his appearance before the Warren Commission, Olsen also confirmed that he had become closer to Jack Ruby in the month before the assassination due to the fact that his new girlfriend, Kay Coleman, was one of Ruby's strippers. Of more immediate interest, however, is the fact that Officer Olsen met Jack Ruby sometime after midnight on the very night of the Kennedy assassination. Not only did Ruby meet Olsen and Kay Coleman sometime between midnight and 3:00 a.m., he concealed this meeting from the authorities and never disclosed it until his appearance before the Warren Commission on June 7, 1964. Ruby then stated that Olsen had also made a threatening remark about Oswald at that time. Ruby testified that Olsen "stated they should cut this guy [Oswald] inch by inch into ribbons and so on."[23] Interestingly, Ruby also incorrectly identifed his friend of three years as "Harry Carlson," rather than Harry Olsen. Ruby told the Commission he had met Officer Olsen and his girl friend at around 2:00 a.m. as he was driving downtown on a couple of "late night chores":

> As I was driving toward the *Times Herald* with the intention of doing these things, I heard someone honk a horn very loudly, and I stopped. There was a police officer sitting in a car. He was sitting with this young lady that works in my club, Kathie Kay . . . and I remained with them . . . did I tell you this part of it?
>
> I didn't tell you this part because at the time I thought a lot of Harry Carlson as a police officer, and either it slipped my mind in telling this, or it was more or less a reason for leaving it out, because I didn't want to involve them in anything . . . Anyway, I did leave it out. His name is Harry Carlson. Her name is Kathie Kay.
>
> . . . he stated they should cut this guy [Oswald] inch by inch into ribbons and so on.

I left them after a long delay. They kept
me from leaving. They were constantly
talking and were in a very dramatic mood
. . .[24]

Ruby's testimony about this rather strange late
night meeting with Officer Olsen, the night of the
assassination, is interesting for a number of reasons.
At the time he met up with Olsen, Ruby was driving
back from the police station where he had been
standing within three feet of Lee Harvey Oswald
while Oswald was being moved by police officials. In
this instance — which was so similar to Ruby's fatal
encounter with Oswald just two days later — Ruby
somehow had made his way right into the police
headquarter offices where Oswald was being interrogated. Ruby told the Warren Commission:

I am in the hallway there — there is a narrow hallway and I don't recall if Capt.
Fritz or Chief Curry brings the prisoner
out, and I am standing about 2 or 3 feet
away from him . . . I was standing about
3 feet away from Oswald.[25]

Ruby's first known appearance in the same room
with Oswald — on the very night of the assassination
— occurred at around 11:30 p.m.[26] It was then that
Ruby verbally corrected District Attorney Henry
Wade during a press conference. Wade stated that
Oswald had belonged to the "Free Cuba Committee,"
an anti-Castro Cuban exile group with strong CIA
connections.[27] Ruby corrected him by shouting that
Oswald actually belonged to the pro-Castro "Fair
Play for Cuba Committee." Ruby later told the
Warren Commission:

I corrected Henry, because listening to the
radio for KLIF, it stood out in my mind
that it was "Fair Play Cuba." There was a
difference.[28]

Of further note is the fact that during Ruby's testimony concerning his meeting with Olsen, he made a plea to the Warren Commission to take him to Washington where he would give them some additional "vital" information. The only two Commission members present at this time were Congressman Gerald R. Ford and Chairman Earl Warren, in addition to staff aides Leon Jaworski, Lee Rankin, Arlen Specter, Joseph Ball, and several Dallas police officers.[29] Ruby interrupted his description of his late-night meeting with Olsen to tell Warren and Ford: "Gentlemen, unless you get me to Washington, you can't get a fair shake out of me. If you understand my way of talking, you have got to bring me to Washington . . . "[30] During that same Commission session, Ruby asked Dallas County Sheriff J. E. Decker and the other Dallas police officers present to leave the room. He then told Earl Warren and Gerald Ford:

> Gentlemen, if you want to hear any further testimony, you will have to get me to Washington soon, because it has something to do with you, Chief Warren . . . I want to tell the truth and I can't tell it here. I can't tell it here. Does that make sense to you?[31]

Following that plea by Ruby, the official Warren Commission transcript records the following exchange:

Mr. Ruby: Can I make a statement?

Chief Justice Warren: Yes.

Mr. Ruby: If you request me to go back to Washington with you right now, that couldn't be done, could it?

Chief Justice Warren: No, it could not be done. It could not be done. There are a

419

good many things involved in that, Mr. Ruby.[32]

Ruby's pleas to go to Washington "and tell the truth," which came during his testimony about Officer Harry Olsen, offer substantial loose ends that were never pursued by the Warren Commission. And yet the story of Officer Olsen does not end there.

During Olsen's own Commission testimony he disclosed that he had been present several blocks from the scene of the Tippit shooting.[33] Olsen testified that he had been working as a guard during his off-duty hours at an estate near the scene of the Tippit murder. He'd been standing in for another policeman who couldn't be there that day. Yet Olsen couldn't remember who owned the estate, or who he was substituting for that day.[34] He also testified that he had quit the Dallas Police force about a month after the assassination, and had moved to Long Beach, California. Olsen stated that he had been asked to resign from the Department by Dallas Police Chief Jesse Curry, for "several" reasons.[35] However, the Warren Commission never asked Chief Curry for an explanation of why Officer Olsen was asked to resign.[36] Harry Olsen's present whereabouts are unknown.

Paul Bentley

Paul Bentley worked in the Identification Bureau of the Dallas P.D. at the time of the Kennedy assassination. Like Sergeant Gerald Hill, he'd arrived at the scene of Tippit's murder shortly after it occurred, and also rode in the car in which Hill and two other officers drove suspect Lee Oswald to police headquarters, following his arrest. **Officer Bentley** actually removed Oswald's wallet from his pocket during the ride in the police car:

> When I asked for his identification — of course he was handcuffed — he said, "If you want it, take it yourself." He leaned over and I took his wallet from his hip pocket. This was the end of his conversation. He did not say another word all the way to City Hall.[37]

Bentley states that he found identification cards in the alias of "Alek Hidell" in addition to Oswald's real ID cards. Bentley has claimed that he and the other officers in the car then radioed this information to police headquarters. Bentley has stated, "We radioed in that we had a prisoner an and gave the names. And I say names, this was taken from his wallet. He used several different names, as you know. But we gave the names. This was when they told us that he was a suspect in the assassination of the President. So we were instructed to bring him directly to Capt. Fritz . . . "[38] Yet the official FBI transcript of all the dispatcher and squad car transmissions from that afternoon shows no such radio transmission. The transcripts show that Sergeant Hill made no mention of any wallet or alias identification cards during his radio call to headquarters.[39] Also, despite the fact that the Dallas Police Department later prepared an official report setting forth the accounts of Hill and Bentley about finding the two sets of identification on Oswald, Bentley's first official memorandum to Chief Curry made no mention of alias identification being found in Oswald's wallet. In the memo, Bentley stated only that, "On the way to the City Hall I removed the suspect's wallet and obtained his name."[40] A thorough review of this incident reveals the whole matter to be highly complex and wrought with significant contradictory testimony. Much of the difficulty in presently resolving such questions stems from the refusal of various key members of the Dallas Police force to respond to questioning regarding these areas. Officer Paul Bentley left the Dallas force in the late 1960s and is now director of security for the First National Bank of Dallas.

Dallas Squad Car #106, 107, or 207

One of the most interesting pieces of information related to the possible activities of the Dallas Police Department in the aftermath of the Dallas assassination was provided by Mrs. Earlene Roberts, the housekeeper of the rooming house where Lee Oswald lived.[41] This episode — which has extremely serious implications — was only partially investigated by the Warren Commission and remains the subject of considerable speculation today. The Warren Report set forth the basic details of the episode:

> The possibility that accomplices aided Oswald in connection with his escape was suggested by the testimony of Earlene Roberts, the housekeeper at the 1026 North Beckley rooming house. She testified that at about 1:00 p.m. on November 22, after Oswald had returned to the rooming house, a Dallas police car drove slowly by the front of the 1026 North Beckley premises and stopped momentarily; she said she heard its horn several times. Mrs. Roberts stated that the occu-

pants of the car were not known to her . . . She testified that she first thought the car she saw was No. 106 and then said it was No. 107. In a FBI interview she had stated that she looked out the front window and saw Police Car No. 207. Investigation has not produced any evidence that there was a police vehicle in the area of 1026 North Beckley at about 1:00 p.m. on November 22, 1963. Squad car 207 was at the Texas School Book Depository Building as was car 106. Squad car 107 . . . (was) sold in April 1963 . . .[42]

Ironically enough, Robert Oswald has provided one of the more cogent rebuttals to the Commission's summary of Earlene Roberts' account:

> I find this summary completely inconclusive. Mrs. Roberts was treated as a responsible witness by the Commission, and her testimony alone placed Lee at the house at 1026 North Beckley at 1:00 p.m. on November 22, 1963. How could the Commission decide that she was right when she supplied that information, but wrong when she made her firm statement about the police car stopping and honking? Her uncertainty about the precise number does not seem surprising to me. She did say flatly that it was a police car, that it did honk several times, and that this happened while Lee was in the rooming house.[43]

He further said:

> I think this will remain forever one of the mysteries surrounding the assassination. Mrs. Roberts is now dead. The occupants of that police car — and I

personally believe they did stop in front of the house and honk just as Mrs. Roberts said — apparently decided four years ago to keep silent. They may have been on some relatively innocent mission. Perhaps they were policemen who were off their assigned beat and had stopped at the wrong house to greet a friend. Or they may have had some less innocent purpose in mind.[44]

Officer J. D. Tippit

Officer J. D. Tippit was the Dallas Patrolman shot to death roughly 45 minutes after the President's assassination, on a street a mile from Lee Harvey Oswald's boarding house. Minutes later, the Dallas Police arrested Oswald in a nearby theater — after he allegedly pulled a gun on the arresting officer — and accused him of the Tippit murder. Subsequently, Oswald was also charged with the assassination of President Kennedy.

The Warren Commission later stated that the Tippit murder provided strong corroborative evidence of Oswald's capacity to kill as well as his desperate attempt to escape after murdering John F. Kennedy.

However, serious questions have been raised regarding the entire Tippit episode: in particular, the rather clouded circumstances relating to Tippit's movements and actions following the assassination; the less-than-solid identification made of his killer (or killers) by various witnesses; and other potential aspects of conspiratorial involvement as well.

Almost from the beginning it was rumored both that Tippit was assigned to murder Oswald to effectuate the "closed case" of a "single assassin," and that Oswald shot his way out of this supposed "double cross" or "frame."

Several accounts of varying degrees of credibility soon surfaced regarding possible relationships between Tippit and Oswald or Tippit and Ruby. In December, 1963, the FBI interviewed a Dobbs House waitress, Mary Dowling, who stated that both Oswald and Tippit had visited the restaurant at the same time on the morning of November 20, 1963, two days prior to the assassination.[45] Although she said they were not seated together and didn't speak with each other, the FBI expressed no interest in following up her recollection of this alleged random Oswald-Tippit link.[46] Interestingly, it was not until seven months later on July 31, 1964, that the FBI sent a copy of the Mary Dowling interview to the Warren Commission.

The FBI also waited six months before interviewing another waitress at the same restaurant who also claimed that Oswald had frequented the premises during late 1963. Delores Harrison provided a detailed account of Oswald's visit to the restaurant a day or two before the assassination that closely corroborated the Dowling statement.[47] Strangely enough, the FBI never asked Mrs. Harrison if Officer Tippit had been in the restaurant during Oswald's last visit — as Mary Dowling had earlier recalled.[48]

Probing the associations and activities of Officer J. D. Tippit has proved quite difficult. The Warren Commission was virtually devoid of any investigative efforts aimed at dealing with the allegations surrounding Tippit's associations. Author Sylvia Meagher has noted:

> Tippit, the policeman and the man, is a one-dimensional and insubstantial figure — unknown and unknowable. The Commission was not interested in Tippit's life, and apparently interested in his death only to the extent that it could be ascribed to Oswald...
>
> The Commission's profound lack of interest in Tippit may be measured by its failure to take testimony from his widow, who probably saw him two hours before his death... or from any of his friends or neighbors.[49]

In his June 7, 1964 Commission testimony (during an abbreviated Commission attendance, featuring members Warren and Ford, as well as counsels Specter, Jaworski, Rankin, and Ball) Jack Ruby was asked "Did you know Officer Tippit?"[50] Ruby replied that he did in fact know an "Officer Tippit," but that he believed this was a different "Officer Tippit" than the one who had been murdered.[51] Ruby stated that "there was three Tippits on the force," of whom he'd known only one.[52] There were no further questions pertaining to the various Tippits, or to whether Ruby was sure about which one he'd known.[53]

General Counsel Rankin then questioned Ruby about "a story that you were seen sitting in your Carousel Club with Mr. Weissman [a right-wing Dallas political figure], Officer Tippit, and another who has been called a rich oil man, at one time shortly before the assassination."[54] After digressing from the question at hand for a moment, Ruby answered that the story was untrue, and that, "I am as innocent regarding any conspiracy as any of you gentlemen in the room..."[55]

Over five weeks later, on July 18, 1964, Ruby was questioned a second and last time by the Commission. The only member present, in addition to Dallas authorities was counsel Arlen Specter whose interrogation of Ruby on this point could only be regarded as inconclusive:

> *Mr. Herndon:* Did you know Officer Tippit?
> *Mr. Ruby:* This is off the record for a minute, please?
> *Mr. Specter:* Mr. Ruby, I think it would be unwise for us to go off the record on this question.
> *Mr. Ruby:* Well, all right. There were three Officer Tippits in the Police Department. I only knew one.
> *Mr. Specter:* Was that Officer J. D. Tippit?
> *Mr. Ruby:* He's the one who was slain?
> *Mr. Specter:* Yes — Officer J. D. Tippit.
> *Mr. Ruby:* No; I don't think he was the one.
> *Mr. Specter:* Did you know Officer Tippit who was slain?
> *Mr. Ruby:* No; I don't know him. You see, I know so many officers and there are three Tippits, but I know one Tippit, and which one that is — if I would see him personally and see his physical features and knowing him — of course, I wouldn't have time to — I was incarcerated too soon to find out...[56]

Though DA William Alexander interjected that he believed the Officer Tippit whom Ruby knew was not J. D. Tippit, Specter pursued the matter no further and never inquired as to the details of exactly which Tippit Ruby knew.[57]

In an effort to determine why J. D. Tippit was patroling an area four miles from the Texas School Book Depository, the Warren Commission ordered the Dallas Police Department to prepare a transcript of the police radio log. The Commission concluded that Tippit had received radio instructions at 12:45 p.m., 15 minutes after the assassination, to move into the Oak Cliff area where he was soon shot. However, the way in which the police gave the Commission information about these purported instructions to Tippit raises disturbing possibilities.

The transcript of radio dispatches relating to the Kennedy and Tippit shootings contained no reference to any order to Tippit to proceed into the suburb of Central Oak Cliff,[58] while every other available patrol car in the Dallas vicinity had received immediate instructions to go to Dealey Plaza.

In April, 1964, the Commission asked the Dallas police for a more detailed radio dispatch record — a verbatim transcript — in an effort to resolve the matter.[59] The new transcript, finally contained radio instructions to Tippit to move into the Oak Cliff area, as well as simultaneous orders to a second patrolman, Officer Nelson, to proceed into the same section.[60] Thus, it now appeared that Tippit was not the only patrolman assigned to go somewhere other than the Book Depository.

However, the alleged orders to Officer Nelson were soon questioned, also. A police report, later entered as Warren Commission Exhibit 2645, discloses that Officer Nelson, like every other patrolman, had actually been dispatched to the Texas Book Depository, and further, that Nelson had remained on guard at the Depository entrance for the rest of the afternoon.[61] The police contention that Tippit was not the only officer ordered to Oak Cliff was seemingly shattered. Meanwhile, Dallas Police Chief Curry had informed the Commission that the purported orders to Tippit had been missing from the first radio transcript due to technical difficulties.[62]

Sylvia Meagher, a specialist on matters pertaining to the Tippit murder and related aspects of the case, has pointed out:

> If the Instruction to Tippit — and Nelson — is authentic, we must ask why the dispatcher singled out those two officers for special and quite curious treatment. They

> were the only officers contacted by the dispatcher with instructions unrelated to the assassination and lacking any other apparent purpose. During the half hour after the President was shot there was no breach of law and order in Central Oak Cliff, and no strategic reasons for sending reinforcements there. The assassination took place at a point some four or more miles from Central Oak Cliff. As it turned out, a Book Depository employee who was missing and under suspicion was en route to his furnished room in Oak Cliff at 12:45 p.m. but there was no [known] way for the dispatcher to know that. Oswald's absence had not yet been noticed at 12:45; his Oak Cliff address was not known to his wife or employer, much less to the Dallas police.[63]
>
> The dispatcher had sent out a general order for all downtown squads to proceed to the Book Depository. Aside from Tippit and Nelson, the dispatcher did not contact any specific squad cars, nor did he give any general order to men in the outlying district to move elsewhere. We are asked to believe that, in the midst of this consternation, the dispatcher took the time to call Tippit and Nelson and give them instructions which make no sense.[64]

Officer J. D. Tippit was last heard from at 12:54 p.m., nine minutes after he had supposedly received the 12:45 instructions to proceed to Oak Cliff.[65] At 12:54, the radio dispatch recorded that Tippit notified the dispatcher that he was in Oak Cliff at the intersection of Eighth and Lancaster Street.[66]

The dispatch record shows that six minutes later, at 1:00 p.m., Tippit was signaled by the radio dispatcher — but did not reply. The Dallas Police, FBI, and Warren Commission concluded that Tippit was shot to death at about 1:15 p.m. If Officer Tippit had not yet been murdered at 1 p.m., the questions immediately at hand were: Where was he? Why had he not responded to the radio signal of 1 p.m.? And what had Tippit been doing in the immediate minutes before his murder?

In 1976, the National Archives disclosed that "tape recordings of Dallas Police Department radio broadcasts" were among the items from the Warren Commission's records missing from the Archives Building in Washington.[67]

Strangely enough, Tippit's last reported position, the intersection of Eighth and Lancaster, happens to have been either at or right near the estate where Jack Ruby's close friend, Officer Harry Olsen, was spending his off-duty hours substituting for another private guard. Olsen, the boyfriend of one of Ruby's strippers who met him early in the morning the next day,[68] told the Commission that he'd been guarding an estate on Eighth Street in Oak Cliff, about two blocks from the Freeway[69] when he learned of the assassination, and had discussed it with a couple of passersby.[70] Eighth and Lancaster, adjacent to the Freeway, is almost the exact location from which Tippit was last heard from alive.[71]

David W. Belin, the former Warren Commission counsel and staff director for the Rockefeller Commission appointed by President Ford, has stated that the Tippit murder is the "Rosetta Stone" which ties a desperate escaping Oswald to the Kennedy assassination. However, critics of the Warren Commission point instead to such things as the extraordinarily confusing physical evidence relating to the bullets recovered from the officer's body; the cartridge shells found at the murder scene; and the bullets found in the alleged Oswald pistol after his arrest, as well as those allegedly found in his pocket.

The Warren Commission, while seeking to downplay the apparent inconsistency between the bullets recovered from Tippit's body and the bullet shells recovered at the scene, sets forth the following confusing information:

> When Oswald was arrested six live cartridges were found in the revolver. Three were Western .38 Specials, loaded with copper-coated lead bullets, and three were Remington-Peters .38 Specials, loaded with lead bullets. Five additional live cartridges were found in Oswald's pocket, all of which were Western .38 Specials, loaded with copper coated bullets.
> Four expended cartridge cases were found near the site of the Tippit killing. Two of these cartridges were Remington-Peters .38 Specials and two were Western .38 Specials.[72]

Finally, the Warren Commission came to the central inconsistency in this physical evidence:

> Based on the number of groove, groove widths, groove spacing, and knurling on the four recovered bullets, three were copper-coated lead bullets of Western-Winchester manufacture [Western and Winchester are divisions of the same company], and the fourth was a lead bullet of Remington-Peters manufacture. This contrasts with the four recovered cartridge cases, which consisted of two Remington-Peters and two Westerns.[73]

Thus, the problem is clear: the shells found at the scene of the Tippit shooting (two Remington-Peters and two Westerns), did not fit the bullets found in Tippit's body (one Remington-Peters and three Westerns).

The Warren Commission proposed an extraordinarily difficult three-pronged theory as to how this clear variance in the physical evidence might be explained away:

> There are several possible explanations for this variance (1) the killer fired 5 cartridges, 3 of which were Western-Winchesters and 2 of which were Remington-Peters; 1 Remington-Peters bullet missed Tippit [at point-blank range]; and a Western-Winchester cartridge case and the Remington-Peters bullet that missed were simply not found. (2) The killer fired only 4 cartridges, 3 of which were Western-Winchesters and 1 of which was Remington-Peters; prior to the shooting the killer had an expended Remington-Peters case in his revolver which was ejected with the 3 Western-Winchesters and 1 Remington-Peters cases; and 1 of the Western-Winchesters cases was not found. (3) The killer was using hand-loaded ammunition, that is, ammunition which is made with used cartridge cases, to save money, thus he might have loaded one make of bullet into another make of cartridge case. This third possibility is extremely unlikely, because when a cartridge is fired the cartridge case expands, and before it can be reused it must be resized. There was, however, no evidence that any of the 4 recovered cartridge cases had been resized.[74]

The Warren Commission, during the first three months of its probe, had only received one of these four recovered bullets from the Dallas Police Department. According to the FBI, the police had given the Bureau only one of the bullets on November 23rd, the day after the assassination. The Dallas Police had informed FBI ballistics expert Cortlandt Cunningham that only one of the four bullets had been recovered.[76] Finally, in March of 1964, the Warren Commission requested the FBI to locate the other three bullets or bullet fragments, and soon found that the Dallas Police Department did in fact have the other recovered bullets in a file at Department headquarters.

In 1976, the National Archives disclosed that "photographs showing [the] area of [the] shooting of Officer J. D. Tippit" are among the items which are missing from the Warren Commission records in the Archives Building in Washington.[77]

The testimony of Acquilla Clemmons, a witness who stated that she saw two men running from the scene of the Tippit shooting, neither of whom she claimed was Oswald, will be set forth in the chapter on "Neglected or Spurned Witnesses."

While some researchers have pointed out that at the time of his death, Tippit was working weekends at a barbecue diner owned by an active member of the Dallas John Birch Society, little is known of Tippit's political beliefs.[78]

In the days and weeks after his murder, J. D. Tippit became a hero of sorts to many people, and the recipient of various posthumous awards. In the immediate months following the assassination, his widow received a large number of cash gifts from the public at large, reportedly as much as $100,000. Yet to this day, the man remains an enigma.

Jesse Curry

Jesse Curry, the Chief of the Dallas Police, was

in overall charge of the investigation conducted by the local police. Police Chief Curry has been criticized for a number of actions related to the police investigation, but Commission critics have focused more attention and criticism on Captain Will Fritz, the head of the Dallas Police Homicide Bureau. Captain Fritz, the officer directly in charge of handling the specifics of the investigation, was responsible for assembling the bulk of the evidence obtained by the Department.

Police Chief Curry was privately reported to have had doubts about the conclusions of the Warren Commission and the roles of at least a couple of his own officers. However, Curry voiced no such doubts or criticism for over six years. Finally, in early 1970, the *New York Times* reported that Curry would soon publish a book which would reveal his strong doubts about key areas of evidence. Curry's *JFK Assassination File*, a privately printed work published in Dallas for a generally limited circulation, detailed his comprehensive doubt about many facts of the investigation, and also disclosed new information taken from his personal files. Curry embraced several of the key areas of information long cited by Commission critics as evidence of a possible conspiracy. Curry wrote:

> The physical evidence and eyewitness accounts do not clearly indicate what took place on the sixth floor of the Texas School Book Depository at the time John F. Kennedy was assassinated. Speculative magazine and newspaper reports led the public to believe that numerous eyewitnesses positively identified Lee Harvey Oswald as the

sniper in the sixth floor window. The testimony of the people who watched the motorcade was much more confusing than either the press or the Warren Commission seemed to indicate.[79]

Stating that the true circumstances surrounding the Kennedy assassination may not have been told, Curry spoke of strong contradictions in the affidavits and testimony of key eyewitnesses, including testimony of an eyewitness and his wife who told the FBI during an official interview that they had seen two men with a rifle in the same window from which Oswald had allegedly fired alone. Curry noted however that, "No statement about the 'second man or mention of an accomplice appeared in the FBI report.' "[80] He also voiced criticism and doubt about the manner in which the FBI and Warren Commission had handled the investigation of physical evidence relating to the autopsy:

> Dr. Malcolm Perry at Parkland Hospital had maintained that the President had been shot from the front. Investigators were awaiting the results of the autopsy with the naive assurance that the government would release a detailed autopsy report which could be used in the investigation. The photographs and autopsy evidence were never released by the government. Apparently portions of the material have even been destroyed. The Warren Commission yielded to political pressure and never examined the autopsy photographs.[81]

The way J. Edgar Hoover's FBI handled the investigation, including their desire to "seize evidence" later during the day of the assassination came under fire from Curry:

The evidence gathered during the assassination weekend was dispersed in many directions. The FBI had already begun to seize evidence at the scene. Secret Service Agents had seized the President's body before the required autopsy could be performed. Although most of the evidence was gathered by the Dallas Police Department, it did not remain in our hands very long. Early Friday evening [November 22, 1963] FBI Agents were anxious to have all physical evidence released to them.[82]

Curry voiced particular criticism over what he felt was a disruptive influence by FBI Agents and other Federal representatives during the interrogation of prisoner Oswald. According to Curry:

> Although Captain Fritz in the Dallas Homicide Bureau should have been solely in charge of the interrogation of Oswald, an orderly and private interrogation proved impossible. Because of the constant pressure from other investigative agencies, Captain Fritz was never allowed to carry out an orderly private interview with Lee Harvey Oswald.
> I have also wondered whether or not Captain Fritz could have obtained crucial information from Oswald if he had been allowed to spend two to three hours alone with him under normal interrogative conditions.[83]

Curry was upset with some of the men in his own department for their failure to prevent Jack Ruby from gaining access to the police basement where he murdered Lee Harvey Oswald on November 24, 1963. Curry stated that he had planned on being personally present during the transfer of Oswald through the basement, but had ultimately missed being there:

> As Capt. Fritz was leaving his office I mentioned that I would go on down to the basement to watch the transfer. As I was walking down the corridor, I was called to take a phone call from Dallas Mayor Cabell in my office. He was interested in the progess of the investigation. Since other officers were in charge of moving Oswald and everything was in order, I stayed in my office to give the report to Mayor Cabell . . . I was sitting in my office talking to Dallas Mayor Cabell on the phone when an officer burst in with the news.[84]

In an interview in May, 1973, Curry stated that there had been some evidence that another gunman had fired a shot (perhaps the fatal shot to Kennedy's head) from the grassy knoll area in front of the Presidential limousine. Curry stated, "I don't have a strong feeling that there was someone there, but, on the other hand, it wouldn't surprise me at some time, at some point in history, that more proof will show that there was somebody up there."[85]

In 1976, the National Archives disclosed that two sets of a report pertaining to the "operation security involving [the] transfer of Lee Harvey Oswald" were among the items missing from the Warren Commission records in the Archives. The report was contained in a larger file prepared by the Texas Attorney General's office in 1963 and early 1964, with the assistance of Leon Jaworski, then a Special Assistant to the Attorney General in that state.[85a]

William Alexander

William Alexander, Assistant District Attorney of Dallas, was of course involved in key aspects of the investigation, and later headed the legal team that conducted the only prosecution that ever grew out of the case: the successful prosecution of Jack Ruby. Alexander was also closely involved in the investigation into the shooting of Officer J. D. Tippit, and had arrived on the scene soon after the policeman was

shot. While it may be reasoned that Alexander already suspected some connection between the Tippit shooting and the Kennedy assassination, his on-the-scene involvement in the Tippit murder probe was unusual. In fact, it was beyond the scope of activities allowed by the DA's office.

District Attorney Henry Wade himself later told the Warren Commission: ". . . it has never been my policy to make any investigations out of my office of murders or anything else for that matter. We leave that entirely to the police agency . . . The only time we investigate is after they are filed on, indicated . . . [86]

Alexander was apparently one of the key sources of the mysterious allegations that Lee Harvey Oswald had been on the payroll of the FBI. These rumors of an Oswald-FBI connection were a major subject of discussion during the Commission's earliest sessions, particularly that of January 27, 1964.[87] During these early discussions, it became evident that a reporter for *The Houston Post*, Alonzo Hudkins, was a primary source of the rumors about Oswald. At a January

24th meeting between Chairman Earl Warren, General Counsel Lee Rankin, District Attorney Wade, Assistant District Attorney William Alexander, Texas Attorney General Waggoner Carr, and Carr's Special Assistant, Leon Jaworski, the Texans reported that Hudkins may indeed have been the prime source for the Oswald-FBI allegations. Sometime during the same period, Rankin wrote an undated memorandum for the files which he titled "Rumors that Oswald was an undercover agent."[88] The Rankin memo, released by the National Archives several years ago, shed further light on the source of the rumors. Rankin stated that he had learned from a Secret Service interview on January 23rd that reporter Alonzo Hudkins had told the Secret Service that he had received the information from Allan Sweatt, a Dallas Deputy Sheriff.[89] Rankin further noted he'd learned on the previous Friday that Deputy Sheriff Allan Sweatt had informed the Secret Service that William Alexander, the Assistant DA, was the person who'd told him of the alleged Oswald-FBI connections. Thus, the Warren Commission's efforts to trace the source of these allegations had finally come full circle, ending up with William Alexander as the primary source. As George O'Toole has written:

> All this is very strange. The Commission first heard of the FBI-Oswald rumor from Texas Attorney General Waggoner Carr, and he, in turn, said he heard it from Dallas District Attorney Henry Wade. Then Carr and Wade met with Justice Warren and they brought along Wade's assistant, William Alexander. Alexander turned out to be the real authority on the matter and he attributed the story to the press in general and Alonzo Hudkins in particular. But Hudkins got the story from Deputy Sheriff Sweatt, and Sweatt said he got the story from Bill Alexander. All roads lead to the assistant district attorney.[90]

The transcript of the Warren Commission session of January 22, 1964, reveals the members were puzzled by their efforts to determine what the Texas state authorities knew about Oswald's contacts with the FBI. In discussing the Oswald-FBI allegations, the Commission members had the following exchange:

> *Rep. Boggs:* What role did this man Alexander play in this?
>
> *Mr. Rankin:* Well, it appeared to have started earlier than — he was active, but it is possible, I don't know —
>
> *Justice Warren:* I think he is the fellow who blew the whistle so far as this Commission is concerned. I think that is where Carr got his information, don't you think?
>
> *Rep. Boggs:* From Alexander?
>
> *Justice Warren:* From Alexander, yes.[91]

Little else is know about Assistant District Attorney William Alexander's role in this area, the accuracy of his information, or where or how it was obtained.

Roger D. Craig

Deputy Sheriff Roger Craig was involved in two significant aspects of the on-the-scene investigation. Craig, who had once been honored as Dallas's "Deputy Sheriff of the Year," has provided two important pieces of information which cast doubt on key

findings of the Warren Report.

Craig was one of the policemen who searched the Texas School Book Depository immediately after the assassination, and along with another deputy first discovered the alleged assassination rifle in the corner of a room on the sixth floor. And along with the other deputy, Roger Craig has stated that this gun was not the 6.5 caliber Mannlicher-Carcano that the Warren Commission and FBI say it was, but a 7.65 mm German Mauser. In a letter to assassination researcher Edward Tatro in March, 1975 (cited in Robert Sam Anson's book, *They've Killed the President!*) Craig wrote: "Deputy Eugene Boone and I found the rifle, which I might add was a 7.65 Mauser, so stamped on the barrel."[92]

Another Deputy Sheriff who also first discovered the rifle, Seymour Weitzman, agreed with Craig that the gun was a 7.65-mm German Mauser, and signed an affidavit later that day identifying it as such.[93] Thus, serious questions arose the very afternoon of the assassination as to what type of rifle was found on the sixth floor of the Depository. As Commission critics have long pointed out, this point raises strong possibilities as to whether there was a second gun and thus, a second gunman, involved — both of which apparently disappeared — or whether the Italian Mannlicher-Carcano allegedly owned and used by Oswald was later planted to replace the German Mauser that the two deputies swore they found.

Roger Craig has raised a further question about the rifle and rifle shells found in the Book Depository. Immediately after the assassination, the official police photographer took pictures of the three rifle shells found on the floor of the room which was supposedly

Oswald's sniper's nest. According to the police, the rifle casings were photographed just the way they were found — and hadn't been moved or touched in any way — scattered on the floor beneath the sixth floor corner window. Yet, Craig, who reaffirmed his recollection in April of 1975, claims, "they [the rifle shells] were in uniform [position] lying on the floor no more than two inches apart all facing the same direction when I found them."[94] Thus, if Deputy Craig's account is accurate, someone must have moved or touched or possibly switched the shells before the police photographs were taken and after Deputies Craig and Weitzman first saw them.

Craig also testified before the Warren Commission that just minutes after the assassination, he saw a man, whom he was sure was Oswald, running from the area of the Book Depository toward the Freeway Triple Underpass, a half block away from the Depository,[95] and jump into the passenger side of a light colored Rambler station wagon which sped away from the scene.[96] The Commission later concluded that he had probably misidentified this man as Lee Oswald: "Although Craig may have seen someone enter a station wagon 15 minutes after the assassination, the person he saw was not Lee Harvey Oswald, who was far removed from the [Book Depository] building at that time."[97]

Roger Craig was subsequently fired from the Dallas Police force for unspecified reasons. Beginning in 1967, he claimed he was threatened and harassed by unknown individuals. In October, 1970, Craig was seriously injured when his automobile engine mysteriously exploded. According to his family, he was then threatened in other ways. On May 15, 1975, Craig shot himself to death, leaving a suicide note to his father which stated "I am tired of this pain."[98]

In 1976, the National Archives disclosed that a "letter from Capt. Fritz to the [Warren] Commission, June 9, 1964, on spent shells found in the Texas

School Book Depository," was among the items missing from the Archives collection of Commission records.[98a]

Seymour Weitzman

Deputy Sheriff Seymour Weitzman, the other officer who identified the alleged weapon as a German Mauser, signed an affidavit on November 22 stating that the rifle he found was indeed a Mauser.[99] Weitzman

should have been an accurate judge of rifles, as he'd managed a sporting goods store and was known as something of a firearms expert.[100] However, when the Warren Commission began its official investigation, Weitzman changed his story, saying he'd misidentified it as a Mauser. In a 1967 CBS interview Weitzman said, "I looked at it, and it looked like a Mauser which I said it was. But I said the wrong one because just at a glance I saw the Mauser action, and — I don't know — it just came out words, it's a German Mauser which it wasn't."[101] Weitzman stated that he had made an "honest mistake" in wrongly identifying the rifle, and that he had only taken "a glance" at the weapon.[102]

The controversy over what kind of rifle was really found at the Book Depository has never subsided. A recently declassified CIA document, written three days after the assassination, identifies the Kennedy murder weapon as a Mauser. The CIA analysts wrote: "The rifle he [Oswald] used was a Mauser which OSWALD had ordered (this is now known by handwriting examination) from Klein's Mail Order House, Chicago, Illinois. He had the rifle sent to a Post Office Box which Lee OSWALD had rented. In the order for the rifle, OSWALD used the name Alex HIDELL. "OSWALD also had in his possession at the time of his arrest (after he also killed a Texas policeman) a U. S. Selective Service Card in the name of Alex HIDELL."[103] The CIA has refused to comment on this memorandum.

Deputy Sheriff C. L. Lewis

Deputy Sheriff C. L. Lewis was one of the first Dallas police officers to arrive at the Texas School Book Depository. He quickly arrested an out-of-town man whom he believed was "behaving suspiciously" across from the Book Depository, just minutes after the fatal shots were fired.[104]

The man arrested by Lewis, Jim Braden, was briefly questioned and then released — without being fingerprinted or a check made of his past records. It was not until the late 1960s that former CBS producer Peter Noyes began an investigation of Jim Braden and soon determined that he actually had another identity. Braden had legally changed his name from Eugene Hale Brading in the weeks just prior to the assassination. Thus, his real identity was never known to the Commission.

Peter Noyes' intensive probe into Brading's background quickly revealed that he was long-associated with powerful Mafia figures in virtually every national crime syndicate jurisdiction, including several professional killers who worked for the syndicate. Noyes compiled an extensive amount of national and state law enforcement records on Brading and found that federal authorities had identified him, as of the early 1970s, as a key courier of Meyer Lansky.

Noyes also established, through such sources as Brading's parole records and documentation on his travels and business activities in 1963, that he was a man with several possible connections to both Jack Ruby and David Ferrie.

Following his arrest by Deputy Sheriff C. L. Lewis, Jim Braden [Brading] signed a brief statement at police headquarters recounting the circumstances of his arrest:

> I am here on [oil] business and was walking down Elm Street trying to get a cab and there wasn't any. I heard people talking, and saying "My God, the President has been shot." Police cars were passing me, coming down the triple underpass and I walked up among other people and this building was surrounded by police officers with guns and we were all watching them.
>
> I moved on up to the building across the street from the building which was surrounded and I asked one of the girls if there was a telephone I could use . . .[105]

According to his brief statement, after he unsuccessfully tried to make a phone call, a "colored man" ran up to him and said, "You are a stranger in this building and I was not supposed to let you [in] ..."[106] The black elevator operator then ran out and brought Deputy Sheriff Lewis in, who then arrested Braden, whose only identification was a credit card.[107]

Two FBI agents re-interviewed Jim Braden on January 29, 1964, but never discovered his actual identity as Eugene Brading, a known Mafia figure. The official FBI report concluded: "Braden has no information concerning the assassination and both Lee Harvey Oswald and Jack Ruby are unknown to him."

In 1976, the National Archives disclosed that two records of the Warren Commission, pertaining to the arrest of Jim Braden, are missing. These include "Records of the Dallas Police and County Sheriff's Office concerning arrests on November 22, 1963," as well as a "photograph . . . showing a man being arrested or under arrest near the Dal Tex Building," in Dealey Plaza, on November 22, 1963.[108] Other photographs of the Braden arrest do however still exist.

1. Warren Commission Report, p. 224.
2. Meagher, *Accessories After The Fact*, p. 422.
3. Warren Commission Exhibit 1467.
4. Meagher, *Accessories After The Fact*, p. 422.
5. Warren Commission Volume 4, p. 420.
6. Butler, Warren Commission Report, p. 793; Arnett, Warren Commission Exhibits 1467 and 1615; Swain, Warren Commission Exhibit 2002, p. 171; Kaminski, Warren Commission Exhibits 1549 and 1592; Gilmore, Warren Commission Exhibits 1592 and 2329, Warren Commission Volume 12, pp. 76-78; Eberhardt, Exhibit 5026; Warren Commission Volume 13, pp. 181-187; Standifer, Warren Commission Volume 15, p. 617; McGee, Gee, Warren Commission Exhibit 2002; Cutchshaw, Lowery and Harrison, Meagher, *Accessories After The Fact*, p. 425; Blankenship, Warren Commission Exhibits 1611 and 1628; Carlson, Warren Commission Exhibits 1612 and 2080; Neal, Warren Commission Exhibit 1542; Walton, Ibid.
7. Warren Commission Volume 4, p. 238.

8. Ibid.
9. Ibid.
9a. "National Archives — Security Classification Problems Involving Warren Commission Files and Other Records," Hearings before the House Subcommittee on Government Information, 1976.
10. Warren Commission Volume 5, pp. 34, 37.
11. Ibid.
12. *New York Times*, September 2, 1975.
12a. "National Archives — Security Classification Problems Involving Warren Commission Files and Other Records," Hearings before the House Subcommittee on Government Information, 1976.
13. Warren Commission Volume 7, p. 64.
14. Ibid.
15. Ibid.
16. Warren Commission Volume 7, pp. 45-49; *CBS News Inquiry*, "The Warren Report," Part One, June 25, 1967.
17. Warren Commission Volume 24, p. 239.
18. George O'Toole, *The Assassination Tapes* (New York: Penthouse Press Ltd., 1975), p. 157.
19. Ibid.
20. Warren Commission Volume 24, pp. 804-805; O'Toole, *The Assassination Tapes*, p. 158.
21. O'Toole, *The Assassination Tapes*, p. 148.
22. Warren Commission Volume 14, p. 631.
23. Warren Commission Volume 5, p. 191.
24. Ibid.
25. Ibid., p. 189.
26. Ibid.
27. E. Howard Hunt, *Undercover* (New York: Berkley Publishing Corporation, 1974), p. 141; Weisberg, *Oswald In New Orleans*, pp. 344-348.
28. Warren Commission Volume 5, p. 189.
29. Ibid., p. 181.
30. Ibid., p. 191.
31. Ibid., pp. 191-194.
32. Ibid., p. 195.
33. Meagher, *Accessories After The Fact*, pp. 263-264.
34. Ibid.
35. Warren Commission Volume 14, p. 637.
36. Warren Commission Volume 4, pp. 150-152; Warren Commission Volume 12, pp. 25-42; Warren Commission Volume 15, pp. 124-133.
37. O'Toole, *The Assassination Tapes*, p. 160.
38. Ibid.
39. Warren Commission Volume 23, pp. 875-877.
40. Warren Commission Volume 24, p. 234; Warren Commission Volume 23, pp. 875-877.

41. Warren Commission Volume 6, p. 433-434.
42. Warren Commission Report, pp. 253-254.
43. Oswald, *Lee*, pp. 223-224.
44. Ibid.
45. Warren Commission Exhibit 3001.
46. Ibid.
47. Ibid.
48. Ibid.
49. Meagher, *Accessories After The Fact*, pp. 253-254; Warren Commission Exhibit 2985.
50. Warren Commission Volume 5, p. 203.
51. Ibid.
52. Ibid.
53. Ibid.
54. Ibid.
55. Ibid.
56. Warren Commision Volume 14, p. 559.
57. Ibid.
58. Sawyer Exhibits, Nos. A and B, Warren Commission Records Section.
59. Warren Commission Exhibit 705.
60. Ibid.
61. Warren Commission Exhibit 2645.
62. Warren Commission Volume 4, pp. 185-186.
63. Meagher, *Accessories After The Fact*, p. 262.
64. Ibid.
65. Warren Commission Exhibit 2645.
66. Ibid.
67. "National Archives — Security Classification Problems Involving Warren Commission Files and Other Records," Hearings before the House Subcommittee on Government Information, 1976.
68. Warren Commission Volume 5, pp. 189-191.
69. Warren Commission Volume 14, p. 629.
70. Ibid.
71. Dallas City Directory, Oak Cliff; Warren Commission Exhibit 2645.
72. Warren Commission Report, p. 559.
73. Ibid.
74. Ibid., p. 560.
75. Warren Commission Volume 3, pp. 473-474.
76. Ibid.
77. "National Archives — Security Classification Problems Involving Warren Commission Files and Other Records," Hearings before the House Subcommittee on Government Information, 1976.
78. Meagher, *Accessories After The Fact*, pp. 253-254.
79. Jesse Curry, *JFK Assassination File* (Dallas: American Poster and Printing Company, Inc., 1969), p. 61.
80. Ibid., pp. 61-62.

81. Ibid., p. 122.
82. Ibid., p. 81.
83. Ibid., pp. 72-73.
84. Ibid., pp. 127, 133.
85. O'Toole, *The Assassination Tapes*, p. 7.
85a. "National Archives — Security Classification Problems Involving Warren Commission Files and Other Records," Hearings before the House Subcommittee on Government Information, 1976.
86. Warren Commission Volume 5, p. 215.
87. Weisberg, *Whitewash IV*, pp. 36-121.
88. J. Lee Rankin memorandum, "Rumors that Oswald was an undercover agent," undated, National Archives.
89. Ibid.
90. O'Toole, *The Assassination Tapes*, p. 216.
91. Warren Commission Session Transcript, January 27, 1964; Weisberg, *Whitewash IV*, p. 90.
92. Anson, *"They've Killed the President!,"* p. 77.
93. Warren Commission Exhibit 2003, p. 63.
94. Anson, *"They've Killed the President!,"* p. 77.
95. Warren Commission Volume 4, p. 245.
96. Ibid.
97. Warren Commission Report, p. 235.
98. Dallas Police Department, Homicide Bureau Report, May 15, 1975.
98a. "National Archives — Security Classification Problems Involving Warren Commission Files and Other Records," Hearings before the House Subcommittee on Government Information, 1976.
99. Warren Commission Exhibit 2003, p. 63.
100. Warren Commission Volume 7, p. 108.
101. *CBS News Inquiry*, "The Warren Report," Part One, June 25, 1967.
102. Ibid.
103. CIA memorandum, November 25, 1963, title unknown, document #1367, declassified in spring of 1976.
104. Warren Commission Documents 385 and 401.
105. Warren Commission Document 816.
106. Ibid.
107. Ibid.
108. "National Archives — Security Classification Problems Involving Warren Commission Files and Other Records," Hearings before the House Subcommittee on Government Information, 1976.

CHAPTER TEN

The New Orleans Probe

In early 1967, as increasingly serious doubts were being raised about the Warren Commission's conclusions (particularly its ballistics and forensic findings about the shots that struck President Kennedy and Governor Connally), the Kennedy case reached a new peak.

While events seemed to be moving in the direction of a new inquiry — spurred to a great extent by the investigative efforts of *Life* magazine, the *Saturday Evening Post*, CBS, and other news organizations — this movement was suddenly superseded by a wholly unexpected investigation of the assassination by someone else: New Orleans District Attorney Jim Garrison.

The Garrison investigation came upon the national scene like a sonic boom, instantly becoming the subject of more intensive press interest than any other event that year. While the controversial District Attorney had initially received favorable reviews in probing what he claimed was "a powerful assassination conspiracy," later events began to run against Garrison to a degree he had never foreseen. The Garrison probe — noted for its carelessness and sensationalism, as well as its bizarre cast of characters or "suspects" — finally ended in shambles.

Years later, many assassination investigators were still trying to sort out the various areas of information left behind by the New Orleans probe — some good, some useful, a good many bad. As will also be seen, new information continues to surface about the Garrison investigation even today.

Clay L. Shaw

Clay Shaw, a millionaire New Orleans businessman, was one of the men named by Garrison as a conspirator behind the JFK assassination. Shaw was officially indicted by Garrison in early 1967 for "participation in the conspiracy to murder John F. Kennedy." With the death of Garrison's other top suspect, David Ferrie, Clay Shaw became the only person Garrison prosecuted as an actual alleged conspirator. In early 1969, just two years after his arrest, Shaw was acquitted following a lengthy trial. Shaw, who'd previously served as Director of the New Orleans Trade Mart and had long been prominent in New Orleans society, exclaimed "You've got to be kidding," when Garrison arrested him at his home in New Orleans.

During his trial, Garrison attempted to prove that Shaw had worked with David Ferrie, plus a number of Cuban exiles and other CIA-connected conspirators in planning the assassination. Garrison's prosecution became the subject of intense and comprehensive criticism by several legal groups, the press, and a number of Commission critics. For his part, Garrison complained of heavy Federal interference in the prosecution of his case; the unwillingness of five states to extradite witnesses; the refusal of the Justice Department, FBI, and National Archives to respond to some of his subpoenas relating to actual physical evidence from the assassination; and such incidents as the mysterious theft of a copy of his trial brief — and the alleged delivery of it to Shaw's attorneys — shortly before the trial began.

While Garrison, in 1969, was unable to produce solid evidence of the alleged CIA connections of his suspects, such information became available years later. Former CIA executive Victor Marchetti disclosed in 1975 that Richard Helms had privately admitted that some of Jim Garrison's suspects had indeed once been connected to the Agency.[1] While Marchetti's information does not lend any direct support to Garrison's allegations about the assassination itself, it does establish that he was at least accurate in ascribing a CIA affiliation to these men. Marchetti disclosed that Helms had often spoken privately of Shaw's CIA connections during the course of his trial in January and February of 1969.[2]

According to Marchetti's information, Helms repeatedly instructed his top aides to "do all we can to help Shaw" during his trial.[3] Marchetti further stated that he remembers that CIA General Counsel Lawrence Houston told Helms that the Agency was "on top of the Shaw situation."[4] Depending upon how Helms and the CIA may have helped Shaw during his trial, an obstruction of justice may have occurred. Although the CIA has refused to comment on Victor Marchetti's recollections, recently released documents offer substantiation of key parts of his information. In the spring of 1976, a newly declassified CIA document revealed Clay Shaw's connection to the CIA. This CIA "Memo for Deputy Director for Support," dated May 1, 1967, disclosed: "The CI [Counterintelligence] staff, in a detailed staff study of the Garrison investigations, has noted past CIA contact with only two figures named in the inquiry, Clay L. Shaw and Carlos Bringuier, in both cases the contact was limited to domestic contact service activities."[5] Further details about Clay Shaw's "domestic contact service activities" for the CIA are not presently available as substantial portions of the memo were withheld by the Agency.[6]

Unconfirmed reports say that some of Clay Shaw's work for the CIA centered on an alleged CIA proprietary company named CMC-Permindex which had been expelled from Italy following allegations that it had been illegally involved in financing political activities there. Victor Marchetti remembered CIA officials mentioning some information regarding Shaw's ties to a company in Rome. In early 1976, the scope of the CIA's subsidizing of Italian political activity was publicly disclosed for the first time. The Final Report of the House Intelligence Committee, headed by Congressman Otis Pike, (which was published in the *Village Voice* on February 16, 1976) revealed that the CIA — in 1972 alone — "expended some $10 million in contributions to political parties" in Italy.[7] The secret Pike Report, leaked to the *Village Voice* by CBS newsman Daniel Schorr, disclosed that the CIA had disbursed payments to the Italians in 1972 in the following amounts:

> A major political party received $3.4 million; a political organization created and

supported by CIA, $3.4 million; other organizations and parties, a total of $1.3 million.[8]

The Report also disclosed that President Nixon may have been influenced by some unnamed "international businessmen" before making his 1972 decision to authorize more CIA payments to Italian politicians.[9]

> It is known that during this period the President was indirectly approached by prominent international businessmen, who were former nationals of [Italy]. Their communications to the President were not available to the Committee.[10]

Following his acquittal in early 1969, Clay Shaw retired to his home in New Orleans, a "broken man" in the words of his friends and associates. Shaw had virtually depleted his entire fortune in his long legal battle, and had reportedly been deeply anguished over the disclosure of his homosexual activities.
Clay Shaw died of cancer in 1974.

Gordon Novel

Gordon Novel, a young electronics expert, had first become involved in Jim Garrison's investigation in 1967 when he volunteered to provide information relating to Cuban exile activities. However, after working with him a brief period, Garrison accused Novel of being a "plant" and announced that he was investigating his connections to both David Ferrie and the CIA. Novel was subsequently involved with Watergate conspirator Charles W. Colson in a

mysterious plan to erase some of President Nixon's secret Watergate tapes (in 1974). The details of this Novel-Colson plan, first reported by columnist Jack Anderson, received little attention.

In March, 1967, DA Garrison subpoenaed Gordon Novel to testify about an August, 1961 munitions burglary in Houma, Louisiana which had allegedly been carried out by David Ferrie, Cuban exile leader Sergio Arcacha Smith — and according to Garrison — Gordon Novel. On March 16, 1967, shortly before appearing before the Grand Jury, Novel told reporters that he would testify "about activities during 1961 which are related to Mr. Sergio Arcacha Smith."[11] When Garrison issued another subpoena for Novel to testify the following week, he disappeared. Reporters learned that Novel had sold his New Orleans bar several days after his first Grand Jury appearance, and had left town.[12] On March 23, 1967 he was located in Columbus, Ohio, by a UPI reporter, who quoted him as saying, "I don't believe [Garrison's] case and from the method he's used I think he's a fraud."[13] Though he claimed he had nothing to hide, Novel said he was not ready to respond to the New Orleans subpoena. On that same day, Garrison ordered his arrest as a "material witness" relating to events surrounding the Kennedy assassination, and a New Orleans judge ordered Novel's immediate arrest unless he voluntarily returned to New Orleans under a $50,000 bond.[14]

Gordon Novel was soon the subject of nationwide headlines as "Garrison's Missing Witness." He was next reported to be on his way to Chicago, but instead ended up in Washington, D.C. There, on March 26, 1967, the *Washington Evening Star* reported that he'd taken a lie detector test which he claimed cleared him of any involvement in the Kennedy assassination or events surrounding it.[15] Novel, however, refused to comment on Garrison's allegations that he'd been associated with both of Garrison's leading suspects, David Ferrie and Clay Shaw.

Soon after Novel had fled from New Orleans, authorities discovered a secret letter which he'd hidden in his former apartment. In the note, which his attorney admitted was authentic, Novel seemingly was warning a former intelligence contact that Garrison was investigating Novel's connection to the Bay of Pigs. His attorney stated that the note had "little or nothing to do with the assassination of President Kennedy," but that "everything in the letter as far as Novel is concerned is actually the truth."[16]

> This letter is to inform you that District Attorney Jim Garrison has subpoenaed myself and an associate to testify before his Grand Jury on matters which may be classified TOP SECRET. Actions of individuals connected with DOUBLE-CHEK CORPORATION in Miami in first quarter of 1961.
>
> Our connection and activity of that period involves individuals presently . . . about to be indicted as conspirators in Mr. Garrison's investigation.
>
> Mr. Garrison . . . is unaware of Double-Chek's involvement in this matter but has strong suspicions. I have been questioned extensively by local FBI recently as to whether or not I was involved with Double-Chek's parent-holding corporation during that time . . . Bureau unaware of Double-Chek's association in this matter. Our attorneys and others are in possession of complete sealed files containing all information concerning matter. In the event of

our sudden departure, either accidental or otherwise, they are instructed to simultaneously release same for public scrutiny . . .[17]

While the exact details of Novel's activities "in Miami" during the "first quarter of 1961" are not known, it is widely believed that he was referring to his work in the Bay of Pigs invasion, which the CIA coordinated from Miami. The Double-Chek Corporation, the Miami electronics "front" which Novel admitted being "connected with" in his letter, was reportedly used by the CIA. After this letter came to light, Novel and his attorney admitted that he had indeed worked as a CIA operative. On April 25, 1967 the *New Orleans States-Item* reported that Novel "told a number of friends and intimates he was a CIA operative and will use this role to battle Garrison's charges."[18]

In CIA documents declassified in 1976, the Agency admitted having "one tenuous link" with Gordon Novel. In a CIA memorandum dated May 1, 1967 ("Memo for Deputy Director for Support") the CIA's analysts disclosed:

> The CI [Counter Intelligence] staff, in a detailed staff study of the Garrison investigation, has noted past CIA contact with only two figures named in the inquiry, Clay L. Shaw and Carlos Bringuier . . .
>
> During the course of our inquiry into Novel's charges, one tenuous link was developed which conceivably could be exploited and distorted in attempts to link this Agency with Novel and others.[19]

On March 29, 1967, when he was still in hiding to avoid Garrison's subpoena and a New Orleans arrest warrant, Les Whitten of the *New York World-Journal Tribune* reported that Novel had secretly recorded several telephone conversations with Jim

Garrison's closest financial contributor, Willard Robertson, in which Robertson discussed the progress and direction of the Garrison investigation.[20] Whitten, who apparently received copies of the Novel tapes, disclosed that Novel had made these illegal tape recordings in an effort to find out what information Garrison was pursuing about him.[21]

Novel was finally compelled to return to New Orleans for questioning by the Grand Jury in early April, 1967, and made his first appearance in court on the afternoon of April 3, 1967, to post bond for his arrest. Novel then "hinted" at some kind of cover-up in the case, and was suddenly interrupted by his lawyer while beginning to mention the name of a Cuban exile.[22] News coverage of the appearance was quite heavy, and the following day the *New York Times* carried the Novel story under a headline reading, "Witness in Plot Investigation Hints a Cuban Link."[23]

On the night following Novel's court debut, President Johnson's top aide, Marvin Watson, called J. Edgar Hoover's top aide, Cartha deLoach, and informed him that President Johnson "was now convinced" that the CIA had been involved in the Kennedy assassination.[24]

Gordon Novel was also mysteriously linked to President Nixon's Special Counsel, Charles Colson, a key Watergate conspirator convicted in 1974. On August 15, 1974, columnist Jack Anderson disclosed that Colson and Novel had met in March, 1974 and had discussed a plan to magnetically erase some of Nixon's secret Watergate tapes, through the use of an experimental "de-gaussing" machine.[25] Anderson reported that Colson and Novel conferred several times during that period, and that Novel had spent considerable time on the secret tape-erasing plan. According to Anderson, Colson told Novel that the proposed tape device could be used not only on some of Nixon's Watergate tapes, but on some secret tapes kept by the CIA as well, and described these secret recordings as tapes that "could cause the President grief."[26] Anderson further disclosed that Gordon

Novel had flown to Texas in March 1974 to confer with another man about the proposed tape erasure plan.[27]

At the time that Anderson wrote the column, he was apparently unaware of Novel's prior involvement in Garrison's assassination investigation, as no mention was made in the column of his past activities. Anderson further reported that while Charles Colson admitted meeting with Gordon Novel and admitted discussing such a tape-erasing plan, he denied that he had ever taken it seriously, saying, "I laughed at it. It was a little bit of comic relief."[28]

Jim Garrison

In early 1967, New Orleans District Attorney Jim Garrison shook the nation by announcing that he had uncovered what he claimed was a conspiracy behind the assassination of President John F. Kennedy. The ensuing investigation and prosecutions by Garrison provided a new peak in the widespread public doubts about the conclusions of the Warren Commission. While Garrison's long investigation produced new areas of evidence and focused substantial attention on many past deficiencies in the "lone assassin" conclusions of the Warren Commission, his efforts and allegations became the subject of intense criticism and raging controversy.

In an extensive interview in October, 1967, Garrison set forth the basic outlines of what he claimed was the conspiracy:

> ... a number of the men who killed the President were former employees of the CIA involved in its anti-Castro underground activities in and around New Orleans. The CIA knows their identity. So do I.
>
> We must assume that the plotters were acting on their own rather than on CIA orders when they killed the President. As far as we have been able to determine, they were not in the pay of the CIA at the time of the assassination ...
>
> ... The CIA could not face up to the American people and admit that its former employees had conspired to assassinate the President; so from the moment Kennedy's heart stopped beating, the Agency attempted to sweep the whole conspiracy under the rug ... In this respect, it has become an accessory after the fact in the assassination.[29]

His investigation brought to light a number of unresolved and highly intriguing bodies of information pertaining to the Cuban exile and CIA connections of men who'd also been scrutinized by the Warren Commission. Yet, his probe increasingly came under criticism for the "circus atmosphere" surrounding it. Part of Garrison's problems stemmed from the extraordinary mixed bag of tipsters, eccentrics, volunteers, and publicity seekers who flooded into New Orleans to be part of "the history" that was to be made by uncovering the alleged conspiracy. Garrison's own tendency to be both talkative and incautious also was, in the eyes of many observers, a strong factor in his eventual decline.

In the spring and summer of 1967, as Garrison sought to cope with the loss of his top suspect, David Ferrie, allegations of investigative misconduct mounted against him. In mid-May, *Newsweek* magazine reported that two of his investigators had allegedly offered a $3,000 bribe to Alvin Beauboff, a former roommate of the late David Ferrie, in return for some fabricated testimony.[30] A month later, on June 19, 1967, a nationally-televised NBC investigative report on the Garrison case amplified the *Newsweek* claims and added further charges of intimidating witnesses, implanting evidence, and falsifying other testimony.[31] NBC subsequently provided a half-hour of television time for DA Garrison to fashion a rebuttal.

Garrison, well aware of the strong controversy he had provoked, once stated, "To read press accounts of my investigation, I'm a cross between Al Capone and Attila, the Hun — bribing, threatening innocent men."[32] He added, "In over five years of office I have never had a single case reversed because of the use of improper methods — a record I'll match with any other DA in the country."[33]

Though his lengthy investigation became increasingly mired in controversy, Garrison still retained strong support from a surprisingly large percentage of the American public as well as more than a few officials around the country. Perhaps a typical response came from Cardinal Cushing of Boston, the long-time friend and advisor of the Kennedy family, when he voiced his support: "I think they should follow it through . . . I never believed that the assassination was the work of one man."[34]

But the embattled DA often publicly charged that his investigation was being subjected to strong and, of course, very secret interference from the Federal government, presumably the CIA, FBI, and Justice Department, and that at least two people who had originally assisted him had been planted on his staff as infiltrators or saboteurs by some unknown party, possibly the CIA. In late 1967, Garrison stated:

> Let me put it this way: If you were in charge of the CIA and willing to spend scores of millions of dollars on such relatively penny-ante projects as infiltrating the National Student Association, wouldn't you make an effort to infiltrate an investigation that could seriously damage the prestige of your agency?[35]

With the acquittal of Clay Shaw in early 1969, and something approaching universal condemnation of various aspects of his prosecution, Garrison began to wind down his investigation. In his brief book, *A Heritage of Stone*, published in 1970, Garrison wrote about the problems that he believed contributed to the unraveling of his case, including what he regarded as a biased press corps: "Undoubtedly, they were as unaware of the Federal government's role as I was when I first began to look into the case. It must have appeared to them that I was presenting a scenario which featured abominable snowmen as the assassins."

As his investigation stretched on into late 1969 and then on into 1970, he became the subject of new charges. This time, Garrison was alleged to have had dealings with Louisiana organized crime figures, in particular New Orleans Mafia leader Carlos Marcello. Though Garrison admitted being personally acquainted with the top Mafioso, and further admitted that his office had "inevitably" come into contact with the Marcello empire during the course of numerous investigations, he denied any improper dealings with the underworld. Garrison claimed he would hardly be investigating Carlos Marcello's own former investigator and pilot, David Ferrie, as a top assassination suspect if such allegations of his close relationship with Marcello were true.

Yet, the broadside of allegations against Garrison continued, allegations of an increasingly serious nature. On August 29, 1969, *Look* magazine reported that during the course of Garrison's dealings with Marcello's New Orleans empire, the DA had managed to buy an expensive home at a cut-rate price from a top Marcello lieutenant.[36] A year later, on August 10, 1970, *Life* Magazine reported further allegations regarding Garrison's mob "ties," including the charge that he'd "managed to hush up the fact that last June, a Marcello bagman, Vic Corona, died after suffering a heart attack during a political meeting held in Garrison's own home."[37] Even though Garrison admitted that he was "stunned" by such reports, there was in fact another side to his record — namely his long-established image in New Orleans as a tough "no-holds-barred crime fighter" and "rackets buster." In a critical analysis in *Playboy*, Garrison's record as New Orleans DA was set forth in some detail, including his effort against organized crime in that city:

> . . . his toughest fight . . . came in 1962, when he announced that the refusal of the city's eight criminal court judges to approve funds for his investigations of organized crime "raised interesting questions about racketeer influences." The judges promptly charged Garrison with defamation of character and criminal libel — and a State court fined him $1,000.00. Garrison appealed the Court all the way to the Supreme Court, and on November 23, 1964, in a landmark decision on the right to criticize public officials, the nation's highest tribunal reversed his conviction, contending that "speech concerning public affairs is more than self-expression; it is the essence of self-government." Never the one to turn the other cheek, Garrison subsequently employed his

political influence to unseat a number of the judges when they came up for re-election.[38]

By 1975, though Garrison was frequently viewed as a "paranoid conspiracy theorist" who maintained the CIA was continuing to cover up the alleged Kennedy assassination conspiracy, he continued to have a substantial number of defenders across the nation, and was the recipient of praise from another somewhat unusual source: Jimmy Hoffa. In an interview just weeks before his disappearance Hoffa stated, "Jim Garrison's a smart man . . . Goddamned smart attorney . . . . Anybody thinks he's a kook is a kook themselves."[39]

Perhaps the lowest point in his fortunes came in 1971, when he was indicted on Federal charges of bribery and conspiracy. Despite being twice found not guilty, the clouds of controversy and acrimony that had long surrounded Garrison finally took their toll. On December 17, 1973 he was defeated in an extremely close election for nomination to a fourth consecutive term as District Attorney.

While Garrison still assists various assassination researchers around the country, and has provided information to several Congressional investigators, his work is now distinctly low key. In 1975, when told of Victor Marchetti's disclosure that Richard Helms had privately revealed CIA officials had been instructed to "do all we can" to help Clay Shaw, Garrison was uncharacteristically silent, and then replied, "That's not really news, is it?"

When informed that declassified documents revealed at least three of his suspects had indeed had CIA connections, Garrison was somewhat morose in his response: "I guess we can just say that, yes, there were CIA operatives running all around in these areas of assassination evidence but that they were all actually fine, innocent men. Isn't that about where everyone wants to leave it?"

Kerry Thornley

Kerry Thornley was a close friend of Lee Harvey Oswald during their service together in the U.S. Marine Corps in the late 1950s.[40] According to Thornley, who appeared before the Warren Commission as well as in the Garrison investigation, "You might say I was his [Oswald's] best buddy, but I don't think he had any close friends. I was a close acquaintance."[41]

Oswald had been stationed at Atsugi Air Base in Japan, which was one of the CIA's largest and most important installations in Asia. Previously classified Warren Commission documents show that the CIA's top-secret U-2 flights were staged from Atsugi during the period Oswald was a radar technician there.

Upon his discharge from the Marines, Kerry Thornley became a free-lance writer. According to Thornley, he'd kept a journal that contained an account of Oswald's activities in the Marines, and which traced his emotional development during the period that Thornley knew him. Thornley says he found Oswald to be an unusually interesting person, and thus planned to turn his journal into a book about Oswald, using the format of a novel. Interestingly, Thornley's plans were developed about two years before the assassination, as revealed in a series of articles he wrote about his friend in *Men's Digest* magazine following the assasination:

> The book was about the gradual moral breakdown of a Marine who finally defects to Russia. In earlier drafts, certain sections were based almost entirely on Oswald.
>
> As a matter of fact, my main character's name originally was Lee — Lee Shellburn.
>
> . . . [the book] certainly reflects Lee's character in many pages.[42]

While Thornley never published a novel about Oswald, he later wrote a "psychological study" of his friend in 1965, for a Chicago publisher.[43] The book, *Oswald*, did not sell well.

In his testimony before the Warren Commission in 1964, Kerry Thornley stated that the last time he'd ever seen Lee Harvey Oswald was in 1959, before Oswald left the Marines. On January 9, 1968, Jim Garrison subpoenaed Thornley, who was then living in Tampa, Florida, and accused him of concealing other contacts with Oswald in the years since 1959,[44] from the Warren Commission other contacts with Oswald in the years since 1959.[44] Garrison charged:

"In September of 1963 Kerry Thornley was closely associated with Lee Oswald at a number of locations in New Orleans."[45]

The Miami Herald reported:

"Thornley said he has found out that both he and Oswald were in New Orleans for about two weeks at the same time and both had been to the same bar during that time."[46]

From Tampa, Thornley announced that while he had nothing to hide, and even though he had denied Garrison's charges, he would not honor the subpoena unless extradited. Thornley explained: "I won't have anything new to tell the Grand Jury because I didn't see Oswald after 1959 and had no contact with him."[47] Thornley also stated that on the day of the assassination, he'd been working in a restaurant in the French Quarter of New Orleans.[48] He admitted he may have made some disparaging remark about JFK's murder:

"I was rather light and flippant about it . . . . That upset a few people in the restaurant."[49] Thornley also said he was "very, very skeptical" about whether his friend had in fact assassinated President Kennedy.

On February 8, 1968, after Garrison's subpoena had been enforced, Thornley finally appeared before the Grand Jury in New Orleans. Two weeks later, on February 21, 1968, the DA formally charged him with perjury, accusing him of lying about his contact with Oswald during his Grand Jury testimony.[50] In a UPI interview that day, Thornley stated that he may have once seen Oswald in New Orleans without actually recognizing him. Thornley said that, "I may have passed him and not recognized him and as far as I know he never saw me."[51]

While Thornley strongly maintained that he had never had any contact with Oswald after their hitch in the Marines, Thornley conceded that he'd once considered visiting Oswald in 1962, when ex-defector Oswald, flew back to the United States after living in Russia. Thornley, who was still then planning his book on Oswald, wrote in *Men's Digest*: "At that time I thought seriously about going to see him before starting the rewrite. He could provide invaluable information."[52]

In tracing Thornley's movements across the country, a Garrison investigator came across at least one reliable witness who stated that Thornley himself had once admitted being in contact again with Oswald in 1963. Mrs. Doris Dowell, the assistant manager of Shirlington House, a well-known apartment complex in Arlington, Virginia, disclosed that Thornley had been employed there from December of 1963 to mid-1964. Thornley had been hired on the basis of a strong recommendation from his previous job in New Orleans, which Thornley quit shortly after the assassination.[53] Mrs. Dowell and another manager of the Virginia apartments stated that Thornley had left his job in Virginia and had gone to California in the middle of 1964.[54] Then, according to the official summary of her interview:

Mrs. Dowell said that about one month before THORNLEY left for California he told her that he had been in the Marine Corps with LEE HARVEY OSWALD, and also that they were buddies in New Orleans. He said that he had met OSWALD again in New Orleans, and that they had met at a place in the French Quarter that she would probably not like.[55]

With Clay Shaw's acquittal in early 1969, the perjury charges against Kerry Thornley were dropped. In the years since, Thornley has refused comment on his relationship with Lee Oswald, and has resisted efforts to establish exactly what kind of work he was assigned to while serving with Oswald in the Marines. At last report, he was involved in a direct mail business project in Atlanta, Georgia.

The CIA Station Chief
In New Orleans

A distinguished New Orleans attorney, whose name has never been revealed publicly is believed to have served as Station Chief of the New Orleans CIA Office at the time of the Kennedy assassination, according to informed sources. The large New Orleans CIA station has long been one of the key CIA offices within the United States, and has been active in connection with the various Cuban exile groups in the city as well as in monitoring the international shipping activities of the New Orleans area port complex. It is believed to be located in the Masonic Building in the downtown section of the city.

While solid documentation linking Lee Harvey Oswald to the CIA in an official capacity has thus far never been established, most investigators agree that if such an Oswald-CIA connection is ever officially documented, the connection will have probably originated with the CIA's station in New Orleans.

There were at least two disclosures in 1976 which indicated that the CIA may at one time have recruited Lee Oswald for some unknown purpose. On October 1, 1976, the Associated Press disclosed a previously classified CIA memorandum which noted that several CIA officials "showed intelligence interest" in defector Lee Oswald, sometime in 1960, and "discussed . . . the laying on of interviews."[56] The November 25, 1963 CIA memo further noted that the Agency had considered using Oswald for several purposes, including to "help develop [foreign] personality dossiers."[57] The startling CIA document directly contradicts the sworn testimony of Richard Helms.[58] In May of 1964, in his Warren Commission testimony, Helms had claimed that "there's no material in the Central Intelligence Agency, either in the records or in the mind of any of the individuals that there was any contact had or even contemplated with" Lee Harvey Oswald.[59] Interestingly, the Agency officer who wrote the memo also noted that he "[did] not know what action developed thereafter" with the future alleged Presidential assassin.[60]

In June, 1976, four months before the de-classification of this memo, the Church Committee revealed:

> The CIA also took an interest in the Fair Play for Cuba Committee with which Oswald was associated. According to . . . FBI documents, on September 16, 1963, the CIA advised the FBI that the "Agency is giving some consideration to countering the activities of [the FPCC] in foreign countries."[61]

On November 26, 1976, *Washington Post* reporter Ron Kessler disclosed that the CIA had destroyed several secret tape recordings of Oswald's telephone conversations with the Cuban and Soviet Embassies in Mexico City, which had been made in September, 1963, during his mysterious ten-day visit to Mexico. The *Washington Post* claimed that the CIA had not only withheld portions of the Oswald tape transcripts from the Warren Commission, but had also hidden the same material from the FBI.[62]

Beyond the possible connections between Lee Oswald and David Ferrie, there are at least two other men who crossed paths with Oswald in New Orleans — men who may very well have been connected to the large CIA station in that city: William Gaudet and Albert Osborne. (See the chapter on "The Intelligence Community.")

Any final determination of who was or wasn't involved with the CIA apparatus in New Orleans will, of course, have to await further official investigation.

Interestingly, in 1976, the Senate Intelligence Committee disclosed at least one instance in which CIA officials in New Orleans had run a secret mail intercepting program which had lacked the standard required authorization from higher authorities:

> A third CIA mail intercept project, encrypted "Project SETTER," was conducted in New Orleans for two-and-one-half weeks during 1957. This project . . . involved the screening and opening of first class international surface mail transiting New Orleans enroute to and from South and Central America.
>
> There is no record of any internal authorization above the level of Deputy Director of Security and Deputy Chief of the CI [Counterintelligence] staff, and the only apparent external approval was by a Division head in the Customs Service, who stated that he was unaware the project involved the opening of mail.

... James Angleton, the Chief of the CI staff at the time, testified that he had no contemporaneous knowledge of it.[63]

The Station Chief is now retired and is believed to live on St. Charles Street in New Orleans, one of the city's most fashionable areas. He refuses requests for interviews by members of the press.

James Hicks

James Hicks, a young civil service employee who became another "material witness" in the Garrison investigation, had been an actual witness at the scene of the assassination, and had an unobstructed view of President Kennedy being hit. Various films and photographs taken by members of the public in the crowd, particularly a photograph by witness Phil Willis, showed James Hicks standing near the Presidential limousine as the fatal shots were fired. Hicks, however, was never called to testify by the Warren Commission. The Commission neglected to call or even identify a significant number of people who had been actual witnesses to the shooting. It was not until 1967 that author Josiah Thompson compiled a nearly complete compendium of these witnesses in his book, *Six Seconds in Dallas.*[64]

In January, 1968, James Hicks was called to testify

before the New Orleans Grand Jury. It was soon learned that he was going to testify that he was certain that at least one shot had been fired from the grassy knoll area to the front of the President's car. On January 11, 1968, the Dallas *Morning News* reported that James Hicks would testify that he had also seen two men acting suspiciously behind the picket fence on the grassy knoll prior to the assassination.[65]

Hicks was scheduled to testify before the New Orleans Grand Jury on the next day, January 12, 1968. However, late the night of January 11th, two men broke into his room at the Fountainebleau Motel, woke him up, beat him severely and finally smashed him through a plate glass door that led to the balcony of his sixth floor room.[66] The intruders were never apprehended.

Before appearing for questioning in Garrison's office the next morning, Hicks told reporters that he did not believe the attack on him had been connected in any way to the assassination investigation.[67] However, Hicks stated he had received previous threats on the lives of his wife and son and was now quite nervous about testifying. Hicks went on to describe how he had witnessed the fatal shot that had hit President Kennedy during the Dallas motorcade: "It's really hard to say what happened because it happened so fast, but I do remember the President being shot and I knew he was shot when it happened because I saw his whole head explode. It didn't look like one shot . . . his whole head exploded."[68] James Hicks claimed that four shots were fired at the Presidential car and that one of these had been fired from the grassy knoll.[69] On January 12, 1968 the *New Orleans Times Picayune* reported further details of Hicks' testimony:

> Hicks said he heard four shots, and one bullet passed his head and struck a traffic caution sign, which he said was removed almost immediately after the assassination. He said as far as he knows it was never men-

tioned in the Warren Commission Report.

Hicks said the sign was removed by men "I assumed to be members of the Dallas Police Force. I assumed they would use it as evidence."[70]

When reporters inquired about the traffic sign, it was discovered that it had indeed been removed shortly after the assassination, though no records were available as to who ordered the removal or why. Hicks claims he specifically remembers seeing a bullet hole in the sign on the day of the assassination.[71]

Reverend Raymond Broshears

Reverend Raymond Broshears, a former roommate of the late David Ferrie, was one of the more eccentric figures who first came to light during the Garrison probe. Reverend Broshears, also known as "Brother Ray" Broshears, was active in several rather strange church organizations and had been involved in other equally unusual groups.

Like David Ferrie, Reverend Raymond Broshears was an active homosexual. "Brother Ray" first publicly disclosed that he was a former roommate of Ferrie in an interview broadcast by a Los Angeles television station on July 8, 1968.[72] He said he had lived with

Ferrie in 1967 (actually from August 1965 to late 1966) and that Ferrie had confided to him that there had in fact been a conspiracy behind the Kennedy assassination — a conspiracy in which Ferrie allegedly claimed to have served as a key participant.[73] On August 9, 1968, Broshears appeared for questioning at the office of District Attorney Garrison. He later stated that "I told him [Garrison] about David Ferrie and some of his work for the Central Intelligence Agency." Broshears had previously voiced strong anger over Garrison's investigation, but subsequently stated that he wished to cooperate fully. While Garrison's staff never arrived at any final determination of the accuracy of the eccentric Broshears' information, the DA's investigators questioned him extensively. A Garrison investigative report states:

> BROSHEARS described JACK RUBY as a "clown — a pompous little clown — a dime store Napoleon who hated JOHN F. KENNEDY and loved him out of the other side of his mouth." He stated that RUBY did not know FERRIE but that FERRIE knew of RUBY.
>
> BROSHEARS said that OFFICER J. D. TIPPITT was supposed to kill OSWALD but that OSWALD KILLED TIPPIT INSTEAD. Jack Ruby had to kill OSWALD to preserve the secrecy of the plot. (BROSHEARS says that OSWALD did not fire at PRESIDENT KENNEDY.)
>
> He later added that OSWALD was a bisexual who had had relations with FERRIE. FERRIE told BROSHEARS that OSWALD was with the CIA.[74]

According to Broshears' account of the alleged assassination conspiracy, two of the actual Kennedy assassins had been killed in a plane crash near Corpus Christi, Texas, while making their escape just hours after the assassination.[75] Broshears also stated that he had once conferred in 1966 with Richard Lauchli, a leader of the violent right-wing group, The Minutemen, concerning some "emotional problems" that roommate Ferrie was having.[76] Broshears did not elaborate.

In 1965 and 1966, Broshears was investigated by the Secret Service for having allegedly made a threat on the life of President Johnson, and was once briefly held in November 1965 in connection with that threat.[77] He claimed he had made the threat on Johnson's life in order to be placed under protective custody, where he would be safe from unspecified "harassment." He later escaped prosecution by basing his defense on mental illness. Curiously, he surfaced again in 1975 in an investigation of an assassination attempt on the life of Gerald Ford in San Francisco.

Hugh Ward

Hugh Ward worked as a private investigator for Guy Banister's detective agency at 544 Camp Street in New Orleans which figures prominently in several areas of information relating to Lee Oswald, David Ferrie, anti-Castro Cuban exiles, and various Mafia and intelligence connections. Banister's employee, Hugh Ward, reportedly worked with another employee, David Ferrie, on a number of investigations and had also been taught to fly by Ferrie.[78] There have also been unconfirmed reports that Hugh Ward had active connections to the violent right-wing Minutemen organization.[79]

Ward was killed in the crash of a small plane in Mexiço in 1964, which also took the life of New Orleans Mayor DeLesseps Morrison.[80]

Dean Andrews

Dean Andrews, like several other of Garrison's witnesses, had originally been interviewed by the Secret Service, FBI, and Warren Commission in the months after the assassination. Andrews told the Secret Service that Lee Oswald, accompanied by three Latin homosexual companions, had visited his law office several times in the summer of 1963 seeking help in trying legally to change Oswald's dishonorable Marine Corps discharge.[81] Andrews told the Secret Service that on the day after the assassination, he received a phone call from a New Orleans man who was closely connected with the large homosexual community in that city.[82] The man, whom he stated used the name "Clay Bertrand" asked him to go to Dallas to defend Oswald.[83] Andrews turned him down. Garrison later conducted an investigation to attempt to determine the true identity of "Clay Bertrand." Previous New Orleans police reports had in fact spoken of a wealthy homosexual known as either Clay or Clem Bertrand.

Garrison tried to prove that the mysterious Bertrand was actually Clay Shaw, his top assassination suspect, but no solid evidence of that was ever produced. Dean Andrews later changed his story about Oswald and Bertrand, said he had made part of it up, finally said he had made all of it up, and then subsequently stated that "most" of it was actually true.[84]

The fast-talking Andrews was widely regarded as one of the more colorful figures to emerge from the controversial Garrison investigation.

Judge Edward A. Haggerty

Judge Edward Haggerty, the judge who presided over the Clay Shaw conspiracy trial, soon after became the subject of strong controversy. In fact, on November 24, 1970, he was ordered removed from the bench by a six-to-one ruling of the Louisiana Supreme Court,[85] which had been set in motion following his arrest in a New Orleans motel during a vice squad raid.[86] Haggerty had originally been charged with assault on an arresting policeman, resisting arrest, soliciting for prostitution, and conspiracy to commit obscenity. The Louisiana State Judiciary Commission subsequently charged Judge Haggerty with "public misconduct off the bench . . . so seriously delinquent as to bring disgrace and discredit upon the Judicial office."

In the aftermath of the Clay Shaw conspiracy trial, Judge Haggerty stated that he was unaware of any federal interference in the case.

1. Anson, *"They've Killed The President!,"* pp. 123, 376; Interview with Victor Marchetti, October 7, 1975.
2. Ibid.
3. Ibid.
4. Ibid.
5. May 1, 1967 CIA Memorandum, "Memo for Deputy Director For Support."
6. Ibid.
7. "The Report On The CIA That President Ford Doesn't Want You To Read," *The Village Voice*, February 16, 1976, p. 84 (Final Report of the House Select Committee on Intelligence).
8. Ibid., p. 85.
9. Ibid., p. 84.
10. Ibid., p. 85.
11. Weisberg, *Oswald In New Orleans*, p. 366.
12. Ibid.
13. Ibid., p. 367.
14. Ibid.
15. *Washington Evening Star*, March 26, 1967.
16. James and Wardlaw, *Plot or Politics*, p. 11.
17. Letter draft of Gordon Novel, District Attorney's Office, New Orleans, March 1967.
18. *New Orleans States-Item*, April 25, 1967.
19. May 1, 1967 CIA Memorandum, "Memo for Deputy Director for Support."
20. *New York World-Journal-Tribune*, March 29, 1967.
21. Ibid.
22. *New York Times*, April 4, 1967.
23. Ibid.
24. *Senate Intelligence Committee Report*, Volume 6, p. 182.
25. Jack Anderson column, August 15, 1974.
26. Ibid.
27. Ibid.
28. Ibid.
29. *Playboy* magazine, Interview with Jim Garrison, October 1967.
30. *Newsweek*, May 15, 1967.
31. *NBC News*, "The J.F.K. Conspiracy: The Case of Jim

Garrison," June 19, 1967.
32. *Playboy* magazine, Interview with Jim Garrison, October 1967.
33. Ibid.
34. Ibid.
35. Ibid.
36. "The Persecution of Clay Shaw," *Look*, Warren Rogers, August 29, 1969.
37. *Life*, August 10, 1970.
38. *Playboy* magazine, October, 1967.
39. *Playboy* magazine, Interview with James R. Hoffa, December, 1975.
40. Warren Commission Report, p. 612.
41. *Miami Herald*, March 11, 1968.
42. *Men's Digest*, Four Part Series on Lee Harvey Oswald, January-April 1967.
43. Kerry Thornley, *Oswald* (Chicago: New Classics House, 1965).
44. *Miami Herald*, January 10, 1968.
45. Ibid.
46. Ibid.
47. *Miami Herald*, March 11, 1968.
48. Ibid.
49. Ibid.
50. *Tampa Tribune*, February 22, 1968.
51. Ibid.
52. *Men's Digest*, Four Part Series on Lee Harvey Oswald, January-April 1967.
53. April 2, 1968 Interview with Mrs. Doris Powell, New Orleans District Attorney's Office, New Orleans, Louisiana.
54. Ibid.
55. Ibid.
56. *Washington Post*, October 1, 1976.
57. Ibid.
58. Ibid.
59. Ibid.
60. Ibid.
61. *Senate Intelligence Committee Final Report on the Kennedy Assassination*, p. 65.
62. *Washington Post*, November 26, 1976.
63. *Senate Intelligence Committee Final Report, Book Three*, pp. 620-622.
64. Josiah Thompson, *Six Seconds In Dallas* (New York: Bernard Geis Associates, 1967), pp. 252-271.
65. *Dallas Morning News*, January 11, 1968.
66. New Orleans Police Report, January 12, 1968.
67. *New Orleans Times-Picayune*, January 12, 1968.
68. Ibid.
69. Ibid.

70. Ibid.
71. Ibid.
72. "Tempo I," Stan Bohrman television panel, Interview with Raymond Broshears, July 8, 1968.
73. Ibid.
74. Staff summary report of interview with Raymond Broshears, New Orleans District Attorney's Office, April 12, 1968.
75. Ibid.
76. Ibid.
77. Ibid.
78. "The Garrison Commission on the Kennedy Assassination," *Ramparts*, William Turner, January 1968.
79. Ibid.
80. *Playboy*, Interview with Jim Garrison, October, 1967.
81. Warren Commission Volume 9, pp. 326-329.
82. Ibid.
83. Ibid.
84. Epstein, *Counterplot*, p. 41.
85. *New Orleans Times-Picayune*, November 25, 1970.
86. Ibid.

CHAPTER ELEVEN

The Cubans

On Sunday morning, November 24, 1963, just hours before he was shot to death by Jack Ruby, Lee Harvey Oswald was asked about his feelings toward Cuba.[1] The only comment young Oswald had was: "Will Cuba be better off with the President dead? Someone will take his place, Lyndon Johnson, no doubt, and he will probably follow the same policy."[2]

In her analysis of remarks made by Oswald during his brief imprisonment — statements that have been laboriously pieced together from various reports of Dallas and federal authorities — author Sylvia Meagher has written:

> Time has confirmed Oswald's prognostication. The radical right, which has been enamored of the theory that Oswald assassinated the President on instructions from

Castro or for pro-Castro reasons, has not taken into consideration the elementary facts that Oswald recognized at once: That the substitution of Lyndon Johnson for John F. Kennedy offered no advantage to Castro or to any socialist or leftist faction, whether national or external. Can the same thing be said in regard to the conservatives or adherents of the radical right? [3]

While competing accusations of right-wing anti-Castro or left-wing pro-Castro involvement in the Kennedy assassination have continued through the years, the mystery surrounding Oswald's simultaneous involvement in his own "Fair Play for Cuba Committee" as well as his offers to work with anti-Castro Cuban exiles also continues unabated.

In late June, 1976, the Senate Intelligence Committee Report criticized both the FBI and CIA for inadequately investigating these Cuban connections. It noted that the CIA had restricted its investigations into potential areas of anti-Castro Cuban exile or pro-Castro Cuban involvement, and disclosed that the CIA had a staff division uniquely equipped to conduct such an investigation: the Special Affairs Staff — which had been prohibited from joining the assassination investigation in any substantive way:

> Cuban operations were uniquely compartmented within CIA. As one witness described the Special Affairs Staff, it was "sort of a microcosm of the Agency with emphasis on Cuban matters."
>
> SAS had its own counterintelligence staff...
>
> However, the Warren Commission staff did not work directly with anyone from SAS. Although the CIA centered its work on the assassination in its Counterintelligence

Division, the Chief of SAS Counterintelligence testified that the SAS had no "direct" role in the investigation of the assassination.

. . . there is no evidence whatsoever that SAS was asked or ever volunteered to analyze Oswald's contacts with Cuban groups. The chief of SAS/CI testified he could recall no such analyses.

Indeed all the evidence suggests that the CIA investigation into any Cuban connection, whether pro-Castro or anti-Castro, was passive in nature.[4]

The Report disclosed that the CIA's own investigators had not been told by their superiors about the anti-Castro CIA-Mafia conspiracies:

Even though CIA investigators did not know that the CIA was plotting to kill Castro, they certainly did know that the Agency had been operating a massive covert operation against Cuba since 1960. The conspiratorial atmosphere of violence which developed over the course of three years of CIA and exile group operations, should have led CIA investigators to ask whether Lee Harvey Oswald and Jack Ruby who were known to at least have touched the fringes of the Cuban community, were influenced by that atmosphere. Similarly, arguments that the CIA domestic jurisdiction was limited belie the fact CIA's Cuban operations had created an enormous domestic apparatus, which the Agency used both to gather intelligence domestically and to run operations against Cuba.[5]

The Bay of Pigs amalgamation of CIA men, militant Cuban exiles, and various Mafia sponsors, as well as the simultaneous CIA-Mafia plots, provide the backdrop for continuing inquiry. JFK aide Theodore Sorensen has written of the extreme secrecy surrounding the Bay of Pigs invasion, which led to Kennedy's inability to exercise his necessary critical role:

> Only the CIA and Joint Chiefs had an opportunity to study and ponder the details of the plan. Only a small number of officials and advisors even knew of its existence; and in meetings with the President and this limited number, memoranda of operations were distributed at the beginning of each session and collected at the end, making virtually impossible any systematic criticisms or alternatives. The whole project seemed to move mysteriously and inexorably toward execution without the President being able either to obtain a firm grip on it or reverse it.[6]

Serious deficiencies in the plan stemmed from the intense in-fighting within the CIA's Cuban exile groups, as well as the President's lack of knowledge about how serious those internal difficulties actually were. Sorensen further states:

> Cooperation was further impaired by the fact some of the exile left-wing leaders were mistrusted by the CIA, just as some of their right-wing leaders and brigade members were mistrusted by the Cuban Underground. . .
>
> Their assumptions were not made known to the President, just as his were not made known to them: and the Cuban Revolutionary Council was similarly kept largely uninformed on the landing and largely out of touch with the brigade.[7]

Richard N. Goodwin, Kennedy's Special Assistant for Cuban Affairs, recalled "I shared the absurd belief — which was then general, but far from universal — that Castro's rule over Cuba was somehow inimical to our interests."[8] The question of alleged Cuban involvement in the Dallas assassination would now seem to revolve around who would have believed that Kennedy's rule over the United States was somehow inimical to their interests.

In addition to the extensive areas of information pertaining to Cuban activities and Cuban exiles covered in earlier chapters, there are several significant figures who have emerged as prime sources of speculation regarding a possible Cuban "connection" to the Kennedy assassination.

Fidel Castro

Though many observers immediately suspected he was behind JFK's murder, the only documented evidence relating to Fidel Castro and assassination plots establishes the exact opposite. In November, 1975, the Church Committee disclosed "concrete evidence of at least 8 plots involving the CIA to assassinate Fidel Castro from 1960-1965"[9] which employed "assassination devices [that] ran the gamut from high-powered rifles to poison pills, poison pens, deadly bacterial powders, and other devices which strain the imagination."[10]

It was partly out of fear of Castro's involvement that President Johnson appointed the Warren Commission, as he noted in 1971 in his memoirs:

> We were aware of stories that Castro ... only lately accusing us of sending CIA agents into the country to assassinate him, was the perpetrator of the Oswald assassination plot. These rumors were another compelling reason that a thorough study had to be made of the Dallas tragedy at once.[11]

Johnson's suspicions that Castro and the Cuban government were involved were later replaced by even stronger suspicions that the CIA was somehow responsible for the assassination. While many critics have raised further questions about Castro's possible role, this theory has generally been downgraded over the years, and in 1975 and 1976, new information became available which pointed to the lack of a rational motive. Castro came to view JFK as the "lesser of all evils" on the American political scene, and had, following the 1962 Cuban Missile Crisis, become more convinced of Kennedy's own increasing "reasonableness" in dealing with American-Cuban relations. Castro and his top advisors, though still somewhat wary of Kennedy, saw him as the main counter-balance to other political forces in the United States, in particular Senator Barry Goldwater, former presidential candidate Richard Nixon, and various Pentagon officials who advocated much more militant opposition to the Castro regime. As Castro himself said in an interview with American journalists, "There was no reason to wish him personal harm. Besides, Kennedy could be followed by someone worse ... I always used to say that at least we knew Kennedy."[12]

The Church Committee confirmed rumors that Castro and Kennedy had secretly begun an effort in 1963 to "discuss opening negotiations on an accommodation between Castro and the United States."[13]

McGeorge Bundy, JFK's National Security Affairs advisor had proposed this effort toward Cuban detente in a confidential memo as early as January 4, 1963.[14] The President's "Special Group" of advisors on Cuban policy, which was coordinated by his brother Robert, had approved a policy decision on June 3, 1963 to explore "various possibilities of establishing channels of communication to Castro."[15]

President Kennedy had already taken action to curtail some of the more militant anti-Castro activities of militant Cuban exiles, many of whom had either once worked or were presently working with the CIA. Frank Fiorini Sturgis, the future Watergate burglar, had been a key anti-Castro militant affected by Kennedy's crackdown on such activists. In May, 1976, the former chief of the CIA's vast Miami-based intelligence network told of the Kennedy Administration's efforts to curtail the exile operations launched against Cuba: ". . . the whole apparatus of government, Coast Guard, Customs, Immigration and Naturalization, FBI, CIA, were working together to try to keep these operations from going to Cuba."[16]

Fidel Castro expressed "great displeasure" over Kennedy's death, and spoke of JFK's willingness to challenge the assumptions of his more conservative political opponents who maintained that the only way to deal with the Cuban dictator was through force: ". . . we would have preferred that he continue in the Presidency of the United States. Because if there was a President of the United States who could have had the courage to change policy, or at least to question American policies toward Cuba, that was Kennedy."[17]

Castro placed the actual blame for the Bay of Pigs invasion on a man who had also been a long time opponent of President Kennedy: Richard M. Nixon. Castro told American journalists: ". . . when he [Kennedy] became President, this whole plan of training troops and of invading Cuba had already been organized. And he had great doubts . . . It must not be forgotten, as I have mentioned, that it was Nixon who had proposed that the Marines and the Armed Forces to be used."[18]

The Church Committee has shown that the tenor of the developing Kennedy-Castro rapprochement increased significantly in the Fall of 1963, with secret discussions through intermediaries commencing in September, 1963. President Kennedy was personally coordinating these expanded efforts toward improved relations as the testimony of his Special Advisor to the United Nations, William Attwood, shows:

> Attwood testified that from September until November 1963, he held a series of talks with the Cuban ambassador to the United Nations to discuss opening negotiations on an accommodation between Castro and the United States.
>
> Attwood said that at the outset he informed Robert Kennedy of these talks and was told that the effort "was worth pursuing".
>
> . . . Attwood stated that he was told by Bundy that President Kennedy was in favor of "pushing towards an opening toward Cuba" to take Castro "out of the Soviet fold and perhaps wiping out the Bay of Pigs and maybe getting back to normal."

The Senate Intelligence Committee Report went on to note:

> Attwood said he believed that the only people who knew about his contacts with the Cubans were the President, Ambassador Averell Harriman, McGeorge Bundy, Bundy's assistant, and journalist Lisa Howard.

On November 18, 1963, Attwood spoke by telephone with a member of Castro's staff in Cuba persuant to White House instructions, Attwood informed Castro's staff member that the United States favored preliminary negotiations at the United Nations . . . Attwood reported this conversation to Bundy who told him that after the Cuban agenda was received President Kennedy wanted to see Attwood [after he returned from his trip to Dallas] to "decide what to say and whether to go or what we should do next."[19]

In a series of exclusive interviews published in 1975, Fidel Castro expressed at great length his views on the assassination, and told interviewers Frank Mankiewicz and Kirby Jones:

"For a while, the CIA was attempting assassination of some of our revolutionary leaders. Some say the decision was on Kennedy's desk several times. We do not know. It's as much of a mystery as Kennedy's own assassination. It would be a good thing if the truth were known. I have heard that there are certain documents that will not be published for 100 years and I ask myself why. What secret surrounds the Kennedy assassination that these papers cannot be published? I ask myself why the man who commits such an act tries to come here? As you know, he applied for — and was denied — a permit to travel to Cuba. And one must take into account the fact that a few days after killing Kennedy, he himself was killed. How can the conclusion be avoided that there are others behind all this?

"Who knows what goals they were seeking by killing Kennedy? Sometimes we ask ourselves if someone did not wish to involve Cuba in this, because I am under the impression that Kennedy's assassination was a conspiracy organized in the United States by reactionaries with possible connections to the CIA. This is my opinion, and my opinion is that the man who carried it out was an agent-provocateur. The other mystery is that this other man, Ruby, who had no moral ideals, no political ideals, no political passions, becomes so enraged by Kennedy's assassination that he kills the assassin right in front of the police. It was incredible, inconceivable. That does not happen even in the most mediocre of movies."[20]

Nancy Perrin Rich

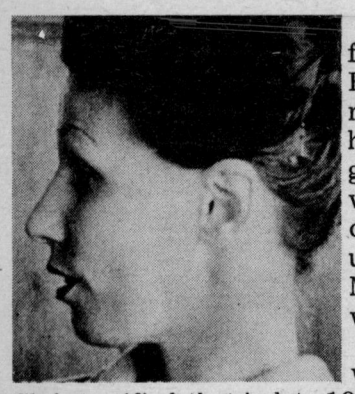

Nancy Perrin Rich is former employee of Jack Ruby whose Warren Commission testimony linked him to a Cuban exile gun-running operation which was apparently co-ordinated by various figures connected with the Mafia and extreme right-wing politics.

Nancy Perrin, a cocktail waitress in Ruby's Carousel Club testified that in late 1961 and 1962, she and her husband Robert had attended secret meetings, at which a Cuban exile gun-running scheme was planned.[33]

These sessions were attended by several people, including an Army Colonel and a man who reportedly was the son of Vito Genovese,[34] the New Jersey Mafia boss who had replaced Frank Costello as the most powerful and violent Mafioso in the nation.

According to Nancy Perrin, her husband was offered $15,000 to pilot a small craft to Cuba to deliver a cache of arms during a clandestine landing, and to pick up some escaping refugees.[35] Mrs. Perrin said her former employer, Jack Ruby, entered the room during one of these meetings, discussed the gun-running plan with the army colonel, and then apparently gave him a bulging envelope containing a substantial amount of cash.[36] The Perrins subsequently decided to end their involvement in the proposed Cuban gun-running plan.[37]

Unfortunately, Robert Perrin was not alive in 1964 to corroborate his wife's testimony. Robert Perrin died in late 1962 from arsenic poisoning in a death that was never fully explained. The Commission staff raised some doubts as to the reliability of Nancy Perrin and her testimony. Mrs. Perrin did in fact have a background befitting any female who worked in Jack Ruby's nightclub. She had a series of criminal associations in her past and had reportedly been linked to questionable activities in Dallas among other cities. By her own admission, she had also come to dislike Ruby, and had quit the Carousel Club following a dispute with him.

Nonetheless, the fact that Mrs. Perrin came forward with her story of the gun-running plan detailing Ruby's involvement, immediately after he shot Oswald, led investigators to take her account seriously.

The Warren Commission staff included her information in an official memorandum sent to CIA Deputy Director for Plans Richard Helms requesting any and all related CIA information on Jack Ruby. In this memo, of February 24, 1964, the Warren Commission noted:

... Ruby is also rumored to have met in Dallas with an American Army Colonel [L.N.U.] and some Cubans concerning the sale of arms:

A Government informant in Chicago connected with the sale of arms to anti-Castro Cubans has reported that such Cubans were behind the Kennedy assassination..."[38]

It is possible that Ruby could have been utilized by a politically motivated group either upon the promise of money or because of the influential character of the individual approaching Ruby.[39]

No further investigation was ever made of Nancy Perrin Rich's information about Ruby.

Carlos Bringuier

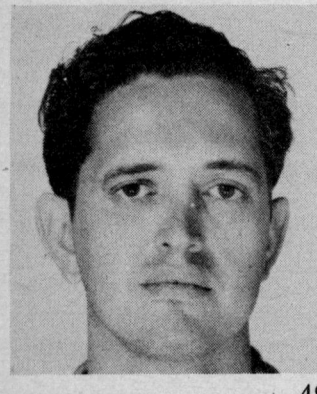

A leading Cuban exile leader whose hatred for Fidel Castro was surpassed only by his penchant for publicity, Carlos Bringuier had been featured in a radio debate with Lee Harvey Oswald on August 21, 1963 in New Orleans.[40] Oswald and Bringuier engaged in a heated discussion about Cuba — a debate set in motion by

Oswald's recent publicity as an "activist" of the New Orleans-based "Fair Play for Cuba Committee."[41] Bringuier had been a former member of the Cuban Revolutionary Council, the main Cuban exile organization set up and coordinated by the CIA for the Bay of Pig invasion.[42]

Earlier that same summer, Oswald had approached Bringuier and offered to help train anti-Castro Cuban exiles in para-military operations.[43] Oswald's strange offer, of course, directly conflicted with his "pro-Castro" activities during that same period, and has never been explained. Bringuier says Oswald came into his store on August 5, 1963 and "asked me for some literature against Castro, explained that he had experience in guerrilla warfare, and expressed that he was willing to help train anti-Castro Cubans in guerrilla activities."[44]

When he met Oswald handing out his pro-Castro leaflets on a New Orleans street corner, Bringuier was outraged to see that he was apparently "pro-Castro" instead of "anti-Castro." Bringuier and Oswald then got into a brief fistfight which resulted in Oswald's arrest — whereupon he immediately requested to meet with a representative of the FBI.

Carlos Bringuier has fervently maintained that Fidel Castro either directly or indirectly influenced Oswald to assassinate JFK, stating that the President "was murdered by the Communist movement."[46] Bringuier, known for his extreme anti-Communist fervor, has said the Warren Commission staff was composed of "persons who at one time or other defended the travel of students to Communist Cuba, or opposed anti-Communist laws in their respective states,"[47] and that most of the Commission's critics are either Communists or Communist sympathizers, stating that author Mark Lane's "defense of Oswald, in my opinion, is indirectly a defense of Communism in general and Castro in particular."[48] Bringuier has also charged that "pro-Castro forces" are "trying to bring about a revolution in this country. They are saying that anti-Castro Cubans were involved in the assassination. . . . They know as long as the people of the United States believe in the institutions of the Nation, such as the FBI, they cannot take over."[49]

Bringuier is still active in various anti-Castro exile circles, and has stated that any re-investigation of the assassination will produce nothing to refute the Warren Commission's conclusion that Oswald acted alone.

The "Cuban-American" Passenger on Cubana Airlines

In June of 1976, the Church Committee disclosed that CIA and FBI files relating to the assassination contained references to the mysterious movements of a pro-Castro "Cuban-American" who flew to Cuba shortly after the Dallas assassination.[59] While it did not divulge the Cuban-American's identity, the Committee did note that the man's strange actions should have been brought to the attention of the Warren Commission — something which the FBI and CIA had failed to do. The Senate Committee reported:

> On December 1, 1963, CIA received information that a November 22 Cubana Airlines flight from Mexico City to Cuba was delayed some five hours, from 6:00 p.m. to 11:00 p.m. E.S.T., awaiting an unidentified passenger. This unidentified passenger arrived at the airport in a twin-engined aircraft at 10:30 p.m. and boarded the Cubana Airlines plane without passing through customs, where he would have needed to

identify himself by displaying a passport. The individual travelled to Cuba in the cockpit of the Cubana Airlines plane, thus again avoiding identification by the passengers.[51]

At least one "source" told the CIA that this twenty-three-year-old Cuban-American might have been "involved in the assassination,"[52] and had reportedly been involved with the Tampa, Florida branch of the "Fair Play For Cuba Committee," to which Lee Oswald had once written. The Senate Committee stated that this entire incident should have prompted a far more thorough and timely investigation than the FBI conducted and the results should have been volunteered to the Warren Commission..."

Sergio Arcacha Smith

Sergio Arcacha Smith was the New Orleans Director of the "Cuban Democratic Revolutionary Front," also known as the FRD or *Frente Revolucionario Democratico* — one of the key Cuban exile groups coordinated by the CIA for the Bay of Pigs invasion. E. Howard Hunt has written of his close involvement with the FRD and its key role in the ill-fated CIA operation.[54]

Sergio Arcacha Smith, long regarded as one of the more conspiratorial Cuban exile leaders, was also a key official in two of the other CIA-sponsored Cuban exile organizations: the "Crusade To Free Cuba Committee," and the largest of the CIA exile groups, the "Cuban Revolutionary Council."[55] CIA officials have long admitted the Agency's involvement in coordinating both of these exile groups.[56]

Harold Weisberg has cited various Secret Service reports that set forth Sergio Arcacha Smith's involvement with these groups. Critic Weisberg has noted that a December 9, 1963 Secret Service report reveals that the "Cuban Revolutionary Council" maintained an office in New Orleans at 544 Camp Street from October 1961 to February 1962.[57] Another Secret Service report on other militant anti-Castro exiles notes that Smith was one of six Cuban exile officials authorized to sign checks for the CIA-sponsored Revolutionary Council, along with Luis Ravel, Manuel Gil, Arnesto Rodriquez Sr. and Jr. and Joiquin Villodas.[58]

Sergio Arcacha Smith provides the clearest example of David Ferrie's links to militant Cuban exiles, the anti-Castro zealots who were employed by both the CIA and the Mafia. Smith's close association with Ferrie, Carlos Marcello's private investigator and pilot, traced back to the Bay of Pigs, when Smith and Ferrie were both engaged in the activities of the FRD. In the summer of 1961, New Orleans FRD director Sergio Arcacha Smith wrote to Captain Eddie Rickenbacker, Chairman of the Board of Eastern Airlines to request a leave of absence for Eastern pilot David Ferrie. Smith told Rickenbacker in his letter of July 18, 1961:

> When the FRD was originally organized, under the demands of the U.S. Government, the FRD was to "front" for the effort of the CIA to reinstate democratic government in Cuba. The effort of April

17 failed, as you know thereafter, the morale of the Cubans in exile and the Underground within Cuba fell to zero. Then along came Captain Ferrie. He strongly prodded our whole organization until it was revitalized. Thereafter, dissident elements were removed. Fund collecting began. The Underground was reorganized and the reharassment of Castro has begun.

The reinvigorating of our program was the result of the prodding of Captain Ferrie, and his associates, here in New Orleans. Through him we've been able to get the best advice in affairs political, economic and military. In addition Captain Ferrie has been assisting in obtaining needed equipment...

Since events are approaching a climax we thoroughly need his advice on a day-to-day basis . . . we are requesting that Captain Ferrie be given either a 60 or 90 day leave with pay so that the work at hand can be completed. At this time he holds in his hands so many threads which pertain to the security of the Caribbean area that no reasonable substitution can be made.[59]

A New Orleans police report, dated August 30, 1961, containing an account of the arrest of Smith's top deputy, Layton Martens, also sets forth the Ferrie-Smith association: "Layton Martens is second in command to one Arcacha Smith . . . who is conducting a counter revolution movement in New Orleans, against Fidel Castro of Cuba. Also connected with this organization is one Captain David Ferrie . . ."[60]

The close relationship between Smith and Ferrie continued over the years, with Ferrie maintaining contact with the Cuban exile leader right up until the time of his death. Smith firmly denied that Ferrie had any connection to the JFK assassination, and denounced Jim Garrison's probe as "a witch hunt." Smith has stated he believes Oswald carried out the assassination alone, due to his alleged pro-Castro leanings.

1. Meagher, *Accessories After The Fact*, p. 236.
2. Ibid.
3. Ibid.
4. *Senate Intelligence Committee Report on the Kennedy Assassination*, pp. 57-58.
5. Ibid., p. 59.
6. Sorensen, *Kennedy*, p. 341.
7. Ibid., p. 339.
8. Richard N. Goodwin, *The American Condition* (New York: Doubleday and Company, Inc., 1974; Bantam Edition, 1975), p. 267.
9. *Senate Intelligence Committee Report on Foreign Assassinations*, p. 71.
10. Ibid.
11. Lyndon B. Johnson, *The Vantage Point* (New York: Holt, Rhinehart and Winston, 1971), p. 26.
12. Frank Mankiewicz and Kirby Jones, *With Fidel* (New York: Ballantine Books Edition, 1975), p. 147.
13. *Senate Intelligence Committee Report on Foreign Assassinations*, p. 173.
14. Ibid.
15. Ibid.
16. Ibid., p. 11.
17. Mankiewicz and Jones, *With Fidel*, p. 145.
18. Ibid., pp. 141-142.
19. *Senate Intelligence Committee Report on Foreign Assassinations*, pp. 173-174.
20. Mankiewicz and Jones, *With Fidel*, pp. 145-146.
33. Warren Commission Volume 14, pp. 345-354.
34. Ibid.
35. Warren Commission Volume 14, pp. 345-354.
36. Ibid.
37. Ibid.

38. Warren Commission Exhibit 2980; Warren Commission Volume 26, pp. 467-470.
39. Ibid.
40. Warren Commission records, Stuckey Exhibit No. 3.
41. Ibid.
42. Hunt, *Give Us This Day*, pp. 182-185; Wise and Ross, *The Invisible Government*, pp. 20, 27.
43. Warren Commission Volume 10, pp. 33-34, 82-83.
44. Charles Bringuier, *Red Friday* (Chicago: Charles Hallberg and Company, 1969), p. 25.
45. Warren Commission Volume 4, p. 437; Warren Commission Volume 17, pp. 758-762.
46. Bringuier, *Red Friday*, Introduction.
47. Ibid., p. 3.
48. Ibid., pp. 15-19.
49. *New Orleans Times-Picayune*, January 5, 1968.
50. *Senate Intelligence Committee Report on the Kennedy Assassination*, pp. 60-61.
51. Ibid.
52. Ibid.
53. Ibid., p. 63.
54. Hunt, *Give Us This Day*, pp. 44-54, 182-185.
55. Warren Commission Document 87.
56. Wise and Ross, *The Invisible Government*, pp. 20, 27; Hunt, *Give Us This Day*, pp. 44-56, 182-185.
57. Weisberg, *Oswald In New Orleans*, p. 338.
58. Ibid.
59. July 18, 1961 letter of Sergio Arcacha Smith to Captain Eddie V. Rickenbacker.
60. New Orleans Police Department Arrest Report, August 30, 1961, Item No. H-13903-61.

CHAPTER TWELVE

Links to Watergate

In the beginning, Watergate, the greatest criminal conspiracy in the recent history of the United States, was indirectly blamed on Fidel Castro.

The initially apprehended conspirators — most notably Bay of Pigs field coordinator Bernard Barker — claimed that their crime was the result of Fidel Castro and the Cuban government. Messrs. Barker, Sturgis, Martinez, and Gonzales claimed that their crime was actually only a "national security" operation that had been set in motion because money from Castro — Communist money — was secretly financing the Democratic Party.

At the conclusion of the earliest Watergate trial, before any "higher-ups" had been exposed, a *New York Times* editorial referred to some of the apparent assumptions upon which the Watergate burglary conspiracy had been based:

> Chief Judge John Sirica spoke for a host of incredulous observers at the Watergate trial when he told defendant Bernard Barker that he simply did not believe his story that $144,000 had arrived in unmarked envelopes from sources unknown . . . Guided only by hallucinations akin to the anti-Castro fanaticism that motivated the hirelings in the Watergate plot, an individual or group could feel free to take up arms or utilize any other repressive measures their paranoid supporters dictated. Such a political law of the jungle might readily lead from protective espionage to defensive assassination.[1]

It will be shown that in the four years since those words were written, a surprisingly large and surprisingly overlooked number of questions have been raised regarding the possible connection of various Watergate events and participants to circumstances surrounding assassination-plotting, and, in particular, the JFK assassination.

The alleged Kennedy assassination conspiracy had the central purpose of killing Kennedy physically. The Watergate "plumbers" conspiracies had as one of their central purposes killing a Kennedy politically. The JFK plot (if it was a plot) was aimed at criminally controlling who would be President — by removing John Kennedy from the White House. The Nixon intrigues in large part were also aimed at criminally controlling who would be President — by removing Edward Kennedy (and subsequently Edmund Muskie) from serious contention as Richard Nixon's 1972 opponent. That Ted Kennedy, and Kennedy associates such as Larry O'Brien, were in fact viewed by the Nixon circle as the prime targets for illegal surveillance, smear, and sabotage, is obvious.

As many of the Warren Commission's critics see

it, the alleged Kennedy assassination conspiracy was quite a bit more than met the eye:

— Oswald could not have acted alone or without guidance; there must be higher-ups involved;

— There were mysterious footprints all around, leading to an odd assortment of Cubans as well as shadowy ex-FBI and ex-CIA characters;

— With intrigue in Texas and Mexico City figuring prominently somewhere within;

— Beyond that, an awesome federal cover-up, with the CIA being pressured to conceal the plot's true dimensions and the FBI withholding evidence of a wider conspiracy (with J. Edgar Hoover even apparently authorizing the destruction of a secret letter by Oswald himself).

And then Watergate, the proven conspiracy:

— The apprehended burglars could not have acted alone or without guidance, there must be higher-ups involved;

— There were mysterious footprints all around, leading to another odd assortment of Cubans as well as shadowy ex-FBI and ex-CIA characters;

— With some Texans' laundering of the break-in funds through Mexico City figuring prominently somewhere within;

— Beyond that, an awesome federal cover-up, with the CIA being pressured to conceal the plot's true dimensions and the FBI withholding evidence of a wider conspiracy (with L. Patrick Gray even destroying secret files taken from the vault of E. Howard Hunt himself).

"The only thing about Watergate that ever surprised me," a veteran Senate investigator recently remarked, "was that we never had an honest-to-God murder before it was over with." With the deadly nature and background of the various Watergate conspirators becoming all too clear over the past four years, such thoughts are almost commonplace.

Before going on to the wide range of specific information that connects some of these same mysterious men to events surrounding the assassination of President Kennedy — information that some researchers believe indicates that the alleged cover-ups in the two cases may in some ways be one and the same — it might be pertinent to recall other aspects of the Watergate mystery. One need only remember some of the darker reports emanating from the scandal to fully appreciate the dangerous forces at work therein:

— Early concern by federal prosecutors that Alfred Baldwin, the man who served as the "lookout" during the Watergate break-in (and who escaped, but later turned himself in) might be "endangered" by associates of the Cuban exile burglars;

— The roughing-up of Martha Mitchell by her husband's security aides a day or two after the capture of the burglary team, an assault that resulted in a slashed hand and battered shoulder on the wife of Richard Nixon's former Attorney General, as well as drug induced hysteria, resulting from a forced injection of a strong "knockout" drug;

— Conspirator G. Gordon Liddy's offer to fellow conspirators Robert Mardian and Fred LaRue (John Mitchell's two top aides) to "have himself [shot to death] on any street corner" if they didn't trust his ability to remain silent, an offer made three nights after the capture of the burglary team;

— Fears voiced by burglar Frank Fiorini Sturgis (to his friend Andrew St. George) that he might be murdered in his D.C. jail cell;

— The disclosure (by conspirator Jeb Magruder) that G. Gordon Liddy had once mistakenly believed that he had been instructed to carry out the murder of columnist Jack Anderson;

— The disclosure by Magruder that Liddy had also once threatened to "break every bone" in his (Magruder's) body;

— The disclosure by Bob Woodward that E. Howard Hunt was once ordered to either drug and/or murder columnist Jack Anderson, orders that allegedly originated with Nixon counsel Charles Colson;

— Recurring speculation that the jet crash death of Mrs. E. Howard Hunt (the day after the existence of the secret Plumbers Unit was confirmed, and two weeks after she had delivered her husband's threatening memo to Nixon campaign officials) was the result of a murder/sabotage plot;

— James McCord's Senate testimony that secret Nixon investigator John Caulfield delivered what McCord believed was a threat on his life, shortly before McCord decided to break open Watergate by turning state's evidence;

— A Nixon campaign secretary's fear of being physically harmed or possibly murdered as a result of her knowledge of Nixon campaign finances;

— Reports by *Time* magazine and others that FBI Director L. Patrick Gray had considered committing suicide as his own involvement in covering up for President Nixon began to be exposed;

— The assignment of round-the-clock U. S. Marshal protection for conspirator John Dean, following his decision to disclose the criminal involvement of Richard Nixon and his closest aides;

— The subsequent disclosure that John Mitchell had also once pondered committing suicide as his role as an architect of the Watergate burglary became known;

— The Woodward and Bernstein disclosure that President Nixon himself had spoken of suicide ("I don't have a pistol") during a conversation with General Haig; that White House physicians were ordered to withhold any potentially lethal sedatives or medicines from Nixon; and that other aides and associates of Nixon had feared that their leader would either "blow his brains out" or take a fatal overdose.

Frank Fiorini Sturgis

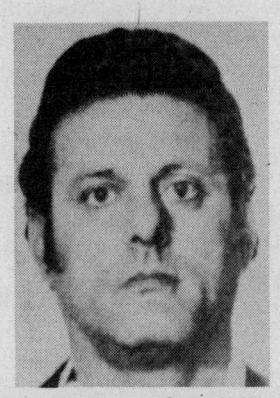

Frank Sturgis, one of the five Watergate burglars arrested inside the Democratic National Committee offices on June 17, 1972, had been recruited for the burglary squad by Bernard Barker, the man who had served as CIA official E. Howard Hunt's top deputy during the Bay of Pigs.

Sturgis had long been a key organizer of anti-Castro Cuban exile operations in Miami, and was, according to extremely reliable reports, heavily involved with the Mafia, particularly the Santos Trafficante-Meyer Lansky syndicate in Florida. In a confidential FBI memorandum that L. Patrick Gray prepared two days after the Watergate arrests, on June 19, 1972, Sturgis' activities were set forth in some detail. Gray has testified that he originally intended to send the memo to H. R. Haldeman on June 19th, but had decided against doing so.[2] It stated in part:

> Frank Anthony Fiorini, also known as Fred Frank Fiorini, Attila F. Sturgis, Anthony Sturgis and Edward Joseph Hamilton, was arrested on July 30, 1958 for illegal possession of arms in Florida. Prosecution was declined concerning the matter. Sources in the Miami area report he is a "soldier of fortune" and allegedly was a gunrunner to Cuba prior to the Castro regime. Sources in Miami say he is now associated with organized crime activities, the details of which are not available.[3]

As early as 1962, Sturgis had been identified as an associate of various Mafia leaders who had run gambling operations on Cuba. In his 1962 book on Cuba, *Counter-Revolutionary Agent*, Hans Tanner described Frank Sturgis and his Cuban exile group, "The International Anti-Communist Brigade" as being "financed by dispossessed hotel and gambling owners who operated under Batista."[4]

Interestingly, Sturgis has confirmed that he served as Fidel Castro's chief gambling inspector in 1959, during the period before Castro turned openly Communist. Sturgis and many other Cuban associates had originally supported the Castro revolution, prior to Castro's turn to Marxism. In an interview in August, 1974, Sturgis confirmed that he had served as Cuba's "Superintendent of Games of Chance" in Havana during 1959.[5] As some researchers have pointed out, this position would quite likely have placed Sturgis in some contact with Lewis McWillie, Jack Ruby's close friend who managed the large Tropicana Casino. Ruby had visited McWillie in Havana and had discussed becoming involved in gambling operations there himself.

Though not much press attention has been focused on it, Frank Sturgis had been investigated by the FBI shortly after the Kennedy assassination, due to reports that he had been in contact with Lee Harvey Oswald.

Warren Commission Document 59 contains an FBI report prepared several days after the President's murder. The FBI had investigated an article in the November 26, 1963 *Sun Sentinel* in Florida, which had stated that Sturgis had a good deal of significant information about the accused assassin,[6] and that he claimed Oswald had been in touch with Cuban intelligence officials in November of 1962, and had been in touch with Castro agents in Miami.[7] Upon being interviewed by the FBI on November 27, 1963, Sturgis claimed that the information attributed to him in the *Sun Sentinel* article was false and inaccurate.[8] However, according to the FBI report, Jim Buchanan, the reporter who wrote the article, was a close associate of Sturgis.

Warren Commission Document 395, titled "Lee Harvey Oswald — Internal Security" contains another FBI report concerning another article written by Buchanan. This second article, of December 4, 1963, stated that Sturgis claimed to have actually been in contact with Oswald at one time.[9] Oswald had tried to infiltrate the Sturgis "International Anti-Communist Brigade" in Miami, but Sturgis had rejected his membership application[10] because he had been unable to ascertain enough information about Oswald's background.[11]

Upon being interviewed by the FBI for a second time, Frank Fiorini Sturgis once again denied the article's accuracy, and claimed that he had been completely misquoted on all of the remarks about Oswald attributed to him.[12]

Weeks later, yet another FBI report was prepared on Sturgis, a report subsequently contained in Warren Commission Document 1020. This third report is much shorter than the first two, and centered upon allegations that Lee Oswald had once been in a brawl with a member of the Sturgis "International Anti-Communist Brigade."[13] When interviewed by the FBI for a third time, Sturgis denied any knowledge of the alleged incident.[14]

In a series of interviews in 1976, Frank Sturgis claimed that Fidel Castro and Che Guevara were behind the Kennedy assassination, and that Oswald had been a Castro agent of some kind.

While Sturgis's passionate hatred of Fidel Castro's government has increasingly tarnished his reputation (many reporters regard him as a mistrusted and unreliable source) his early role in disclosing the true scope of the Watergate conspiracy was significant. A detailed account of the secret hush money payments of higher-ups, as well as records of the burglars' other spying activities written by Sturgis and Andrew St. George, became a central part of *New York Times* reporter Seymour Hersh's important Watergate disclosures of January 1973. The Sturgis information was disclosed two months before James McCord's decision to talk, at a time when Woodward and Bernstein were, in their own words, "in danger of running out of steam."

Interestingly, Frank Sturgis has provided a highly intriguing and almost universally overlooked piece of information regarding what the burglars were looking for inside the Watergate offices of Democratic Chairman Larry O'Brien, as well as why the break-in was actually ordered. Sturgis first disclosed the information to his friend Andrew St. George, a well-known writer, during his early imprisonment in October, 1972.[15] Sturgis asked St. George not to publish the information until Sturgis got out of jail, and it was not until August of 1974 that St. George finally did so in an article for *True* magazine.[16] During his jail cell interview with St. George, Sturgis told him, "I will never leave this jail alive if what we discussed about Watergate does not remain a secret between us. If you attempt to publish what I've told you, I am a dead man."[17] Sturgis stated that the Watergate burglary team had been instructed to look for "any dirt" on prominent Democrats which might be contained in the files of Larry O'Brien's offices, as well as "anything on Howard Hughes."[18]

At that point, Sturgis told of something else the burglary team was instructed to find: "a thick secret memorandum from the Castro government," which consisted of two main parts.[19] First, a "long, detailed listing" of CIA and DIA covert actions against Cuba, and secondly, a "long" section which "said that the Castro government suspected the CIA did not tell the whole truth about these operations even to American political leaders; therefore, the Cubans were providing an itemized list of all such 'abuses.' The complaints were especially bitter about various attempts made to assassinate the Castro brothers."[20]

The Senate Watergate Committee was ending its investigation at the time the St. George article appeared, and thus, no investigation of Sturgis' account was ever made. And, as noted earlier, the information has received little if any press attention since.

E. Howard Hunt

E. Howard Hunt, the mysterious mastermind of much of the Watergate conspiracy, had of course earlier served as the CIA coordinator of the Bay of Pigs invasion. It was Hunt's blackmail of the Nixon inner circle that had led to the President's direct involvement in approving secret hush money pay-offs for the Watergate burglars.

The past activities of E. Howard Hunt were also

the key topic of conversation in the mysterious June 23, 1972 White House tape — the Nixon/Haldeman tape that the President had been forced to disclose in August of 1974, which led to his resignation days later. Nixon's strange references to Hunt are still a prime source of mystery and speculation to many observers. Among other things on the highly incriminating tape, Nixon said:

> . . . this Hunt, that will uncover a lot of things. You open that scab there's a hell of a lot of things . . . This involves these Cubans, Hunt and a lot of hanky-panky . . .
>
> . . . just say [unintelligible] very bad to have this fellow Hunt, ah he knows too damned much, if he was involved — you happen to know that? If it gets out that this is all involved, the Cuba thing, it would be a fiasco. It would make the CIA look bad, it's going to make Hunt look bad, and it is likely to blow the whole Bay of Pigs thing which we think would be very unfortunate —both for the CIA and for the country...[21]

In 1974, Tad Szulc, the highly-respected former *New York Times* correspondent, disclosed some information that would indicate that E. Howard Hunt may have been involved in the CIA's mysterious monitoring of Oswald's activities during his mysterious trip to Mexico City in September, 1963. Szulc, who was responsible for several of the early Watergate disclosures, wrote that Hunt had served as a top official (perhaps acting Station Chief) of the CIA station in Mexico City during Oswald's visit in September of 1963.[22]

The Warren Commission established that the CIA had secretly overheard Oswald on wiretaps during his phone conversations with the Cuban and Soviet Embassies there.[23] On November 26, 1976, the *Washington Post* disclosed that tape recordings of these secret wiretapped Oswald calls had been destroyed by the CIA sometime before the assassination.[24] The CIA had also taken photographs of a man they incorrectly identified as Oswald walking in or out of these same Embassies.[25]

In any event, if Szulc's account is correct (it has thus far never been confirmed) there would seem to be a strong possibility that Hunt would have had knowledge of the Oswald surveillance and would have been privy to the CIA's other information on him.

While Hunt has admitted working at the Mexico City CIA station on at least two occasions, including during the 1960 Bay of Pigs planning, he has denied being there at any time in 1963.

Bernard Barker

Bernard Barker, the leader of the Watergate burglary team, had of course earlier served as E. Howard Hunt's top deputy during the Bay of Pigs. Barker was the CIA's chief liaison to the various Cuban exile groups recruited for the disasterous invasion, and was "paymaster" for all exile work for the Agency.

Interestingly, Barker was another Watergate burglar who had once been associated with the Mafia. Like Frank Sturgis, the reported Barker involvement with the mob had centered around the Miami area controlled by syndicate bosses Santos Trafficante and Meyer Lansky. Confirmation of Barker's past Mafia "relationship" had come from CIA Director Richard Helms himself. In executive session testimony before the Senate Foreign Relations Committee on February 7, 1973, Helms was questioned by Chairman William Fulbright about the work which several of the Watergate conspirators had done for the CIA at one time or another. Under questioning by Senator Fulbright, Helms disclosed that Bernard Barker had been "fired" by the CIA "some time in the middle" of the 1960s because "we found out he was involved in certain gambling and criminal elements."[26] Barker apparently provided at least one CIA-Mafia connection which the Agency didn't wish to continue. Helms' testimony remained classified for over a year, and was finally released by the Committee on March 5, 1974.[27]

The key CIA-coordinated exile group, the "Cuban Revolutionary Council," had been personally coordinated by Hunt and Barker. Several Cuban exiles whose names have surfaced in regard to the Kennedy assassination were at one time or another involved with the "Council." Interestingly, Lee Harvey Oswald had once given the address of a building used by the New Orleans branch of the "Cuban Revolutionary Council" as his own address. Oswald had stamped this Camp Street address on his own pro-Castro leaflets, an action which the Warren Commission admitted couldn't be explained.

Barker has also been linked to a man who was once arrested for Cuban gunrunning with an associate of Jack Ruby. The Barker associate is Carlos Prio Socarras, a wealthy financier of Cuban exile activities in Miami. Both Barker and Frank Sturgis have admitted being close to Socarras, and Socarras himself has admitted coordinating Cuban exile demonstrators at the 1972 political conventions — under the initial guidance of his friends, Barker and Sturgis.[28]

Carlos Prio Socarras had once been arrested in a gunrunning conspiracy with Robert McKeown, the man whom the Warren Commission established had discussed various Cuban exile operations with Jack Ruby (See reference to Robert McKeown in the chapter on "The Mafia Connection"). McKeown had discussed "running jeeps to Cuba" with Ruby, among other smuggling schemes.

An April 17, 1964 FBI letter, sent from J. Edgar Hoover to Warren Commission General Counsel J. Lee Rankin, mentioned Socarras's gunrunning involvements:

> ". . . Carlos Prio Socarras and a number of others including McKeown, was involved in a conspiracy to ship arms, munitions, and other war materials to Fidel Castro to assist him in his efforts to overthrow the Batista regime in Cuba.[29]

Thus, a Cuban gunrunner associated with Jack Ruby has also been arrested for gunrunning with Socarras, a close friend of two of the Watergate burglars, Bernard Barker and Frank Sturgis.

Manuel Artime

Manuel Artime, the well-known Bay of Pigs exile leader, has been E. Howard Hunt's closest friend for over a decade. Artime had been the organizer of the early "Cuban Defense Fund" which had been used to funnel secret hush money payments to the Watergate burglars, before the Nixon inner circle took over the personal handling of the pay-offs. Artime's role had been detailed by the Watergate Special Prosecutors when his name appeared on a "flow chart" of the

hush money payments, introduced as evidence at the 1974 Watergate cover-up trial of Haldeman, Mitchell, Ehrlichman, and Mardian.

J. Anthony Lukas, the Pulitzer Prize winning former *New York Times* reporter, has written of Artime's involvement in the Watergate conspiracy:

After his wife's death, Hunt had funneled $21,000 to Manuel Artime, his old friend from the Bay of Pigs days. Artime had earlier formed an informal committee to aid the Miami defendants; as a leader of the Cuban exile community and the godfather of Hunt's youngest son, he was an ideal man to assume this role. When Artime came to Washington in December [1972], Hunt gave him $12,000 in a manila envelope for distribution to Barker and his men. Later Hunt arranged to have three envelopes containing $3000 each left in Artime's mailbox. In February Fred LaRue passed $12,000 more to Artime.[30]

The Senate Intelligence Committee established that Manuel Artime had earlier served as the key assassination conspirator in a CIA plot to assassinate Fidel Castro. Though the Senate Committee used the CIA code name "B-1" in referring to Artime (and also referred to him as "the leader of an anti-Castro group") his identity was subsequently confirmed by Senate Intelligence Committee sources as well as the *Washington Post*.

The Senate Committee disclosed that Artime had

been involved with another CIA assassin, code named AM/LASH, in plotting the assassination of Fidel Castro in 1963 and 1964.[31] AM/LASH has since been identified as former Cuban official Rolando Cubela by Senate Committee members.

The Committee disclosed that "the CIA put AM/LASH [Cubela] in contact with B-1 [Artime] to set up another assassination plan against Castro."[32] An internal CIA report noted that "B-1 needed a man inside [Havana] and AM/LASH wanted a silenced weapon, which CIA was unwilling to furnish him directly. By putting the two together, B-1 might get its man inside Cuba and AM/LASH might get his silenced weapon — from B-1."[33] A subsequent CIA document cited by the Senate Committee stated that "B-1 is to provide AM/LASH with a silencer for the FAL [rifle]; if this is impossible, B-1 is to cache in a designated location a rifle with a scope and silencer . . ."[34]

Later, Manuel Artime and Rolando Cubela did in fact exchange various assassination weapons. A CIA cable indicated that Cubela [AM/LASH] would receive "one pistol with silencer and one FAL rifle with silencer from B-1's [Artime's] secretary."[35] Another CIA cable indicated that "B-1 had three packages of special items made up by his technical people and delivered to AM/LASH."[36]

The implications of the involvement of E. Howard Hunt's closest associate in this assassination conspiring are serious. It is known that the Senate Intelligence Committee is continuing an inquiry into Manuel Artime's involvement in the AM/LASH activities. In June of 1976, the Senate Intelligence Committee concluded:

> In hindsight, the AM/LASH operation seems very relevant to the investigation of President Kennedy's assassination. It is difficult to understand why those aware of the operation did not think it relevant,

and did not inform those investigating President Kennedy's assassination of possible connections between that operation and the assassination.[37]

... information on the AM/LASH operation, an operation which those who investigated the assassination of President Kennedy now believe would have been relevant to their inquiries, was not supplied to either the Warren Commission or the FBI. Even the CIA personnel responsible for investigating the assassination were not informed of the operation.[38]

Investigators are pursuing at least two lines of thinking about a possible connection between the plots to assassinate Castro, and the assassination of President Kennedy. First, that Fidel Castro may have learned of the CIA-Mafia-Cuban exile plots against him, and then, blaming them on Kennedy, decided to retaliate by killing the American President. Or secondly, that some of the same mysterious Mafia leaders, militant Cuban exiles, or CIA contacts involved in the plots against Castro, may have subsequently decided to assassinate President Kennedy himself, whom they hated almost as much as Fidel Castro.

Whether E. Howard Hunt was aware of his close friend and "blood brother's" involvement as "B-1" in this assassination plot against Castro is not presently known. However, based upon their close relationship and long mutual involvement in other CIA operations it appears quite likely.

Hunt himself has written that during the Bay of Pigs planning he had urged his CIA superiors, Tracy Barnes and Richard Bissell, to "Assassinate Castro before or coincident with the invasion . . ."[39] Additionally, it seems probable that Hunt would have been aware of the CIA's assassination plots since the first ones were in fact timed to coincide with the Bay of Pigs — for which he himself had served as political coordinator.

Hunt's fellow Watergate conspirator, Bernard Barker, is another close associate of Manuel Artime. Barker recalled, in an NBC interview in April, 1974, that "Mr. Hunt personally always had the theory that the physical elimination of Fidel Castro was the proper way for the liberation of Cuba."

Frank Sturgis has similarly recalled: "Hunt was different: he was a professional. He'd been a clandestine services officer all his life. That's another thing everyone is snickering about — how Howard tried to assassinate Castro, and Castro is still around bigger than ever. Alright, but hey, listen: Howard was in charge of a couple of other CIA operations that involved 'disposal' and I can tell you, some of them worked."[40]

The Senate Watergate Committee investigation disclosed that President Nixon had personal knowledge of Manuel Artime's early hush money payments to the Watergate burglars — payments passed to Artime from E. Howard Hunt — and directly instructed John Dean to maintain the "cover" of the Manuel Artime "Cuban Defense Fund." The crucial cover-up meeting between Nixon and John Dean, which was taped on the morning of March 21, 1973, included the following discussion:

> *Dean:* All right, so arrangements were made through Mitchell, uh, initiating it, in discussions that — I was present — that these guys [the Watergate burglars] had to be taken care of ... Uh, [Nixon lawyer] Kalmback raised some cash.
>
> *Nixon:* They put that under the cover of a Cuban Committee or [unintelligible]
>
> *Dean:* Yeah, they had a Cuban Committee and they had — some of it was given to

Hunt's lawyer [William Bittman] who in turn passed it out. This, you know, when Hunt's wife was flying to Chicago with the ten thousand, she was actually, I understand after the fact now, was going to pass that money to, uh, one of the Cubans — to meet him in Chicago and pass it to somebody there.

Nixon: [Unintelligible]. Maybe — Well, whether it's maybe too late to do anything about it, but I would certainly keep that, [laughs] that cover for whatever it's worth.[41]

During this same climactic discussion Nixon spoke of "getting" another million dollars in cash for the Watergate burglars, saying "it's not easy," but "you could get a million dollars. And you could get it in cash. I, I know where it could be gotten."[42] Nixon had then asked Dean "would you put that through the Cuban Committee?"[43] Nixon further noted "that would give a little bit of a cover" for the secret payoffs.[44] Later during the conversation, Nixon had given his now famous orders to go ahead and continue paying off E. Howard Hunt and the burglars, saying of the secret cash, "Well for Christ's sake, get it."[45]

While little attention has been focused on him, Manuel Artime was a continuing presence throughout the Watergate scandal, with repeated contact with Hunt and the other conspirators on many occasions. In addition to setting up the fraudulent "Cuban Defense Fund," Artime was involved in other ways as well. Artime had met with Hunt and Barker during Hunt's April 1971 trip to Miami during which Hunt met with a couple of the men who later served as Watergate burglars.[46] Artime was later called before the original Watergate grand jury on September 8, 1972 to testify about his frequent contact with Hunt and Barker.[47]

Artime later conferred with Hunt during the course

of the first Watergate burglary trial, on January 8, 1973.[48] Hunt has stated that on that day he and Artime discussed Hunt's decision to plead guilty, and that Artime also then met with Barker and the Cuban exile burglars — who were deciding whether to plead guilty also.[49] Later, during that same month of January 1973, Artime was invited by the Nixon Administration to attend the second inauguration of President Nixon.[50]

Shortly before their sentencing in March of 1973, Artime had again flown to Washington to confer with Hunt and the Cuban exile defendants.[51]

Several other militant Cuban exiles that Hunt and Barker recruited for such secret tasks as the Ellsberg break-in, the "casing" of the Watergate building, as well as the physical attack on Daniel Ellsberg and other anti-war protestors on the steps of the Capitol on May 2, 1972 [52] have received little attention from the press over the years. Among these other little known Watergate participants were Felipe DeDiego, Pablo Fernandez, Reinaldo Pico, Humberto Lopez, and Angel Ferrer.[53]

John Caulfield

John Caulfield served as a secret White House investigator for President Nixon, H. R. Haldeman, John Ehrlichman, and John Dean. Caulfield had previously served as a member of Vice President

Richard Nixon's Secret Service detail in the 1950s.

Caulfield, and his partner, Anthony "Tony" Ulasewicz, became key witnesses before the Ervin Watergate Committee, and had astonished the nationwide viewing audience during their televised testimony about the "dirty projects" they had undertaken for the Nixon inner circle.

Caulfield and Ulasewicz engaged in extensive surveillance and smear operations against leading Democratic Senators and Congressmen during their work for the Nixon men, and focused their greatest attention on Senator Edward M. Kennedy.[54] As the Senate Watergate Committee hearings established, in 1971 Caulfield had been assigned to set up round-the-clock surveillance of Sen. Kennedy, complete with a tailing of all the Senator's movements.[55]

Another Caulfield assignment involved sending Ulasewicz to the island of Chappaquiddick, hours after Kennedy's car plunged off the Dyke Bridge there. Ulasewicz began an immediate on-the-scene probe of the accident for the White House. Still later, according to the Ervin Committee, Caulfield and Ulasewicz had planned an extensive secret program to sexually "entrap" the various women who had been present at the Kennedy yachting party at Chappaquiddick.[56]

The Senate Committee reported that Caulfield believed the young women could be lured into having relationships with undercover agents working for the Nixon circle — and thus be "blackmailed" into disclosing what they "really knew" about Chappaquiddick.[57] This particular Caulfield plan progressed to the point where Ulasewicz actually rented a New York apartment with which to "lure" the young women.[58]

The staff of the Senate Watergate Committee withheld part of this Caulfield-Ulasewicz plot, when it was decided that some details were too crude to be included in the Senate Committee's Final Report.

Caulfield had also collected extensive amounts of alleged "dirt" on various "enemies" of the Nixon Administration. The Ervin Committee published a fifty-item list of various Caulfield/Ulasewicz "investigations" for the Nixon circle, the vulgarity of which had astonished even some hardnosed Senate investigators.[59]

An obscure FBI memorandum of May 28, 1964, titled "Lee Harvey Oswald, Internal Security — R— Cuba," discloses that "Detective John Caulfield, Bureau of Special Services, New York City Police Department," had investigated various anti-Castro Cuban exiles in New York, during the course of the Warren Commission investigation.[60] Caulfield had provided information on the DRE, (the Cuban Student Directorate) which was an anti-Castro group with which Oswald had allegedly had some contact.[61]

Caulfield reported on one incident in which anti-Castro militant exiles had "demonstrated against recent United States Government orders imposed upon Cuban exiles carrying out armed attacks against Cuba."[62] Caulfield continued his investigation activities in December, 1963, and reported no further militant actions in the New York area during that period.[63]

The Warren Commission was then concerned with the activities of the DRE and its members due to continuing allegations that Oswald had been associated with DRE members in New Orleans and Miami. However, no documented connection of Oswald to the group was ever established.

Caulfield, who is reportedly now writing a book to cash in on his Watergate notoriety, has not been available for comment on his investigations for the Warren Commission during that period.

Charles W. Colson

Charles Colson, President Nixon's Special Counsel and widely hated hatchetman from 1969 to 1973, was the man who originally selected E. Howard Hunt to set up the secret White House Plumbers. Colson, with the single exception of H. R. Haldeman, seems to have been involved in more of the horrors of the Nixon rogues gallery than any other aide.

During his years with Nixon, Colson attained a well-deserved reputation as one of the meanest, most slippery, and dangerous men ever to serve in American government. Nixon himself had once remarked, "Colson would do anything."

Colson had once been involved with one of Jim Garrison's former "suspects" in a mysterious plan to erase the Nixon Watergate tapes, in March of 1974.[64] This strange information first came to the surface in August of 1974, when Jack Anderson[65] disclosed that Colson had met with New Orleans electronics specialist Gordon Novel in March, 1974 and had begun developing plans for the magnetic erasure of various Nixon tapes.[66] Novel, who had received national attention in 1967 as District Attorney Garrison's "missing witness," when he was under investigation for his reported contacts with both David Ferrie and Clay Shaw. Novel and Colson discussed the use of an experimental "de-gaussing" machine which could project a magnetic beam into the Nixon tapes and erase them without having to handle them in any way.[67] Anderson reported that Colson had described some of the tapes as containing conversations that "could cause the President's grief," and that Novel recalled that Colson had also spoken of using the erasing machine to obliterate some secret recordings maintained by the CIA as well.[68]

Following his discussion with Colson in March 1974, Gordon Novel flew to Texas to see an associate, and drew up a blueprint for the erasing plan, which he cryptically referred to as "the El Paso matter" when he later sent the blueprint to Colson, by hand courier, in Washington.[69]

Colson claimed that the whole erasing idea was just a "joke," and that he had discussed the plan only for "a little bit of comic relief."[70]

In another episode involving the Watergate tapes and the assassination, Colson and Nixon wanted Attorney General Elliott Richardson to use a specific New York attorney as a "neutral arbiter" to review and "edit" certain "national security" segments of the President's taped conversations. According to Richardson, the man personally selected by Colson was J. Lee Rankin — who'd run the Warren Commission investigation when he was its controversial General Counsel.[71]

Former *New York Times* reporter J. Anthony Lukas has said Special Prosecutor Archibald Cox considered the suggestion for a time, but the proposal was ultimately rejected.[72] In the intervening years, the Rankin episode has received scant attention.

Charles Colson was also involved in a still-mysterious plan to break into the Milwaukee apartment of Arthur Bremer — a few hours after Bremer shot Governor George Wallace of Alabama.[73] E. Howard Hunt testified that Colson had ordered him to fly to Milwaukee and break into Bremer's apartment, but that Colson subsequently cancelled the orders following Hunt's objections.[74]

Colson, who denied Hunt's account, has stated that he merely discussed Bremer's psychological make-up during this conversation with Hunt.[75] On January 5,

1976, CBS News correspondent Dan Rather disclosed a previously classified Secret Service report which stated that Bremer's apartment had subsequently been sealed off by the FBI, under the personal orders of President Nixon — orders that had been relayed through Colson,[76] who refuses to comment on the matter.[77]

Washington Post reporters Woodward and Bernstein have written that Colson and his law partner, David Shapiro, seemed to hint that they would "help out" the two reporters with other articles if they would "kill" their original plans to publish the story of the Bremer break-in plans. According to the two reporters, Woodward told Colson and Shapiro that he had uncovered the mysterious Bremer plan, during an interview with them on June 19, 1973.[78] Colson and Shapiro then indicated that they might be able to provide Woodward with copies of two other Watergate documents — an offer that Woodward thought may have been contingent upon not publishing the Bremer disclosure.[79] Woodward and Bernstein described the incident in *All The President's Men*.

Colson and Hunt have also been linked to a reported conspiracy to murder columnist Jack Anderson. The proposed murder was to have taken place a few weeks before the Watergate break-in.

On September 21, 1975, Bob Woodward disclosed that E. Howard Hunt had "told associates after the Watergate break-in that he was ordered in December, 1971 or January, 1972, to assassinate syndicated columnist Jack Anderson."[80] Woodward reported that the murder contract on Anderson had been assigned to Hunt by a "senior official in the Nixon White House," and that the killing was "cancelled at the last minute but only after a plan had been devised to make Anderson's death appear accidental."[81]

Anderson — who several years earlier had disclosed the CIA-Mafia assassination conspirators' uses of poison — was to have been killed that way himself. According to the *Post* account, Hunt's plan ". . . involved the use of a poison to be obtained from a former CIA physician . . . who added that the poison was a variety that would leave no trace during a routine medical examination or autopsy."[82]

When the *Post* story was published, there was immediate speculation that the murder had been ordered by Charles W. Colson. Colson was Hunt's closest associate in the Nixon circle, and had served as Hunt's superior in most of his mysterious projects. Additionally, the widely hated Colson was known to have had a fanatically passionate dislike for Anderson.

The Senate Committee began an investigation of the alleged conspiracy, and on January 11, 1976, Hunt testified that he had in fact received orders from Colson to "get" Anderson, but his orders had only been to drug Anderson — not murder him.[83] In his own testimony of March 6, 1976, Charles Colson denied being involved in either a murder or drugging conspiracy against Anderson.[84] Nevertheless, Bob Woodward stated that the *Post* account of a murder plot was accurate. Hunt testified that he suspected Colson's mysterious orders had actually originated with President Nixon himself, and that he believed Colson had met with Nixon before ordering the plot.[85]

In his own Senate testimony, Colson seemed to back away from a flat denial under oath of the mysterious allegations. While stating that he "never heard anyone discuss any plan to kill Jack Anderson," he could not "discount the possibility of having said something in jest" along those lines.[86] Colson said Nixon had asked him "many times" to take action to "discredit" Jack Anderson, but that he was unsure of what actions were taken in response to these requests.[87]

The Senate Intelligence Committee established that the Colson-Hunt meeting regarding Anderson had probably taken place on March 14, 1972,[88] and that Hunt and G. Gordon Liddy had subsequently met with a former CIA physician at the Hay-Adams Hotel in Washington to discuss various non-traceable drugs.[89] The Senate Committee disclosed:

> According to Hunt, they discussed various means of administering a drug: painting the steering wheel of a car "for absorption through the palms of the hand," switching bottles in a medicine cabinet [by breaking into the target's home], or dropping a pill into a cocktail.
>
> Hunt said they considered the possibility that Anderson's car was chauffeured and, if he drove his own car, that he would be wearing gloves in the wintertime or would have moist palms in the summer, eliminating the possibility of absorption of a drug on the steering wheel.[90]

G. Gordon Liddy, the one Watergate conspirator who has never discussed what he did for the Nixon White House, of course refused to comment on his involvement in this plan.

In another still unexplained instance regarded as highly mysterious by the Ervin Watergate Committee, Colson used E. Howard Hunt to try and set up the "framing" of a past political enemy on charges of being involved in an assassination conspiracy. Hunt was ordered by Colson to personally forge several documents which would be used to implicate President John F. Kennedy in the 1963 assassination of President Diem of South Vietnam and Diem's brother-in-law Ngo Dinh Nhu, as a means of diminishing the political popularity of JFK's sole surviving brother, Edward Kennedy.[91]

In late 1975, the Senate Intelligence Committee reaffirmed that President Kennedy and his Administration hadn't been involved in the Diem killing in any way.[92] Contrary to Colson's ideas, its investigation of foreign assassinations concluded that there was "no available evidence to give any indication of direct or indirect involvement" of the Kennedy Administration in the South Vietnamese murder.[93]

They established that Hunt had fabricated two

secret State Department cables which he turned over to Colson,[94] who subsequently tried to "plant" the story with *Life* magazine reporter William Lambert.[95] Later, the forgery plot fell through when Lambert began to suspect that the cables were fraudulent. The Senate Watergate Committee concluded that Colson's law partner, Charles Morin, also had knowledge of the fabricated assassination evidence.[96]

Richard M. Nixon

Richard M. Nixon, who was in Dallas, Texas, on November 22, 1963, left the city a couple of hours before the Kennedy assassination occurred, and he later told the FBI that he hadn't been in Dallas at all that day. Later still, Richard Nixon also gave an inaccurate accounting of when he had actually arrived in Dallas.

Before going on to the brief facts surrounding this episode — in which the future President was apparently among the ranks of the very, very few who could not recall exactly what they were doing on the day Kennedy was shot — perhaps a word of caution is due. Although some of the more radical critics of the Warren Commission are now suggesting that Richard Nixon be added to the list of possible candidates or suspects who may have been behind the Kennedy murder, one must admit that such thinking is decidedly incautious. While there is no shortage of amply documented and amply disturbing "connections" or "links" between events surrounding the Kennedy assassination and events surrounding the Watergate conspiracy, some observers do of course note that "conspiracy theorists" have a long way to go before they attain the "legitimacy" which many so fervently seek.

If, during his Presidency, Nixon was able to give fruit to, harness, and direct what seem to have been the most frightening criminal forces in the history of American politics, under the full glare of attention focused upon any occupant of the Oval Office, some people shudder to think of what he and his equally shady associates were capable of during his embittered years of political exile during the early 1960s, when he was, in his own words, "in the shadows."

In any event, the facts surrounding Richard Nixon's presence in Dallas on November 22, 1963 are set forth herein as just that: facts. As with so many other Nixon actions, one is free to draw any conclusions one chooses.

Richard Nixon, the defeated Republican Presidential candidate of 1960, flew to Dallas on November 20, 1963. Nixon was then working as an attorney for the Pepsi-Cola Company, and was in Dallas to attend a Carbonated Bottler's convention. Nixon remained in Dallas for two days, leaving the city about three hours before President Kennedy was shot to death, on November 22nd.

In an interview with political reporter Jules Witcover in early 1967, Nixon told of his November, 1963, trip to Dallas, and his reaction to the Kennedy assassination:

> "I was in a taxicab when I got the news. I had been in Dallas attending a meeting. I flew back to New York the next morning. It must have happened just as my plane was landing. My cab was stopped for a light in Queens, and a guy ran over and said, 'Have

you got a radio? The President's been wounded.' I thought, 'Oh, my God, it must have been one of the nuts.'

"A half hour later I got to my apartment, and the doorman told me he was dead. I called J. Edgar Hoover and asked him, 'What happened? Was it one of the nuts?' Hoover said, 'No, it was a Communist.'"[97]

However, just three months after the assassination, Richard Nixon told the FBI another version of his trip to Dallas when he and his secretary, Rose Mary Woods, were contacted by the FBI during the Warren investigation, because Marina Oswald alleged that Lee had also thought about killing Nixon, sometime in the spring of 1963.[98] The Warren Commission was seeking to determine if Nixon had ever actually been in Texas during that period.

During his FBI interview on February 28, 1964, Nixon inaccurately stated that he'd left Dallas on November 20th — rather than on November 22nd. An FBI report contained in Warren Commission Exhibit 1973 states the following:

> On February 28, 1964, the Honorable Richard M. Nixon, former Vice President of the U.S., was contacted by Assistant Director in Charge of the New York Office, John F. Malone, and furnished the following information:
>
> Mr. Nixon advised that the only time he was in Dallas, Texas during 1963 was two days prior to the assassination of President John F. Kennedy.[99]

While his early 1964 account of when he had left Dallas was obviously inaccurate,[100] his interview with Jules Witcover in 1967 was equally erroneous con-

529

cerning his arrival in the city. Nixon told Witcover, "I had been in Dallas attending a meeting. I flew back to New York the next morning. It must have happened just as my plane was landing."[101] Thus, while Nixon admitted in 1967 he had in fact been in Dallas a couple of hours before the shooting, he incorrectly told Witcover that he had come to Dallas the day before the assassination, November 21st, rather than November 20th, the date he actually arrived in the city.

In his highly detailed account of what various public figures were doing on the day of JFK's assassination, William Manchester recorded in 1967 that Richard Nixon had departed Dallas on the morning of November 22nd on American Airlines Flight 82.[102]

While one hesitates to draw a conclusion of any kind from the episode, it does seem somewhat peculiar that Nixon managed to forget where he was on November 22, 1963 during his February 1964 FBI interview. The often repeated cliche, "No one will ever forget where they were and what they were doing the day President Kennedy was assassinated," seems to have been inaccurate in at least this one case.

Efforts to review the Nixon episode were further hindered when the National Archives disclosed in 1976 that a "Letter of FBI of June 29, 1964 concerning Richard Nixon," was one of the items missing from the Warren Commission records stored in the Archives building in Washington, D.C. The contents of the letter are unknown.[103]

There has been an increasing amount of interest during the past couple of years regarding the reported connections of Richard Nixon and his close associates to various Mafia figures. As was detailed earlier, the *Washington Post*, *New York Times*, and other news organizations have disclosed what now clearly appear to be numerous links or relationships between Nixon and his close associates and organized crime. While the media perhaps inevitably shied away from trying to interpret such various documented connections during the unravelling of Watergate — Nixon's men would of course have mounted a strong backlash against "sensationalism" — the associations remain. These Mafia relationships, favors, and deals can be traced back to the earliest years of Nixon's political career, as Drew Pearson and Jack Anderson first disclosed, and increased significantly during his stormy years in the Presidency.

On December 5, 1976, the *Washington Star* disclosed that two months before Nixon resigned, General Alexander Haig had ordered the Army's Criminal Investigation Command to conduct a secret investigation into President Nixon's possible ties to organized crime, specifically, the powerful Mafia leaders who run the Southeast Asian narcotics traffic. This information had never before surfaced during the long chronology of Watergate, and was confirmed for the *Star* by Army officials involved.[104]

The *Washington Star*'s respected investigative reporter, Jeremiah O'Leary, said that the June, 1974 investigation was ordered by Gen. Haig during a meeting with the Army's Criminal Investigation Command Chief, Colonel Henry H. Tufts, at Fort McNair. The chief investigator for the Haig probe was CIC Special Agent Russell L. Bintliff, an official bodyguard for past Secretaries of Defense, and a former special operations officer for the Army and CIA.[105]

In confirming the previously secret investigation, Bintliff told the *Washington Star*:

> ". . . Haig wanted some things checked out on the President.
>
> "It involved Caulfield and Ulasewicz. Haig wanted to know whether Caulfield and Ulasewicz had been to the Far East and carried back any money for Nixon. He also wanted to know whether Nixon had ever been mixed up with organized crime . . .
>
> "I never could find that Caulfield and

Ulasewicz had gone to the Far East, but in my verbal reports to Col. Tufts I pointed out that in those days an American didn't need a passport to get into Vietnam. . .

"I concluded that they probably had gone to Vietnam, and I considered there were strong indications of a history of Nixon connections with money from organized crime."[106]

General Haig was of course unavailable for comment.

Ironically, several of President Nixon's key lieutenants later became exposed to the Mafia in a different fashion; by being sent to prison. During a lengthy portion of their individual prison terms, most of the key convicted Nixon aides were confined in Federal facilities or "safe houses" specifically maintained for convicted members of the Mafia. Jeb Magruder, Charles Colson, and John Dean have each either spoken of or written about their anxiety over finding themselves confined with key organized crime figures. In her book, Mrs. Jeb Magruder has described the joint imprisonment of her husband and his fellow Watergate conspirators, John Dean, Herbert Kalmbach, and Charles Colson, in the federal "safe house" at Fort Holabird, Maryland: "Except for the four Watergate witnesses who were housed there as a convenience, the fourteen other inmates were mostly Mafia hit men and members of several international drug-smuggling rings."[107]

John Dean in his book *Blind Ambition*, told of his imprisonment in Maryland, three weeks before the final Watergate cover-up trial began, "As best I could piece it together, the twenty-some prisoners broke down as follows: four 'Watergate guys' . . . three members of the French Connection conspiracy; a con artist; a key figure from the Tony Boyle/Yablonski murders; three Latin [Cuban exile] heroin traffickers; a man who had slit the throat of a female government informant and burned her corpse (Chuck [Colson] was working with him); a seasoned hit man with twenty-eight murders under his belt; and an assortment of Mafia figures whose crimes ran from murders to heavy narcotics trafficking."[108]

G. Gordon Liddy

G. Gordon Liddy was the former FBI agent selected by Watergate conspirators Egil Krogh and John Ehrlichman to become a member of the White House Plumbers. Liddy, a man of extraordinary violence, served as the Nixon circle's authority on a wide variety of "intelligence" matters, as well as a key architect of the Nixon campaign's massive illegal fundraising "techniques." More importantly, he was the author and coordinator of what came to be known as "the Liddy Plan" — the secret break-in and bugging blueprints which culminated in the Watergate captures. Liddy had planned much of the Watergate break-in conspiracy in conjunction with Attorney General John Mitchell and H. R. Haldeman's protegé, Jeb Magruder.

As will be seen, G. Gordon Liddy has now been reliably linked to two separate alleged murder plans during his work for Nixon's top aides, and one other actual completed murder, during his previous FBI service. As with so much other data on the Watergate conspiracy, much of this information has come to the surface only after the Senate Watergate Committee ended its investigation and went out of existence. While Liddy is well known to the American public as perhaps the most frightening of the various Watergate conspirators, his darker activities have still not received full attention.

During their sworn Senate testimony in 1973, John Dean and Jeb Magruder admitted that "the Liddy Plan," first unveiled in Attorney General Mitchell's office on January 27, 1972, had originally involved not only break-ins and buggings, but also kidnapping — a capital offense — and muggings. Magruder has written: "It was, as John Dean said later, mind boggling. It included mugging squads, kidnapping, sabotage, the use of prostitutes for political blackmail [which Liddy described as "high-class girls, only the best"] break-ins to obtain and photograph documents, and various forms of electronic surveillance and wiretapping."[109]

Magruder also disclosed that Liddy "explained that the proposed kidnap squads would seize radicals, and inject them with some drug that would render them unconscious . . ."[110] Magruder recalls Liddy saying, "They'd never even know who had them or where they were."[111]

Interestingly, Liddy was apparently in a position to obtain the various drugs and/or poisons that were envisioned in his original Watergate plans. As noted previously, the Senate Intelligence Committee established that Liddy accompanied E. Howard Hunt to a secret meeting with a former CIA physician, during Hunt's alleged plot to drug and/or murder columnist Jack Anderson.[112] The Senate Committee disclosed Hunt did not ask the former CIA physician to procure any drugs because "he felt confident . . . that if the time came when any controlled substance were needed, that Mr. Liddy could secure what was necessary through a 'secure source' within the Treasury Department where Liddy previously worked."[113]

Frank Sturgis has spoken of Gordon Liddy's "hit man" complex, recalling that he "was a nut about guns and silencers . . . and so on. And he was always talking about 'disposal' — about killing people."[114] Robert Odle, a middle echelon official in Richard Nixon's last campaign, has told of the time his wife first met Liddy, and had later exclaimed, "Rob, I just met the most amazing man. He showed me how you could kill someone with a pencil."[115] On another occasion, Liddy approached Magruder and asked, "Jeb, did you know I have a gun that will shoot underwater?"[116]

Intriguingly, Magruder wrote that Gordon Liddy once confided some astonishing personal information to him: namely, that he had once secretly murdered a man while serving on a sensitive FBI assignment.[117]

Even before these latest allegations about Liddy became publicly known, there was considerable speculation about his mysterious activities. Just five months after the Watergate conspiracy began to break open, CBS News reporter Dan Rather suggested the possibility of some kind of connection between the Kennedy assassination and Watergate. In a CBS radio commentary in August of 1973, titled "Rethinking the Unthinkable," Rather stated:

> "Lee Harvey Oswald, the man who shot President Kennedy. Did he ever know or have contact with E. Howard Hunt or Gordon Liddy or any of the others in that mysterious and dangerous crew convicted in the Watergate crime?
>
> "Under normal circumstances, and in normal times, these questions would not be asked. Unfortunately for us all, circumstances are not normal. These are not normal times."[118]

With the then increasing barrage of astonishing Watergate disclosures, Rather commented that it was perhaps time to ask "some of the tough questions about such characters as Hunt and Liddy and their Cuban contacts and whether they had at any time any connection with Oswald..."[119]

While considerable information continues to surface about the mysterious and highly dangerous Liddy, he has never broken his long silence to respond to the various allegations. With a minimum prison term of six years for his part in the Watergate burglary, Liddy would have served longer than any of the several dozen convicted Watergate conspirators had it not been for the commutation of his sentence by President Carter.

Robert Mardian

Senate Intelligence Committee sources have disclosed that some remarks about the Kennedy assassination made by Assistant Attorney General Robert Mardian in the spring of 1971 became the subject of inquiry by Senate investigators in 1976.

The incident began on the afternoon of April 27, 1971, when Assistant Attorney General Mardian delivered a Law Day address at a banquet of the Federal Bar Association in Washington. Mardian spoke about what he claimed was a pressing need for increased internal security measures on the state and federal level.

Mardian also delivered some criticism of the FBI's

handling of the internal security case of Lee Harvey Oswald. According to the *New York Times* account of the following day, Mardian has "said that the assassination of President Kennedy might have been made possible by what the Warren Commission called the Federal Bureau of Investigation's restrictive view of it's duty to investigate Lee Harvey Oswald."[121]

Interestingly, as Senate investigators have noted, on the same day as Mardian's speech, FBI Director Hoover took a sudden action which alarmed the Nixon circle by ordering the abrupt cancellation of all FBI COINTELPRO operations, the secret counterintelligence functions targeted against dissident groups, one of the prime domestic intelligence activities of the Nixon administration. Senate investigators were interested in determining if Hoover's cancellation of COINTELPRO had been intended as a form of retaliation against Mardian's criticisms of the FBI, and sought to determine at what time he had first been informed of the remarks about Oswald. As Senate probers noted, Hoover's long-time tendency to take strong action against those who raised doubts about the FBI performance in investigating the Dallas case was only too well known.

Although the episode remains intriguing, former members of the Hoover circle profess to have no knowledge of any Hoover "retaliation" over the Mardian speech, and suggest that the COINTELPRO cancellation had been on Hoover's mind for several weeks prior to the Mardian episode.

John N. Mitchell

In November, 1970, President Nixon's Attorney

General, John Mitchell, ordered the Justice Department to block the release of crucial ballistics evidence from the Kennedy assassination on grounds of national security. Mitchell's personal involvement in fighting the release of this material came at a time when Commission critics were in an unprecedented position to secure the release of such evidence under the Freedom of Information Act.

The evidence at stake was the FBI's secret spectrographic analyses of the bullet and bullet fragments recovered following the fatal shooting of JFK and the near fatal wounding of Governor Connally. Spectrographic testing — a highly exact method of scientific measurement and analysis — can determine whether two or more projectiles have a common source. These analyses are believed to be "the key" to determining the validity of the "single-bullet, lone assassin" findings of the Warren Commission. Warren Commission critics have long asked: if the spectrographics tests supported the findings of the Warren Commission, why were they never released?

Harold Weisberg began an investigation in 1965 to determine if the FBI had run such spectrographic tests and, if so, where the results were. Weisberg discovered that FBI spectrographic examination was not mentioned in any of the thousands of pages of Warren Commission exhibits. However, when Weisberg asked the National Archives if such tests had ever been carried out, he was notified that the FBI had indeed run such tests and had kept the only copies.[122]

Upon requesting the results from the FBI, Weisberg and the National Archives were told that no such material actually existed.[123] However, Weisberg soon demonstrated that sworn FBI testimony clearly indicated that an FBI spectrographic report did in fact exist, somewhere within the FBI.[124] As Weisberg has noted, "the failure — then the refusal — of the government to make [the] spectrographic analysis public leads inevitably to the conclusion that the evidence does not support the [Warren Commission] Report..."[125]

Efforts to establish exactly what spectrographic material the FBI actually had were repeatedly stymied over the years, despite intensive probing by Weisberg and other qualified investigators. Finally, on August 3, 1970, Warren Commission critic Weisberg filed an unprecedented Freedom of Information lawsuit against the federal government to gain access to this material.[126]

In the suit, *Weisberg v. Department of Justice*, Civil Action No. 2301-70, the Warren Commission critic sought the release of "spectrographic [FBI] analysis of bullet, fragments of bullet and other objects, including garments and part of vehicle and curbstone said to have been struck by bullet and/or fragments during assassination of President Kennedy and wounding of Governor Connally."[127]

On October 6, 1970, the Justice Department, under Attorney General John Mitchell, filed a motion to dismiss the suit. Subsequently, a hearing was set for November 16, 1970.[128] In the meantime, the Justice Department filed an unusual supplemental motion to dismiss the spectrographic suit on the grounds that the release of the FBI analyses "would seriously interfere with the efficient operation of the FBI," and would also "create a highly dangerous precedent in this regard."[129]

Finally, on November 16, 1970, the climactic hearing was held. During the oral argument, Assistant U.S. Attorney Robert Werdig, representing the Justice Department, repeated the FBI's claims that the release of the tests would "interfere" with FBI functions, and that such release was not actually intended under the provisions of the Freedom of Information Act.[130]

However, during the course of the hearing, Werdig disclosed a new and unusual contention that took legal observers by surprise: "In this instance the Attorney General of the United States [John Mitchell] has determined that it is not in the national interest to divulge these spectrographic analyses."[131] Shortly thereafter, the Weisberg suit was dismissed.[132]

Interestingly, in 1974, in a little-noticed Senate floor debate, Senator Edward M. Kennedy defended the legal merits of the Weisberg spectrographic suit under the provisions of the Freedom of Information Act, and spoke in favor of an amendment offered by Senator Philip Hart of Michigan which struck to the very heart of the attempted use of the Freedom of Information Act by Weisberg and Fensterwald.[132] Kennedy asked Hart, "Does the Senator's amendment in effect override the court decision in the Court of Appeals on the Weisberg against the United States [Department of Justice]?[133] Kennedy further queried, "As I understand it . . . the impact and effect of your amendment would be to override [this decision]. Is that correct?"[134] To which Senator Hart had responded, "The Senator from Massachusetts is correct."[135]

The FBI's handling of JFK spectrographic tests is one of the most compelling examples of the suppression of information pertaining to the actual physical evidence from the assassination. Previous reasons for the suppression of other evidence — that such material was of a grisly medical nature — were certainly not applicable to the spectrographic analyses, which were nothing more than detailed laboratory examinations of the metal in the bullet and bullet fragments recovered after the shooting.

Despite Attorney General Mitchell's 1970 orders to withhold the spectrographic analyses, further information has become available in the intervening years. In 1976, the National Archives disclosed that among the records of the Warren Commission missing from the Archives building in Washington are: "FBI Laboratory technical records concerning spectrographic analysis of ballistics evidence," as well as "FBI Laboratory report concerning examination of Presidential limousine."[137]

J. Lee Rankin

Charles Colson has disclosed that he and his law partner, David Shapiro, tried, on behalf of President Nixon, to recruit former Warren Commission General Counsel J. Lee Rankin to serve as the first Watergate Special Prosecutor. Colson's disclosure that he and Shapiro tried to arrange the appointment of Rankin as Special Prosecutor in March of 1973, days after James McCord broke open the Watergate cover-up, came before the House Judiciary Committee on Impeachment on July 15, 1974.[139] Colson testified that Shapiro had "made a date to see him [Rankin] on March 21,"[140] to determine "if Rankin would be interested should the President wish to ask him to do that."[141] Colson further testified that he had discussed the appointment of J. Lee Rankin with Nixon on the night of March 21, 1973, several hours after Nixon had given his now famous "hush money" instructions to John Dean and H. R. Haldeman.[142] Colson testified that during a call from Nixon at about 8:00 that night, he "described to him J. Lee Rankin's background" and told Nixon "that while Rankin had not indicated that he would or would not accept it, it was our judgment... that if the President asked him, he would accept."[143] Subsequently, Nixon decided to delay the appointment of a Special Prosecutor. In 1976, the National Archives disclosed that two letters written to Warren Commission General Counsel Rankin were missing from the National Archives collection: a "Letter of David Belin to J. Lee Rankin, January 23, 1964, on interrogation of Oswald by Dallas Police Department," and also a "Memorandum of Griffin to Rankin in August 1964 dealing with a number of inquiries to be made of various agencies, one of which had to do with unidentified prints found on the cartons in the Texas School Book Depository."[144]

Charles Shaffer

John Dean selected as his defense attorney another man intimately familiar with the assassination of President Kennedy. In April of 1973, Dean retained Charles Shaffer shortly before he went to the federal prosecutors and turned state's evidence against the Nixon circle. Charles Shaffer had served as Administrative Aide to the Warren Commission and unlike other top Commission aides had been recommended for the position by Robert Kennedy.[145] During the course of the Watergate investigation, Dean reportedly felt that his life was in danger at various times, which led to his eventual protection by U.S. Marshals. Woodward and Bernstein have written that Woodward learned from Deep Throat on May 16, 1973 that Nixon had "threatened Dean personally" at one point, warning him not to reveal certain secret matters that Nixon claimed were "national security."[146] Dean has publicly stated (as late as last year) that there are still "very big" revelations yet to emerge from the Watergate mystery.

Joseph A. Ball

In April, 1973, John Ehrlichman also selected as his first defense attorney another man connected to the Warren Commission: Joseph A. Ball. Ehrlichman was then facing initial charges relating to his key role in the Ellsberg burglary, Joseph A. Ball had served as Senior Counsel to the Warren Commission and had been in charge of "Area II" of the Commission's investigation: the "Identity of the Assassin."[147] In his recent novel, *The Company*, Ehrlichman has written about a President and a CIA Director who are blackmailing each other over a past assassination plot that had involved CIA elements. Some observers have speculated that the Ehrlichman novel may actually be referring in some way to the Kennedy assassination. Ehrlichman refuses comment on this.

543

In 1976, the National Archives informed the House Subcommittee on Government Information that two documents of Joseph Ball were missing from the Warren Commission records stored at the Archives: "Memorandum (60 pages) of Ball and Belin Concerning Identity of the Assassin," and a "Draft Chapter Submitted by Ball and Belin in Early June 1964."[148]

Leon Jaworski

In their 1976 book, *The Final Days*, Woodward and Bernstein reported that President Nixon had wanted to appoint Leon Jaworski as Special Prosecutor sometime in April of 1973 — over five months before Jaworski finally did become Prosecutor, following the "Saturday Night Massacre" firing of Archibald Cox. Leon Jaworski had served as Special Counsel to the Warren Commission while also serving as Special Counsel to the Attorney General of Texas. The Warren Commission had given Jaworski the assignment of investigating various allegations in Texas that Lee Oswald had been a government agent of either the FBI or CIA.[149] Jaworski, after a brief investigation, reported back to the Commission that there was absolutely nothing to the story."[150] Woodward and Bernstein reported that Jaworski had turned down Nixon's first offer, and upon being offered the job for a second time, on

544

October 30, 1973, asked Alexander Haig, "General Haig, are you aware of the fact that I, in effect, turned down the job once [before]?"[151] In his own 1976 book, Jaworski wrote that he had turned down the position the first time because he "didn't think the independence to act was there."[152] In 1976 the National Archives disclosed that two of his letters to the Warren Commission were missing from the records of the Commission, including a "Letter of December 18, 1963," expressing a continuing "willingness to assist in any way," as well as a "Letter of Leon Jaworski to J. Lee Rankin, May 8, 1964."[153]

John J. McCloy

In early 1976, former Attorney General Eliot Richardson revealed that President Nixon had suggested on April 29, 1973, that Richardson appoint John J. McCloy as Special Prosecutor for Watergate.[154] John McCloy, as previously noted, had served as one of the actual Members of the Warren Commission. Along with former CIA Director Allen Dulles and Congressman Gerald R. Ford, McCloy had been a leading proponent of the controversial "single-bullet theory" of a lone assassin.[155] McCloy still remains an ardent defender of the Warren Commission findings, claiming that no evidence of a conspiracy was ever found.

Gerald R. Ford

On October 12, 1973, President Richard Nixon nominated Congressman Gerald R. Ford to succeed Spiro T. Agnew as Vice President. Gerald Ford had served in the House for over twenty years and had been a member of the Warren Commission. Ford became the most active member of the Commission, and went on to become the most vocal defender of its conclusions. In 1965, he wrote a book, *Portrait of the Assassin*, which set forth his belief that Lee Harvey Oswald was a lone, deranged, assassin, inspired by Communist beliefs. In 1976, the National Archives disclosed that a "Letter of Gerald Ford, April 7, 1964, concerning expediting the FBI investigation," was among the Warren Commission documents missing from the Archives building in Washington.[156]

J. Lee Rankin

President Nixon and close confidante Charles Colson attempted to retain J. Lee Rankin in October of 1973 to serve as a "neutral party" in evaluating which of the secret Nixon Watergate tapes would be turned over to Special Prosecutor Archibald Cox, and

which should be withheld on "national security" grounds. J. Lee Rankin had served as General Counsel to the Warren Commission and thus held the single highest ranking position on the Commission staff. Rankin supervised the entire investigation and had served as the Warren Commission liaison to both the CIA and FBI. It was Rankin who was the target of heavy internal Commission discontent for his decision to end any further investigation into the crucial "single-bullet theory" at a time when other staff counsel were convinced that the theory was probably impossible.[157]

Rose Mary Woods

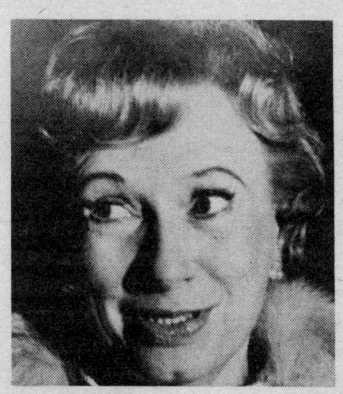

President Nixon's longtime personal secretary, Rose Mary Woods, was advised by Nixon to retain an attorney to defend her against possible charges growing out of the mysterious eighteen-minute tape erasure on the Nixon/Haldeman June 20, 1972 Watergate tape. Woods had become a prime suspect in the tape erasing probe. On November 22, 1973, Miss Woods selected as her attorney a man who had also worked closely with the Warren Commission investigation: Charles Rhyne.[158] Rhyne, a personal friend of Richard Nixon, had served as an official observer in monitoring the Warren investigation and advising on the individual rights of various witnesses.[159]

Arlen Specter

In early December, 1973, President Nixon reportedly asked former Philadelphia District Attorney Arlen Specter to become the head of his Watergate legal defense team. The *Philadelphia Bulletin* reported that Specter had met with Alexander Haig to discuss the defense position and had also discussed the increasing likelihood of an impeachment investigation.[160] Specter subsequently turned down President Nixon's request for legal assistance and James St. Clair (a former lawyer for Charles Colson) was chosen for the position instead.

Arlen Specter had served as Counsel to the Warren Commission and had been assigned to the crucial "Area I" of the Commission investigation: the "Basic Facts of the Assassination." Specter had emerged as the controversial architect of the "single-bullet theory."[161] Which he had seemingly devised to explain away several important pieces of evidence which seemed to indicate the presence of more than one rifleman. Specter's theory — upon which the Warren Report's central conclusion of a single assassin was based — postulated that a single bullet had traveled through both men, since Connally was seated directly in front of Kennedy. Beyond a sizable body of actual ballistic and medical evidence which seriously negates the probability of the Specter theory, recent analyses of the Zapruder film strongly undermine the entire basis of the theory.

In addition to being a protegé of Attorney General John Mitchell, Specter had also served as a co-chairman of the Pennsylvania division of CREEP in 1972.

Albert Jenner

In early January of 1974, President Nixon approved the selection of Albert Jenner to serve as the GOP's Minority Counsel for the Impeachment Investigation of the House Judiciary Committee. Jenner was to have served as Nixon's chief legal counsel on the Committee but later abandoned that role after the massive evidence of impeachable offenses began to mount against the President. Albert Jenner had been a Senior Counsel to the Warren Commission and had been in charge of investigating "Area III": Oswald's Background History,

Acquaintances, and Motives.[162] Jenner is credited with having been one of the key authors of the final Report.[163]

SUMMARY OF SEQUENCE

("WC" Indicates Warren Commission)

March 1973: Nixon considers *Rankin* as Prosecutor (WC *General Counsel*)

April 1973: Dean hires *Shaffer* (WC *Administrative Aide*)

April 1973: Ehrlichman hires *Ball* (WC *Senior Counsel*)

April 1973: Nixon suggests *Jaworski* for Prosecutor (WC *Special Counsel*)

April 1973: Nixon suggests *McCloy* for Prosecutor (WC *Member*)

Oct. 12, 1973: Nixon appoints *Ford* as Vice President (WC *Member*)

Oct. 15, 1973: Nixon selects *Rankin* to "edit" the tapes (WC *General Counsel*)

Nov. 5, 1973: Nixon appoints *Jaworski* as Prosecutor (WC *Special Counsel*)

Nov. 22, 1973: Rose Mary Woods hires *Rhyne* (WC *Legal Observer*)

Dec. 5, 1973: Nixon asks *Specter* to head his defense (WC *Counsel*)

Jan. 7, 1973: Nixon approves *Jenner* as Impeachment Counsel (WC *Senior Counsel*)

1. *New York Times*, January 18, 1973.
2. "Nomination of L. Patrick Gray as FBI Director," Hearings before the Senate Judiciary Committee, 1973, pp. 45-48.
3. June 19, 1972 Memorandum from L. Patrick Gray to H. R. Haldeman, Gray Hearings, p. 47.
4. Hans Tanner, *Counter-Revolutionary Agent* (New York: G. T. Foulis, 1962), p. 127.
5. *True*, Andrew St. George, August 1974.
6. Warren Commission Document 59.
7. Ibid.
8. Ibid.
9. Warren Commission Document 395.
10. Ibid.
11. Ibid.
12. Ibid.
13. Warren Commission Document 1020.
14. Ibid.
15. *True*, Andrew St. George, August, 1974.
16. Ibid.
17. Ibid.
18. Ibid.
19. Ibid.
20. Ibid.
21. June 23, 1972 White House Transcript, meeting between President Nixon and H. R. Haldeman.
22. Tad Szulc, *Compulsive Spy* (New York: The Viking Press, 1974), pp. 98-99.
23. *Washington Post*, November 26 and 27, 1976.
24. Ibid.
25. Warren Commission Documents 631 and 1287.
26. "Nomination of Richard Helms as Ambassador to Iran," Hearings before the Senate Foreign Relations Committee, 1973, p. 25.
27. Ibid., p. 1.
28. *True*, August 1974.
29. April 17, 1964 FBI letter from J. Edgar Hoover to Warren Commission General Counsel J. Lee Rankin.
30. J. Anthony Lukas, *Nightmare* (New York: The Viking Press, 1976) pp. 278-279.
31. *Senate Intelligence Committee Report on Foreign Assassinations*, pp. 89-90.
32. Ibid., p. 89.
33. Ibid., pp. 89-90.
34. Ibid., p. 90.
35. Ibid.
36. Ibid.
37. *Senate Intelligence Committee Report on the Kennedy Assassination*, p. 72.

38. Ibid., p. 75.
39. Hunt, *Give Us This Day*, p. 38.
40. *True*, August 1974.
41. "Transcripts of Eight Recorded Presidential Conversations," House Judiciary Committee Impeachment Hearings, 1974, p. 90.
42. Ibid., p. 94.
43. Ibid.
44. Ibid.
45. Ibid., p. 121.
46. Hunt, *Undercover*, p. 144.
47. Ibid., p. 272.
48. Ibid., p. 289.
49. Ibid., p. 296.
50. Ibid., p. 292.
51. Ibid., p. 296.
52. Lukas, *Nightmare*, p. 197.
53. Ibid., pp. 167-168, 195-196.
54. *Senate Watergate Committee Report*, GPO edition, 1974, pp. 17, 52-55, 63-65, 109-117.
55. Ibid., pp. 116-117.
56. John Dean, *Blind Ambition* (New York: Simon and Schuster, 1976), pp. 77-78; Lukas, *Nightmare*, p. 16.
57. Ibid.
58. Ibid.
59. *Senate Watergate Committee Report*, GPO edition, 1974, pp. 232-236.
60. May 28, 1964 FBI memorandum for the Warren Commission, "Lee Harvey Oswald, Internal Security — R — Cuba."
61. Ibid.
62. Ibid.
63. Ibid.
64. Ibid.
65. Ibid.
66. Ibid.
67. Ibid.
68. Ibid.
69. Ibid.
70. Ibid.
71. *New York* magazine, April 29, 1974.
72. Lukas, *Nightmare*, p. 425.
73. *Senate Watergate Committee Report*, GPO edition p. 129.
74. Ibid.
75. CBS Reports Inquiry, "The American Assassins," Dan Rather, Part IV, January 5, 1976.
76. Ibid.
77. Ibid.

78. Bob Woodward and Carl Bernstein, *All The President's Men* (New York: Simon and Schuster, 1974), p. 327.
79. Ibid.
80. *Washington Post*, September 21, 1975.
81. Ibid.
82. Ibid.
83. Senate Intelligence Committee Final Report, Book IV, p. 134.
84. Ibid., pp. 134-135.
85. Ibid.
86. Ibid.
87. Ibid.
88. Ibid.
89. Ibid.
90. Ibid., pp. 136-137.
91. *Senate Watergate Committee Report*, pp. 126-127.
92. *Senate Intelligence Committee Report on Foreign Assassinations*, p. 262.
93. Ibid., p. 223.
94. Hunt, *Undercover*, p. 179; *Senate Watergate Committee Report*, pp. 126-127.
95. Ibid.
96. Ibid.
97. *Saturday Evening Post*, Jules Witcover, February 25, 1967.
98. *Warren Commission Report*, GPO edition, pp. 187-189.
99. Warren Commission Exhibit 1973.
100. Ibid.
101. *Saturday Evening Post*, Jules Witcover, February 25, 1967.
102. William Manchester, *The Death Of A President* (New York: Harper and Row, 1967), p. 117.
103. "National Archives" Hearings before the House Subcommittee on Government Information 1976.
104. *Washington Star*, December 5, 1976.
105. Ibid.
106. Ibid.
107. Gail Magruder, *A Gift Of Love* (Philadelphia: A. J. Holman Company, 1976), p. 105.
108. John Dean, *Blind Ambition* (New York: Simon and Schuster, 1976), p. 373.
109. Jeb Stuart Magruder, *An American Life* (New York: Atheneum, 1974), p. 178.
110. Ibid., p. 179.
111. Ibid.
112. Senate Intelligence Committee Final Report, Book IV, p. 136.
113. Ibid., pp. 136-137.
114. *True*, August, 1974.

115. Magruder, *An American Life*, p. 174.
116. Ibid.
117. Ibid., p. 175.
118. CBS Radio Commentary, Dan Rather, August 10, 1973.
119. Ibid.
121. *New York Times*, April 28, 1971.
122. Harold Weisberg, *Post Mortem* (Frederick, Maryland: Harold Weisberg, 1975), pp. 16-17.
123. Ibid., p. 18.
124. Warren Commission Volume 5, p. 69; Weisberg, *Post Mortem*, p. 18.
125. Weisberg, *Post Mortem*, p. 19.
126. Civil Action No. 2301-70, *Weisberg v. Department of Justice*.
127. Ibid.
128. Weisberg, *Whitewash IV*, pp. 173-178.
129. Ibid.
130. *Weisberg v. Department of Justice*, U.S. District Court, November 16, 1970; Weisberg, *Whitewash IV*, pp. 173-178.
131. Ibid.
132. *Congressional Record*, Senate proceedings, May 30, 1974.
133. Ibid.
134. Ibid.
135. Ibid.
137. "National Archives — Security Classification Problems Involving Warren Commission Files And Other Records," Hearings before the House Subcommittee on Government Information, 1976.
138. Senate Watergate Committee, Book One, 1973, Testimony of James W. McCord, p. 141.
139. House Judiciary Committee, "Testimony of Witnesses," Book Three, 1974, Testimony of Charles W. Colson, pp. 331-332.
140. Ibid., p. 332.
141. Ibid.
142. Ibid., p. 333.
143. Ibid., p. 333-334.
144. "National Archives — Security Classification Problems Involving Warren Commission Files and Other Records," Hearings before the House Subcommittee on Government Information, 1976.
145. Edward Jay Epstein, *Inquest* (New York: Bantam Books Edition, 1966), p. 13.
146. Woodward and Bernstein, *All The President's Men*, pp. 316-320.
147. Epstein, *Inquest*, p. 59.
148. "National Archives" Hearings before the House Subcommittee on Government Information, 1976.

149. Epstein, *Inquest*, p. 35.
150. Ibid.
151. Bob Woodward and Carl Bernstein, *The Final Days*, (New York: Simon and Schuster, 1976), p.75.
152. Leon Jaworski, *The Right And The Power* (New York: Reader's Digest Press, 1976), p. 2.
153. "National Archives" Hearings before the House Subcommittee on Government Information, 1976.
154. *The Atlantic*, Eliot Richardson, March, 1976.
155. Epstein, *Inquest*, pp. 121-122.
156. "National Archives" Hearings before the House Subcommittee on Government Information, 1976.
157. Epstein, *Inquest*, pp. 115-119.
158. Congressional Quarterly, *Watergate: Chronology of a Crisis* (Washington: Congressional Quarterly, Inc., 1975), p. 444.
159. Sylvia Meagher, *Subject Index to the Warren Report and Hearings and Exhibits* (New York: Scarecrow Press, Inc., 1966), p. 133.
160. *The Philadelphia Bulletin*, December 5, 1973.
161. Epstein, *Inquest*, pp. 13, 60-63.
162. Ibid., p. 13.
163. Ibid., pp. 20-23.

CHAPTER THIRTEEN

Neglected or Spurned Witnesses

The public has been confronted with innumerable allegations by countless people who have come forward claiming to have new information relating to the assassination. As with many criminal investigations, the JFK murder probe produced no shortage of loose ends before it had run its course in late 1964.

Though the Warren Commission's critics have amassed significant amounts of information relating to numerous witnesses who were neglected during its nine-month investigation, a handful of the more interesting "neglected witnesses" provides a vivid illustration of the variety of accounts that have come to light over the years.

Seth Kantor

Seth Kantor, a veteran reporter who now covers Washington for the *Detroit News*, is probably the country's leading expert on Jack Ruby, and author of the definitive book on him. Kantor's acquaintance with Ruby pre-dates the assassination to his Dallas days as a Scripps-Howard reporter. Because Ruby was one of the town "characters," he was known to all local newsmen; he'd even spent hours hanging around the papers, "supervising" the composition of his nightclub advertisements. Kantor knew Jack Ruby very well; in fact, Ruby had helped him with a number of stories.[1]

Although Kantor had been transferred from Dallas to Washington before November, 1963, he'd been sent to Texas to cover JFK's political trip, and was in the press bus behind the President.

When JFK was rushed to Parkland Hospital, Kantor was close behind. During the ensuing confusion, every reporter was having a hard time sorting out fact from rumor. Kantor got a break when Malcolm Kilduff, an Assistant White House Press Secretary, motioned Kantor to follow him, saying that he was going to make an announcement. As they were fighting their way through the crowd, Jack Ruby stopped Kantor.[2] Kantor greeted Ruby but pushed on, following Kilduff.[3]

His chance meeting with Ruby was inconsequential, but Kantor believed it should be reported to the federal authorities.[4] What he did not anticipate was the hostility and disbelief his seemingly minor piece of news evoked. Despite a confirming witness, both the FBI and the Warren Commission refused to believe that Kantor saw and talked with Ruby at Parkland Hospital. They did not exactly call him a liar: it was just that he was mistaken. He either saw someone else at Parkland or saw Jack Ruby at some other place. According to the FBI, Ruby wasn't at Parkland Hospital that day, and that was that. Anyone with evidence to the contrary was simply not to be believed.

Julia Mercer

Julia Mercer, a Dallas housewife who drove past the Texas School Book Depository several hours before the assassination, has long been cited by Commission critics (notably Sylvia Meagher and Mark Lane) as a typical example of an important witness ignored by the Warren Commission, FBI, and Secret Service.[5] Following news of the events in Dealey Plaza, Mrs. Mercer went to Dallas Police Headquarters and swore out an affidavit in which she stated that when she drove past the plaza, on her way to work, she saw a man carrying what appeared to be a rifle case[6] walking toward the grassy knoll area from where many Commission critics insist that at least one shot was fired. (In fact, detailed analysis of eye-witnesses established that at least fifty-one persons stated that a shot or shots had been fired from the area to the right-front of JFK's limousine.[7]) Secret Service Agent Forrest V. Sorrels, a key figure in the probe, later testified that while he had been informed of Mrs. Mercer's information, he had decided not to investigate it: ". . . this lady said she thought she saw somebody that looked like that he had a gun case. But then I didn't pursue that any further — because then I had gotten the information that the rifle had been found in the building and shells and so forth."[8]

Acquila Clemmons

Acquila Clemmons, an eyewitness to Tippit's murder, was never questioned by the Warren Commission. She has stated she saw two men — one tall and thin, the other short and heavyset — talking to Officer Tippit[9] after he got out of his patrol car moments before he was shot by the heavyset man.[10] The pair then ran away in opposite directions. Ms. Clemmons also contended that the thin man was definitely *not* Lee Oswald.[11]

Critics have pointed out that the Commission never called on at least ten other witnesses who had direct information pertaining to the Tippit murder, and instead chose to rely on the testimony of thirteen others — only two of whom said they had actually seen the murder.[12]

The Commission's key witness in identifying Oswald as Tippit's murderer, Mrs. Helen Markham, has long been a key focus of criticism. Her testimony that she'd clearly seen the man who shot Tippit, and her subsequent identification of Oswald in a Dallas police line-up,[13] has severe inconsistencies. She originally stated that the Tippit murder occurred earlier than the Commission says it did — in fact, too early for Lee Harvey Oswald to have even been present. The Report merely notes Mrs. Markham was "uncertain" about the exact time.[14] Even more odd is Mrs. Markham's testimony that she'd knelt and talked to the dying officer minutes after the shooting.[15] The Commission and medical experts reported he'd been killed instantly.[16] According to Mark Lane, Mrs. Markham had also once described Tippit's killer as "dark and bushy-haired," — entirely inconsistent with Oswald.[17] Finally, the official police report noted that Mrs. Markham was "quite hysterical" when she made her crucial identification of Oswald.[18]

Several weeks after the Warren Report was released, Joseph Ball, a Senior Counsel, described Mrs. Markham as an "utter screwball."[19]

Meanwhile, the testimony of Acquila Clemmons, an eyewitness, was never heard.

Abraham Bolden

Abraham Bolden, the first black to serve on the Secret Service's White House detail, was appointed by JFK, but his service was short-lived. He later served a long federal prison sentence: according to Bolden, he was framed, convicted, and sentenced

because he attempted to give information about Kennedy's murder to the Commission.[20]

Abe Bolden grew up in a poverty-ridden family in the poverty-ridden city of East St. Louis, Illinois, but nevertheless became an outstanding young police officer who was eventually accepted by the Secret Service. He did not get along well with his fellow White House officers; he considered the Secret Service detail there to be terribly lax, and was quite vocal in his criticism. Consequently, he was transferred to Chicago and assigned to routine anti-counterfeiting duties.[21]

In October, 1963, an emergency occurred in the Chicago Secret Service office. JFK was scheduled to attend an Army-Air Force football game and parade on November 2nd, and word had reached the Secret Service that an attempt would be made upon his life by four Cuban gunmen. According to Bolden, the investigation which was top-secret, involved all of the Chicago Secret Service squad; inexplicably few, if any, records were kept. However, the gunmen could not be located, and JFK was persuaded to cancel his trip.

Three weeks later, when JFK was killed, Bolden assumed the Secret Service would give the Warren Commission all the details about the recent plot in Chicago. According to Bolden, he discovered that nothing was to be revealed, and though he was warned to keep his mouth shut, he attempted to impart the information to Lee Rankin. Bolden's fatal error was placing the call from a White House telephone.

According to Bolden, he was bundled back to Chicago within twenty-four hours, held incommunicado, and charged with discussing a bribe with a counterfeiter.[22] He was convicted on the testimony of two witnesses. Both were counterfeiters: one had been convicted in a case "made" by Bolden; the other was awaiting trial. Though, one of the witnesses admitted that he had perjured himself, Bolden was refused a re-trial and was forced to serve a long term in federal penitentiary.

Several documented aspects to Bolden's case merit further investigation. In recent years, documentation regarding this reported Chicago threat has become available. Though Chicago Secret Service officials have confirmed the threat and the ensuing probe of possible Cuban exile involvement in it, they have refused further comment on the incident.

Raymond Krystinik

Raymond Krystinik, who worked with Michael Païne at Bell-Helicopter Research Laboratory, is one of the few known links, however tentative, between Oswald and Ruby —a link which was known, but totally ignored, by the Warren Commission.

According to Warren Commission documents, Krystinik and his wife attended an American Civil Liberties Union meeting in Dallas in October, 1963 where his good friend and fellow employee, Michael Paine, introduced him to Lee Harvey Oswald.[23] The introduction was natural enough because Oswald's wife, Marina, was living with Michael's estranged wife, Ruth.

Krystinik spent a good part of the evening in political discussion with Oswald, arguing at length the differences between Marxism, Leninism and socialism.[24] After the meeting, Mr. and Mrs. Krystinik decided to go to a nightclub.[25] This was more than a bit unusual because, as Krystinik later told the FBI, neither he nor his wife drank nor smoked, and neither had ever been to a club before.

The Dallas nightclub they went to was none other than Jack Ruby's Carousel Club.[26]

In his FBI testimony, Krystinik was vague on two points: (1) whether Oswald accompanied them; and (2) whether they actually met Jack Ruby. His "best recollection" was that Oswald did not accompany them but that they probably did meet Jack Ruby.[27] There is no record that either Mrs. Krystinik or Ruby was ever questioned about the occasion. When Counsels Griffin and Liebeler questioned Krystinik on March 24, 1964, they debriefed him in massive detail about the ACLU meeting and Oswald's political beliefs, but asked not one question about his visit to the Carousel Club.[28]

Raymond Krystinik still works for Bell Helicopter, and lives in suburban Arlington, Texas.

1. Warren Commission Volume 15, pp. 80-82; Kantor Exhibit No. 8.
2. Ibid.
3. Ibid.
4. Ibid.
5. Meagher, *Accessoriess After The Fact*, p. 21.
6. Warren Commission Volume 19, p. 483.
7. Meagher, p. 9.
8. Warren Commission Volume 7, p. 352.
9. Lane, *Rush To Judgment*, p. 124.
10. Ibid.
11. Ibid., pp. 193-194.
12. Anson, *"They've Killed The President!,"* p. 57; Lane, *Rush To Judgment*, p. 176.
13. Warren Commission Report, p. 157.
14. Ibid.
15. Warren Commission Volume 3, p. 320.
16. Warren Commission Report, p. 155.
17. Lane, *Rush To Judgment*, p. 180.
18. Warren Commission Volume 7, p. 252.
19. Lane, *Rush To Judgment*, p. 190.
20. *New York Herald Tribune*, May 22, 1964.
21. Ibid.
22. Ibid.
23. Warren Commission Document 75, No. 2.
24. Ibid.
25. Ibid.
26. Ibid.
27. Ibid.
28. Ibid.

CHAPTER FOURTEEN

Bit Players And Victims

While many stories have circulated for years about the alleged murders of a substantial number of witnesses, and while some critics still speak of "the many mysterious deaths" connected to the Kennedy case, the factual basis to most of these alleged murders is exceedingly thin.

Some of the more sensational tabloids have long seized upon the notion that many key witnesses were "murdered" in alarmingly disproportionate numbers to what could reasonably be expected of a couple hundred witnesses over a thirteen year period. However, even upon discarding the many unsupported reports of various "mysterious deaths," one is left with a handful of cases which do in fact appear quite interesting. And perhaps significantly, each of these particular incidents occurred during the course of the Warren Commission investigation, when the actual interviewing of assassination witnesses had not yet been completed.

Priscilla Johnson MacMillan

Priscilla Johnson, the reporter in Moscow who conducted the longest known interview with Lee Harvey Oswald on record had been given this extensive interview while Oswald was living in Moscow's Metropol Hotel, applying for Soviet citizenship. In the years since, Priscilla Johnson (now Priscilla Johnson MacMillan) has become recognized as an "expert" on Oswald, and her articles have appeared in *The New York Times*, the *Washington Post*, the *Boston Globe*, *Harper's*, and other publications.

As Oswald's activities in the Soviet Union have come under increasing scrutiny, questions have been raised about the exact circumstances of Priscilla Johnson's interview, and, beyond that, her activities as a reporter in Moscow. In an April, 1964 article on Oswald for *Harper's*, Mrs. MacMillan set forth some of the circumstances of their contact in Russia. She had approached the defector on the advice of "an American colleague in Moscow"[1] who said "He won't talk to any of us."[2]

The Warren Report disclosed that on December 5, 1963, Mrs. MacMillan informed the State Department that her "colleague" was John A. McVickar, an Assistant Counsel to the United States Embassy. Not only was he neither a reporter nor a writer, he was a State Department official who, due to his sensitive Embassy position in Moscow, may well have worked closely with American intelligence operatives.

She later informed McVickar of the substance of her five-hour interview with Oswald.[3]

The interview covered Oswald's political beliefs about both the American and Soviet political systems. It began late at night in her Moscow hotel room, and stretched on into the early morning hours of the following day. She described Oswald as a young "college student" type. Many Warren Commission critics have pointed out Priscilla Johnson's interview raises questions as to her exact relationship with the Embassy in Moscow, but a more substantive question arises from a declassified FBI report of November 23, 1963. The FBI report, submitted as an official Warren Commission document, stated that "On November 23, 1963, Mr. Jack Lynch, U.S. Department of State (USDS), Security Office, telephonically advised Special Agent in Charge (SAC) Allen Gilles, Oswald had been contacted in Moscow by three employees of the State Department, whom he identified as John McVickar, Priscilla Johnson, and Mrs. G. Stanley Brown. Lynch indicated each of the above persons had interviewed Oswald in Moscow."[4]

Mrs. MacMillan has since denied being a State Department employee in the Moscow Embassy, and has denied working in any undercover capacity for either that Department or the CIA. She states that the State Department's Security Office, which does in fact handle intelligence work for the CIA, was simply incorrect in the information sent to the FBI on the day after the assassination.

Priscilla Johnson, who was then representing the North American Newspaper Alliance in Russia, has since portrayed Lee Harvey Oswald as a classic example of an embittered psychological "loner." Writing in the *Boston Sunday Globe* as early as November 24, 1963, MacMillan recalled her meeting with Oswald in 1959: "I soon came to feel that this boy was of the stuff of which fanatics are made."

In the late 1960s, reports began to circulate in publishing circles that Marina Oswald was considering writing a book about her husband. Many Commission critics hoped that the elusive Marina Oswald might finally disclose new information in her book and resolve many of the inconsistencies in her testimony. However, when an announcement came from Harper & Row, Publishers, that Priscilla Johnson MacMillan had been selected as a co-author to translate and edit the book, the hope was ended.

The book has not yet been completed. One reason reportedly behind the delay was Priscilla MacMillan's involvement in another literary project: assisting Svetlana Stalin to write her memoirs.

Madame Nhu

Madame Nhu, widow of Ngo Dinh Nhu, is one of the potential mystery figures in any reinvestigation of the Dallas murder.

Although her brother-in-law Ngo Dign Diem was the Premier of South Vietnam in 1963, her husband was the power behind the throne, and she is said to have been the power behind her husband. She was an

active and powerful force in Vietnamese politics when both her husband and his brother were assassinated on November 1, 1963. There were loud rumors, which persist to this day, that the CIA was involved in both the *coup* and the assassinations. The Senate Intelligence Committee concluded in November of 1975 that CIA officilas had been involved in the Diem overthrow. Madame Nhu herself placed "the personal blame" for the coup on President Kennedy.

After the twin killings in Saigon, on November 1, 1963, Madame Nhu did not join her children and family in Paris as expected. Surprisingly, she went to the United States, and even more startling, she went to Texas — even to Dallas — all before November 22nd.

The details and purpose of her strange trip are a mystery. They might, however, bear some investigation, if for no other reason than to clear up the mystery.

General Edwin A. Walker

Major General Edwin A. Walker, a controversial right-wing extremist who was removed from his command in 1961, was the target of an unsuccessful assassination attempt by Lee Harvey Oswald in April 1963, according to the FBI and Warren Commission.[6]

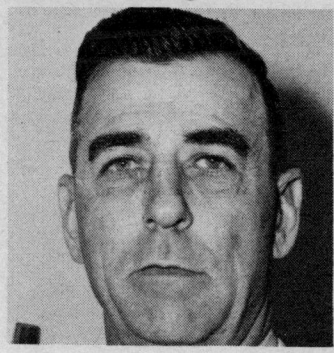

Largely on the basis of Marina Oswald's testimony, the Report stated that Oswald's alleged attempt was further evidence of his capacity to kill and propensity to assassinate.[7] However, serious questions have been raised about the credibility of that Commission conclusion.

General Walker had been removed from his European Command after he made a series of wild allegations about "Communist control" of the U.S. government and armed services. Following his forced resignation from the Army, Walker became identified with various right-wing activities, including the John Birch Society, and again received considerable attention in 1962 when he was arrested in Mississippi for inciting a group of white rioters protesting the admission of James Meredith, the first black man, to a white university in Mississippi.[8]

On April 10, 1963, as Walker sat in his study in his Dallas home, a sniper fired one shot which narrowly missed the former General.[9] Largely on the basis of Marina Oswald's testimony, the Warren Commission concluded that Oswald had been the unsuccessful assassin. Mrs. Oswald testified that Lee had informed her, shortly after the widely reported sniper attack, that he had been the perpetrator,[10] and that he had then buried his rifle in the ground not far from Walker's house. Though her testimony about the incident was vague, Marina Oswald stated that she believed her husband had indeed been involved in the Walker shooting.

However, on the day after the Walker shooting, the *Dallas Morning News* reported that the bullet recovered from the General's house was "identified as a 30.06," which could not have been fired from Oswald's Italian rifle.[11] Thus, if Oswald actually shot at Walker, he must have used a rifle which the Warren Commission never found out about, and which has never been located. The Commission made no mention of this ballistics inconsistency in their Report on the Walker episode.[12]

Sylvia Meagher has further noted "Two nights before [the Walker shooting], two men had been observed lurking about the Walker house and had fled in an unmarked car. This had been reported to the Dallas police before the shot at Walker on April 10. When the shot was heard, a young neighbor saw two men leave the scene in cars."[13]

According to Warren Commission Exhibits 2958 and 3114, the neighbor boy, Walter Coleman, was never asked to testify by the Commission.

Critics have also voiced skepticism over the circumstances in which Marina Oswald first told that Lee had shot at Walker: during an FBI interview on December 3, 1963. The Commission determined that Walker himself had been involved in setting forth a similar allegation several days earlier. On November 23, 1963, Walker had discussed Oswald during a transAtlantic telephone call with a reporter for a rightist newspaper in Munich, West Germany.[14] Days later, in its November 29th edition, that same paper published a sensational story alleging that both Jack Ruby and Lee Oswald had perpetrated the Walker shooting, and that the two assassins had known each other for a considerable period of time. A version of the same story, later published by the *National Enquirer*, later entered into evidence as a Warren Commission Exhibit.[15]

Five days after the West German newspaper account, Marina Oswald first informed the FBI that she believed Lee fired the shot at Walker.

The controversial general later faded into obscurity and was seldom heard from. But on June 23, 1976, Walker was arrested for allegedly making a homosexual advance to a plainclothes policeman in a men's room at Dallas's Cole Park.[16] The sixty-six-year-old former Major General was charged with public lewdness and was released on a $200 bond the next day.[17] He still lives in Dallas.

H. L. Hunt

The name of H. L. Hunt, the late Texas oil billionaire, has often been mentioned in regard to several areas of information surrounding the assassination. Hunt, who was perhaps the richest man in the United States, was a key financier and sponsor of various

right-wing political activities during the early 1960's, and was the head of a business empire noted for both its toughness and important political connections. Hunt was also a bitter critic of President Kennedy and his brother Robert.

The Warren Commission noted that many rumors and allegations had arisen following the assassination concerning the possible involvement of H. L. Hunt and other Texas oil men, and that the name of H. L. Hunt's son, Lamar Hunt, had been found in a notebook belonging to Jack Ruby.[18]

The Commission also established that on the day before the assassination, Jack Ruby had "visited with a young lady who was job hunting in Dallas," and had driven the woman around in her search for employment that day.[19] The woman, Connie Trammel, had become friends with Ruby several weeks earlier. The Warren Report didn't mention where Ruby drove Trammel on November 21, 1963, but an FBI interview report did: to the office of Lamar Hunt, at the H. L. Hunt headquarters in Dallas.[20]

Ruby's visit to the H. L. Hunt offices on the afternoon before the assassination occurred at roughly the same time that Mafia figure Jim Braden was visiting there. Strong possibilities exist of Braden connections to both Jack Ruby and David Ferrie in the days and weeks immediately preceding the assassination.

In a Commission memo of February 24, 1964 to Richard Helms, it requested any information the CIA could provide on possible Ruby ties to H. L. Hunt and his son Lamar.[21] This request was contained in the extensive memo on Jack Ruby's background that Helms did not respond to until the Warren Commission Report was already being set in type.[22] The Commission requested any CIA information relating to the following facts:

> H. L. Hunt and Lamar Hunt. May be same person. Name Lamar Hunt found in notebook of Ruby. Ruby visited his office on November 21. Hunt denies knowing Ruby. Ruby gives innocent explanation. Ruby found with literature of H. L. Hunt [in his apartment] after shooting Oswald.[23]

The extensive and usually subterranean right-wing political financing of H. L. Hunt and his sons, Lamar and Nelson, has received considerable attention recently. Various Hunt contributions to conservative politicians Joseph McCarthy, Richard Nixon, and George Wallace, have also been reported. On January 2, 1975, columnist Jack Anderson disclosed that various investigators were probing an alleged illegal payment of a large sum of money from the H. L. Hunt empire to the conservative Chairman of the Senate Judiciary Committee, James Eastland of Mississippi.[24] In early February of 1971, the Associated Press reported that a petition filed in Los Angeles Superior Court by the former employers of retired Air Force General Curtis LeMay, contained an allegation that he had received a one million dollar investment fund from billionaire Hunt's son, Nelson Hunt,[25] following LeMay's selection as George Wallace's running mate in 1968.[26]

When the Drew Pearson's diaries (from 1949 to 1959) were published in 1974, an allegation about H. L. Hunt's possible financing of an earlier Vice Presidential candidate also surfaced. According to the entry for October 29, 1952, an associate of Pearson had " . . . telephoned me from Texas . . . to tell me about a conspiracy which began about two years ago by H. L. Hunt, the big oil man, and a publicity firm called Watson Associates, to put Nixon into the Vice Presidency. He claims an untold amount of oil money had been behind Nixon for some time, and that all this was put over on Eisenhower without his knowing it. Later, some calls to Texas indicated the story is probably true. . . "[27]

In 1968, prior to Wallace's selection of LeMay as his third-party running mate, H. L. Hunt had apparently lobbied on behalf of another Vice Presidential prospect for Nixon's Republican ticket. According to the *Texas Observer* of August 23, 1968, the oil billionaire had personally button-holed various party officials at the Republican Convention in Miami to recommend a favorite conservative congressman as Richard Nixon's running mate: Rep. Gerald R. Ford.[28]

In early 1975, two declassified CIA memorandum became available relating to the Agency's apparent interest in allegations that H. L. Hunt had been behind the Kennedy assassination.

The first memorandum, from February 14, 1969 (titled "H. L. Hunt Interest in Garrison Investigation of Kennedy Assassination") was sent from the CIA's office in Houston, Texas, to the CIA Director of Domestic Contact Service.[29] The partially deleted memo, written by CIA officer J. Walter Moore, indicates that Hunt had recently been in contact with CIA officials:

> Mr. H. L. Hunt has been very concerned that District Attorney Garrison will try to involve him in the Kennedy assassination. He asked his Security Director [Paul Rothermel] a former FBI agent, to keep up with developments in the case.[30]

The CIA memo goes on to note that an investigator for Jim Garrison, whom the DA had recently fired, had been in touch with H. L. Hunt's aides:

> Since [DELETION] has been fired by Garrison, he has approached [DELETION] for a job with the H. L. Hunt Company. He is interested in writing a book about the assassination and wants Mr. Hunt to sponsor him...
>
> ... [DELETION] said he would relay any information he might receive that Garrison planned to involve the Central Intelligence Agency or subpoena any of its representatives in the trial against Clay Shaw.[31]

The second CIA memo, from April 18, 1969 (titled "Hunt, H. L. — Interest in Investigation of the Kennedy Assassination") had been sent from a CIA SRS/OS official, Sarah K. Hall, to the Chief of the CIA's

LEOB/SRS and Deputy Chief of SRS.[32] In this memorandum, which discusses new developments relating to the Garrison investigation, CIA official Hall notes that a new book on the Kennedy assassination, *Farewell America*, contains several references to billionaire H. L. Hunt. The memo states, "A copy of the book is held by undersigned if you desire to review the portions referring to Hunt."[33]

Farewell America was a controversial work alleging that the CIA and FBI — and perhaps H. L. Hunt — had carried out the Kennedy assassination.[34] The book alleged that Hunt had fled from Dallas with his bodyguards shortly after the assassination on the afternoon of November 22, and had then gone into hiding for a month, where he conducted a series of secret meetings with various right-wing figures.[35]

In January, 1970, the H. L. Hunt empire was shaken by a cloud of intrigue that settled over Hunt's activities following the arrest of a Houston detective who had tapped the phones of four top Hunt aides. Within days, it was disclosed that H. L. Hunt's sons had authorized and financed the secret bugging at a reported cost of over $100,000.[36] Among those who had been bugged was Paul Rothermel, the former FBI agent who had served as Hunt's Director of Security.[37] Rothermel, the aide whom Hunt had assigned to "keep up with developments" in the assassinaton, because he was afraid of being linked to the murder,[38] subsequently filed suit against the Hunts, and the case has been in the courts for several years.

The *Dallas Times Herald* further reported that more than 100 tapes of recorded conversations were seized in the motel room where one of the wiretappers was staying,[39] and that at least five men had been involved in the extensive bugging operation.[40]

Hunt's sons later claimed that the secret wiretapping had been carried out due to "allegations" that Security Director Paul Rothermel and others were embezzling funds from the Hunt empire.[41]

Warren Reynolds

Warren Reynolds was an eyewitness to the shooting of Dallas Police Officer J. D. Tippit on November 22, 1963.[42] When interviewed by the FBI on January 21, 1964, he stated that he could not make a positive identification of Lee Harvey Oswald as the man he saw shoot Tippit.[43]

On January 23, 1964, two days after his FBI interview, Warren Reynolds was shot in the head by an unknown assailant.[44] Despite the fact that he had been shot in the basement of the car lot where he worked, the assailant had not stolen anything or committed any other crime.[45] The Dallas Police did not notify either the Warren Commission or the FBI of the Reynolds shooting.

Several days after the attack, which Reynolds survived with brain damage, a suspect was arrested for the shooting: Darrell "Dago" Garner, a seamy character with a significant police record. However, days later, on February 5, 1964, a woman stepped forward to provide an alibi for Garner, saying that she had been with him at another place at the time the Reynolds attack occurred.[46] The woman was Betty Mooney MacDonald[47] — a former stripper at Jack Ruby's nightclub.[48] With MacDonald's statement in hand, the Dallas Police released Garner, and he was never prosecuted for the shooting.

On July 22, 1964, Warren Reynolds had recovered from his head wound enough that he was able to be questioned by the Warren Commission.[49] Upon once again being shown photographs of Lee Harvey Oswald, Reynolds "positively" identified him as the man he had seen murder Officer Tippit.[50] Reynolds stated that his mind was much clearer than during his FBI interview in January.[51]

Betty MacDonald

On February 13, 1964, Betty MacDonald, the former Ruby stripper who provided the alibi for the man accused of shooting Warren Reynolds, Darrell Garner, was arrested by the Dallas police.[52] The arrest occurred eight days after she had gone to the police with her statement and alibi on behalf of Garner.

She was charged with breach of the peace, following a reported fight with her roommate.[53] Two hours after being placed in a Dallas jail cell, Betty MacDonald was found dead.[54] Jail attendants reported finding her hanging from a fixture in her cell — with her own toreador pants having served as the noose.[55] The MacDonald death was ruled a suicide.

On February 23, 1964, Bob Considine, the nationally known reporter for the *New York Journal-American*, disclosed the mysterious circumstances surrounding the Warren Reynolds shooting, the related MacDonald alibi, and the subsequent death of the former Ruby stripper.[56] While the Warren Commission and the FBI both knew of the Considine article (it later became part of a Commission exhibit) neither made any known investigation into the episode.[57]

Jack Ruby was never questioned about Betty MacDonald during the course of his own Warren Commission testimony, and Warren Reynold's "positive identification" of Oswald as Tippit's killer was cited by the Commission as key evidence of Oswald's guilt.

Bill Hunter

Bill Hunter, a reporter for the *Long Beach Independent Press Telegram*, had flown to Dallas to cover the immediate aftermath of President Kennedy's assassination, and had succeeded in becoming part of a journalistic scoop of sorts: he was one of the first people to gain entrance to Jack Ruby's Dallas apartment, several hours after Ruby murdered Oswald. On the night of November 24, 1963, Hunter, accompanied by Ruby's roommate, lawyer, and another reporter, went to Ruby's apartment to inspect the premises.[58]

Strangely, both reporters present at Ruby's apartment that night were brutally killed before the Warren Commission's investigation ended, nine months later.

On April 23, 1964, as Bill Hunter was conducting an interview at the Long Beach Police Station in his home city he was shot in the head and killed instantly.[59] A Long Beach policeman was charged with the shooting, but was later released, following a ruling that he had accidentally shot the reporter while handling a gun.

Jim Koethe

Jim Koethe, a reporter for the *Dallas Times Herald*, was the other reporter who visited Ruby's apartment

 on the night of November 24, 1963.

On September 21, 1964, three days before the *Warren Commission Report* was issued, Jim Koethe was killed by a karate chop to the throat, while stepping from the shower in his own Dallas apartment.[60] Dallas Police officials reported that the Koethe killing had been very carefully executed. No motive for the murder was ever established, and it has never been solved.

Hank Killam

Hank Killam, a man whom the Warren Commission itself cited might have "possible links" to both Lee Oswald and Jack Ruby,[61] was also brutally murdered during the course of the Commission's 1964 investigation. And, like the preceding deaths cited, the Warren Commission and the FBI never investigated the Killam murder.

The Report described possible association of Killam and his wife with Oswald and Ruby as follows:

> The Commission has also examined the

known friends and acquaintances of Ruby and Oswald for evidence that the two were acquainted, but it has found very few possible links. One conceivable association was through John Carter, a boarder at 1026 North Beckley Avenue while Oswald lived there. Carter was friendly with Wanda Joyce Killam, who had known Jack Ruby since shortly after he moved to Dallas in 1947 and worked for him from July 1963 to early November 1963.[62]

Wanda Joyce Killam was Hank Killam's wife. As can be seen from the Commission's accounting of these relationships, the following information is apparent: a man living in the same small boarding house as Oswald — John Carter — is a good friend of a woman — Wanda Killam — who had known Jack Ruby for sixteen years and had in fact been working for him until a couple weeks before the assassination.

The Warren Commission Report went on to note, however, that "Mrs. Killam . . . did not believe Carter ever visited the Carousel Club . . . or knew Ruby."[63]

Carter stated that he had not heard of Ruby until Oswald was shot, had talked briefly with Oswald only once or twice, and had never heard Oswald mention Ruby . . . The Commission has no reason to disbelieve either Mrs. Killam or Mr. Carter.[64]

In the early morning hours of March 17, 1964, Hank Killam was found dead in Pensacola, Florida, where he had been visiting his mother.[65] Mrs. Wanda Killam's husband had been found lying on a sidewalk with a slashed jugular vein.[66] A store window beside Killam's body had been broken.[67] Pensacola police — and subsequently the coroner — concluded that Killam had probably been killed by accidentally falling into the window, being knocked unconscious by the glass, and then bleeding to death.

1. *Harper's*, April 1964.
2. Ibid.
3. Warren Commission Exhibit 911; Priscilla Johnson testimony, July 25, 1964.
4. Warren Commission Document 49, p. 24.
5. *Boston Sunday Globe*, November 24, 1963.
6. *Warren Commission Report*, GPO edition, pp. 183-187.
7. Ibid.
8. *New York Times*, October 2, 1962.
9. *Warren Commission Report*, pp. 183-187.
10. Ibid.
11. *Dallas Morning News*, April 11, 1963; *New York Times*, April 12, 1963.
12. *Warren Commission Report*, pp. 183-187.
13. Meagher, *Accessories After The Fact*, p. 283.
14. Warren Commission Volume 11, p. 425.
15. Warren Commission Exhibit 837.
16. *Washington Post*, July 9, 1976.
17. Ibid.
18. Warren Commission Exhibit 2980.
19. *Warren Commission Report*, GPO edition, p. 333.
20. Warren Commission Exhibit 2270.
21. Warren Commission Exhibit 2980.
22. Ibid.
23. Ibid.
24. Jack Anderson column, January 2, 1975.
25. *Washington Star*, February 4, 1971.
26. Ibid.
27. Tyler Abell, editor, *Drew Pearson Diaries, 1949-1959* (New York: Holt, Rinehart and Winston, 1974), pp. 228-229.
28. *Texas Observer*, August 23, 1968; Kirkpatrick Sale, *Power Shift* (New York: Vintage Books Edition, 1976), p. 101.
29. February 14, 1969 CIA memorandum, "H. L. Hunt Interest in Garrison Investigation of Kennedy Assassination."
30. Ibid.
31. Ibid.
32. April 18, 1969 CIA memorandum, "Hunt, H. L. — Interest in Investigation of the Kennedy Assassination."
33. Ibid.
34. James Hepburn [pseudonym, actual author or authors unknown], *Farewell America* (Vaduz, Liechtenstein: Frontiers Publishing Company, 1968), pp. 245-252.
35. Ibid., pp. 251-252.
36. *Dallas Times Herald*, February 1, 1970.
37. *Washington Post*, September 26, 1975; *Dallas Times Herald*, February 1, 1970.

38. February 14, 1969 CIA memorandum, "H. L. Hunt Interest in Garrison Investigation of Kennedy Assassination."
39. *Dallas Times Herald*, February 1, 1970.
40. Ibid.
41. *Washington Post*, September 26, 1975.
42. *Warren Commission Report*, GPO edition, pp. 169, 175, 652.
43. Warren Commission Volume 11, p. 435; Warren Commission Exhibit 2523.
44. January 23, 1964 Dallas Police Department Report, Warren Reynolds shooting.
45. Ibid.
46. Warren Commission Exhibit 2589.
47. Ibid.
48. Ibid.
49. Warren Commission Volume 11, pp. 435-437.
50. Ibid.
51. Ibid.
52. February 13, 1964 Dallas Police Department Arrest Report.
53. Ibid.
54. February 13, 1964 Dallas Police Department Report, Death of Betty MacDonald.
55. Ibid.
56. *New York Journal-American*, February 23, 1964.
57. Warren Commission Exhibit 342.
58. Meagher, *Accessories After The Fact*, pp. 298-300.
59. *San Francisco Chronicle*, April 24, 1964.
60. *Dallas Times Herald*, September 22, 1964.
61. Warren Commission Exhibit 2882.
62. *Warren Commission Report*, GPO edition, p. 363.
63. Ibid.
64. Warren Commission Exhibit 2883; *Warren Commission Report*, p. 363.
65. March 17 and March 18, 1964 Pensacola Police Department Reports.
66. Ibid.
67. Ibid.

AFTERWORD

The Committee to Investigate Assassinations has no "pet theories" as to who killed President Kennedy and why. We could speculate endlessly on plots by the Mafia, dissident CIA types, anti-Castro Cubans, or pro-Castro Cubans. . . or a combination of several of them. . . . .but we refrain. *We simply do not know.*

What we do know is that the murder is unsolved. Wittingly or unwittingly, the Warren Commission never came close to getting to the bottom of the case. We know from the physical evidence alone that Oswald was not a "lone-nut" assassin. Using the lowest common denominator, we know that there had to be at least two rifles at work, hence two riflemen, hence a conspiracy.

What has been presented in the preceeding pages has been a bewildering series of "coincidences" which, laid end to end, point toward a much larger and more complex conspiracy than *may* have been at work. We know that many of the coincidences will turn out to be just that — coincidences — once the truth is known. We suspect that a certain number will prove to be more and that they will lead official investigators inexorably to the truth.

A recent Gallup poll indicated that 80% of the American public disbelieves the conclusions of the Warren Commission . . . . and many of them care who killed their President and why.

Some day soon they will know the truth.

INDEX

Accardo, Tony, 276, 347
Adonis, Joe, 357
Agnew, Sprio T., 546
Aléman, Jose, 321-3
Alexander, William, 438-440, 74, 427, 439-40
Allen, George, 334
Alo, Vincent, 370
Anastasia, Albert, 320-21
Anderson, Jack, 78-9, 128, 171, 179, 191, 210-11, 335-7, 370, 455, 458-9, 503-4, 522, 524-6, 531, 534
Andrews, Dean, 476-7
Angleton, James, 183-6, 182, 224, 471
Annenberg, Moses, 281
Anslinger, Harry, 309
Anson, Robert Sam, 122,139, 340-2, 385-6, 441
Arbenz, Jacobo, 238
Arnett, George, 409
Artime, Manuel, 513-19, 161
Attwood, William, 488-9

Baker, Sen. Howard, 103, 123, 149-50, 184, 336
Baker, Barney, 357-8, 356
Baker, T.L., 413
Baldwin, Alfred, 503
Ball, Joseph, 543-4, 37, 419 426, 560
Banister, Guy, 225-7, 296, 298, 391, 475
Barker, Bernard, 511-13, 225, 321, 500-1, 505, 514, 517-19
Barnes, Tracy, 161, 516
Batista, Fulgencio, 282, 318
Beauboff, Alvin, 461
Belin, David W., 82, 106-7, 137-8, 182-3, 410, 430, 541, 544
Bellino, Carmine, 271
Bennett, Robert, 337
Bentley, Paul, 420-4

Bernstein, Carl, 505, 508, 524-5, 543-4
"Bertrand, Clay," 476-7
Bintliff, Russell L., 531
Bioff, Willie, 346
Bischoff, Willie, 286, 324
Bissell, Richard, 81-2, 156-8, 161, 163, 198, 204-5, 210, 236, 238-9, 341, 516
Bittman, William, 518
Blankenship, D.L., 409
Bogard, Albert, 392-3
Boggs, Hale, 96-105, 45, 83, 86, 93, 134, 440
Boggs, Lindy, 96
Boggs, Thomas Hale, Jr., 100-1
Bolden, Abraham, 560-2
Bookhout, James, 410
Boone, Eugene, 441
Borenstein, Lorenzo, 229
Bowen, John H., 232-5
Boyle, W.A. "Tony", 152
Braden, Jim, 287-9, 290, 292, 302-4, 314, 444-6, 572
Brading, Eugene Hale, 287-9, 445-6
Bradlee, Ben, 185, 356
Breen, Bunny, 279-80
Breen, James, 279-80
Brener, Milton, 219
Bremer, Arthur, 523-4
Brennan, Earl, 177
Bringuier, Carlos, 492-4, 303, 366, 453, 457
Broshears, Rev. Raymond, 473-5
Brown, Anthony Cave, 177-8
Brown, Mrs. G. Stanley, 567
Buccieri, Fiore, 339-40
Buchanan, Jim, 507
Bundy, McGeorge, 188-9, 325, 487-8
Butler, George, 276-8, 409

Cabana Motel, 288, 291-4
Cabell, Gen. Charles T. 235-40, 82, 158
Cabell, Earl, 237, 437

584

Cain, Robert T. (Prods.), 346
Califano, Joseph, 125
Cannon, Howard, 135, 337
Capone, Al, 156, 269-70, 339, 345-6, 364, 367
Carlson, E.E., 409
"Carlson, Harry", 417
Carr, Waggoner, 439
Carter, Clifton, 185
Carter, Jimmy, 92, 125
Carter, John, 579-80
Castro, Fidel 485-90, 18, 31, 74-5, 77-80, 81-2, 107, 124, 149, 155-71, 174-76, 186-8, 197-9, 201-2, 204, 209, 212, 236, 260, 302, 309, 312, 314, 318-19, 321, 323, 328-333, 341, 343, 348, 365, 368-9, 482, 485, 493, 496-7, 500, 506-9, 513-17
Caulfield, John, 519-21, 103, 504, 531
Celler, Emanuel, 248
Cellini, Dino, 286, 324
Cerone, Jackie, 282-3
Chavez, Frank, 362-3, 354, 356, 360
Chotiner, Murray, 128-9
Church, Frank, 123
CIA/Support Chief, 209-212, 236
"Clark, Lefty", 286, 324
Clark, Ramsey, 113-117
Clemmons, Aquilla, 559, 433
Cohen, Mickey, 128, 347
Colby, William, 22
Coleman, Kay, 417
Coleman, Walter, 570
Coleman, William B., 89, 111-113, 390
Colson, Charles, 91, 128, 131-2, 336, 454, 458-9, 504, 532-3, 541-2, 548
Columbo, Joe, 315
Combest, B.H., 41-2
Conein, Lucien, 180
Connally, John B., 126-7, 24, 45, 123, 355, 450, 538-9, 549

Connally, Nellie, 126-7
Considine, Bob, 577
Cook, Fred J., 320
Cooke, Leon, 275
Cooper, John Sherman, 86, 96, 99
Coppola, Mike, 357
Cordona, Dr. Jose Miro, 27
Corona, Vic, 463
Costello, Frank, 176, 178, 347, 320, 367, 491
Cox, Archibald, 523, 544, 546
Craig, Roger D., 440-3
Crichton, Jack, 240-1
Crile, George, 180, 321-3
Cronkite, Walter, 125
Cruz, Miguel, 360
Cuban Revolutionary Council, 225, 258, 484, 493, 496, 512
Cuban Revolutionary Democratic Front, 302-3, 495
Cubela, Roland, 515
Cunningham, Cortlandt, 433
Curry, Jesse, 433-7, 253, 411-2, 418, 420, 422, 428
Cushing, Cardinal, 461

Dalitz, Moe, 334-5
Dan, Uri, 369
Dannelly, Lee, 393-4
Danner, Richard, 335-6
Davis, George, 322-3
Davison, Alexei, 219-221
Dean, John, 103, 129-31, 504, 517-19, 532-4, 542-3
Dean, Patrick, 108-110
deBrueys, Warren C., 256-258
DeCarlo, Angelo "Gyp", 130-1
Decker, J.E., 419
DeLoach, Cartha, 76, 117, 124-5, 251, 264, 458
delValle, Eladio, 303-4
DelValle, Maria, 360
Demaris, Ovid, 116-7, 277, 309, 346-7
DeMohrenschildt, George, 212-14, 38
DeMohrenschildt, Jeanne, 212-13

Deslatte, Oscar, 390-1
Dewey, Thomas E., 179
Diem, President, 32, 526, 568
Dobrynin, Anatoly, 33-4
Donovan, James, 31-2
Dorfman, Allen, 133
Dorfman, Paul, 274-5, 356
Dorman, Michael, 308
Dowell, Doris, 467-8
Dowling, Mary, 425
Downing, Thomas N., 146, 343
Ducos, Leopoldo Ramos, 359-362, 356, 362-3
Dulles, Allen, 80-85, 33, 43, 86-7, 92, 107, 157-8, 163, 186, 189, 198, 208, 235-6, 238, 302, 546
Duran, Silvia, 394-6

Eastland, Sen. James, 573
Eboli, Thomas, 315
Edwards, Don, 148, 255
Edwards, Sheffield, 81-2, 156-8, 166-8, 191, 210, 236, 328, 348
Ehrlichman, John, 131, 514, 519, 533, 543
Eisenberg, Melvin, 72-3
Eisenhower, Dwight D., 333, 573
Eisenhower, Dr. Milton, 31
Elder, Walter, 200-1
Ellsberg, Dr. Daniel, 40, 519
Epstein, Edward Jay, 37, 86, 89, 134, 390
Exner, Judith Campbell, 340-2

Fain, John, 262-3
Fair Play For Cuba Committee, 22, 97, 112, 226, 229, 261, 296, 298, 366, 418, 469, 482, 493, 494
Fay, Paul B., 26-27
Fensterwald, Bernard Jr., 103-5, 182, 184, 229, 540
Ferrie, David, 295-305, 115, 226-7, 258, 288, 290, 293-4, 309-14, 391, 445, 451-2, 454-7, 461-2, 470, 473-5, 496-7, 522, 572
Fitzgerald, Desmond, 31-2
Fitzsimmons, Frank, 133, 353
531 Lafayette Street, 225
544 Camp Street, 225, 296, 298, 475
Flynn, Charles W., 260
Ford, Gerald R., 133-136, 546, 43, 49, 71, 86, 99, 111, 123, 337-8, 372, 419, 426, 430, 475, 545, 573
Fox Brothers, 371
Frank, Richard A., 385
Frankenheimer, John, 35
Free Cuba Committee, 218-19, 418
"Friends of a Democratic Cuba", 391
Fritz, Will, 409-410, 408, 418, 421, 434, 436-7, 442
Fulbright, J.W., 24, 512

Gage, Nicholas, 339-40, 369
Gambino, Carlos, 315
Gambino Family, 306
Garner, Darrell, 576, 577
Garrison, Jim, 459-64, 77, 114, 117, 225-6, 237, 293-4, 295, 297-300, 314, 450-77, 498, 522, 574-5
Gaudet, William George, 228-230, 470
Genovese, Vito, 181, 315, 320, 491
Giancana, Sam, 338-342, 82, 124, 157-160, 163, 165, 186-7, 199, 202, 209-11, 236, 260, 276-7, 285, 302, 307, 312, 314, 317, 319, 328, 331, 343, 370
Giancana-Accardo Mob, 277, 279, 282
Gil, Manuel, 496
Gill, G. Wray, 304-5, 314
Gillies, Allen, 567
"Gold, Sam", 211, 317
Goldwater, Barry, 346, 401, 486

Gonzalez, Henry, 147
Gonzalez, Virgilio R., 500
Goodwin, Richard N., 141, 485
Gorey, Hays, 142
Granello, Salvatore "Sally Burns", 181
Grant, Eva Rubinstein, 280
Gray, L. Patrick, 502, 504, 505
Gregory, Paul, 38
Greenspun, Hank, 336
Griffin, Burt, 108-110, 291-2, 541, 563
Groden, Robert, 146
Guevara, Che, 508
Gurfein, Murray, 177, 179
Guthrie, Steve, 276-8
Gwirtzman, Milton, 141

Haggerty, Judge Edward A., 477-8
Haig, Alexander, 531-2, 545, 548
Haldeman, H.R., 103, 130, 505, 514, 519, 522, 533, 542, 547
Hall, Bruce, 257
Hall, Loran, 389
Hall, Sarah K., 574-5
Hammon, J.W., 304
Harriman, Averell, 488
Harrison, Delores, 425
Hart, Sen. Gary, 150-1, 145, 251
Hart, Sen. Philip, 540
Harvey, William, 187-192, 31, 163-71, 174, 186, 198-9, 201-2, 204, 210-11, 323, 332, 347-8, 369
Hazlitt, Bill, 129
Hedgman, Victor, 207
Helms, Richard, 193-203, 20, 21, 31-2, 59, 62-3, 102, 163-5, 168, 182, 187, 189, 204, 210, 239, 298, 317, 328, 359, 361, 452, 464, 469, 491, 512
Herman, George, 115

Herndon, Bell, 284, 427
Hersh, Seymour, 87, 137, 156, 182, 508
Hicks, James, 471-3
"Hidell, Alek", 414-15, 421, 444
Hill, Gerald, 412-416, 420-1
H.L. Hunt Oil Company 288
Hoffa, James R. 349-357, 133, 274, 307, 321, 334-5, 344, 357-60, 362-3, 464
Hoover, J. Edgar, 250-3, 19, 20, 75-87, 90, 96, 99, 101, 105, 115-117, 124, 148, 184, 215, 233, 247, 332, 341, 354, 384-5, 389, 391, 458, 502, 512, 529, 537
Hosty, James, 18-19, 255-6, 410-11
Houston, Lawrence, 166-7, 191, 299, 452
Howard, Lisa, 488
Howard, Tom, 56, 66, 284
Hubert, Leon, 41-2
Hudkins, Alonzo, 438-9
Hughes, Howard, 327-338, 78, 82, 156, 163, 210, 238, 401, 508
Humphrey, Hubert, 24
Hunt, E. Howard, 509-11, 28, 40, 129, 160-1, 213, 225, 238, 302, 336-7, 495, 502, 504, 511-19, 522-6, 534-6
Hunt, Mrs. E. Howard, 504
Hunt, H.L., 571-5, 292
Hunt, Lamar, 292, 572-3
Hunt, Nelson, 573
Hunter, Bill, 578
Hsi-wen, General Tuan, 180

I.N.S. Inspector, 404-5
Isaacs, Professor Harold, 217-18

Jackson, Henry M., 367
Jackson, William, 239-40
Jaworski, Leon, 544-5, 74, 419, 426, 437, 439
Jenkins, Walter, 251

Jenner, Albert, 549-50
Joeston, Joachim, 102-3
Johnson, U. Alexis, 188, 325
Johnson, Haynes, 28
Johnson, Lyndon B., 24, 72-3, 76, 78, 113, 121, 123-5, 167, 180, 239, 255, 333, 355, 458, 475, 481-2, 486
Johnson, Tom, 255
Jones, Kirby, 489
Jones, Paul, 276-9

Kalmbach, Herbert, 517, 532
Kaminski, Erich, 409
Kantor, Seth, 557-8
Karamessines, Thomas, 63, 195, 299, 361
Katzenbach, Nicholas, 251
Kavner, Richard, 360-1
Kay, Kathie, 417
Kefauver Senate Committee, 179, 270, 272, 276, 279, 345
Keeher, James, 39
Kelley, Clarence, 343-5
Kempster, Norman, 256
Kennedy, Edward M., 140-2, 501, 520, 526, 540
Kennedy, John F., 24-36, 84, 184-5, 235, 249, 272, 310-11, 321, 326, 333, 349, 355, 451, 459, 482, 486-9, 515-16, 561, 568, 571
Kennedy, Jacqueline, 56, 64, 66, 284
Kennedy, Joan, 141
Kennedy, Robert F., 18, 31, 33-4, 85, 116, 122-3, 140-1, 147, 163, 165-169, 188-90, 196, 249-50, 268-271, 274, 282, 300, 307, 309, 317, 332, 339, 342, 347, 349-58, 360, 362-3, 487-8, 542, 571
Kessler, Ron, 78, 100, 396, 469
Khruschev, Nikita, 33, 53-4, 190
Kilduff, Malcolm, 557

Killam, Hank, 579-80
Killam, Wanda Joyce, 579-80
Kumsey, Herman, 401-4
King, Martin Luther, 115-116, 147, 152
Kohn, Aaron, 307
Kohn, Howard, 128
Krogh, Egil, 533
Krystinik, Raymond, 562-3
Ky, 179-80

Labriola, Paul, 276-7
Lambert, William, 527
Lane, Mark, 101-3, 108, 139-40, 493, 558, 560
Lansdale, General Edward, 187-8
Lansky, Jake, 286, 324, 370-1
Lansky, Meyer, 367-372, 124, 128, 162, 176, 178, 282, 286, 287, 306, 308-9, 320, 324, 357, 367, 445, 505, 511
Lanza, Joseph "Socks", 178
LaRocca, John, 180
LaRue, Fred, 503, 514
Lauchli, Richard, 474
LeMay, Curtis, 573
Levi, Edward, 344-5
Lewis, C.L., 287, 444-6
Liddy, G. Gordon, 533-37, 336-7, 503-4, 525-6
Liebeler, Wesley, 41, 89, 390, 563
Lincoln, Evelyn, 24
Luciano, Lucky, 176-9, 309-10, 347, 368
Lukas, J. Anthony, 336, 514, 523
Lumumba, Patrice, 205-6
Lynch, Jack, 567

MacDonald, Betty, 577, 576
MacMillan, Priscilla Johnson, 566
Magruder, Jeb, 336, 503-4, 532-5
Maheu, Peter, 335-6
Maheu, Robert, 327-338, 78, 80, 82, 124, 156-7, 161,

163, 165-6, 199, 209-11, 227, 236, 238, 286, 307, 314, 317, 319, 370
Malone, John F., 529
Manchester, William, 141-2, 530
Mankiewicz, Frank, 141, 489
Mannlicher-Carcano Rifle, 44, 49-50, 441
Mansfield, Mike, 92
Marcello, Carlos, 306-16, 226, 288, 290, 293, 296, 299-301, 341, 462, 496
Marchetti, Victor, 22-23, 221, 298, 452-3, 464
Mardian, Robert, 536-7, 503
Markham, Helen L., 560
Martens, Layton, 497
Martin, David C., 190, 192
Martin, Jack, 227
Martin, Jack S., 296-7
Martin, John, 275
Martinez, Eugenio R., 321, 500
Mastriana, Louis, 367
Maynard, Harry, 265
McCarthy, Joseph, 573
McClellan Committee, 271-3, 279, 282, 307, 349-50
McCloy, John J., 545, 71-2, 84, 85-8, 99
McCone, John, 23, 31, 162-4, 166, 170, 187-90, 197-201, 317, 328
McCord, James, 336, 504, 508, 541
McCoy, Alfred W. 179, 318
McDonald, Hugh C., 400-404
McGovern, George, 175
McKeown, Robert, 364-6, 512-13
McLaney, Mike, 366-7
McLaney, William, 366-7
McManus, George, 199-200
McNamara, Robert, 188
McVickar, John A., 566-7
McWillie, Lewis J., 61, 260, 285-6, 324-6, 366, 370-1, 506

Meagher, Sylvia, 38, 46, 98, 215, 408, 425-6, 428-9, 481-2, 558, 570
Mercer, Julia, 558-9
Messick, Hank, 309, 368-9, 370
Meyer, Mary, 184-5
Meyers, Edward, 290-5
Meyers, Lawrence, V., 290-5
Miller, Dusty, 358
Mitchell, John, 537-40, 99, 131-2, 249, 503-4, 514, 517, 533-4, 549
Mitchell, Martha, 131-2, 503
Mondale, Walter, 123, 143-4, 240
Moore, J. Walter, 574
Morgan, Edward P., 78-9
Morin, Charles, 527
Morse, Wayne, 24
Mudge, Rose, Guthrie & Alexander, 294
Mulroney, Michael, 205-6
Murret, Lillian, 38
Murret, Marilyn, 217-218, 38
Muskie, Edmund, 501

Neal, Glen, 409
Nelson, Jack, 129, 137, 224
Nelson, R.C., 428-9
Newman, Mert, 277
Nhu, Madame, 568
Nhu, Ngo Dinh, 526
Nitti, Frank, 346-7, 364
Nixon, Richard M., 527-533, 17, 45-6, 91, 122, 123, 127-33, 139, 294, 327, 333, 335-6, 355, 454, 458, 486-8, 501, 503-5, 509-10, 513, 517-525, 533-5, 542-9, 573
Nosencho, Yuri, 138, 222-4
Novel, Gordon, 454-9, 522-3
Noyes, Peter, 287-8, 300-1, 444-5

O'Brien, Larry, 501, 508
Odio, Sylvia, 387-390, 89, 111, 361

Odle, Robert, 535
O'Donnell, Kenneth, 24, 28, 33, 123, 249, 271
"Olds, Jim", 211
O'Leary, Jeremiah, 531
Olsen, Harry, 416-420, 430
Orth, Maureen, 39
"Osborne, Albert", 232-5, 470
Oswald, Lee Harvey, 36-42, 18, 19, 20, 21, 22, 23, 40, 43, 44-58, 63-7, 73, 79, 83, 4, 85-7, 89, 92-5, 96, 109-113, 126, 132, 134-5, 138-40, 145, 148, 150-1, 158, 183, 194-6, 212-235, 248, 251-8, 253-65, 273, 274, 278, 293-4, 296-304, 349, 357, 361, 364-5, 384-405, 407-418, 420-6, 431, 434-40, 442, 444, 446, 465-71, 474-7, 481-4, 491-5, 502-8, 510-12, 521, 529, 535-7, 542, 546, 560, 562, 566, 570, 572, 576-7
"Oswald, Leon", 388-9
Oswald, Marguerite, 51-55, 196
Oswald, Marina, 43-48, 132, 134-5, 212, 214-15, 219-20, 240, 253-4, 529, 562, 567, 569-71
Oswald, Robert, 40-1, 48-51, 263, 423-4
Otepka, Otto, 230-1
O'Toole, George, 413-16, 439

Paine, Michael, 214-16, 138, 562
Paine, Ruth, 214-16, 563
Partin, Edward, 351-3
Patrick, Lenny, 280-2
Pearson, Drew, 74-80, 128, 211, 531, 573
Pena, Orest, 257-8
Penkovskiy, Col. Oleg, 220-21
Perrin, Nancy, 490-2
Perrin, Robert, 490-1
Perry, Dr. Malcolm, 435
Pike, Otis, 453

Pindling, Lynden, 367
Popkin, Richard, 387
Powers, David, 249-50
Powers, Francis Gary, 83, 231-2
Plumeri, James, 181
Powell, Lewis, 139-40, 123
Presser, Jack, 133
Prouty, L. Fletcher, 181
Provenzano, Anthony, 133

"QJ/WIN", 203-209
Quigley, John, 261

Ragen, James M., 281-2
Rankin, J. Lee, 88-91, 541-2, 546-7, 19, 47, 62-3, 73, 93-95, 98, 101, 194, 196, 233, 259, 281, 389-90, 410, 419, 426, 439-40, 512, 523, 545, 561
Rather, Dan, 22-23, 125, 257, 265, 365-6, 524, 535
Ravel, Luis, 496
"John Rawlston", 211
Ray, James Earl, 115-6
Rebozo, Bebe, 128, 130, 132, 327, 335-6
Redlich, Norman, 43
Reid, Ed, 300, 306, 311-12, 346-7
Reily, William, 218-19
Revill, Jack, 410-12
Reynolds, Warren, 576, 577
Rhyne, Charles, 548
Rich, Nancy Perrin, 490-2
Richardson, Eliot, 523, 545
Rickenbacker, Eddie, 496
Roberts, Earlene, 422-4
Robertson, Willard, 458
Rocca, Raymond, 182-3
Rockefeller, Nelson, 136-138, 123
Rodriguez, Arnesto, 496
Roosevelt, Eleanor, 31
Roselli, John, 343-348, 78-80, 156-163, 166, 168-71, 186-7, 192, 199, 209-12, 236, 260, 307, 314, 317-319,

323, 328-9, 331, 334-5, 339, 370
Ross, Barney, 364
Ross, Thomas B., 218, 226, 238-9
Rothermel, Paul, 574-5
Rowley, James J., 75
Rubinstein, Jack (Ruby), 275
Ruby, Hymie, 279
Ruby, Jack, 56-57, 259-60, 273-284, 18, 19, 20, 41, 96-7, 108-110, 145, 148, 158, 194-6, 229, 248, 251, 254, 285-6, 288, 290-295, 324, 325-6, 349, 357-9, 360, 362-6, 368, 371-2, 386, 407-9, 412, 416-20, 425-7, 430, 436, 438, 445-6, 474, 481-4, 490-2, 506, 513, 557-8, 562-3, 570, 572, 576-80
Rusk, Dean, 188, 230, 239
Russell, Dick, 132
Russell, Richard, B., 91-5, 86, 96, 134, 235

St. Clair, James, 548
St. George, Andrew, 503, 508-9
Salerno, Ralph J., 272-3
Salinger, Pierre, 24, 27-8, 36, 236, 271-2
"Saul", 401-4
Schlesinger, Arthur, 35, 85, 141
Schorr, Daniel, 107, 111, 197, 223-4, 331, 453
Schweiker, Sen. Richard S., 144-5, 81, 103, 123-4, 143, 150-1, 251, 264
Scranton, Paul, 322-3
Sevareid, Eric, 272
Shaffer, Charles, 542-3
Shanklin, Gordon, 255-6, 253, 410-11
Shapiro, David, 524, 541
Shaw, Clay L., 451-4, 114, 298, 456-7, 462, 464, 468, 477-8, 522, 574

Sheridan, Walter, 271, 355, 363
Shimon, Joseph, 331-2
Sidey, Hugh, 180
Siegel, Bugsy, 357
Sinatra, Frank, 340
Sirica, John, 501
Slawson, David, 111-113, 384, 390
Smathers, George, 32
Smith, R. Harris, 176
Smith, Sergio Arcacha, 258, 302, 455, 495-8
Snyder, Richard, E., 221-2
Socarras, Carlos Prio, 512-13
Sorensen, Ted, 29-31, 35, 484
Sorrels, Forrest V., 559
Specter, Arlen, 548-9, 419, 426-7
Sprague, Richard A., 151-2
Stafford, Jean, 53
Stanecki, Gerry, 356
Stern, Lawrence, 78
Stevenson, Adlai, 24
Stiles, Jack, 134
Storey, Bob, 74
Sturgis, Frank Fiorini, 505-9, 487, 500, 503, 511, 513, 517
Sullivan, William, 251-2
Swain, R.E., 409
Sweatt, Allan, 439
Szulc, Tad, 134, 510-11

Tanner, Hans, 506
Tatro, Edward, 441
Taylor, Gen. Maxwell, 29
Teresa, Vincent, 312
Thieu, 180
Thomas, Helen, 132
Thompson, Josiah, 471
Thornley, Kerry, 465-8
Tippit, Officer J.D., 424-433, 49, 65, 413-14, 420, 438, 474, 559-60, 576-7
Tolson, Clyde, 263-4, 76, 124, 251
Tonahill, Joseph, 56
Torello, James, 339-40

Tourine, Charles, 370
Trafficante, Santos, 316-327, 59, 82, 124, 157-8, 162-3, 169, 180, 186-7, 199, 210-11, 236, 260, 285-6, 302, 307, 309, 312, 314, 328, 341, 368-70, 505, 511
Trammel, Connie, 572
Trujillo, Rafael, 32
Tufts, Henry H., 531-2
Turman, Reagan, 408

Ulasewicz, Tony, 520-1, 531-2

Valachi, Joe, 270, 312
Vestal, Bud, 337-8
Villodas, Joiquin, 496
Voebel, Edward, 40, 299

Wade, Henry, 74, 418, 438-9
Walinsky, Adam, 141
Walker, Gen. Edwin, 45-6, 569-71
Wallace, George, 147, 523, 573
Walsh, Kevin, 216
Walter, William, 264-5
Walton, Truet, 409
Ward, Hugh, 475-6
Warren, Earl, 43, 48, 72-80, 83, 87, 99, 123, 284, 411-12, 419-20, 426, 439-40

Watson, Marvin, 76, 124, 264, 458
Wecht, Dr. Cyril, 138
Weinberg, Jim, 276-7
Weiner, Irwin S., 358-9, 356
Weisberg, Harold, 73, 82, 92, 95, 135, 182, 496, 538-40
Weitzman, Seymour, 443-4, 441-2
Wells, Tom, 142
West, Jean, 291, 293-4
Werdig, Robert, 539
Whitten, Les, 457
Willens, Harold, 101, 196
Willis, Phil, 289, 471
Wilson, John, 325-6
Wilson-Hudson, John, 325-6
"WI/ROGUE", 205, 207-9
Wise, David, 218, 226, 238-9
Wisner, Frank, 238
Witcover, Jules, 528-30
Woods, Rose Mary, 547-8, 45, 529
Woodward, Bob, 504-5, 508, 524-5, 543-4

Yablonski, Joseph, 152
Yaras, Dave, 280-3
Yarborough, Ralph, 24

Zapruder film, 146, 549
"ZR/RIFLE", 204, 209